From Empire to Nation State

Many scholars perceive ethnic politics in China as an untouchable topic due to lack of data and contentious, even prohibitive, politics. This book fills a gap in the literature, offering a historical-political perspective on China's contemporary ethnic conflict. Yan Sun accumulates research via field trips, local reports, and policy debates to reveal rare knowledge and findings. Her long-time causal chain of explanation reveals the roots of China's contemporary ethnic strife in the centralizing and ethnicizing strategies of its incomplete transition to a nation state – strategies that depart sharply from its historical patterns of diverse and indirect rule. This departure created the institutional dynamics for politicized identities and ethnic mobilization, particularly in the outer regions of Tibet and Xinjiang. In the twenty-first century, such factors as the demise of socialist tenets and institutions that upheld interethnic solidarity, and the rise of identity politics and developmentalism, have intensified these built-in tensions.

Yan Sun is Professor in the Department in Political Science at Queens College and at the Graduate Centre, The City University of New York.

From Empire to Nation State

Ethnic Politics in China

YAN SUN
City University of New York

CAMBRIDGE
UNIVERSITY PRESS

CAMBRIDGE
UNIVERSITY PRESS

University Printing House, Cambridge CB2 8BS, United Kingdom

One Liberty Plaza, 20th Floor, New York, NY 10006, USA

477 Williamstown Road, Port Melbourne, VIC 3207, Australia

314–321, 3rd Floor, Plot 3, Splendor Forum, Jasola District Centre, New Delhi – 110025, India

79 Anson Road, #06–04/06, Singapore 079906

Cambridge University Press is part of the University of Cambridge.

It furthers the University's mission by disseminating knowledge in the pursuit of education, learning, and research at the highest international levels of excellence.

www.cambridge.org
Information on this title: www.cambridge.org/9781108840293
DOI: 10.1017/9781108885454

First published 2020

A catalogue record for this publication is available from the British Library.

ISBN 978-1-108-84029-3 Hardback
ISBN 978-1-108-79441-1 Paperback

To my father, Sun Zhixiang

October 11, 1933–June 23, 2019

Distinguished Professor of Russian Language

Contents

Figures and Tables

FIGURES

TABLES

Acknowledgments

This book represents almost a decade of work since I first became interested in the topic of China's ethnic politics in the wake of the Lhasa riot of March 2008 and the Urumqi riot of 2009. It is an accumulation of extensive field trips, conversations, and archival research in different regions of China. Ethnic politics is such a politically sensitive topic in China that few foreign (especially US) based scholars may be willing to undertake a project like this, for a lack of local access in China. Thus, I wish to thank the hundreds of people across China who have shared their time and knowledge to help me understand a highly delicate subject. Without them, this project would not have been possible, either physically or intellectually.

For introducing me to research resources, contacts, and trips in minority regions in China, I extend my heartfelt thanks to Professor Ma Rong of Beijing University, Professor Yang Minghong of Sichuan University, Mr. Ming Hao of the research office of the State Ethnic Affairs Commission (SEAC), and Mr. Rigzin Losel of the Tibetology Center of China. They are among the many scholars and policy analysts whom I have met at conferences on minority issues in China. Between them they represent four different ethnicities and diverse perspectives on China's ethnic policy. Professor Ma first introduced me to Xinjiang in the early 2010s by bringing me to two conferences in Xinjiang and then on field trips with his research team across southern Xinjiang. He also introduced me to a forum of ethnic scholars in Qinghai, a heavily multiethnic province. Professor Yang, during three summers between 2014 and 2017, brought me along with his research teams on field trips in Tibetan prefectures of Sichuan and several prefectures in Tibet itself. Mr. Ming Hao introduced me to several forums on minority issues in China, and through his assistance I was able to take field trips in Yanbian, a Korean autonomous prefecture. Mr. Losel, a Tibetan historian, introduced me to many aspects of intraelite politics in Tibetan history and local politics in contemporary Tibetan communities. Throughout my project I have benefited greatly from their local knowledge, their generosity to answer my questions, and their assistance with local access and resources.

For intellectual guidance and support, I owe enormous debts to Professor Dingxin Zhao of the University of Chicago and my colleague at CUNY, Professor Lenny Markovitz. Professor Zhao's astute knowledge of historical empires, and of Chinese political and social institutions both historically and in contemporary times, helped to sharpen my conceptual framework and empirical analyses. Despite his busy schedules between Chicago and Hangzhou, he took time to make informed and constructive comments throughout the entire manuscript. I am also grateful to him for opportunities to present parts of my project at the East Asia Forum at the University of Chicago and the western development symposium at Zhejiang University. Professor Markovitz, my long-time colleague at CUNY, has given me much moral and intellectual support throughout my career. He took time to read and comment on the entire manuscript. As co-editor for the *Journal of Comparative Politics* for decades, he has a knack for critical insights and valuable feedback. Without the encouragement and wisdom of these two professional colleagues, I may not have had the confidence to carry to completion a study whose subject matter can seem too contentious to handle with balance, dispassion, and patience. In addition, I am grateful to Dr. Andrew Mertha, previously at Cornell University and now at Johns Hopkins University, for reading my entire manuscript and offering constructive comments. In this connection, I also thank the anonymous reviewers for Cambridge University Press, whose criticisms and corrections helped to improve my manuscript.

For assisting me in local accommodation, travel, and research, I am indebted to many relatives in southern Xinjiang. Given the current political climate in the region, it is prudent to mention just three who would unlikely face any risk for having hosted a foreign-based relative/researcher. My cousin Ling, who passed away in 2017 at the age of forty-eight, was an agricultural specialist who worked with Uighur farmers throughout his career in a rural county of the Uighur south. My cousin Ping, unemployed since the late 1990s, introduced me to her world of downsized workers from local state factories. Finally, her husband Yong, who passed away in 2017 at the age of fifty-eight, was a staff member in a local government with rich knowledge of local politics. I benefited greatly from staying with them, joining in and observing their daily activities, interacting with their local communities, and visiting places which I could not have done otherwise. Born locally, their fluency in spoken Uighur gave me the necessary tools for local communication. I am also grateful to two other local cousins in whose homes I stayed, and to these and other relatives whose local knowledge and experiences have remained a source of reality checking for me.

Other people who have given me various forms of support deserve my sincere appreciation. Patricia Rachal, my chair at Queens College, has unfailingly supported my research project with schedules and course loads that afforded me the time and environment to complete my project. Andrew Hacker, my senior colleague at Queens College, has been supportive with his deep interest in ethnic politics and his role model as a productive scholar. Ruth O'Brien, my colleague at the CUNY Graduate Center, has supported me with her continuing interest in my project and her readiness to help. Professor Yang Yang of Yunnan University provided valuable assistance in compiling economic data for the autonomous regions. Dr. Ma Bo, my doctoral student, provided assistance in turning the economic data into graphs. Dr. Hu Shaohua, of Wagner College, read parts of my earlier draft and offered comments. Ms. Shen Wenjin, my former editor at the Chinese magazine *Lingdaozhe*, invited me to a volunteer project in the Tibetan village of Diqing, a Tibetan prefecture in Yunnan province, where I interacted with local Tibetan students up close. I thank two scholars at the Minzu University of China; one invited me to the campus for a week and the other facilitated an interview with a dissident Uighur faculty member. I thank my friend Faye Maris for her moral support and tolerance of my absence.

At Cambridge University Press, my sincere appreciation goes to Senior Editor Robert Dreesan and retired Senior Editor Lewis Bateman, for their interest in my project and their editorial advice. My thanks also go to Editorial Assistant Erika Walsh and Content Manager Catherine Smith for their efficiency and assistance in the production of the book. My thanks also go to the fine work of Project Manager Podhumai Anban at Integra Software Services, Copy-Editor Dan Harding, and Indexer Jim Diggins. I especially thank Dan Harding for his superb work cleaning up the manuscript.

For providing resources to help in the research and writing of this study, I gratefully acknowledge two grants from the PSC-CUNY Research Foundation and one grant from the Chiang Ching-kuo Foundation for International Scholarly Exchange.

I acknowledge the *Journal of Contemporary China*, which published my article "Debating Ethnic Governance in China" (28.115, January 2019: 118–32). Chapter 5 of this book, "Ethnic Autonomy and Its Discontents," is adapted and expanded from that paper.

For my education in the English language and political science, I thank three great institutions of higher education. At Nanjing University and Foreign Affairs College in Beijing, where I majored in English, the foreign language faculty eagerly taught the first group of students since the college entrance exams resumed in China in the late 1970s. At Johns Hopkins University, where I pursued my doctoral study in political science, I am grateful to my mentors Drs. Germaine A. Hoston and William T. Rowe, as well as Drs. Richard S. Katz and Steven David in the Political Science Department. As one of the early graduate students from post-Mao China who had no prior exposure to Western social sciences, I benefited greatly from their welcoming attitude, their patience with my novitiate, their stimulating seminars, and most of all their intellectual guidance.

A special note of appreciation goes to my family. My parents, retired college professors in Chongqing, worried about me going to "unstable" minority regions but appreciated and supported my research pursuits. My children Ben and Kenny, and my husband Gang, tolerated my summer absences and one sabbatical absence as I carried out this research project. To them all is this book dedicated, but especially to my father, who passed away in the middle of my final preparation for the manuscript, in June 2019.

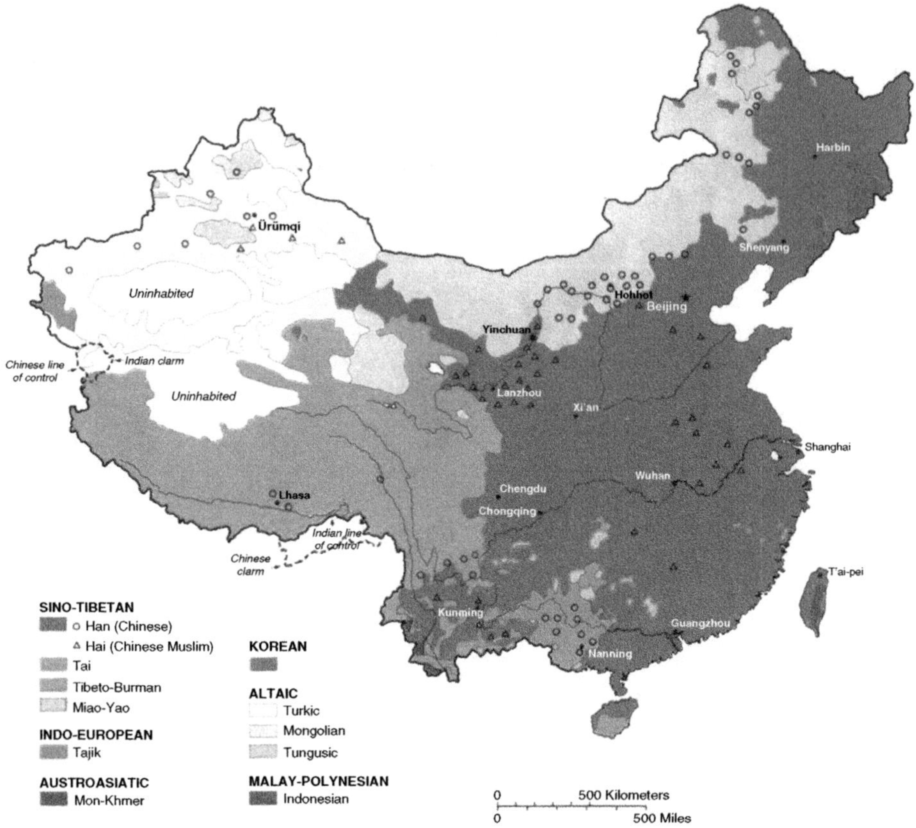

China: ethnolinguistic groups

Source: US Central Intelligence Agency, 1983. The map shows the distribution of ethnolinguistic groups according to the historical majority ethnic group by region.

INTRODUCTION

What Is Destabilizing about China's Ethnic Regions?

Since mid-2017, reports of massive "re-education camps" in Xinjiang have set off global outcries over China's treatment of Muslim Uighurs in western China. Witnesses and personal accounts reveal that a large number of Uighur residents, including returnees from overseas, have been detained and sent to so-called "training centers" for "deradicalization." The latest scholarship provides corroborating evidence from unusual increases in social stability spending and from public tenders for construction of such centers in Xinjiang (Zenz 2018a and 2018b). The estimated number of detainees, ranging from several hundred thousand to over one million, raises serious questions about the state's definition of "religious extremism" and presents a human rights crisis. In November of 2018, the United Nations Universal Periodic Review began its assessment of China's human rights record, amid growing global scrutiny over arbitrary internment of Muslim Uighurs.

Why does China feel so threatened by so-called radicalism that it has resorted to draconian methods to combat it? Granted, the emergence of massive camps in Xinjiang has much to do with Chen Quanguo's assumption of power at the helm here since August 2016. But the central state condones rather than condemns his policies. Moreover, after initial denial of their existence, the central state now acknowledges and justifies it at home and abroad. It is a sign that China feels that it has not yet brought under control those destabilizing forces that had caused many episodes of state-defined terrorism and one major incidence of ethnic riot.

That riot occurred on the evening of July 5, 2009 in the southern section of Urumqi, the capital city of Xinjiang Uighur Autonomous Region (XUAR). Thousands of Uighur youths went on a violent rampage, setting ablaze public buses, private vehicles, stores, shops, government buildings and commercial structures. In particular they targeted Han pedestrians for brutal killings. With the region's party secretary Wang Lequan away that night, it took nearly an hour for his order to arrive, finally allowing armed police to respond to the violence. Local police forces could not have used force earlier because of an official ordinance in 1983, known as dual legal standards, which prevented police from using violence against minority offenders without orders from above.

By next morning, the area looked like a war zone. The official account reported 197 people killed and 1,721 injured, and the destruction of 260 vehicles, 203 stores, fourteen residential houses, and two buildings.[1] The street violence was so shocking that the state banned video footage and other images online, so as to avoid inflaming the Han Chinese majority across the country. Actual casualties could be much higher than the official account, with accusations made by citizens on both sides of the ethnic divide to the contrary.

The Urumqi riot was ostensibly in response to the Shaoguan incident that occurred ten days earlier, on June 26, 2009. This incident involved a brawl among hundreds of Han and Uighur workers in a factory in Shaoguan, Guangdong province. The clash resulted in the death of two Uighur workers and over a hundred injured workers. The Han workers had harbored resentment of Uighur workers because of an online post, which alleged that six Uighur workers had raped two Han women. Local police later found the online account to be false (*NFRB* 2009). Exaggerated versions of the Shaoguan incident, in turn, became a rallying point for Uighur youths in Xinjiang. They mobilized in the capital of the province on the evening of July 5, 2009 to vent their accumulated frustration and anger.

The Urumqi riot also brought into the open the long suppressed resentment of local Han residents. Often perceived as meek and atomized individuals, Han residents found themselves frequently "bullied" in the streets of Xinjiang. The violence of July 5 seemingly roused an ethnic awakening. Angry at the local government's slow response, thousands of them swarmed onto the streets of Urumqi with clubs on July 7, seeking revenge. On September 3 and 4, tens of thousands of Han residents held public protests against a new round of violence involving syringes tainted with poison, which were used to prick Han pedestrians. In an unprecedented move, Han protesters called for the resignation of Wang Lequan, the party secretary of Xinjiang. The series of events eventually led to the dismissal of two top officials of Urumqi's municipal government in late 2009 and Wang's ousting in April 2010. Wang had originally tried to avoid reporting the incident to Beijing, so as to evade political liabilities. But authorities at the Xinjiang Production and Construction Corps (PCC) broke the news to Beijing.[2] The PCCs are composed largely of Han

[1] See the news archive of the riot at *Guoji zaixian*, http://news.cri.cn/gb/27824/2009/07/06/Zt1965s2554780.htm. Accessed May 10, 2019.

[2] According to conversations with a former official of the State Ethnic Affairs Commission, Beijing, fall 2013.

people and are administratively semi-independent from Xinjiang's provincial government.

The Urumqi riot was the worst incidence of ethnic violence in the history of the People's Republic of China, but not the only one. Hundreds of major episodes of violence have taken place in Xinjiang since the early 1990s, including many defined by the state as terrorist attacks. In the three years since the Urumqi riot, between 2009 and 2012, Xinjiang's local police cracked down on over a hundred "security threat" groups each year, including more than 190 "terror cases" in 2012 alone.[3] By late 2013, violence from Xinjiang reached outside the province, first in Tiananmen Square where three tourists were killed on November 28, and then at the Kunming train station in Yunnan where twenty-eight people were killed on March 1, 2014. Several more "major cases of terrorism" were reported in Xinjiang in that year, including an attack on a vegetable market in Urumqi that killed forty-three civilians, an attack in Yarkant county of Kashgar that killed thirty-seven, and a market attack in Bachu county of Kashgar that killed twenty-two civilians (see Chapter 6). After Xinjiang's intensified crackdowns since mid-2014, one massive attack still occurred in 2015, taking the lives of over forty miners in an Aksu county. In the three years between 2013 and 2016, 127 police officers in Xinjiang were killed while "fighting terrorists," according to an official media report (*China* 2017).

Another restive region is the Tibet Autonomous Region (TAR). On March 14, 2008, a rampage of a lesser magnitude than the Urumqi riot broke out on the streets of Lhasa, capital of the TAR. In what came to be known as the 3.14 Incident, eighteen innocent civilians were burned to death, along with the destruction of 908 stores, seven schools, 120 residential homes, five hospitals, thirty buildings, ten banking services, and eighty-four vehicles.[4] Sporadic protests by Tibetan monks have occurred since the late 1980s, as did over a hundred cases of self-immolation since February 2009.

Nationwide, the Lhasa and Urumqi riots of 2008 and 2009, along with violent incidents incurred by ethnic assailants outside Xinjiang, brought into the open the country's "ethnic problems" that had been neglected or hidden from public view. But heightened awareness has also added to ethnic tensions, igniting fiery debates and verbal feuds in online forums. As one Chinese analyst puts it, ethnocentrism on all sides has helped to intensify biases and radicalize ethno-nationalism; slanderous and radical comments often enjoy greater freedom than critically fair and rational ones in the blog sphere; the "Shangri-La"-rized image of

[3] According to data from Xinjiang's provincial police, reported in "Xinjiang qunian fasheng 190 yuqi kongbao an" [Over 190 terror cases in Xinjiang last year]. *Liaowang dongfang zhoukan*, October 30, 2013. Web.

[4] The event is archived at "Lasashi 3.14 da za qiang shao shijian" [The Lhasa 3.14 incident of violence, destruction, pillage and arson]. *China*, March 22, 2008, http://news.china.com/zh_cn/focus/tibet08/. Accessed June 3, 2013.

Tibetans is replaced by one of viciousness and ungratefulness; "pickpockets from Xinjiang" are attacked online; and the singing and dancing "earthy ethnic folks" are now viewed as "backward and lazy thugs" (Yao 2013b). It was precisely such polarized emotions that drove interethnic mistrust, resulting in the Shaoguan incident of 2009 that ignited the Urumqi riot on July 5 that year.

RESEARCH QUESTION

Why have ethnic mobilization and violence occurred only in the two outer peripheral regions of China? That is, Xinjiang and Tibet, the two regions that are geographically, ethnically, and culturally most remote from China. The issue is important at the theoretical level for understanding ethnic conflict and ethnic policy and at the empirical level for understanding a volatile problem in a large multiethnic country. For China as a historical empire and a former Soviet-type regime, it is also important to understand the linkage between ethnic mobilization and national integration or disintegration. As such, ethnic strife also constitutes a security issue for China, when the combined areas of Tibet and Xinjiang comprise nearly a third of China's territory and China's minority regions as a whole encompass nearly two-thirds of the country's territory.

The upsurge of ethnic tensions in contemporary China has received much scholarly attention. Existing perspectives may be grouped into two broad schools. The first highlights the effects of post-Mao reform policies and processes, arguing that minority grievances and interethnic disparities have been sharpened by China's modernization and developmental drive (Hillman and Tuttle 2016; Fischer 2005, 2012, and 2013; Williams 2008; Koch 2006; Dreyer 2005 and 2006; Clarke 2007; Heberer 2005; Moneyhon 2004; Becquelin 2004; Goodman 2002 and 2004; Gladney 1995 and 2009; Mackerras 1994; Harrell 1995). The second broad school emphasizes the lack of political autonomy that allows little independence of action or expression (Han and Paik 2014; Bovingdon 2004 and 2010; CECC 2005; Starr 2004; Stein 2003; Moneyhon 2002; Becquelin 2000; Yash 2000; Heberer 1989). These two perspectives are not mutually exclusive. Both see an interplay of limited autonomy and imposed development that coalesces minority grievances in four areas: religion and culture, resource distribution, social discrimination, and political autonomy (Dreyer 2005).

While on target, these analyses do not provide a consistent long-term causal chain of explanation. That is, why more limited autonomy did not lead to more ethnic unrest in the Mao era, or why some minority regions in the reform era have experienced more unrest than others and in more volatile ways, or why such unrest should differ qualitatively from protests by disadvantaged members among the Han Chinese majority over similar issues of socioeconomic discontent and rights violations. A recent study does address the intergroup divergence by highlighting how external factors make a difference. That is, ethnic groups with extensive external kinship networks – specifically the Tibetans and Uighurs – are most likely to perceive a capacity to achieve better circumstances and thus more likely to politically mobilize and contest national identity (Han 2016). However, the size of the internal minority group matters when it comes to external kinship support in internal conflict, as it affects power considerations. External kinship support is more likely and potentially more impactful when the internal minority group is relatively large (Cederman Girardin and Gleditsch 2009). For relatively small groups, external kinship support matters little even if present. Although Uighurs and Tibetans comprise relatively large groups among China's minority groups (fourth and ninth largest, respectively) and are concentrated in two major borderlands, they each constitute less than 1 percent of China's overall population (respectively 0.7555 percent and 0.4713 percent in the 2010 census).

My study is intended to understand the long-term causal chain of factors from a historical-political perspective. By "historical," I refer to the relevance of the patterns of historical transition from a dynastic empire to the modern nation state in the Mao era, and then to the current system of ethnic governance in the post-Mao era. Because modern China largely inherited the territories of the preceding imperial dynasty, the dynamics of that transition must be considered as part of a long-term causal chain of explanation. As Wimmer and Min argue (2006), change in the institutional form of states is itself a major cause for war, and the rise of empires and the global spread of the nation state are the most important institutional transformations in the modern age. Although China was a historical empire rather than a modern one, the dynamics of transition to the modern nation state were fundamentally similar to those identified by Wimmer and Min: competing nationalist doctrines of the national majority and ethnic minorities, competing projects of nation and state building, and ensuing power struggles over the ethno-national character of the state. For China, thus, the dynamics of the transition to the modern nation state is central to understanding sustained or renewed internal strife associated with state building. China did not undergo modern state formation by way of violent destruction or disruption of multiethnic regions and peoples, as was notably the case following the disintegration of the Ottoman Empire (Ungor 2012; Akçam 2004 and 2013). Nor has China lapsed into contemporary state re-formation, as was the case following the disintegration of the Soviet Union. The legacies of China's historical transition, thus, bear importantly on its contemporary ethnic politics.

Indeed, the characteristics of the Chinese transition make the Chinese case unique as well as universal in comparative contexts. The (forced) transition from empire to the modern state was universal, as with other major historical empires such as the Ottoman Empire (1299–1922) and the Russian Empire (1721–1917). But the unique features of China's historical legacy helped to avoid the disintegration experienced by the Ottoman Empire and the Soviet Union. Among those unique features, Dingxin Zhao notes, were the consistent imperial system of two millennia, the strongest state tradition among major civilizations, the only world civilization where transcendental world religions exerted no influence on politics, civilian rule, a huge territory due to expansion by nomadic conquests, and a large core population with a shared identity (over 90 percent of the country's population by the nineteenth century) (2015: 7, 374–5).

From the point of transition to the modern nation state, most important was the persistence and dominance of the Confucian state, which had given rise to a geographic/demographic feature unique to pre-modern China. That is, the core of the Chinese Empire had a very large size and a huge population with a similar cultural identity.[5] This territorial/demographic feature was interrelated: by assimilating cycles of nomadic conquerors from surrounding communities, China had expanded via what Henry Kissinger calls "cultural osmosis" (2012: 529). That is, incorporating rounds of frontier communities into the empire's territorial/demographic core. This incorporation also entailed a contiguous – though tiered – topography for China's pre-modern empire, with inner peripheral regions more incorporated than outer peripheral ones. This contiguity helped to preserve China's ethnic borderlands in pre-modern and modern times, and it also facilitated state building in contemporary times. Together, China's demographic/territorial legacy has made it difficult for even the least assimilated groups to break away; that is, the Tibetan and Uighur communities on the far western frontiers. As previous research shows, the ethno-demographic make-up of a state is a principal predictor of whether the shift to the nation state will be accompanied by interstate war (Wimmer and Min 2006: 875). China's demographic/territorial advantage, nevertheless, has not obviated the persistence of the two least assimilated groups. It is not incidental that only these two groups have fueled ethnic strife in contemporary times.

The context and legacy of China's national integration, thus, are central to understanding its contemporary ethnic problems. To the extent that modern China avoided secessionist civil wars and saw just one region break away (outer Mongolia), its transition to the modern nation state may be seen as largely successful. Its transition to the post-socialist era, likewise, has avoided a disintegration of the Soviet type. However, China's transitions have not been without tribulations, which cannot be understood through contemporary forces alone. If the existing literature blames limited autonomy, economic modernization, and contested identities for China's contemporary ethnic woes, their root causes should also be understood in the historical patterns of China's ethnic governance and their modern fate.

ARGUMENT

My study attempts to understand China's contemporary ethnic strife from the perspective of its twofold transition from empire to a modern nation state. That is, the integration of frontier regions into a nation state with predominantly

[5] I thank Professor Dingxin Zhao for these insights.

ethnic Han Chinese. Instead of individual policies, my perspective places emphasis on the institutional arrangements of the twofold transition and how they have become sources of contemporary problems. The first transition was from empire to the modern nation state, via the autonomous system in the socialist era. The second transition was from the socialist era (1949–78) to the reform era (1978–present).

This twofold transition, I argue, has laid down the root causes or the institutional dynamics of China's contemporary ethnic strife. Those dynamics may be summed as political centralization on the one hand and ethnic particularism on the other, or simply: centralization and ethnicization. Centralization narrowly refers to a uniform system of ethnic governance under the centralized political leadership, and broadly refers to state policies with centralizing functions and consequences. Ethnicization refers to the grounding of identity, administrative units, and policy benefits on the ethnic criterion, as well as its ethnicizing effects. Centralization is centripetal, while ethnicization, by consolidating different local identities into a cohesive cross-regional ethnic identity, is centrifugal. These institutional tensions have been manifest during each phase of the twofold transition.

During the first transition, from empire to nation state, those institutional tensions were laid down but tempered, I argue. Centralization materialized in the Chinese Communist Party's (CCP) three strategies of nation state building: state classification of identities, a system of autonomous regions, and socialist egalitarianism. Ethnicization inhered from the same three strategies: politicized identities, titular ethno-territorial units, and policy prerogatives along ethnic and ethno-territorial lines. The tensions therein were temporarily mitigated by a new class universalism, whereby the communist sense of history was able to provide a basis for elite consensus. Based on social class solidarity, this new universalism helped to buttress both national integration and particularistic policies for the ethnic proletariat.

In the second transition, from the Mao era to the post-Mao era, the mix of centralization and ethnicization has particularly affected Xinjiang and the TAR. This is because they have remained the *only* two outer peripheral regions in the geographic, demographic, and cultural sense: far flung, with ethnic majorities and distinct ascriptive features. In this reform era, centralization stems from two main sources: state facilitation of identity politics and control of its directions on the one hand, and state developmentalism on the other. Ethnicization, meanwhile, stems largely from uncontrolled growth of identity politics and interethnic competition in the marketplace. The centrifugal nature of identity politics and interethnic competition, in turn, has necessitated more political centralization to enhance integration, but also more ethnic accommodation to placate centrifugal forces. The intensified institutional strains therein – more centralization but also more ethnicization – are the key sources of ethnic strife in Tibet and Xinjiang in the contemporary era.

What contributed to the paradox of centralization and ethnicization in the twofold transitions? In the first transition, a number of historical legacies and modern strategies were highly relevant to the patterns of the transition and to contemporary ethnic strife. These may be seen at three levels. First, the CCP's ethnic classification displaced historical legacies of ethnic neutrality and localized identities by creating centrally politicized identities. Pre-modern ethnic identities could also be politicized, but they were predominately politicized at local levels, and local ethnic identities also crosscut. Such localization and crosscuts prevented local identities from consolidating into a sustained cross-regional ethnic or proto-nationalistic political identity. Second, the CCP's autonomous system displaced historical legacies of indirect, diverse, and de-ethnicized rule over minority regions by creating direct and uniform rule based on the titular minority. Third, the CCP's socialist egalitarianism displaced historical legacies of elite co-optation through penetrating minority societies with transformative preferential policies. Together, the CCP's strategies, by departing dramatically from historical legacies and mixing centralization with ethnicization, created the built-in institutional dynamics for ethnic strife in contemporary times.

What makes the causal chain of explanation here particular to the Chinese case? After all, the CCP's strategies were universal in other multiethnic contexts. The first two strategies, that is the creation of centrally politicized identities and centrally directed rule, were universal in the early modern transition from empire to nation states. The third strategy, socialist egalitarianism, was universal in former Soviet-type countries that were multiethnic. The mix of centralization and ethnicization, as reflected in these strategies, also echoed those of almost all pre-modern empires that relied on sticks and carrots to rule diverse populations. What made these strategies peculiar to the Chinese case was the embedding of new institutions in local contexts.

This embedding may be seen in three ways. First, while reliance on some type of universalism was universal in pre-modern empires as well as during their transition to nation states, the strength of China's Confucian universalism eased the transition to a new universalism based on social class solidarity. Both emanated from a strong central state and were reinforced by a large demographic/territorial core. Second, China's pre-modern patterns of ethnic governance, based in "loose rein," made the transition to nation state relatively smooth for those ethnic regions that had been historically incorporated into China's imperial bureaucratic system. Only two outer peripheral regions, Tibet and Xinjiang, experienced belated incorporation and possessed ethnic majorities at the time of the modern transition. Third, while China adopted the Soviet model of ethno-federalism, it did so without accepting the Soviet tenet of ethnic self-determination. This partial ethno-federalism precludes legal grounds for independence, which contributed to the dissolution of the Soviet Union. Together, the unique Chinese features – a strong demographic/geographic core, pre-modern patterns of ethnic rule, and an adaptation of the

Soviet model – have been key differences in the patterns of China's transition from empire to nation state.

In the second transition of ethnic governance, that is to the post-Mao era, reform policies have undone the course of the first transition in a few key policy areas. As such, they have helped to create the institutional dynamics for contemporary ethnic strife in Tibet and Xinjiang. First, the abandonment of class universalism has undermined the ideological and political underpinning of centralization. It has created the institutional dynamics for greater reliance on "sticks" as well as "carrots" to uphold centralization. Second, the rise of identity politics has been legitimated by policies to redress leftist wrongs. This has served as an alternative to class universalism and an institutional dynamic for greater ethnic particularism. Third, the demise of the socialist contract – via economic liberalization – has left ethnic masses abandoned socioeconomically but their grievances ethnically charged. It has ushered in the institutional dynamics for interethnic competition and disparities. Fourth, the rise of state developmentalism has facilitated state transformation of minority societies from a pre-modern, rural, and agrarian society to a secular, urban, and industrial society. It has created the institutional dynamics for greater integration in minority regions, and along with it an intensified disruption of their traditional society, sweetened by preferential policies that also enhance ethnicization.

What makes this causal chain of explanation peculiar to the Chinese case? Again, ethnic tensions arise in many places and different contexts in today's world. Modernizing and globalizing forces create winners and losers interethnically in various societies across the globe. Political and economic liberalization contributed to the disintegration of the Soviet Union along ethno-territorial lines. Identity politics spurs ethnic discords even in mature democracies. Within China, different outcomes have resulted from the same four processes of transformation in post-Mao China, that is the demise of class universalism and the rise of identity politics on the one hand, and the demise of the socialist contract and the rise of state developmentalism on the other. Ethnic regions other than the two outer peripheral regions have not experienced the level of ethnic strife seen in Tibet and Xinjiang.

What makes the causal processes – the end of class universalism and the socialist contract on the one hand, and the rise of identity politics and developmentalism on the other – particularly important in Tibet and Xinjiang? It is the strong role of the state in facilitating them, resulting in more politicized outcomes. In the Soviet case, as a contrast, it was the weakness of the central state that contributed to the disintegration of the union in the wake of socialism's demise. In mature democracies, identity politics is driven by societal forces rather than the state, in contrast to China's case. Among developing contexts where economic disparities divide ethnic groups, no central state has been more proactive than China's in driving development. And within China, the state has been most proactive in Tibet and lately Xinjiang.

TABLE I.1 *Historical transition of China's ethnic governance: from empire to the post-Mao era*

	Pre-modern empire	Modern state (Mao era)	Post-Mao era
Identity	Local and crosscut	State classified and consolidated in "class"	State classified and consolidated in "nation"
Governance	Indirect rule	Direct rule and titular	Direct rule and particularistic
Policy strategy	Elite alliances	Egalitarianism	Developmentalism

In short, the twofold transition of ethnic governance has laid down the built-in institutional dynamics for China's contemporary ethnic woes: historical discontinuities have reduced political autonomy for the constituent members of China's pre-modern empire, aggravated by intrusive centralizing forces in the reform era; while the socialist or egalitarian strategies contribute to what Terry Martin calls "an affirmative action empire" of the Soviet type (2001a). The combined result is limited autonomy on the one hand and ethnic particularism on the other. That is, a mix of centralization and ethnicization. This core institutional feature of China's autonomous system is referred to as "socialist autonomy" in this study. The advent of institutional dynamics for ethnic tensions, during the twofold historical transition, is presented in Table I.1.

A further review of the relevant literature, in the three sections below, will provide theoretical contexts to the argument I make in this book.

SOCIALIST AUTONOMY AND A BREAK WITH HISTORY

The literature on interethnic relations in pre-modern China sheds light on historical patterns and puts in perspective China's contemporary system of ethnic governance. Broadly, what was the nature of ethnic relations in pre-modern China? Why have Tibet and Xinjiang remained the only outer peripheral regions in a geographic and cultural sense?

Above all, interethnic relations were conditioned by ecological features in pre-modern China. Western scholarship universally recognizes a prolonged series of interactions between the settled people of the East Asian heartland and their nomadic neighbors of Inner Asia, despite a sharp disagreement over the nature of their interactions (Rawski 1996; Ho 1998). From the ecological perspective, scholars characterize a "political ecology" between the steppe tribes of Inner Asians and their agricultural and sedentary neighbors of the Central Plains, which bound them to rivalry (Lattimore 1940; Barfield 1989 and 2001; Khazanov 2001; Kradin 2002 and 2005). A nomadic society had difficulty raising revenue because its members, unlike settled farmers, could move themselves and their wealth easily, and were skilled fighters; while its chief product, livestock, could not be easily stored, unlike the grain produced in agrarian economies (Khazanov 1984; Zhao 2015: 318–19, 322–3). Whether or not driven by the dynamic of this "needy nomad" (Barfield 1989; Di Cosmo 1994), pre-modern nomads of Inner Asia frequently plundered resources from agrarian societies, by pillaging farm villages, extorting tributes, and controlling trade routes and the terms of trade. They conquered northern China periodically, and twice the entire country (Fairbank 1983: 87–8).

The dynamics of Sino-nomadic relationships, at the same time, were more complex than a "Sino-barbarian" dichotomy. Ancient Chinese statesmen had divergent, and at times contradictory, ideas about how to treat the aliens (Di Cosmos 2002). The same diversity of approaches was true across the prairies (Purdue 2005: 533; Jagchid and Symons 1989; Khazanov 1984). Most importantly, the comparative advantages of each group compelled and contributed to mutual learning and mutual assimilation in the context of competitive struggles for survival (Zhao 2015: 325–9). In fact, the cycles of nomadic incursions, competition/interaction, and migration/fusion were responsible for the evolution of China as a multinational country and of the majority Han people itself (Fei 1988). This interpretation of China's ethnic make-up is supported by historical and archeological evidence (Wang 1934; Lü 1935; Lin 1936) and more recently, by genetic and genealogical evidence (Cavalli-Sforza 1998; Wen et al. 2004; Jin et al. 2005).

The cycles of Sino-nomadic interaction and fusion contributed to a key difference between China and the rest of the world. That is, the persistent domination of Confucianism, along with its acculturation of successive nomadic communities, had given rise to a *geographic/demographic* character unique to pre-modern China: the core of the Chinese Empire had a very large size and a huge population with a similar cultural identity (Zhao 2015: 7, 374–5). By contrast, in the cases of the Ottoman Empire and the Soviet Union, the dominant ethnic or religious group did not amount to a strong majority, or were divided into significant subgroups. The Ottoman Empire had a Christian majority under the rule of a Muslim minority up to the second half of the fifteenth century (Benton 2001: 109–10). The proportion of Muslims rose to 60 percent in the 1820s, 69 percent in the 1870s, 76 percent in the 1890s, and 80.9 percent by 1914 (Içduygu et al. 2008: 363). However, these Muslims subdivided into Arabian, Persian, North Africans, and Balkan Europeans across three continents. For the Russian Empire, the first and only census carried out in the empire, in 1897, recorded that Russian speakers comprised a little less than 45 percent of the total population.[6] On the eve of the Soviet dissolution in

[6] Demoscope.ru, Первая всеобщая перепись населения Российской Империи 1897 г. Распределение населения по родному языку и регионам (First General Russian Empire Census of 1897. Population breakdown by mother tongue and regions). Demoscope.ru, www.demoscope.ru/weekly/ssp/rus_-lan_97.php.

1989, Russians made up 51.4 percent of the population of the Union of Soviet Socialist Republics (USSR), while the fourteen titular minority groups made up the rest (Sakwa 1998: 242–50).

The weakness of a demographic core was compounded by geography in the Ottoman and Soviet cases. The Ottomans' overly expansive empire exerted little reach or influence into the large number of ethnic and religious communities spanning across three continents, who lived separately in segregated domains called millets (Barkey and Gavrils 2016). With little loyalty toward the imperial state, ethnic nationalism – based on distinctive religion and language – provided the centripetal forces that eventually brought down the Ottoman Empire (Quataert 1983). In the Soviet case, territorial contiguity did earlier help to hold together Russia's historical empire across the Eurasian land mass during the transition to the modern nation state. However, the expansive territory of the Soviet Union did not survive the transition to the post-socialist world. Ethnic nationalism, nurtured by Soviet minority policy itself, contributed to the union's dissolution along ethno-territorial lines (Bunce 1999; Leff 1999). The lack of a large territorial/demographic core with a shared Russian identity, certainly, made it difficult to hold the secessionist ethnic republics in check.

In the context of China's demographic/territorial core and its incremental acculturation/incorporation of frontier communities, why have Tibet and Xinjiang remained the only outer peripheral regions? These two regions, along with Mongolia and Manchuria, had historically comprised China's "four Central Eurasian frontier regions" (Millward and Perdue 2004: 62). They were far flung, on the steppes, and semi-nomadic or nomadic. Until the late Qing period (1880s–1911), Tibet and Xinjiang were the only ethnic regions that did not adopt the provincial system or undergo bureaucratization reforms.[7] For Inner Mongolia and Manchuria, central policies during the late Qing period and the Republican era (1911–1940s) had significantly changed the composition and orientation of the local populations, as did the warmer climate after the eighteenth century that made Inner Mongolia cultivatable. By the time the CCP came to power in 1949, Manchuria had been well integrated while Inner Mongolia had a solid Han majority. Tibet and southern Xinjiang were left as the only outer peripheral regions in the demographic, linguistic, and cultural sense.

As such, these two regions remain the principal challenges for China's nation state building. Without China's demographic/territorial core, the two regions might have seceded after the collapse of the Qing empire, much as the lack of such a core facilitated the breakdown of the Ottoman Empire and the Soviet Empire. That unique Chinese feature made it very difficult for Tibet and

[7] Xinjiang became a province in 1884. Manchuria became three provinces during the late Qing: Jilin, Tianxing sheng (Liaoning), and Heilongjiang. Jilin was an en route province during the Yuan dynasty. Tibet never became a province before the CCP came to power in 1949.

Xinjiang to achieve independence then and now. Yet the People's Republic of China's (PRC) socialist autonomy has failed to construct a new national identity that transcends ethnicity. It has even consolidated the ethnic identity of the already peripheral groups, Tibetans and Uighurs. These two cases remain the exceptions among China's ethnic regions (Leibold 2016; Han 2016), but have forced the Chinese state to endure very high costs in contemporary times. This is quite unique to China: a large demographic/territorial core but two highly politicized ethnic majority regions. This politicization, moreover, has been engineered by the modern state itself.

SOVIET-TYPE AUTONOMY AND IDENTITY POLITICS

The literature on Soviet-type ethno-federalism sheds light on two issues central to understanding the linkage between institutional designs and ethnic tensions in China. First, is China's autonomous system ethno-federal? Second, is this system conducive to institutionalizing identity that was largely absent in much of Chinese history?

Ethno-federalism is a federal political system under which component territorial governance units are intentionally associated with the most important ethnic groups in them (Roeder 1991). The Soviet model included multiple levels of administrative units – autonomous republics, provinces, regions, and districts – for non-Russian ethnic groups. Fourteen of the Soviet Union's fifteen Union Republics were based on a titular minority group. Constitutionally, each republic was a sovereign Soviet socialist state, united with its peers in the USSR. Each republic was accorded with language and cultural rights, ethnic representation in local official and professional ranks, separate branches of the Soviet Red Army, Republic-level commissariats for foreign affairs and defense, and most of all, the nominal right to secede from the USSR. At the union level, however, the USSR was a highly centralized entity, with all republics subordinated directly to the central government. A hierarchy of party organizations existed alongside the state administrative one. This allowed the Politburo to exercise control over the republics. The state hierarchy received directions and personnel appointments from the parallel party hierarchy.

Do political centralization and a lack of popular elections render Soviet-type federalism meaningless? Scholars answer in the negative, arguing that this formalistic model has meaningful import (Leff 1999: 210; Roeder 1991 and 2004). First, the official recognition accorded to the titular nationalities in the ethno-regional units, reinforced by language and cultural rights, has unintended consequences for ethnic mobilization, by providing the tools for entrenching and activating national identities. Second, the structures of autonomy provide separate and distinct political marketplaces for developing institutional interests at the ethno-regional level. Finally, ethno-regional units provide territorial bases for the emergence of distinctive regional elites, rooted in the titular nationalities. Having partially emulated the Soviet model, China's autonomous system may be characterized as "latent" or "nascent" ethno-federalism (Hale 2004: 167). Except for the right of secession, the Chinese variant adopted key features of the Soviet model, including ethnic classification, territorial units based on titular minority groups, and minority-specific public policies.

Virtually all explanations of the breakup of socialist ethno-federations fault their ethnicizing effects. That is, such systems have had the effect of (1) strengthening ethnic differences, and (2) providing resources, bases, and networks for political entrepreneurs to play the "nationality card." On the first effect, Valerie Bunce observes that the federal structures of the Soviet Union, Yugoslavia, and Czechoslovakia "worked to build nations (or reinforce such processes, if nations were already formed), along with proto-states at the republic level" (1999: 136–9). Ronald Suny writes that Soviet nationality policies led to "the consolidation of ethnicity rather than to its disappearance," and "rather than a melting pot, the Soviet Union became an incubator of new nations" (1993: 87). The "making nation" approach, rather than the "sleeping beauty" frame, thus explains the breakup of the Soviet Union (Suny 1992: 24). Others call it a revenge of "ethnic particularism" promoted by the USSR itself (Slezkine 1994; Minogue and Williams 1992).

On the second effect, or the provision of resources to play the nationalist card, scholars argue that ethno-federal states differ from other federal states in the political recognition of ethno-territorial identities. In a federal state with a homogenous population or a complex mixed society, federal structures afford neither a clear ethnic territorial base nor a concept of ethnic-regional identity (Leff 1999: 210). The geographical base of the periphery is crucial because it provided the "geographical concentration of the nation as a prime facilitator of the development of group solidarity." Ethno-federalism did combine with economic decline and state repression to consolidate subnational consciousness in the Soviet case, but "in the absence of federalism, geographically concentrated minorities seem to be less prone to either want to leave the state or, if that is desired, to succeed in doing so" (Bunce 1999: 138). A high degree of regional autonomy has also encouraged "ethnic revival" and separatism in Russia in the 1990s, and regions with religious identities, especially Muslim titular minorities, are considerably more separatist (Treisman 1997).

Cultural and linguistic tools add to pernicious tensions in Soviet ethno-federalism. These arise, Anthony D. Smith argues, from the assertion of political control on the one hand but the preservation and enhancing of cultural and linguistic spheres on the other. State attempts to separate the two domains result in a "contradiction between political centralism and cultural diversity," which, given the modern role of culture as the major basis of politics, "bedevils most polyethnic states" and "particularly those polyethnic states that have adopted a Leninist political mode." The situation is rendered yet more explosive by the Herderian legacy of nationalism, Smith argues, which stresses the central role of language in the definition of nations, supplemented by territory. As such, Lenin and Stalin "provided not only a framework for categorizing the many ethnic groupings within Soviet territories, but also the sociological basis for their modern redefinition and regeneration" (Smith 1992: 59).

In short, Soviet-type ethno-federalism attempts to achieve ethnic autonomy and equality, *not through mechanisms of political autonomy*, but through the institutionalization of ethnic and geographical markers. China's adoption of these markers, I argue, was the structural origin of the contemporary problems in Tibet and Xinjiang.

SOCIALIST AUTONOMY AND ECONOMIC LIBERALIZATION

Studies show that political and economic liberalization exacerbates the inherent tensions of ethno-federalism. For while the state may continue to allocate political and economic opportunities along ethnic distinctions, it can no longer control interethnic equality in outcomes.

In the classic literature on nationalism, economic modernization is found to be the root cause of the ascendency of politicized ethnicity. The reasons are straightforward. Economic modernization increases social mobility and creates political economies in which advancement depends increasingly on one's cultural capital. When young men of one ethnic group from the countryside found themselves disadvantaged in the new industrial labor markets or state bureaucracy on the grounds of their first language, they became receptive to political mobilization along ethnic ("national") lines (Deutsch 1953; Gellner 1983). The key idea is that ascriptive barriers to upward mobility – that is, disadvantages according to a criterion that an individual acquires usually at birth – gives political entrepreneurs an eager constituency (Anderson 1983; Fearon 2006).

Why are the advantages or disadvantages of cultural or ascriptive endowments so salient in the modern polity and economy? Gellner emphasizes the nature of modern economies: they require literate workers able to interpret and manipulate culturally specific symbols, thus culture matters in the modern world in a way it never did in the pre-modern, agrarian age. Why not then learn the language and culture of the dominant economic and political group? Gellner, Deutsch, and Anderson suggest that such assimilation may be possible, but only when pre-existing cultural differences are not too great, such as in nineteenth-century France. Where they were, such as in Austria-Hungary, the pace of assimilation may be too slow relative to economic modernization (Deutsch 1953), or psychological biases may lead advanced groups to attribute backwardness to the ethnic differences of less modernized groups (Gellner 1983).

Recent studies of ethnic violence, moreover, point to the role of state institutions in making cultural identity relevant politically. Where the institutions of state and economy make ascription (i.e., cultural and religious distinctions) the criterion for membership and for economic participation and allocation, ethnic identity becomes politically relevant. Specifically, the interaction of high interregional inequality and ethnic concentration increases the likelihood of ethnic conflict (Bakke and Wibbels 2006). Such conflict turns volatile when state institutions of political and economic allocation are weakened. Thus in recent decades, much of the rising ethnic violence across the globe is closely linked to globalizing forces and demands of economic liberalization that have weakened states' capacities, both political and financial, for redistributing resources (Crawford and Lipschutz 1998).

As a result, many states have been forced to break established social contracts, often dramatically changing power relations in heterogeneous societies that had previously been relatively stable. Those power and distributional shifts have been experienced in the form of ethnic and religious discrimination and are often at the root of identity politics and violent "cultural" conflicts (Crawford and Lipschutz 1998). This was especially true of post-socialist multinational states, as they were transitioning from institutions that structured the allocation of political and economic benefits along ethnic lines (Suny 1993; Slezkine 1994; Roeder 1998; Crawford 1998). As those socialist institutions changed, individual or cultural characteristics nurtured and protected by ethno-federalism were slow to adapt. When the unchangeable characteristics, such as one's first language, cultural traits, and religious faiths, became barriers to successful participation in the competitive market, these societies became vulnerable to ethnic conflict.

In China's case, the confluence of ethnic concentration and ascriptive barriers – ingredients of heightened ethnic consciousness and assertiveness – is striking in Tibetan and Uighur regions. In fact they are the only ethnic communities in China where ascriptive barriers – language and culture (in the form of religion) – are present. Adding to this confluence is one of the most intense processes of economic liberalization in the world, and along with it the weakening of the state institutions of economic allocation for ethnic minorities. These processes, not surprisingly, have affected Tibetan and Uighur regions most adversely. This is precisely the second part of my argument: the built-in tensions of the autonomous system have worsened in the outer peripheral regions since economic liberalization.

METHODOLOGY

Baseline

For the first phase of the twofold transition of China's ethnic governance, that is from empire to the modern nation state, the baseline for my case selection will be the entire universe of China's historical ethnic regions. Since a central contention of the book is that this transition laid down the roots of contemporary ethnic tensions, in ways embedded in China's local contexts, it is necessary to include the universe of China's historical ethnic regions. This would help highlight the changing forms of center–peripheral relations, and in particular, distinctions between two major types of ethnic regions, the inner peripheral and the outer peripheral.

For the second part of the twofold transition, from the socialist era to the reform era, my case selection will include only Tibet and Xinjiang. This is because they have remained the only two outer peripheral regions, the only "core" ethnic regions (i.e., autonomous regions with ethnic majorities), the only groups with distinctive ascriptive features (i.e., language and religion), and most of all, the only ethnic regions that have experienced serious ethnic conflict since the 1980s. No other significant case is left out.

Sources

I utilize archival research, supplemented by field research. For the first transition, from empire to nation state, I draw on historical records and government documents in modern and contemporary times, and secondary sources in Chinese and English. For the second transition, or the reform era, I draw on official documents, government data, policy reports, and a variety of local media. I also consult Chinese pundit analyses and academic literature. The archival research is supplemented by fieldwork in a host of ethnic regions.

Official documentary records supply key sources of factual information about the evolution and content of ethnic policies. Official yearbooks on the demography, economy, and education of ethnic regions provide the only source of systematic data for studying minority regions. These data have limitations, but researchers work in an imperfect world. Official statistics, as a scholar of Tibetan regions notes, goes beyond insights extrapolated from sporadic personal and anecdotal accounts (Fischer 2002: 13), thus they overcome another set of imperfections. Official data can often reveal problems or outcomes of state policy in a more systematic way than sporadically extrapolated insights.

Quasi-official and unofficial materials from China provide contextual information and local assessment of relevant political developments. The quasi-official literature includes (1) policy reports by research groups of government agencies (e.g., the State Ethnic Affairs Commission, the National People's Congress, and academies of social sciences); (2) national and local media; and (3) memoirs of former officials and their staff members. The unofficial literature includes (1) investigative journalism from more independent media, for example those based in Hong Kong and Guangzhou; (2) academic debates and reports, published in more independent sources, such as university and local presses; and (3) non-governmental organization or personal blogs and dissident discourse. Blogs have become useful sites to locate unorthodox views or articles that have been blocked in formal venues. Dissident views may be found among those who work within the Chinese system (e.g., Zhang Haiyang, He Fang, Hu Deping, and Tohti) and those who are outside it (e.g., Wang Lixiong, Woeser, and Li Jianglin).

The vast amount and range of this Chinese literature is little noted in the West and is itself part of the ongoing developments in China's ethnic policy. It offers a critical window into the spectrum of policy discussions in a country where doing first-hand research is nearly impossible in the two sensitive regions. During my field trips, private conversations with official and unofficial sources were often candid and informative, but formally consented interviews would only yield stereotypical answers echoing official lines, especially on the type of issues in which I was interested. Even my relatives would not give consented interviews and those employed in local government agencies shunned direct contact with me. Except for leading spokesmen of well-known views, such as Ma Rong and Ilham Tohti, few were willing to offer their real thoughts in consented interviews, even if assured of confidentiality.

Drawing on the variety of quasi-official and unofficial sources offer several advantages. Policy analyses from government agencies and research institutions offer background details otherwise inaccessible to outside researchers. National and local media are rich sources of the latest developments and controversies, including those not reported by authorities. Memoirs of former officials and staff members provide rare insights into behind-the-scenes politics. Local researchers convey varied perspectives and may influence policy making or sway public opinions. As Thomas Mullaney (2010a) documents, Chinese social scientists served as the "eyes" of the state in the state's ethnic classification of the 1950s, and they continue to serve as such eyes today. And as Gilbert Rozman (1987) shows, Chinese debates are not only important for understanding developments in China but also the Chinese worldview on sensitive matters critical to domestic and international affairs.

The richness and complexity of Chinese sources also help to overcome the limitations of access available to foreign-based scholars. Two major types of information can be learned. One is information that is not directly researchable. For example, I encountered brochures on radical religious activities in local state offices in southern Xinjiang, but marked for internal circulation only. However, if local researchers use such documents in their publications, I may utilize the factual information they cite from internal documents. As another example, while visiting southern Xinjiang with a Chinese research team, I was advised not to join them when they did their interviews. However, I can rely on the team's published papers for the content of those interviews. As yet another example, I was able to visit a rural school in southern Xinjiang because a friend worked there. However, his apparent nervousness in having me on campus deterred me from going beyond simple greetings with students and teachers. In these cases, I must rely on published Chinese sources to gather factual information.

The second type of information that can be gleaned from Chinese sources is the subjective assumptions and judgments of Chinese analysts. This helps an outside researcher to overcome limits of local access by providing contextualized insights. Unlike in the Mao era, the Chinese literature no longer uniformly toes the official line or lacks total independence, at least until early 2018. The era of "reform and opening" has made possible a proliferation of diverse perspectives. Treatment of sensitive topics and controversial viewpoints can be found in publications at subnational levels and in academic institutions. Dissident views used to survive online, such as the websites of Ilham Tohti, Wang Lixiong, Li Jianglin, and Woeser. These may still be accessible for local residents who use a virtual private network (VPN). Field research provided opportunities for direct investigation, participant observation, and unstructured conversations. Given the polemics surrounding the issue of Tibet and Xinjiang, it is essential to have first-hand experiences. Mingling with local residents in those and other ethnic regions provided me with opportunities for unrehearsed encounters and conversations. Of the hundreds of people I met in these regions, I held meaningful conversations with well over a hundred people.[8] While they would not formally consent to interviews, they were usually willing to be quoted anonymously. Information gleaned from direct observations and conversations has helped to check out hypotheses, gain contextualized understanding of the nature of existing data, compare the daily life experiences on the ground with what have been written and reported in the outside world, sense the mood on the ground, and find missing pieces. Between 2011 and 2019, my summers and one fall in China involved numerous trips to ethnic regions, participation in academic forums on ethnic issues, and conversations with local scholars, officials, students, and ordinary people of various walks of life and ethnic backgrounds. These conversations were informal, spontaneous, and unstructured, but candid and informative. Or they occurred in the company of groups where I was a passive listener.

My research travels included the ethnically concentrated areas of Sichuan, Xinjiang, Qinghai, Jilin, Yunnan, Beijing, and Chongqing, as well as the TAR. My travels to Xinjiang (mainly southern Xinjiang) included three trips between 2011 and 2015, or before Chen Quanguo assumed the top official post there in mid-2016. Since then it would be nearly impossible to have candid interactions with local residents without causing potential problems for them. Thus, between 2016 and 2019, I made annual summer stops in Suzhou of Jiangsu province, where a migrant community of several thousand Uighurs resides. My travels to Tibetan regions included four trips between 2014 and 2017, covering western Sichuan, northern Yunnan, and the TAR itself. Outside these two major ethnic regions, I made one trip to the ethnic Bai region of Yunnan in 2014, the Korean prefecture in Yanbian of Jilin in 2013, and the multiethnic Xining city of Qinghai in 2012; three trips to ethnic research institutions in Beijing in 2012, 2013, and 2018, multiple trips to Chengdu between 2014 and 2018

[8] This number does not include my relatives in Xinjiang and those who have returned to their hometowns, but may include the networks of people they introduced to me.

(which has thriving Tibetan communities), and annual trips to Chongqing (my hometown which has four ethnic counties, one ethnic district, and fourteen ethnic villages).

My earlier visits to Xinjiang were mostly unconstrained. During a trip across Xinjiang in the early 2010s, I joined in a multiethnic research team, allowing me access to events and people that would otherwise be impossible for a foreign-based researcher. At an academic forum on one Urumqi campus, I was not able to attend as a foreign-based researcher. But this allowed me to develop a good rapport with ethnic scholars in attendance and to converse with them during informal times. During their formal meetings, I spent time visiting the sites of local riots, talking to local residents, and learning about local ethnic politics, all with the help of Uighur students from the Urumqi campus. In the southern prefectures of Hotan, Kashgar, and Aksu, we met with local officials, educators, students, and partner project managers. Because I was advised to stay away from the team's formal meetings with officials, I used the time to visit rural areas, urban bazaars, farmers' markets, small businesses, partner projects, ethnic quarters, public schools, mosques, and hospitals, with the help of Uighur students or my local relatives who speak Uighur. During my research team's informal gatherings, I was able to attend and hear the real conversations take place.

I faced few restrictions in academic activities at other local colleges in Xinjiang during my trips in the early 2010s. I attended forums on bilingual education at which I heard candid discussions about Uighur resentment and passive resistance. I had free chats with faculty members in different academic departments and interacted with Uighur students on campus, delving into topics from religious bans to the futility of classes on Marxism. I was able to examine teaching materials, read short essays by Uighur students, and observe Chinese language classes. I attended talks on research strategies and learned the kind of topics that interested Uighur scholars. I sensed tensions among the multiethnic faculty but also warm feelings between the multiethnic faculty and students. The most educational episodes were the informal meetings and conversations, including interactions with Xinjiang's smaller minorities, the Kazakhs, Mongols, Sibes, and Huis.

During my trips to southern Xinjiang, I stayed at the homes of several relatives who came to southern Xinjiang during the Mao era or were locally born.[9] Together I was able to meet with nearly two dozen local relatives from seven families in southern Xinjiang[10] (and over a dozen relatives who had returned to Sichuan in the 1980s).[11] Those who were born in Xinjiang during

[9] They were first, second, or third cousins.

[10] These relatives were or are employed in both the public and private sectors, including private and state firms, state agencies and banks, public schools, healthcare, insurance, agriculture, catering, and media.

[11] They used to be employed in colleges, state firms, and local police.

the Mao era could speak Uighur and served as interpreters. Despite being mostly Han Chinese,[12] their longtime local roots allowed me to observe different aspects of local society through participating in their daily activities and interactions with their multiethnic neighbors, friends, and colleagues. It is natural to suspect that Uighurs would not tell what is really on their mind to non-Uighurs, especially Han Chinese, but this did not seem a problem among old neighbors, acquaintances, and co-workers. In particular, older Han and Uighurs who worked in the public sector during the Mao era have memories of better ethnic relations in the past and are more open with one another. Through these networks I was also able to converse with a special group of people, so-called "*er zhuangzi*," children of mixed Han-Uighur parentage. Their fathers came to Xinjiang as officers and soldiers of the Kuomingtang (KMT, or the Nationalist Party) in the 1940s or of the People's Liberation Army in the 1950s and 1960s, and married local Uighur women.[13] These mixed offspring, with extended families on both sides of the ethnic divide, are familiar with perspectives on both sides and more even-handed in their assessment of ethnic faults and in their narration of local events. Near the residential compounds of two different relatives, I was able to observe for extended periods the expressions and behaviors of large crowds of Uighur men flowing into major local mosques or idling in front of them. Due to my gender, however, I was not able to go in myself.

Outside Xinjiang I visited Uighur communities in Suzhou multiple times between 2016 and 2019. The city's famed jade-carving industry has drawn several thousand Uighurs here, including jade traders, food caterers, food stand owners, and their family members. They congregate on the main jade street, Shiquanjie, and a few minor jade streets in the city, living mostly in nearby alleys. The bustling jade market a few years ago has made many Uighur traders wealthy, making them the most successful Uighur migrants in interior China. More recently, the slowdown in demand for jade products has left some of them struggling, jarring their experience away from home. Nevertheless, this immigrant community is an alternative and more moderate source of information on Uighur sentiments and well-being, being away from the tense political atmosphere back home. More of them speak Mandarin and are far more relaxed about discussing Xinjiang than they would be in Xinjiang.

My field research in Tibetan regions has included Tibetan regions in the provinces of Sichuan, Qinghai, and Yunnan as well as the TAR. In the summers of 2014 and 2015, I joined a local research group from Sichuan University to

[12] One relative's grandmother was Uighur, so her father was an "*erzhuangzi*" while she herself identifies with the Han. One relative is Manchu.

[13] Apart from relatives, "*erzhuanzi*" I conversed with included two former co-workers of a relative, two employees of a relative's private business, and a nanny in a relative's home. In addition, I met on my own two local soldiers during a long train ride and two private store owners in a local bazaar. All in southern Xinjiang, 2013 and/or 2015.

visit Ngawa and Garzê prefectures of Sichuan, where we visited Tibetan villages, monasteries, and Buddhist schools. These two prefectures have been the sites of a majority of Tibetan self-immolation cases since 2009. We met with villagers, lamas, and local officials, including family members of lamas and local officials in charge of dealing with monasteries. In the summer of 2016, I volunteered at the cultural center of a Tibetan village in the Deqing Tibetan Autonomous Prefecture in Yunnan province. This allowed close interaction with local Tibetan students, village officials, and villagers. In the summer of 2017, I joined a research team from Sichuan University on a field trip to the TAR, which included numerous monasteries, cities, and villages in the three prefectures of Nyinchi, Shannan, and Shigatses, as well as Lhasa. A number of factors – a near absence of tensions compared with southern Xinjiang, introduction through local researchers and my own proficiency in the Sichuan dialect – facilitated interactions with local Tibetan residents, rural families, monks, officials, and students. In between these years I also made visits to the Tibetology Center in Beijing and *minzu* universities in Sichuan, Beijing, and Qinghai. In addition, encounters with Tibetan immigrants from China in New York City exposed me to Tibetans from across the Tibetan plateaus, social strata, and local experiences.

Participation in academic forums in China has also provided valuable field experiences. They allowed me to converse with scholars from different ethnic regions and groups, and sometimes went on field trips with them. On a Qinghai campus, I chatted candidly with local Tibetan scholars about their grievances, while also learning alternative accounts from Hui, Monguor, and Salar members. They briefed me on Qinghai's old and new ethnic feuds. At the Minzu University of China in Beijing, I had conversations with ethnic scholars from a range of ethnicities, localities, and perspectives. In the Yanbian Korean Prefecture, academic exchanges and field trips with local ethnic Korean scholars and officials allowed me to learn about China's model autonomous area. In various localities, I had opportunities to converse with scholars and officials from central or local branches of the State Ethnic Affairs Commission (SEAC).

The many ordinary people I have met, ethnic or otherwise, have allowed me to learn about the real people who live or have lived in autonomous regions. They include public employees and private entrepreneurs, farmers and migrant workers, teachers and students, street vendors and shop owners, the self-employed and the unemployed. Their diverse experiences and thoughts have helped me to put into perspective the scholarly debates and partisan views about the effects of government policy in China's minority regions. These sources will be noted in footnotes where their conversations are cited (in Chapters 4–8).

Question of Bias

From my field experiences, the leading source of Chinese mistrust for a Western-based scholar (especially a US-based one) is the perception of bias, especially on the subjects of Tibet and Xinjiang. Many Chinese scholars and graduate students I met have heard of the "Xinjiang project," referring to the book *Xinjiang: China's Muslim Borderland* (Starr 2004). They have also heard of China's travel ban on the contributing authors.[14] Despite my efforts to explain that a book project funded by a government grant did not mean a "government project," few were fully convinced. In fact, it was a local scholar in Xinjiang who first brought the book to the attention of local authorities.[15]

Even renowned US scholars who are not considered to be "unfriendly" to China are not immune from criticisms of bias by Chinese specialists. Prominent examples include American scholars who have been attacked by some Tibetan exiles as "running dog propagandists" for China (Norbu 2008). Yet they have also been criticized by scholars in China (Losel 2011a; Wang X. 2012). Chinese specialists duly recognize the extraordinary professionalism and objectivity of those US scholars, but also point out their "limitations," particularly a lack of familiarity with Chinese-language sources (Du 2005).

Likewise, my own biases and assumptions were frequently questioned during my fieldtrips. During long rides across the Xinjiang and Tibetan regions, I had many debates with members of the Chinese research teams I traveled with over perceived Western biases on my part. What upset them was their perception that my focus was on the problems of China's ethnic policy, rather than giving equal attention to its positive achievements. Also frustrating to them was a perceived lack of even-handedness on my part in assessing ethnically charged disputes that often do not have clear right or wrong sides. The nature of Western biases, as perceived by Chinese specialists, is aptly described by Gilbert Rozman in his study of Chinese debates on Soviet socialism:

> Chinese specialists remark that their Western counterparts are unable to be objective about the Soviet Union because they start with negative premises about socialism. They are out to prove that socialism does not work. ... I was told that the Yugoslavian press coverage of the Soviet Union was more objective than Western coverage. ... In short, Chinese argue that Western specialists, biased by their desire to prove the superiority of capitalism to socialism, fail to provide objective, well-rounded evaluation of the Soviet Union. (Rozman 1987: 26)

Indeed, the willingness of the Chinese research teams to bring me along on their field trips was in large part due to their desire to "correct" my biases. This included showing me the complex realities of sensitive ethnic regions, the voices of ordinary ethnic members (who are perceived as the moderate majority, in contrast to the nationalistic ethnic intelligentsia), the mundane calm of their daily lives, and most of all, the problems as well as the successes of China's

[14] The ban is reported in Daniel de Vise, "Scholars say their book on China led to travel ban." *The Washington Post*, August 20, 2011.

[15] He is Pan Zhiping of the Xinjiang Academy of Social Sciences. On July 11 and 12, 2011, I attended, in an unofficial capacity, an academic conference on the campus of Xinjiang University, at which Pan presented a critique of the book.

ethnic policy. To their credit, at least they did not think of me as possessing Western arrogance or an "imperialist" mentality, hence not worth bothering with.

Is the Chinese literature not itself ridden with biases? Of course it is, especially given the country's restrictive political context. But an emphatic attention to a wide spectrum of Chinese views should at least compensate for some of the limitations. The spectrum ranges from official sources at one end and dissident sources at the other.

Organization of the Study

The substantive chapters are organized around the twofold transitions highlighted by this study. The first, from empire to the autonomous system of the socialist era, is the topic of Chapters 1–3. Chapter 1 focuses on changing approaches to ethnicity, Chapter 2 on changing forms of ethnic governance, and Chapter 3 on changing policies for ethnic co-optation. The second transition, from the socialist era to the reform era, is the topic of Chapters 4–8. Each of these chapters examines one key aspect of post-Mao ethnic policy, including the political, religious, economic, and educational spheres. The concluding chapter considers why the twofold transition has resulted in institutional sources of instability, weighs various proposals for reform, and considers the implications of ethnic issues for a rising China.

1

Changing Approaches to Identity

From Maintenance to Transformation

This chapter focuses on the transformation of approaches to ethnicity in China's transition from empire to nation state. That is, how and why Chinese approaches evolved from a maintenance-oriented strategy aimed at pacification and stability in pre-modern times to a transformative strategy aimed at institutionalizing identities in the socialist era, with huge unintended consequences.

This classification and engineering, I argue, created the first institutional dynamic for ethnic strife in contemporary times. That is, they contributed to the politicization of identity at national level. Historically, Confucian universalism provided a neutral and inclusive approach to ethnicity, but it could not accommodate the advent of the *minzu* (nation) and the nation state in modern times. Yet the *minzu* discourse was ineffective at nation building during the late Qing and Republican eras. It took the CCP to accomplish this task through a mix of class universalism and politicized identities. The new approach served to incorporate minority members as equal citizens of a new modern state, but it also departed sharply from pre-modern approaches of maintenance and pacification. The contradictions therein – promoting political incorporation but also ethnic identities to fit that goal – would render *minzu* identities a key source of institutional strains in the autonomous system in contemporary times.

This chapter covers the following topics: (1) relevant legacies of pre-modern China's approaches to ethnicity, (2) relevant legacies of modern China's efforts at nation building, and (3) the CCP's transformative approaches to ethnicity as a nation building strategy and its unintended consequences.

PRE-MODERN LEGACIES: UNIVERSALISM, MAINTENANCE, AND PACIFICATION

For China's modern nation building, the most relevant legacies from pre-modern times were Confucian universalism, and a maintenance-oriented approach to ethnicity and localized identities that it helped to foster. Universalism was a common strategy used by empires to deal with different peoples across extensive territorial spans. By proclaiming principles of universal application, universalism embodies inclusiveness and non-racial neutrality. Confucianism and neo-Confucianism comprised the uniqueness of pre-modern Chinese approaches.

The Confucian system of values and governance was adept at ruling an empire and pacifying frontier communities. That is, a maintenance-oriented approach aimed at pacification and stability for different territories and peoples. From John Fairbank to Joseph Levenson, historians characterize a cultural universalism (*tianxia*) in imperial China. As a form of cultural consciousness and identification with the moral values of Confucian civilization, it entailed that culture (as a way of life) was more fundamental than nationalism or race, hence non-racial and inclusive. This universalist culturalism allowed China's dynastic emperors to assert that they ruled civilized mankind without distinction of race or language. It permitted nomadic invaders to rule and assimilate easily. "Barbarian" dynasties, so long as they ruled by the proper Confucian order, reinforced rather than weakened that universalist conception. Successive alien rulers acknowledged this fact and ruled accordingly (Fairbank 1983: 98–9).

Confucian culturalism was conducive to ethnic acculturation but also localized identities. Unlike Christian universalism, Confucian universalism was not messianic with the assumption that the "barbarians are always with us" (Levenson 1971: 24). The comparative advantage of organizational and technological know-how, crystalized in the Confucian bureaucracy, allowed it to prevail once nomadic rulers and invaders settled in: "major dynasties of nomadic or semi-nomadic origins sooner or later adopted Confucianism as a ruling ideology and relied on the Confucian-Legalist state to rule the most populated part of the country" (Zhao 2015: 324). As successive nomadic invaders voluntarily succumbed to the ways of the settled people, Confucian universalism was periodically reinforced. The ideas of the nation and nationalism based on ethnicity or race per se did not exist. As Henry Kissinger puts it, imperial China expanded by "cultural osmosis, not missionary zeal" (2011: 512). It did not seek to convert and change, leaving alone localized identities.

Confucian universalism was conducive to localized and crosscut identities also because it did not preclude cultural pragmatism or alternative beliefs. The Confucian officialdom made constant compromises in order to adapt to "alternative views of the world order," compromises that the Confucian elites would cover with the rhetoric of universalism (Duara 1997: 57). Cultural pragmatism entailed that the creation of a Confucian society "did not diminish the strong presence of numerous religions and other traditions in China," for as long as all religions accepted Confucian orthodoxy, and did not worship ethnically problematic gods or turn against the state, the Confucian state did not repress popular religion or non-Confucian teachings but made efforts to co-opt it (Zhao 2015: 342, 344–5). Whether it was cultural universalism or pragmatism, none denied admissibility to the Chinese political community on the basis of ethnicity, faith, or other ascriptive features.

The rise of neo-Confucianism, between the Song dynasties (960–1279 CE), greatly strengthened the influence and universalizing facility of Confucianism in Chinese society. This helped to further expand and consolidate a large demographic/territorial core in pre-modern China. The expansion of the civil service exam as the defining institution of society spurred academies for Confucian teaching in urban and rural areas, giving rise to a unified elite culture and identity. The expansion of lineage-based networks and other Confucian rituals helped to extend Confucian tenets in local communities. These two developments facilitated the penetration of Confucian ideology and institutions into all spheres of Chinese life as never before, creating a Confucian society (Zhao 2015: 334–8). Confucianism's influence, in terms of territory and population, was greatly expanded as a result. This demographic/territorial core consolidated, notably, before the arrival of two minority dynasties, the Mongols and Manchus. The Manchus, who embraced Confucianism, ruled much more successfully and lasted much longer than the Mongols.

Official records from Qing, China's last imperial dynasty, are illustrative of the imperial court's loose groupings of various subjects under its empire. They show functional, localized, and crosscut groupings of disparate communities. During the period of Emperor Jiaqing (1760–1820), the Comprehensive Gazetteer of Jiaqing used just three categories to classify twenty groups of subjects: soldiers, civilians, and frontier peoples. These were functional rather than ethnic categories. The category of soldiers, or the "banner register," included Manchu, Mongol, and Han soldiers. The category of civilians, or the "household register," included the *Min* (or civilians, covering the Han, Chinese-speaking Muslims, and sinified minority groups in the south), the *Hui* (covering Turkic-speaking Muslims of Xinjiang and Gansu), the *Fan* (or alien tribes, covering Tibetan and Qiangic herdsmen and Taiwanese aborigines), and the rest (covering the *Qiang*, *Miao*, *Yao*, *Li*, *and Yi*). The category of "frontier peoples" included nine Mongol and Manchu subgroups in the northeast. Importantly, these categories were largely for the purpose of differentiating tax rates. Households listed under ethnic categories were placed alongside functional groups, such as soldiers, craftsmen, fishermen, opium smokers, and salt workers. The ethnic categories, moreover, had little internal logic to them. The *Fan* group ranged from pastoral people in western Sichuan to indigenous people in Taiwan, while the Manchu tribes were divided into six subgroups. The Qing court never established a coherent logic of ethnic classification, but only an ethnic description for administrative purposes (Wu 2013). This practice was representative of the general approach to ethnicity in imperial China.

At the micro level, the social unit of identification in pre-modern China helped to reinforce localized identities and crosscuts. This prevented local identities from consolidating into a sustained cross-regional ethnic or proto-nationalistic political identity. Kinship and lineage networks were the focus of localized identities rather than ethnicity or race. Most illustrative is the word "*zu*," the term for ethnicity and race in the contemporary Chinese vocabulary. The etymology of *zu* signifies the role of interclan conflict in the emergence of the concept of *zu* and the clan-based rule of early Chinese society. The conventional usage of *zu* in pre-Qin texts denoted a clan or tribe linked by blood lineage and/or surname (Ma 2010b: 211–15). This "*zu*" was also rooted in the military functions of a community with blood ties: *zu* was bigger than *jia* (family) but smaller than *zong* (interrelated clans). Subsequently, when used in compound phrases in historical texts, *zu* retained the meaning of a social unit based on blood lineage, for example *jiazu* (family clan), *shizu* (surname clan), *zongzu* (interrelated clan), *jiuzu* (multiple interrelated clans), *buzu* (tribal clan), *gongzu* (royal kinsmen), and *wangzu* (royal clan). Until modern times, the word *zu* was never used with an ethnic group in classic Chinese texts (Ma 2010b: 214–16). Like Confucian universalism, the pre-modern understanding of the royal house as a kinship clan allowed the Sinic communities to overlook the ethnic origin of the nomadic and semi-nomadic dynasties.

In short, pre-modern Chinese approaches to ethnicity aimed at pacification and stability. Confucianism served these imperial goals through cultural universalism, pragmatism, and religious tolerance, allowing cycles of nomadic rulers and communities to acculturate. At local levels, family-centered Confucian values reinforced kingship and lineage-based identities, rather than providing a basis for ethnic or proto-nationalistic political identities. All this helped to create a large demographic/territorial core, while also leaving distinct ethnic communities alone.

TRANSITION TO THE MODERN STATE

Confucian universalism came under serious challenges after China's defeat in the Opium Wars (1839–42, 1856–60). The arrival of the West presented the "conceptual shock" of the three millennia of Chinese history, in the words of the prominent Qing official, Li Hongzhang.[1] While alien invaders were nothing new, the earlier ones posed military rather than civilizational challenges to the Chinese society. But the invaders from Europe imposed not only their terms of engagement but also their worldview and world order. In particular, their power politics and racial exclusivity presented conceptual and normative challenges to the longstanding universalism of Confucian culturalism.

For China's nation building, the most relevant legacies from modern times were the challenge from the Western concept of the nation and the subsequent

[1] Cited in Liang Qichao (1901/1963: ch. 6).

regimes' ineffective responses to meeting the challenge of modern nation building. Those failures paved the way for the CCP to embrace the Soviet doctrine of nationality and class universalism, resulting in the adoption of ethnic classification as the CCP's strategy of nation building. Compelled by exigencies of the time, China's accession to the new concepts – the nation and the nationality – disregarded historical and local realities, with unintended consequences for contemporary times.

Problems of the "Nation" Discourse

Late Qing reformers failed to develop an alternative worldview because the Western concept they embraced, the *minzu* (nation) and nation state, did not fit with China's pre-modern realities. After China's defeat in the Sino-Japanese war of 1895 and the failure of the Reform Movement of 1898, frustrated reformers saw Confucian universalism as a fundamental barrier to an effective response to the challenge of the West: domestically it impeded awakening Han nationalism against the inept Qing court, whose rulers were ethnic Manchus, and externally against Western and Japanese encroachments. Qing reformers were convinced that the absence of the nation state, along with its attendant nationalism, put China at a disadvantage in the internal and external politics of the day. They desperately turned to the *nation* discourse for its perceived potency to save the country and Chinese civilization.

Key differences among late Qing reformers illustrated the mismatch of the *nation* concept in the local context, and why they could not come to a consensus. Thanks to the large demographic/territorial core of the Qing empire, or the Han people, the radical reformers equated the Chinese nation with the Han people. This group, represented by Zhang Taiyan, Sun Yat-sen, Wang Jingwei, Chen Tianhua, and Zou Rong, were deeply indignant at the Manchu regime and implored the nation discourse to displace it. However, the moderate reformers or Constitutional Monarchists, represented by Liang Qichao, Yan Fu, Huang Zunxian, and Wang Tao, upheld the Confucian tradition by including the multiethnic constituents of the empire as part of the Chinese nation. Both groups, as modern-minded writers and translators of their times, were bearers of new ideas and terminology to China, including *minzu* and *minzu zhuyi* (nationalism). These terms – mainly through translation of Japanese renderings of Western texts, became profuse in Chinese publications from the late 1800s. The context of such use was so politicized that a century later, the validity of the Japanese renderings was among the first topics debated by Chinese ethnologists in the post-Mao era.

The concept of nation posed serious problems for Chinese nation building in late Qing, contributing in important part to its failure. Foremost was the linkage of race to the nation state. Radical reformers expressed their anger at the Qing court by directing hostility toward the Manchus as an alien group, espousing the infamous slogan "Expel the Manchus and Restore China." This narrow conception of the nation excluded the Manchus as well as other lesser "nations" of the Qing empire. Because Japan was a homogenous country in racial and cultural terms, the Japanese rendering of the Western concept of "nation" as *minzu* denoted a racial-cultural-political community (Wang K. 2003). By appropriating the Japanese term, radical reformers sought to save China by appealing to its large demographic/territorial core, the Han nation.

Another problem of the nation concept was the need to reconstruct a collective memory for this core nation, which ironically had to begin overseas. In 1902 a group of Chinese intellectuals studying in Japan convened a meeting to observe the "242nd anniversary of the fall of China." That is, the fall of the Ming dynasty that preceded the Qing dynasty. Emulating Meiji Japan's construction of emperor worship and the imperial lineage, Zhang Taiyuan implored the Han collective memory by constructing the Yellow Emperor as the Han ancestor (Sun 2004: 18–19). Chen Tianhua held anyone who did not descend from the Yellow Emperor as non-Han and anyone who helped non-Hans as disloyal to his ancestors (Chen 2002: 87). From these Japanese origins, the new cultural symbol of the Yellow Emperor was promoted across China to rally support for the overthrow of the Manchus.

Yet another problem of the nation concept was the inconvenience of the Manchu race, a fellow race of the Han. The dichotomy of the yellow and white races grew out of Chinese exposure to the theory of social Darwinism from 1895. The translator of Darwin's works, Yan Fu, warned of the danger of the "extinction of our country and race" after China's loss in the Sino-Japanese war of 1895 (1986: 4). Fellow intellectuals quickly embraced the new divine law of "natural selection." Fearing that the Chinese nation and race would be "gobbled up" by imperial powers, they depicted a "racial war" between the yellow and white races. But the dichotomy posed dilemmas, since the Manchus were a fellow race. Radical reformers circumvented this inconvenience by dismissing the Manchus as a "Siberian race" (Zou 1958: 25–6) or not part of China's "historical nation" (Zhang 1977: 195, 199). At the same time, they exalted Meiji Japan as a racially pure nation state, thus racializing China's plight inflicted by the Western powers but not its defeat dealt by Japan (Sun 2004: 12).

The most serious problem of the Han nation discourse was the intellectual and political threats that it posed to the "nationhood" of the various non-Han communities in the Qing empire. Major ethnic communities – being Qing subjects – did not necessarily equate the Qing empire with China, and they were equal members like the Han in the constituent territories of Qing; but since they had already accepted the Confucian cultural and normative order, the Manchus and other so-called barbarians should be equal members of *Zhongguo* (China) (Duara 1997: 76). And like the Han, minority groups fought against foreign encroachments as members of the Qing empire (EdB 1979: 23, 95, 216, 223). Moreover, the Han nation discourse inspired some minority groups to assert their own nationalism and nationhood, making it difficult to oppose the growing independence movements in Mongolia and foreign incitation of separatism in Tibet and Xinjiang in the midst of the Qing dynasty's disintegration.

Moderate reformers developed the concept of a composite nation, but were unable to prevail initially. They phrased the Darwinian battle as one between China and foreign powers, rather than between China's internal groups, or in Yan Fu's words, a conflict between the white and yellow races, with the Mongols, Manchus, and Hans all being part of the yellow race (Yan 1986: 9–10). Arguing against internal divisions, Kang Youwei wrote, "If we set ourselves up as weak prey, how can we avoid being attacked? If we set ourselves up for chaos and decline, how can we complain about being bullied?" (Xu and Jin 2008: 37). Instead of a Han nation, they urged the fusion of internal ethnic groups into one modern nation state, a precursor to the idea *Zhonghua minzu* (the Chinese nation) popularized a decade later in the 1911 revolution.

The momentary prevalence of radical reformers contributed to the failure of an elite consensus. When China's first political party – the Chinese Revolutionary League – was established in 1905 under the radical reformer Sun Yat-sen, its major platform was to "Expel the Manchus and Restore China." Moderate reformers countered with the concept of *Zhonghua minzu*, to include the Manchu and other ethnic groups in the new Chinese nation (Huang 2002; Chang 2010), but the Han-centric approach prevailed among the revolutionaries who led the overthrow of the Manchu dynasty in 1911.

Republican Failures

The overthrow of the Qing dynasty, during the revolution of 1911, thrust new challenges of nation building for the ensuing Republican regimes (1911–49). With the Manchu dynasty fallen, the various populations of imperial China could no longer be called Qing subjects (*Qingchao chenmin*), while their potential separatism became a real threat to the new Republic. Clinging to the Han-centric conception of the nation, the Republican regimes (1911–49) attempted assimilationist strategies at nation building, but ultimately failed. This influenced the CCP's embrace of class universalism, which was the major Republican legacy.

One reason for the Republican failures was an expedient approach to the idea of the Chinese nation. Initially the new Republic turned to the multinational narrative largely to inherit the Qing empire. As Sun Yat-sen and other revolutionary leaders realized, Han nationalism, after justifying the overthrow of the Manchus, would now lead to the breakaway of the outer peripheral regions. The new Chinese nation would now have to consist of five major groups, the Manchus, Mongols, Tibetans, Huis (Muslims), and Hans, such that the new Republic could legitimately inherit the territorial boundaries of the Manchu dynasty (Duara 1997: 76–7). In naming the five co-nations, the new Republic acknowledged the major challenges for nation building. The Manchus and Mongols were part of the ruling coalition in the Qing dynasty and must therefore be co-opted by the new regime. Uighurs were incorporated into the regular provincial system less than three decades ago. Tibetans of Ü-Tsang were not yet governed in such a system.

Thanks to the large demographic/territorial core left from imperial times, however, Republican leaders soon returned to a Han-centric conception of the Chinese nation. The demise of the Qing dynasty had left the Manchus and Mongols on the defensive, the Tibetans under British influence, and the Uighurs under regional warlordism. These centrifugal forces put pressure on the Republican regimes to attempt nation building. Merely a year after the revolution of 1911, Sun Yat-sen's revolutionary league openly espoused "racial assimilation." In the same year, the reorganized league, the KMT, vowed to implement "racial assimilation" (Wu 2014: 41). After Chiang Kai-shek came to power in 1928, the KMT formally backtracked on the idea of a multiethnic republic. By the 1930s, when separatist movements surged among all four ethnic co-nations, the KMT repudiated the idea of ethnic minorities altogether. Chiang Kai-chek replaced the idea of the five-*zu* nation with one "*guozu*" (national race), calling ethnic groups "different clans of the same lineage" (*zongzu)* (Wu 2014: 45–6). The intention was to counter the rise of ethno-nationalism and separatism encouraged by foreign powers in all four "co-nations" of the new republic: Japan in Inner Mongolia and Manchuria, Britain in Tibet, and the Soviet Union in Xinjiang.

Without an inclusive universalism, the KMT's assimilationist policies bumped up against ethnic identities in flux. Conventional Chinese historiography on the early Republican period tends to blame foreign powers for inciting ethnic separatism in the outer peripheral regions (Xu and Jin 2008: 69). Recent historiography by China's minority scholars, however, emphasizes the unprecedented dilemma faced by minority elites at that critical historical juncture: to stay with or leave the Middle Kingdom. The collapse of the Qing dynasty had left a power vacuum and an identity crisis in the outer minority regions, whose elites used to be part of the Qing's ruling coalition and were more loyal to the empire than to the new Republic. Across all four ethnic "co-nations," many minority elites struggled with a new national identity and with their uncertain fate in a turbulent period, and some turned to foreign forces in the hope of pursuing separatism (Chang 2011: 13–14; Ma 2011e: 2; Jian 2011: 36). The KMT's assimilationist policies caused a backlash among the already anxious minority elites.

Forced assimilation did not go well even in the more integrated communities of the inner peripheral regions, which would later turn to the CCP. From administrative integration to the banning of ethnic tongues in local urban areas, the KMT's enforcement of assimilation was felt to be too harsh. Rather than secession, the inner peripheral groups sought an equal status in a multinational framework. Without it, they could not legitimately resist the assimilationist drive. In 1935, more than thirty ethnic chieftains from southwestern provinces sent representatives to Nanjing, China's capital at the time, to lobby for recognition and political rights (Wu 2013: 6). Japanese invasions soon damped their hope for reform, but gave them a different boost. From the late 1930s to the mid-1940s, China's leading academic institutions were relocated from eastern China to Sichuan and Yunnan provinces, close to the traditional inner peripheral regions. The relocation boosted scholarly studies on the hitherto neglected ethnic groups in the southwest. The researchers' field experience during this period was to have a major impact on the CCP's ethnic policy in the 1950s.

In short, in the turbulent transition to the modern nation state, the Republican model of five co-nations failed to provide an alternative identity to the pre-modern identity of minority communities as imperial constituents. Extraordinary circumstances aside, the Republican regimes failed because of their intrusive assimilationism, in contrast to Confucian universalism. The demographic weight of the Han majority, no doubt, rendered it easy to take assimilationism for granted and to avoid taking serious measures to forge a modern national identity. The major impact of the Republican legacy was the CCP's turn to the Soviet doctrine of nationality and class universalism.

The Soviet Alternative

The Soviet doctrine allowed the CCP to find a viable new universalism. Based on social class solidarity, class universalism transcended ethnic particularism by emphasizing interethnic affinity as members of the proletarian class, regardless of ascriptive features. By identifying with oppressed masses across the ethnic spectrum, it helped the CCP to overcome the confines of the Republican regimes.

A brief discussion of the Soviet theory and policy on "nationalities" will suffice here, as it has been extensively studied (Martin 2001a; Suny and Martin 2001; Slezkine 1994). For Lenin and Stalin, both ardent advocates of nations and national rights, nations were a matter of historical reality that was taken for granted. In Stalin's classic definition, "A nation is a historically evolved, stable community based on a common language, territory, economic life and psychological make-up manifested in a community of culture," and being here and real, nations had rights: "A nation can organize its life as it sees fit. It has the right to organize its life on the basis of autonomy. It has the right to enter into federal relations with other nations. It has the right to complete secession. Nations are sovereign and all nations are equal" (Slezkine 1994: 416). It did not matter whether they differed in size, power, and level of development, all nations or nationalities were equal because they had the same rights.

How could the Soviet Communist Party build a unitary state while encouraging ethno-nationalism? Terry Martin summarizes the Soviet reasoning: first, "nationalism is a masking ideology that leads legitimate class interests to be expressed, not in an appropriate class-based socialist movement but rather in the form of an above-class national movement"; second, "national identity is not an essential and permanent quality but rather an unavoidable by-product of the modern capitalist *and* early socialist world, which must be passed through before a mature internationalist socialist world can come into being"; third, "since national identity is a real phenomenon in the modern world, the nationalism of the oppressed non-Russian peoples expresses not only masked class protests but also legitimate national grievances against the oppressive Great Power chauvinism of the dominant Russian nationality" (Martin 2001b: 72–3). These reasonings were unsurprising given the Bolshevik leaders' own backgrounds. As Liliana Riga shows, two-thirds of those leaders were members of ethnic minority groups. Culturally assimilated yet socially and politically excluded by state imperial policy, they found revolutionary class universalism especially appealing (Riga 2012).

It followed that in the Bolshevik logic, neither nationalism nor national identity could be unequivocally condemned as reactionary. Some national claims, such as those confined to the national "forms" – territory, language, culture, and elite – are considered legitimate and must be granted in order to fragment the national alliance. Such a policy was expected to speed up the emergence of class cleavages and motivate the non-Russian proletariat and peasantry to support the Communist Party's socialist agenda. In short, nationalism is supposed to be disarmed by granting the forms of nationhood. Two resolutions of the Soviet Communist Party from 1923, along with Stalin's speeches in defense of them, became the standard Bolshevik "proof text" on nationalities policy. Policy implementation soon followed the 1923 resolutions (Martin 2001b: 73). The Soviet conception of the nation, along with the policy based on it, became the standard justifications for Soviet ethno-federalism, or an "affirmative action empire" in the words of Terry Martin (2001a). The Soviet theory and policy also became models for other multiethnic socialist countries, including China.

Soviet theory on nationality attracted the CCP's interest because of its class universalism. Unlike the Darwinist nation discourse, the Soviet theory championed the rights of the weak and oppressed groups. When the CCP first learned about it at the Comintern conference on nationalities in 1922, Lenin's point about the sovereign equality of all nationalities regardless of their size appealed deeply to the Chinese communists. Not only China's minority masses, but China itself, were oppressed by domestic and foreign forces at the time. In the same year, the CCP began to use the concept of "nationality" to refer to China's ethnic groups. By 1928, the CCP formally affirmed the "nationality" status of China's "weak and small" ethnic groups, namely the hitherto unrecognized small groups. It also recognized the right of all nationalities to "self-determination" (*minzu zijue*), which would include the right to "completely separate from or freely associate with" the rest of China (MUF 1991: 87). The rationale, as with its Soviet precursor, was that China's national liberation should include the national liberation of its "weak and oppressed" minorities.

Realities on the ground soon led the CCP to adjust its full embrace of the Soviet theory, or to backtrack on the idea of self-determination. In the mid-1930s, a confluence of factors led the CCP to see China as a composite multiethnic nation, rather than a land of heterogeneous nationalities in separate existence. During the Long March (1933–5), the Red Army spent over a third of their time in remote ethnic terrains, encountering over a dozen minority groups in over ten provinces. The imperative of courting local support compelled the CCP forces to overcome minority groups' mistrust of the Han people (Xiong and Yan 2006: 35). It also helped that in mid-1935 the Comintern cautioned against a "mechanistic" application of the Soviet experience, making it easier for the CCP to move away from the doctrine of self-determination (CCTB 1989: 329). Finally, the anti-Japanese war of 1937–45 made it critical for the CCP to rally minority support in a united war front. Japanese forces, by wooing minority elites, had occupied Manchuria, popping up a puppet regime here and in Inner Mongolia, while also encouraging a Hui homeland in the northwest. These realities compelled the CCP to see the paradox of self-determination and to abandon the idea by the late 1930s.

To retain the support of the minority proletariat, the party kept class universalism and the concept of nationality as part of its revolutionary ideology. The promises of national rights and autonomy helped to draw in left-leaning minority youths, who became the party's links to minority regions. Primary examples included Püncog Wanggyai, the legendary "red Tibetan" who established the first Tibetan Communist Party branch and led the Red Army into Lhasa in 1950, and Ulanfu, the Mongol communist leader who helped to dissuade Mongol separatists and to establish China's first autonomous system in Inner Mongolia in 1948.

Despite the retreat on self-determination, class universalism played a key role in winning over minority allies for the CCP and in laying down the foundation for a new national identity. The function of this new universalism was no longer pacification and stability for frontier groups, but liberation and incorporation of them as equal members of the new nation state.

A TRANSFORMATIVE APPROACH TO ETHNICITY

China's pre-modern and modern approaches to ethnicity left two important legacies when the CCP came to power in 1949. The first was a long tradition of localized and crosscut identities. The second was the accession, under historical exigencies, to the concepts of the nation and nationality. The first legacy entailed that nation-building efforts would help local identities to transcend their previous confines, conducive to cross-regional cohesion. The second legacy entailed that the new concepts of the nation and nationality did not fit

China's historical and local realities, with adverse effects on the transition to nation state.

The conceptual misfit was manifest when the state had to undertake an elaborate project to classify ethnic groups in the 1950s. The fact that these groups needed to be identified by the state meant that they were not established "nations" or "nationalities." The Soviet Union, from which the CCP learned the concept of nationality, relied on census information to enumerate ethnic groups. But promises made to China's small minority groups before the CCP came to power drove its draconian approach: a hands-on classification by the state.

Class Universalism and the Classification

The twin goals of the CCP's ethnic policy agenda, upon coming to power in 1949, were class equality and national integration. The former served the latter: the appeal of class solidarity and equality helped to rally the support of minority masses, facilitating their identification with the new state. Class universalism was best expressed in Premier Zhou Enlai's justification of the party's minority policies: "paying debts" for past oppression suffered by minority groups (Zhou 1957a).

Class universalism carried the day in part because the imperative of national integration helped to sidestep the issue of "class enemy" in the initial years of CCP rule. While class universalism should theoretically exclude former minority elites, they were embraced as "patriotic ethnic bourgeoisie." The rationale was that social class structures were not fully developed in minority regions, due to their "backward" economies. As such, class struggle needed to be toned down in line with their lower level of development. Minority elites were thus given more concessions than Han elites in comparable social strata (Dreyer 1976: 94). The "backwardness" of minority regions entailed Han social solidarity with minority communities as a whole, including the "patriotic ethnic bourgeoisie."

The establishment of the autonomous system was the CCP's key administrative mechanism to achieve equality and integration. It would create territorial units named after the ethnic appellation of their main inhabitants. This system was formally stipulated by the Chinese People's Political Consultative Conference (CPPCC) in 1949 and written into the Chinese Constitution in 1954. It would materialize class universalism by enforcing equal rights, while formally incorporating ethnic members as citizens of the new nation state. Implementing equality, in turn, demanded that all groups, big or small, be recognized as equal groups through a scientific classification, according to Fei Xiaotong (1980: 142), China's preeminent sociologist at the time and a leading researcher in the project. Indeed, to demarcate ethno-territorial units in ways equitable to all self-claimed groups, especially where they historically coexisted, required a taxonomic clarification of the inhabitants. This was the primary driving force for the state's project to classify ethnic groups in the 1950s.[2] Not surprisingly, the classification project began in the longstanding mixed regions, namely inner peripheral regions.

Official records lend credence to the view that many groups had localized identities unknown to outsiders. Official documents – for the entire decade of the 1950s – show no central instruction or discussion about ethnic classification in the state's ethnic policy agenda before or during the height of the classification (Qin 2013: 36, 37).[3] Instead, four provinces – Yunnan, Hunan, Guangxi, and Heilongjiang – added "ethnic classification" to their "regular agenda of social investigation" of minority regions during the 1950s. According to Su Keqin, a deputy head of the SEAC and the only official who mentioned the classification in his work report,[4] the classification was necessitated by the implementation of ethnic equality in the establishment of the autonomous system (1960: 122). All this meant that the state itself had little idea about many "nationalities," because the label was a misnomer in the first place.

Yunnan provided strong evidence for localized, crosscut, and heterogeneous identities. The province became a principal driver of the classification project precisely because this was an inner peripheral region with culturally burred groups. In the PRC's first census conducted during 1952–3, 260 groups reported themselves as separate minority groups in Yunnan, amounting to 65 percent of the 400 self-reported groups nationwide. Conventionally, just eleven ethnic groupings were recognized in the whole of China at the time: the Mongol, Hui, Tibetan, Uighur, Miao, Yi, Korean, Manchu, Yao, Li, and Gaoshan groups. The large number of self-reported groups made it impossible to create an autonomous unit for every self-reported group scattering across the province. As local authorities learned from earlier efforts to create autonomous units, which began in May 1951, the biggest hurdle was to guarantee equality for the myriad minority groups in the province (Shen 2013: 36). It was impossible to accommodate all self-reported groups with a titular territorial unit without some kind of sorting and consolidation. The classification had to ensue as a result.

Disparate and crosscut sources of local identities were further evidenced by the use of local dialects to consolidate self-reported groups. When the Ethnic

[2] Although Thomas Mullaney argues that the classification originated from the need to have representatives from all minority groups for the NPC assembly in September 1954, this did not seem the case empirically. Local scholarship suggests that NPC representatives had been selected months before the first classification took place in Yunnan in 1954. See Qin (2013: 38) and Shen (2013: 36).

[3] Qin (2013) examined all official documents for the period of 1950–3, or before the start of the classification in 1954, and for the period 1954–9, or the height of the classification campaign. Those documents include decrees from the CCP Politburo, the State Council, the CCP Department of United Front, the State Ethnic Affairs Commission (SEAC) as well as the writings and memoirs of the leading officials in the last two agencies.

[4] In over a hundred work reports on state ethnic policy issued in the 1950s, written by central and local leaders involved in this area, Su Keqin was the only official who discussed "ethnic classification," in just two paragraphs. See Qin (2013: 36, 37).

Classification Study Group of Yunnan was founded in May 1954 – comprising forty-six members from local state agencies, national and local universities, and even a local hospital – they solicited the help of the linguist Fu Maoji to sort out the multitude of local ethnic groups. Mao's research team had been in Yunnan during 1952 for the state's language reform project. Based on his investigation in Yunnan, Mao and another scholar proposed that language be the major basis for differentiating ethnic groups (Luo and Fu 1954). According to Ma Yao, president of Yunnan Minzu College and a participant in the Yunnan classification group, Fu's language team was instrumental in helping to sort out local minority groups and their sub-branches, as language provided the organizing tools for ethnic classification (2001: 5). Based on the criterion of independent language possession, Fu concluded in 1954 that Yunnan's 140 appellations of ethnic groups could be consolidated into twenty-five categories (Fu 1954). Later that year, twenty-five minority groups were officially recognized in Yunnan (Qin 2013: 39).

The elevation of localized identities to ethno-political ones was immediate, as state recognition made a difference in group rights. In Yunnan's case, after six new ethnic groups were officially confirmed in late 1954, five new autonomous prefectures and two new autonomous counties were established as a direct result. In one case, an autonomous prefecture had already been created for the Hani group in early 1954, but after the classification project determined that the Yi group also had a sizable presence in the area, the prefecture was renamed to include the Yi as a co-titular group (Qin 2013: 43). The classification helped to raise the number of autonomous prefectures in Yunnan from three before the classification to a total of eight afterwards. There were also increases in the number of autonomous units within the prefectures over the years. By the 1990s Yunnan had a total of twenty-nine autonomous counties and 197 autonomous villages.

Similar dynamics affected other provinces where a multitude of ethnic groups coexisted, mainly inner peripheral regions. These regions had longstanding traditions of ethnic interaction and mixed communities: Guizhou, Guangxi, Guangdong, Fujian, Hunan, Gansu, and Qinghai. Local state agencies here began to investigate self-reported ethnic groups between 1952 and 1954. Guizhou had eighty such groups, the largest number after Yunnan (SEAC 2007a). Whenever local authorities ran into difficulty in assessing self-reported groups and demarcating ethno-territorial units, the central state was notified and research teams would be dispatched by the SEAC to help resolve the problems. These teams were headed by China's best scholars in the field of anthropology and ethnology at the time.[5] Their efforts helped to consolidate and transform localized identities into official and politicized ones.

[5] These included Fei Xiaotong, Huang Xianfan, Lin Yaohua, Xia Nongkang, Qiu Pu, Weng Dujian, Li Youyi, Li Anzhai, Wu Zelin, Fang Guoyu, Yang Chengzhi, Yang Kun, Wu Wenzao, Jiang Yingliang, and Liu Xian.

As expected, in the historically outer peripheral regions, classification of the principal groups was unnecessary, since they were well recognized. This did not necessarily mean that those groups had internal cohesion. When the classification took place in Xinjiang and Inner Mongolia in 1953 and in Tibet in the 1960s, the well-known groups were confirmed and officially registered. In Xinjiang, they included twelve ethnic groups who were already identified in the 1930s: several Muslim groups, Mongols, Sibes, and Russians. In Inner Mongolia they were Mongols concentrated in the pastoral regions. In the TAR they were Tibetans who comprised 99 percent of the local population when the TAR was established in 1965. In these three regions, the focus of classification was the marginal groups: the Daur in Inner Mongolia (and Manchuria), Qiangic and Tibeto-Burman groups in eastern and southern Tibet, and small Central Asian groups in Xinjiang (Fei 1980). Nevertheless, having to identify and give them official labels entailed that these small groups were not "nations" in the first place.

Together the classification formalized forty-four new "nationalities." Twenty-seven of these were classified on the basis of the first national census in 1953 and on field studies. Another seventeen were classified in the next two decades.[6] Along with the traditionally recognized eleven ethnic groups, they added up to a total of fifty-five officially recognized minority groups. Since the late 1950s, every individual's ethnic status was entered into the household registry of the state. Since the mid-1980s, it also appears on the personal identification card issued by the state. Institutionally the official designations embody political "inclusion" in terms of PRC citizenship and "equality" in terms of entitlement to preferential policy benefits.

Class universalism, in the form of political inclusion and ethnic entitlement, marked a major departure from Confucian universalism, which treated acceptance of Confucian norms as the criterion for membership in the Sinic community, without official fixity or ethnic particularism. By politicizing previously heterogeneous and localized identities, the classification resulted in a number of unintended consequences conducive to ethnic mobilization.

Classifying and Engineering Identities

Foremost among such consequences is the creation and engineering of identities that previously did not exist or existed weakly. Many new groups did not match the official definition of "nationalities." Officially, Stalin's definition of nationality was used, namely, the combined presence of four "commons" – common language, territory, economic life, and psychological make-up (1913). But Chinese researchers found few groups who met the criterion. Instead they emphasized "common language" in their classifying efforts, and in its absence

[6] For a comprehensive treatment of the ethnic classification projects, see Huang and Si (2005) and EdB (1989). For Fei Xiaotong's account, see Jiang and Huang (1994: 43–7).

relied on "group characteristics" (Fei 1980). As Yunnan's case showed, the sorting of languages was no easy matter, and that of group characteristics was often subjective, since so many groups self-reported as separate groups.

For multitudes of ethnic communities in inner peripheral regions, ethnic markers were vague while shared features were common. Longstanding interactions with multiethnic areas had created shared historical memories, communal ties, and blurring ethnic boundaries, especially in southwestern provinces. Small numbers and proximity to other groups entailed intermarriages, rendering ethnic and linguistic distinctions ambiguous. Not surprisingly, many communities with shared features and vague distinctions ended up being classified as or merged into different groups in different locations (Wu 2013: 19, 21). As Mullaney finds, ethnic elites in some communities had to be convened and persuaded that rather than their self-reported ethnic categories, they belonged with another label based on linguistic differentiation (2010b: 103). Rather than merely reflecting pre-existing realities, thus, the classification also created "fixed" identifies by political means.

For many of the larger ethnic groups, extended periods of migration and mingling had resulted in the loss of cohesive and collective commons by the mid-twentieth century, but these were plucked from history to fit into official categories. The Manchus, because of their small numbers and conqueror roles, spread across the country and lost all of the four "commons" except in the remote steppes of the northeast. In fact, as a Manchu scholar argues, the Manchu ethnic group was itself a political creation, a fusion of various steppe tribes for the purpose of conquering China; thus its political demise inevitably led to its demise as an ethnic group (Guan 2011: 19). The Huis, thanks to a history of commercial activities on the historical Silk Road and imperial services during the Mongol era, scattered across the country despite a sizable concentration in the northwest. Other than religion and dietary restrictions, many Huis would have more in common with their fellow residents locally than with Huis elsewhere. The Mongols too were diverse and spread beyond the prairies, thanks to the legacy of the Mongol conquest. After centuries of geographical and cultural separation, Mongols in and out of the steppes had different economic lives (pastoral vs. sedentary), spoke different languages, and practiced different cultural customs. In these cases, the criterion of "historical commons" had to be used to sort individuals into their appropriate categories.

.Other groups with disparately localized identities were merged into large groups. What came to be classified as the Miao and Yao peoples inhabited in various southern and southwestern provinces, followed different cultural practices, and spoke mutually intelligible tongues – from variants of the Mien, the Hmong, and the Kadai to Chinese dialects. But they were merged into the two categories, despite weak common identities. In Guangxi, two dozen local groups, who spoke different branches of the Kadai language and shared no clearly traceable common history, were merged into the Zhuang label, while a few others were assigned to different groups in neighboring provinces (Wu 2013: 23). The Zhuang is now the largest minority group in China with 17 million people (2010 census), but weak ethnic markers.

Other groups were classified on the basis of religion, which had its share of internal and historical incongruities as well. Historically the term Hui included all Central Asian Muslims who came to the eastern Tibetan plateau from different parts of the Mongol empire as recruited soldiers during the Mongol conquest of China in the thirteenth century. They shared distinct but mutually intelligible tongues, numbered in the thousands only in population, and were once considered as different branches of the Hui people. On the basis of "group preferences," they came to be classified as separate "nationalities" despite sharing the Muslim faith and historical origins. Two groups were classified as the Bonan and the Dongxiang, who had historically mixed with Mongols, Hans, Huis, and Tibetans (Mi and You 2004: 58; Olson 1998: 66). Another small Muslim group, self-identified as the Salar, migrated to the eastern Tibetan plateau in the twelfth century CE and was identified as a separate nationality by itself. Decades later, many members of these groups still think of themselves as part of the larger Hui or Muslim people except where policy benefits matter (Jian 2006). In countless cases like these, it was artificial to define every individual as a member of a "nation."

Discrepancies in local administrative efforts also helped to fracture previously shared local identities, since the classification was administered locally. A lack of coordination resulted in cases where similar groups were classified as different ethnicities in neighboring localities. Qiangic speakers were variously classified as part of the Qiangic, Tibetan, Pumi, Nakhi, and Mongol groups. The Nakhi people, who lived in areas bordering Sichuan and Yunnan provinces, were identified as the Mongol on the Sichuan side but the Nakhi on the Yunnan side, while the Pumi people were classified as Tibetans on the Sichuan side but Pumis on the Yunnan side (Fei 1980). Various branches of the Zhuang were grouped into different groups in different provinces thanks to administrative divisions (Mullaney 2010a: 88). The Bouyeis of southern Guizhou, who appeared to be no different from the Zhuangs across the border in Guangxi, were grouped as a different nationality (Hu and Zhang 2009: 12). In an extreme case, one self-identified Bouyei group in three Yunnan counties was classified into three separate nationalities, the Bai, Zhuang, and Bouyei, a result largely due to the separate decisions of three provinces bordering the three counties (Wu 2013: 23).

The classifying project also helped to engineer identities because of their linkage to preferential policies. Policy benefits associated with an official ethnic status, especially a titular status, provided incentives for local groups to seek or compete for state classification of an ethnic category, which they otherwise did not know or care about. The category of Tujia people, who were indistinct from the Han people or fellow hilly communities in central China, was created thanks to the lobbying efforts of one determined woman and villagers who wanted to qualify for state benefits, because their long-term neighbors who received classification got tax relief (Chen 2010: 45–6). The Tujia is now the seventh largest ethnic group in China with over 8 million members. The same incentives drove other small groups with vague ethnic features or awareness to seek classification, so that they too could qualify for state benefits (EdB 1987: 216, 217).

As the majority ethnic group, the Han people were not part of the classification project but were still impacted. Most importantly, the Han became defined by virtue of the contrast with the Other. The idea of ethnic classification had as its corollary the assumption that anyone who did not think or know of oneself as belonging to a non-Han group, was automatically part of the Han majority group (Guan K. 2007: 265). It was not uncommon for longtime residents of mixed and border areas to be classified as Han or one of the local ethnic groups. In western Sichuan, some Qiangic speakers were labeled as Tibetans or Hans, while some Pumi speakers were classified as Tibetans or Hans (Wu 2013: 21). When the state's household registry system (*Hukou*) began in 1958, each individual would choose to put an ethnicity in the registry record. Many who had not thought of this question before simply put "Han" as a spontaneous response or were casually advised to do so (Gladney 1998: 118). Indeed, differences within the Han people were significant in terms of language, religion, and culture, but these were neglected in the classification, and those differences became smaller only over time in the modern state-building process. The classification project, thus, also helped to create the Han people.

Between the number of self-claimed and officially recognized groups, a great many were thus made or unmade in the process. Almost a quarter of the fifty-five official groups numbered between a few hundred to a few thousand people, but they were now a "nation" on a par with groups that represented major civilizations. With institutional fixity, the ethnic marker becomes part of the permanent personal information in the official registry that is critical to receiving services and opportunities in the public sector: state benefits, college admissions, job application, and professional promotion. As the everyday symbol of one's politically fixed identity, it departs sharply from historical patterns of ethnic fluidity and political neutrality.

Politicizing Uighur and Tibetan Identities

Politically the most consequential cases involved the Uighurs and Tibetans, as they too were disparate communities that came to be defined and unified by official designation. The politicizing effects of the *minzu* identity have been duly noted in the Western scholarly literature. Scholars share the observation that the institutionalization of *minzu* identities, along with the allocation of privileges along *minzu* lines, has considerably strengthened collective identities among China's minority groups. These include, in particular, the culturally and linguistically distinct groups of the Uighurs (Gladney 1990 and 1991: 301;

Bovingdon 1998, 2004, and 2010) and the Tibetans (Shakya 2012: 24), but also, to a lesser extent, less distinct groups such as the Hui (Gladney 1991 and 1998), the Zhuang (Kaup 2000), the Yi (Harrell 2001; Harrell and Li 2003), the Yao (Litzinger 2000), the Miao (Schein 2000), and the Naxi (White 1998).

In Xinjiang, the classification facilitated the consolidation of a Uighur identity that began in the 1930s. Before the 1930s, the various Uighur groups identified themselves by the oases they came from, not by an ethnic group (Rudelson 1997). Their position on the Silk Road and the crossroads of the East and West civilizations gave them multicultural exposure, while the barriers of desserts and oases gave them geographic identities. They would identify themselves as from Ili, Tarim, Hotan, Kashgar, and Hami, namely, localized identities. With no written script in common use, they varied vernacularly. They also differed physically – ranging from East to Central to West Asian in appearance. The name "Uighur" reappeared from the Uighur Khaganate (mid-eighth to ninth centuries CE) in modern times, after the Soviet Union took the ninth-century ethnonym and reapplied it to all non-nomadic Turkic Muslims of Xinjiang (Bellér-Hann et al. 2007: 32). Though scholars debate how the term Uighur came to be used in its modern ethnic context, they agree on two elements: first, the term appeared in Xinjiang in the mid-1930s, and second, Soviet influence was a factor, if not the only factor (Rudelson 1997: 7, 149).

The diverse ancestry and fluid definition of the Uighurs historically renders uncertain what constitutes true Uighur ethnography and ethnogenesis.[7] They were known by various names in Chinese history, depending on changing groupings, regroupings, and migratory movements: Guifang, Dingling, Gaoche, Tiele, Chile, Huihu, Shatuo, Huiwei'er, and Hui'e'er. They were relatively recent migrants to the Tarim Basin region, dating to the mid-ninth century. Comparing the DNA of the Tarim mummies (1900 BCE–200 CE) to that of modern-day Uighurs, the research team of Victor Mair found some genetic similarities but "no direct links." According to Mair, "[F]rom around 1800BC, the earliest mummies in the Tarim Basin were exclusively Caucausoid, or Europoid. East Asian migrants arrived in the eastern portions of the Tarim Basin about 3,000 years ago ... while the Uighur peoples arrived after the collapse of the Orkon Uighur Kingdom, based in modern-day Mongolia, around the year 842" (*The Independent* 2006). Genetic studies confirm that present-day Uighurs have an admixture of East Asian and European components (Cavalli-Sforza 1998; Li and Kidd et al. 2009).

Soviet influence was most substantial in reshaping Xinjiang's ethnic landscape. In the 1930s, the warlord Sheng Shicai relied on Soviet definitions and methods to classify fourteen "ethnicities" in Xinjiang, including the "Uighurs" (meaning "united"). Ruling Xinjiang ruthlessly with the support of the Soviet Union, Sheng's purpose was to fragment the various groups of

[7] See a review of the academic debate about Uighur ethnography and ethnogenesis in Bovingdon (2010: ch. 1).

Turkic-speaking Muslims so as to weaken pan-Turkic and pan-Islamic movements. According to Benson and Svanberg, the Turkic Muslim peoples of Xinjiang preferred to identify themselves as "Turki," "East Turkestani," or just "Muslim," but the Soviets and the KMT intended to foster a Uighur identity in order to divide the Muslim population (1998: 20–1). The use of the term Uighurs "covered over a whole host of internal differences among the oasis of the Tarim Basin" and the KMT government's classification of the Uighurs "shaped their ethnic identity to a large extent" (Rudelson 1997: 7). In 1954 the CCP officially adopted the Uighur label from the 1930s, along with twelve other ethnic designations in Xinjiang. The establishment of the XUAR, in 1955, further consolidated a Uighur identity (Bovingdon 2010). This identity, moreover, is closely associated with Islam.

This official identity both rewrote and diminished the Uighurs' own history in Xinjiang. Most Uighur inhabitants of west Tarim did not convert to Islam until the fifteenth century. Before Islam established hegemony in Central Asia, communities of Uighurs practiced Shamanism, Zoroastrianism, Manicheanism, Buddhism, and Nestorian Christianity. Before its modern reappearance, Uighur identity had previously been associated with Buddhism and never with Islam (Rudelson 1997: 7). The newly defined Uighur identity neglected this part of Uighur history as well as the other parts. As all of the Turkic history of Xinjiang came to be interpreted as Uighur, the historical fluidity and richness of Uighur identity was lost. In the 1930s Uighurs had powerful incentives to accept their officially assigned label, Rudelson suggests, because it made them the largest "nationality" in Xinjiang and defined them against the competing groups – the Hans, Tungans, and Kazakhs (1997: 7).

The Tibetans too amalgamated from diverse ethnic origins but came to be united by the classification of the 1950s. Dibyesih Anand writes:

> [H]istorians disagree over the extent to which a pan-Tibetan identity existed before 1959. Most (Goldstein; Shakya; Mills; Samuels) argue that while there was a sense of belonging to an overarching tradition (with Lhasa as the main religious and administrative center), local identities were the defining feature in the lives of most people. Even the primacy of the Dalai Lama as the sole, largely uncontested, leader of the Tibetan nation is a product of twentieth-century post-exile politics. (2003: 215)

Tsering Shakya, a Canada-based Tibetan historian, writes, "[T]o some degree the creation of a single Tibetan group owes much to the nationality policies and ethnic categorization system introduced by the communists. Before 1950, there was no single Tibetan group with this name, because local identity was the primary marker of group identity" (2012: 24). Beijing's own Tibetan scholars concede that the subgroups of Tibetans scattered across different altitudes of the Tibetan plateau descended from different ethnic mixes, belonged to bickering religious sects, and spoke mutually unintelligible tongues while sharing dialects with fellow residents of various ethnic descent locally (Losel 2011b: 22, 23).

Inhabitants of Greater Tibet also had mixed origins but many came to be classified as Tibetans. Early settlers in the Amdo area (parts of present-day Qinghai and Gansu), such as the Tuyuhun (a Xianbei or Eurasian nomadic branch), dated back to the third century and were later conquered and absorbed by the Tubo (Tibetan) empire (Li and Li 1992: 14–18; Zhou 1985). The Tanguts (Dangxiang) ruled a greater part of the Amdo area during the West Xia dynasty (1038–1227 CE), till its annihilation by Genghis Khan (Li 2005). Some Tangut survivors possibly fled to the Muya area of the Tibetan Kham region. The Gyarong Tibetans of Kham, who were classified as Tibetans, may have descended from the Tanguts; while the Baima Tibetans of southwestern Kham were classified as Tibetans in Sichuan but the Pumi in Yunnan (Fei 1980). Not surprisingly, Gyarong and Baima groups prefer a reclassification.

In addition, since the Mongol conquest of the thirteenth century, Central Asian soldiers and their Muslim faith had infiltrated the Amdo area. Intermittent Chinese migrations before and after the Mongol empire also accumulated numerous Han Chinese residents in the Amdo and Kham areas (Cai 2008). Tibetans in Amdo and Kham intermarried with all other groups, sharing local Chinese dialects with their ethnic counterparts while speaking Tibetan dialects distinct to their local co-ethnics. What came to be defined as Tibetans in the classifying project was largely by religion, that is, Buddhism.

The consolidation of Uighur and Tibetan identities would have long-term implications for ethnic mobilization, since they remain the only outer peripheral groups. The blurring of inner and outer peripheral groups, which under-recognized the special status of the Uighurs and Tibetans, would have further politicizing effects.

Blurring of Inner and Outer Peripheral Groups

Another unintended politicizing consequence of the classification was the blurring of inner and outer peripheral groups as co-"nationalities." While this entailed formal equality across ethnic groups, it obscured critical differences between them, in particular the greater autonomous status of outer peripheral groups historically: the Uighurs and Tibetans. Underdifferentiation portended challenges for integration, as it obscured historical differences and contemporary needs of the two broadly different groups.

In pre-modern China, cultural and geographic distance made a key difference in imperial and conventional dealings with the frontier groups. Tribes of the inner peripheral regions, such as the southeast and southwest, were called "familiar aliens" (*shu fan*) who were close to Sinic ways and traits. By contrast, tribes of the outer peripheries were called "unfamiliar aliens" (*sheng fan*), who were significantly different. The characters *shu* and *sheng* connoted degrees of their geographic and cultural distances: less versus more divergence from Sinic communities, more versus less contact with them, and more incorporation versus less incorporation with them. First appearing in this usage during the Zhou dynasty (1045 BCE–771 BCE), the character *fan*, literally meaning "fence" and connoting a barrier area, denotes borderland areas and peoples (Liu 2009b: 42; Zhang S. 2010: 106, 107). The "familiar" aliens, due to their agrarian and sedentary ways, would be partially taxed, amounting ironically to a "debarbarization" process. The "less familiar" aliens, largely nomadic, were not formally entered into the imperial household registry nor required to pay imperial taxes.[8]

A classification of all minority groups as "nationalities" overdifferentiated the small groups in inner peripheral regions and underdifferentiated the large groups in outer peripheries. Not surprisingly, as Uighur intellectuals would complain in private, how could "small and isolated primitive tribes" in remote hills of the southwest be comparable to large communities associated with major civilizations? Instead of fifty-five "nationalities," they argued, just three major cultural groups should be distinguished in China: Confucian, Buddhist, and Islamic (Chen 2012: 34). This conception of Tibetans (Buddhist) and Uighurs (Islamic) echoes the definition of a "national minority" by Keith Banting and Will Kymlicka, referring to historically substate groups with national identities and aspirations. Two other minority groups defined by Banting and Kymlicka are "indigenous minorities" and "immigrant minorities" (MCP 2020).

A differentiation of China's minority groups along these lines would have entailed a more layered conception of minority groups, giving more recognition to the special status of Tibetans and Uighurs. A definition of these two groups as a "national minority" would entail their rights to territorial autonomy and its associated prerogatives, such as language and religion. The "isolated primitive tribes" are analogous to indigenous peoples, which would entail their land and cultural rights. Although official Chinese discourse is averse to the term *yuanzhu min* (aboriginal peoples), it is not opposed to the term *xianzhu min* (early settlers). Needless to say, varying degrees of historical incorporation and coexistence will not make a classification of "indigenous peoples" easy. Culturally at least, the small tribal groupings can simply be called "ethnic groups," rather than "nationalities" on a bar with large groups like Tibetans and Uighurs. These two groups, moreover, were the only two that constituted "core ethnic regions" at the time of the classifying project, in other words where they comprised the majority population.

The reasons for the overdifferentiation of minor groups and underdifferentiation of major groups remain controversial. The official justification was class universalism, that is equality of all groups, regardless of their demographic sizes. Ma Rong, a leading ethnologist in China, blames Soviet influence for the way the CCP implemented equality, by registering the ethnic status of every citizen (Ma 2012). A Taiwanese historian impugns the CCP's political motives: granting

[8] Details of the Tang dynasty's differentiated tax rates are described in Du You, *Tong dian* [General Dictionary] (*c.* 766 to 801), ch. 6. Beijing: Zhonghua shuju, 1988.

recognition to the small groups would offset the centrifugal tendencies of the larger groups (Wu 2013: 12). This last thesis suggests a "divide and conquer" strategy, though with little proof of intent. The main evidence cited was that the primary targets of the classifying project were the weaker and smaller ethnic groups in the southwest, rather than large groups such as the Manchus, Mongols, Muslims, and Tibetans (Wu 2013: 27). However, this argument appears to be unfounded. Since the Republican era, the large groups had already been officially recognized as part of the five "co-nations."

Rather, class universalism better explained the CCP's intentions for overdifferentiating the minor groups. During the 1930s and 1940s, the small groups had to fight for official recognition and preferred the CCP to the KMT precisely because of the CCP's willingness to recognize their equal status. As Mullaney's study suggests, the wartime experiences of social scientists in the southwest played a key role in their classifying efforts in this region (2010a). Those social scientists, contrary to the "divide and conquer" thesis, helped to merge many groups in the southwest. This merge was done even in the sensitive case of Tibetan regions. In western Sichuan, there were cases where two dozen disparate local communities in a county were merged into the same Tibetan category (Qin 2013: 35). Some of these communities continue to express their preference to be reclassified (Fei 1980).

For a lack of better evidence, the CCP's revolutionary idealism provided a more plausible explanation for its pursuit of equality, or class universalism. But the blurring of small and large groups only produced nominal equality, with more winning for the former than for the latter. It also portended that the state version of integration and equality would not likely suffice to placate those larger groups with ethno-national aspirations, the Tibetans and Uighurs.

SUMMARY

This chapter focuses on changing approaches to ethnicity in China's transition from empire to the modern nation state. I have argued that the universalism and pragmatism of Confucianism served ethnic maintenance in imperial China, but the ancient approach was unraveled by challenges from the *nation* discourse in modern times. The failure of the late Qing and Republican regimes to construct an effective response opened the way for Soviet influence and the triumph of class universalism. This new approach to ethnicity helped the CCP to complete the incorporation of minority members as citizens of the modern nation state.

Specifically, historical legacies and modern strategies impacted the patterns of China's transition to nation state in two major ways. First, the large demographic/territorial core, while serving as the stabilizing force during and after the decline of the Qing empire, led late Qing revolutionaries and Republican leaders to a Han-centric conception of the nation. The narrow approach hampered them from building a national identity that transcended ethnicity and oriented them toward assimilationist strategies that ultimately failed. Second, the CCP's strategy of nation building, via ethnic classification, had the unintended consequences of politicizing identities and creating "nations." It departed from pre-modern practices by altering the criteria for membership in the Chinese political community. Under Confucian universalism, ethnic markers were not the criteria in defining this community. Under the CCP, they became explicitly so, through the state's classification and the household registry. As such, these groups became institutionalized as constituent members of the new Chinese nation, regardless of their previous relationship or identification with the central state. On the positive side, frontier peoples were no longer relevant to the state largely for reasons of border security. They became political equals in a state of *co-nationalities*. Being such, they were no longer peripheral objects who were subject to "loose rein," but political subjects with nominal equal citizenship.

By mixing centralization and ethnicization, politicized identities lay down the first set of institutional dynamics for ethnic discord in contemporary times, especially for the two outer peripheral regions of Tibet and Xinjiang. One institutional dynamic arose from political integration and the surrendering of historically heterogeneous identities. This centralization entailed that the state assumed the right to command the political loyalty and identity of previously distant and peripheral groups. This was a significant change for the outer peripheral regions, particularly where theocratic institutions had been the basis of political loyalty and identity. Class universalism may mollify the jolt of this change temporarily, but ethnic particularism – encouraged by the state's own titular and other ethnic prerogatives – would pose an inherent challenge to the surrendering of traditional identities imposed by the state. That is, the classification project did not only justify integration on the basis of social class solidarity, but also identity assertion on the basis of "nationality" status, thus offsetting the official goal of nation building.

Another institutional dynamic stemmed from the politicization of localized identities, or ethnicization. The classification helped to overcome parochial factors that localized ethnic identities in pre-modern times, providing cohesion to previously insular and crosscut identities. The politicizing effects would be particularly consequential for major groups of the outer peripheral regions. It formally gave Uighurs and Tibetans cohesive identities that transcended geographical and sectarian barriers, allowing them to consolidate into sustained cross-regional ethnic or proto-nationalistic political identity. As the Tibetan historical Shakya aptly puts it, the Tibetan self-identification as *bod rigs* or "Tibetan nationality" is rather recent and created by the Chinese authority itself. The CCP's classification of the people across the Tibetan plateau as a single *borig* provided fixity to "Tibetanness," homogenizing it typologically (2012: 24).

Yet another institutional dynamic created by the classification was the construction of co-nationalities in the name of equality. For distinct groups with major civilizational heritages, namely the Tibetans and Uighurs, becoming co-nationalities with minor groups entailed diminished parity. Nominal equality was achieved at the expense of these major groups, fueling potential discontent. Moreover, institutional tensions also arose here from the state's own linkage of policy prerogatives to ethnic status, thus energizing minor and indistinct ethnic groups. The politicizing and divisive tendency of this linkage was already manifest during the classification process, when competing groups vied for separate classification for the sake of policy privileges associated with it.

These institutional dynamics for ethnic mobilization were tempered by class universalism during the socialist era. Elevated ethnic identities crosscut with social class identities. Memories of repressive former elites, along with the appeal of social class solidary and the redistributive socialist state, helped to rally the majority and minority masses around the Communist Party. Once these mollifying factors weakened or disappeared, however, those institutional tensions became amplified.

2

Changing Approaches to Ethnic Governance

From Loose Rein to Ethno-territorialism

This chapter focuses on the changing strategies of ethnic governance in China's transition from empire to modern nation state. That is, evolution from a maintenance-oriented strategy aimed at pacification and stability in imperial times, to increased incorporation in modern times, and to a transformative strategy aimed at integration and egalitarianism in the socialist era.

The new system of ethnic governance, I argue, created the second set of institutional dynamics for ethnic discord in the long run. That is, a uniform and direct form of ethnic governance based on titular ethnic status, known as the system of autonomous regions. Historically imperial China had a three-tiered approach to ruling its extensive domain: direct rule over a core region, indirect and diverse rule over inner peripheries, and elite alliances in outer peripheries. This pre-modern "minimalist state" (Crone 1989: 47) came under serious challenge in modern times, when the ideas of sovereignty and nation state arrived in China in the late 1800s. Late Qing and Republican regimes failed to construct a new institutional order to redefine the relationship between the center and peripheral regions, thus opening the way for Soviet doctrine and the CCP. The CCP's approach to ethnic governance, characterized by political centralization and ethno-territorialism, served to incorporate frontier regions and to complete China's institutional transition to the modern state. In the process it departed from pre-modern Chinese practices of diverse and de-ethnicized rule. The contradictions therein – promoting political integration but also ethno-territories to fit that goal – would render the autonomous system as another key source of institutional tensions in contemporary times.

This chapter covers the follows topics: (1) relevant legacies of pre-modern China's strategies of frontier governance; (2) relevant legacies of modern China's attempts at nation state building; and (3) the establishment of the CCP's system of ethnic governance and its institutional repercussions.

ONE EMPIRE, THREE TIERS

For China's transition to the modern nation state, the most relevant legacy of pre-modern times was a three-tiered structure and strategy of rule in the Chinese Empire. There was more direct rule in the core region, but various forms of indirect and ritualistic rule over the semi-frontier and frontier regions. Differentiated rule entailed varying types of central–peripheral relations. This diversity rendered it challenging to build the nation state in modern times.

The differentiated rule of imperial times, concomitant with Confucian universalism, involved a graded and concentric hierarchy under the celestial empire. This empire may be understood restrictively to denote a type of "agrarian state that controlled multiple urban centers and extensive hinterlands, significantly adapted its methods of rule to peoples of different ethnic origins, and, due to its limited pre-modern infrastructural capacity, exercised only indirect rule over local communities and frontier areas" (Zhao 2015: 4). The nature of this rule may be understood through Michael Mann's concept of "compulsory cooperation." Pre-modern empires relied on such cooperation to maintain rule over their subjects, due to their limited infrastructural capacity to establish direct rule over an extended domain (1986: ch. 5).

The three tiers of rule entailed differentiated types of compulsory cooperation in imperial China. A form of direct rule applied in the central zone, the Central Plains, or agrarian regions populated largely by Sinic communities. These areas were governed by the bureaucratic and legal rules of the imperial bureaucracy, entered into the official household registry, and obligated to pay imperial taxes. Despite the diverse origins of the Celestial Emperor, be they Sinic, semi-nomadic, or nomadic, rulers mostly relied on Confucianism as a ruling ideology and on the imperial bureaucracy run by the Confucian elite. The merger of political and ideological power in the Chinese state structure motivated new rulers, indigenous or nomadic, to seek the cooperation of the Confucian elite, to adopt the Confucian-Legalist political arrangement, and to embrace Chinese culture (Zhao 2015: 4, 324). Confucian universalism facilitated nomadic acculturation and de-ethnicized rule.

Various forms of indirect rule applied outside the central zone, that is the tribal and peripheral territories. They relied on ritualistic obligations and titles in a system of "loose rein." Voluntarily or militarily surrendered, the peripheral areas differentiated between an inner and outer peripheral zone. Cultural and geographical distances made a key difference in their relationships and cooperation with the central authority. The inner peripheries, or "familiar aliens" (*shu fan*), were geographically, culturally, and administratively closer to the central zone. Tribal leaders here were obligated with annual tributes and periodic pilgrimage trips. Due to their agrarian and sedentary ways, communities here would be partially taxed as they became increasingly incorporated into the regular governance system. Internal affairs were left to the tribes themselves, though internal rebellions and misrule had sometimes required central intervention. Traditionally these areas consisted of "semi-barbarian" tribes to the east, south, and near west of the Central Plains. At various times they included the Hmong-Mien tribes of central and central south China, the Ba-Shu habitat of Sichuan, the Daic and Mon-Khmer tribes of the southeast and southwest, and the Qiangic hub of western Sichuan.

The outer peripheries, or "unfamiliar aliens" (*sheng fan*), were geographically, culturally, and ethnically more distant. Nomadic or semi-nomadic, communities here were not formally entered into the official household registry nor required to pay imperial taxes. Tribal chieftains were obligated to acknowledge the Celestial Emperor but were required to make less frequent pilgrimage trips (Liu 2009b; Zhao and Wei 2003; Yang 1999; Peng 2004). Internal affairs were left to themselves. At various times these outer peripheries consisted of "barbarian" tribes to the far north and the far west, that is, the four Eurasian frontiers, including the Mongolic north, the Tungusic northeast, the Turkic west, and the Tibetan far west.

The system of loose rein, under which ethnic regions of the two peripheral zones were administered, resulted from cycles of core–periphery rivalry that have taken place throughout Chinese history. As an institution it took shape under the united dynasties of Qin (221–6 BCE) and Han (206 BCE–220 CE), appeared in the historical chronicle of the Han dynasty for the first time, reached its peak during the preeminent Tang dynasty (618–907) and declined during the Ming (1368–1644) and Qing (1644–1911) eras. Sinic dynasties tended to use it as a defensive mechanism against tribal rebellions and nomadic intrusions, while nomadic dynasties tended to use it as an offensive mechanism against frontier rivals rising on their flank. Not surprisingly, the loose rein system experienced the greatest growth under the semi-nomadic dynasty of Tang and the nomadic dynasties of Yuan (1271–1368) and Qing. Tang's founders were of mixed Xianbei and Han origins, while the founders of Yuan and Qing were Mongol and Manchu respectively.

At its height, Tang's loose rein system exemplified pre-modern China's institutional arrangements for differentiated rule: more "rein" in the inner peripheral than in the outer peripheral zone. After an ethnic tribe or region was militarily defeated, self-subdued, or naturalized, a variety of loose rein territorial units were established. In the inner peripheral regions, loose rein structures consisted of administrative hierarchies mirroring the regular prefectures, while some loose rein counties were established under the jurisdiction of regular prefectures if they bordered the Tang proper, such as in the southwest. In the outer peripheral areas, with large and remote frontier regions, loose rein protectorates were established, such as in the Turkic khanates of the western regions (Liu 1998: 120–3; Peng 2004: ch. 3). Security concerns were key motives behind Tang's extensive loose rein system (Peng 2004: ch. 3). To neutralize the Turkic threats on the western frontiers, Emperor Taizhong opted for loose rein territorial units along the lines of individual tribes, or the eastern and western Turkic khanates. Within the more powerful western khanate, a further division was made between a left and right district, each with a Tang command area seated in them.

As a conquest dynasty, the Mongols' Yuan court enforced greater centralization of interior lands and greater incorporation of borderlands, but its territorial span still consisted of three tiers. They included the Central Region (*fuli*), the en-route provinces (*xingsheng*) or much of the inner peripheral areas, and outer peripheral regions managed by the Grand Protectorate (*Daduhufu*) (i.e., Uighur areas in the western regions) and the Bureau of Buddhist and Tibetan Affairs (i.e., the kingdom of Tibet). In the inner peripheral areas, the Yuan court initiated the *Tusi* system, or native chieftaincy, which formally incorporated native ethnic chieftains into the Chinese administrative hierarchy and conferred official posts upon the chieftains with Chinese-style rankings (Took 2005: 44–5). After conquering the Nanzhao kingdom, the Mongols turned it into the province of Yunnan in the thirteenth century. They submitted the kingdom of Tibet to a "patron–priest" relationship, the nature of which remains contentious between China and Tibetan exiles over the former kingdom's sovereign status (Norbu 2001: 139).

Another conquest dynasty, the Manchus' Qing court, faced great challenges of governing all of the surrounding prairies and plateaus it had conquered, with inevitable reliance on diverse and indirect rule. In the inner peripheries, Qing consolidated effective control with greater centralization of the native chieftaincy system. In localities already governed under this system, largely in the southwest, Qing instituted bureaucratization reforms, which transformed a majority of the localities into regular administrative units (Took 2005: 229–32; Yang 1993; Li S. 2001). This reform marked a major step in the historical incorporation of the inner peripheral regions.

In the outer peripheral areas of Mongolia, Xinjiang, and Tibet, Qing ruled with greater centralization but also differentiation. Security concerns, rather than internal control per se, were paramount. In Mongol tribal areas, Qing co-opted local chiefs with military and marriage alliances and retained the banner system, a form of military organization based on tribal and lineage units. But Qing differentiated Inner and Outer Mongolia: in the former, Qing assumed more direct control and did not allow appointed chieftainship to be inherited; in the latter, Qing left more autonomy and allowed inherited appointments. In Uighur areas, Qing improved upon the *beg* (native chief) system by defining the powers of local chieftains, banning them from serving as religious leaders, and requiring imperial approval for their appointment and promotion. In Tibet, Qing used the Galoon system, by which four Galoons (Tibetan aristocrats) would take charge of Tibet's administrative affairs. To reduce the power of elite lamas, only one of the four Galoons could be from the monastery, and later even the sole clergyman was dropped. Beyond the political arrangements at the top, various spheres of local life were left to ethnic chieftains, including economic, religious, commercial, fiscal, and penal affairs (Yang 1993; Li S. 2001).

Qing's separate methods of rule for outer peripheral regions cannot be overemphasized. In fact Qing used a separate central agency, the *Lifan Yuan*, to administer them. Originating from the Manchus' Office for Mongol Affairs, this agency had roots in the Manchus' military alliances with Mongol banners. Its wording in the Manchu language, Office for Managing Affairs of Outer Provinces, provided the accurate meaning of *Lifan Yuan* (Zhang 2004: 26). The agency's jurisdiction covered Inner, Outer, and Western Mongolia, Muslim Xinjiang, Manchu banners, Tibet, and western (Tibetan) Sichuan (Xu and Jin 2008: 43). Qing referred to three of these regions as *waifan* (external fences or aliens), namely Mongolia, Tibet, and Muslim Xinjiang, but distinguished them from foreign countries by treating them as internal aliens rather than external aliens. Qing mandated annual pilgrimages of native chiefs from those internal alien tribes, but used the voluntary tributary system for the external or foreign aliens. This was the essential difference between the two systems (Zhang S. 2010: 106–14). The annual pilgrimages from the internal aliens were part of their "compulsory cooperation," formalistic as they may have been.

In short, three broad patterns of Chinese imperial rule may be characterized: Confucian universalism, administrative diversity, and de-ethnicization. The Celestial Emperor ruled universally in name across three tiers of the imperial domain, but with diverse approaches and ethnic neutrality. This legacy presented formidable challenges in modern times for nation state building, when shared identities and administrative structures were demanded.

TRANSITION TO THE NATION STATE

From the onset of the modern era in China, marked by the arrival of Western powers, imperial rulers were epistemically constrained to understand the concept of the sovereign nation state. For millennia, the Sino-centric order at home and abroad precluded the assumption of sovereign equality among political communities. Rather, a core–periphery hierarchy was presumed. Constituent members were not considered sovereign equals but culturally graded tributaries. The modern concept of sovereignty did not exist. There was the Chinese state, with undefined boundaries (*youguo wuji*). Chinese governance reached where security concerns mattered and imperial capabilities matched. But the foundations of this celestial empire were shaken by China's defeat in the two Opium Wars, and along with it the relationships between the imperial court and frontier regions.

For China's transition to a nation state, the most relevant legacies from modern times were its embrace of the concept of the nation state and the ineffective responses of late Qing and Republican regimes to meet the challenge of nation state building. However, one legacy that made a critical contribution in the long run was the promotion of frontier farming by Han immigrants, which helped to change the demographic and ecological orientation of two of China's four Eurasian frontiers: Manchuria and Inner Mongolia.

Influx of the Sovereign State

As with the concept of the nation, historical exigences played a key role in China's embrace of the idea of the sovereign nation state. Late Qing rulers gradually acquiesced to the idea of equal sovereigns, after being forced to sign a series of unequal treaties in the wake of the Opium Wars. Treaty concessions to the foreign powers formally signified the collapse of the Sino-centric worldview, or the longstanding conception of the world as a concentric hierarchy with China at the top. In this context, reform-minded officials and thinkers began to view the world as a multi-state system and China as one among equals. Difficult negotiations with Western governments allowed them to see how Western powers utilized the concept of sovereignty to protect their national interests.

Ironically, a deep appreciation of the injustice of the treaty concessions facilitated Qing elites' acceptance of the concept of sovereign nation states. It provided Qing reformers with an ideational and legal weapon to recover China's losses made in the unequal treaties, namely, concession of extraterritorial rights, commercial privileges, and territories to foreign powers (Cao and Liu 2004: 87, 88; Guan 2004: 86, 87; Si 2003: 48–9). By the late 1860s and 1870s, the Qing court began to adopt policy measures in the direction of a sovereign state, such as dispatching diplomatic missions abroad and establishing the ambassadorial system overseas. Long accustomed to receiving foreign envoys, such moves signified that China had finally joined the communities of the world as an equal member, thus abandoning the idea of the celestial empire (Si 2003: 50).

Domestically the Qing court made nascent efforts at modern state building, focusing on the outer peripheral regions. Since the late 1880s, the far-flung borderlands had become the targets of vying powers – Russia in Mongolia, Manchuria, and Xinjiang; Japan in Manchuria; and Britain in Tibet. Taking advantage of late Qing's weakness and the rise of the national discourse, those foreign powers made a point of referring to the borderland communities as "nations" and encouraged them to seek self-determination. In response, the Qing court tried to strengthen administrative and cultural incorporation with reform measures. To curb Russian penetration in the north, Qing lifted bans on Han immigration to Manchuria, organized Han immigrants to undertake frontier farming in Inner Mongolia, and established administrative units at local levels in both regions. These policies played a significant role in changing the demographic composition and orientation of the local populations in Manchuria and Inner Mongolia. They paved the way for these two regions to become inner peripheral ones in subsequent decades.

The Qing court did attempt state-building reforms in the remaining outer peripheral regions: Xinjiang and Tibet. In Xinjiang, Qing reduced local autonomy by turning it into a regular province in 1884, formally implementing the political system of the rest of China. In an interesting twist, Qing's reconstruction programs – after Xinjiang's provincialization – resulted in helping Uighurs to migrate from southern Xinjiang to northern and eastern Xinjiang. These areas used to be inhabited almost completely by Han Chinese (Millward 2007: 151). In Tibet, high commissioners Lian Yu and Zhang Yintang promoted "new deal" policies (*xinzheng*). Treating the region no longer as a frontier security matter, the new policies targeted the more fundamental problem of economic development. In western Sichuan or Kham, Qing sped up the incorporation of Tibetan chieftains into the regular bureaucracy during 1905–8, under the stewardship of Governor Zhao Erfeng. Zhao's brutal suppression of monastic and other resistant forces is usually criticized in Chinese histography, but he is also credited with improving the livelihoods of Tibetan serfs and laying the administrative foundations for Xikang province, which was established two decades later in 1928 in the former Kham area.[1]

The Qing dynasty's reforms may be viewed as part of a historical transition from empire to a modern nation state. But they did not amount to a new system of ethnic governance. Nor did they resolve the issue of the ambiguous status of the outer peripheral lands, whose historical relationships with the central state did not accurately fit the modern concept of sovereignty.

Republican Efforts

After the revolution of 1911 that overthrew the Qing dynasty, the Qing empire was nominally transformed into a modern nation state in the Republic of China. However, the Republican regimes – Beiyang (1912–28) and the KMT (1928–45) – faced great difficulties in incorporating the outer peripheral regions. Here the disintegration of the Qing dynasty had resulted in much stronger centrifugal forces than in the inner peripheral regions. With their brief rule, plagued by warlordism at home and invasions from abroad, neither regime had sufficient time or experience to construct a viable new institutional order.

The demise of the Manchu dynasty had left in particular institutional vacuums in outer peripheral regions, along with a legacy of institutional and personal loyalties vested in the imperial order. These regions had not gone through the system of native chieftaincy or bureaucratization reforms, in contrast to inner peripheral regions. The Manchu court, as a minority dynasty with semi-nomadic origins, had ruled its vast empire by aligning with the political and military elites of frontier regions, especially the Mongols. This

[1] See a summary account, "Zhuzang dachen Zhao Erfeng and Xizang" [Governor Zhao Erkang and Tibet], June 10, 2010. http://politics.people.com.cn/GB/14562/11843783.html.

peripheral alliance, "encouraged Mongol leaders to see themselves as part of a greater Qing elite" (Barfield 1989: 276). Qing's demise ended the privileged positions of Mongol elites and their roles in the empire, leaving them discontented and uncertain about their status. Nostalgic about the imperial system and hostile to the new Republic, some Mongol elites turned to independence movements (Chang 2011). Separatist movements surged in outer and eastern Mongolia after the 1911 revolution. Other outer peripheral regions also saw rising ethno-nationalism, compounded by encroachments of foreign powers into those regions: Japan in Manchu and Mongol areas; Russia in Manchu, Mongol, and Uighur areas; and Britain in Tibet. In the northwest, Japan also wooed Hui Muslim elites, with whom the Qing court used to align for local rule.

Top-down approaches characterized the Republican regimes' strategies to hold on to those outer peripheral regions, especially when compared to the CCP's emphasis on lower social classes later on. One Beiyang strategy was to strengthen central mechanisms of control over Mongol, Tibetan, and Muslim regions. Pressured by separatist movements in Mongolia and Britain's conversion of Tibet as a protectorate in 1904, Beiyang created the Commission on Mongolia and Tibet in 1912, with ethnic officials serving at its helm. The agency was to maintain political liaison with and supervision over local aristocracy and elite lamas. To avoid alienating Mongol elites, Beiyang initially refrained from applying the provincial system to Mongol regions and curbed frontier farming by Han farmers. However, after consolidating his presidency by early 1914, Yuan Shikai established special administrative districts in three major Mongol domains, asserting jurisdiction over their military and civilian affairs. In the northwest, Yuan established regional commander systems to strengthen central control over Tibetan, Hui, and Mongol areas of Qinghai, Ningxia, and Gansu provinces, and appointed regional commissioners to Tibet and Xinjiang to administer local affairs. But regional warlordism, rampant across China at the time, made central control fragile and at the whim of regional warlords.

Another Beiyang method of integration, frontier state farming, enriched ethnic elites at the expense of local herdsmen. While banning private encroachment, Beiyang set up state agencies to sponsor frontier farming. In collaboration with Mongol aristocrats, it encouraged Han landlords and farmers to encroach into Mongol areas through claiming uncultivated land or pushing off poor herdsmen. The process allowed Mongol elites to collect fees for the claimed land, but it caused a massive loss of grazing land for local herdsmen. Rather than strengthening integration, frontier state farming infuriated the local communities that opposed it (Chang 2011: 10–11). This opposition drove some Mongol elites to the cause of self-determination, while pushing many Mongol youths to the class universalism of the CCP.

The KMT regime, after assuming power in 1928 under Chiang Kai-chek, attempted a more institutional approach in outer peripheral regions, but it was even more ineffective and unpopular. The KMT de-emphasized the ethnic nature of frontier regions, treating them as a matter of administering borderlands rather than ethnic lands. Mongol intellectuals who were attracted to the KMT's earlier ideas of self-determination were soon disappointed by Chiang's policies (Li 2004a: 84, 85). The KMT placed the Commission on Mongolia and Tibet, inherited from Beiyang, under the executive branch so as to exert greater control over the two regions. Special administrative districts in Mongol areas, established by Beiyang, were replaced with three en-route provinces.[2] Two Mongol banners in the northwest were incorporated into Ningxia, historically a county or en-route province, now made into a regular province in 1928.[3] Although the Mongol banner systems were preserved within the newly created provinces, the fragmentation of Mongol territorial units across several provinces caused fierce opposition from Mongol elites and tribes. But the fragmentation made it difficult for them to mount any united resistance.

The fragmentation of Mongol areas was compounded by the deeper encroachment of frontier farming, which was changing the demographic composition and ecological orientation of Inner Mongolia. The newly created provincial system made it easier for provincial governments and regional warlords to aggressively promote frontier farming by Han immigrants. The consequences – poor herdsmen being forced off prairielands and opium poppy growing on the former grazing land – ignited an intense sense of ethno-nationalism among Mongol elites and educated youths, spurring an autonomy movement led by Prince Demchugdongrub (also known as Prince De) (Chang 2011: 11). Chastised in conventional CCP historiography as a separatist and a collaborator of Japanese forces, he is viewed more positively in recent Chinese scholarship as a champion of Mongols' rightful interests and self-strengthening (Li 2004a: 86). In this new perspective, the real villain was the KMT's oppressive policy.

Indeed, Mongol elites did not allow their native land to turn into an inner peripheral region without a fight. In 1933 the KMT compromised by granting more Mongol autonomy through new legislation and established the Mongol Local Autonomy Political Affairs Committee. This led to the coexistence of a provincial and an autonomous system. Mongol princes were appointed to the new committee. Prince Yondonwangchug (also known as Prince Yun), also a leader of the autonomy movement, served as its chairman. But he soon grew frustrated with the limited power of the committee vis-à-vis the provincial

[2] These included Rehe (at the intersection of Hebei, Liaoning, and Inner Mongolia), Chaha'er (parts of Hebei, Shanxi, and Beijing), and Suiyuan (central Inner Mongolia).

[3] For details of the KMT's administrative changes in the northeast and northwest, see Dreyer (1976: 18–29).

administration and a lack of support from the central government in Nanjing. Autonomy fell apart in just three years, when Prince De responded to Japanese wooing. Since Japan encroached into China's northeast in 1931, some Mongol areas had already been incorporated into the Japanese-created state of Manchukuo (Manchurian state). After war broke out between China and Japan in 1937, the Mongol prince declared the independence of the remaining parts of Inner Mongolia, serving as the head of the new state of Mengkiang, or Mengkukuo, renamed as the Mongolian Autonomous Federation in 1941.

Compounded by the domestic turmoil and foreign encroachments of the 1930s, the KMT fared poorly elsewhere in its nation-building project. In Xinjiang, Uighur nationalists agitated for the first East Turkestan Republic (1933–4), with British support in the south and Japanese support in the north. Only Soviet backing for Sheng Shicai, the KMT warlord ruler, helped to suppress the Uighur movement. But Soviet motives were aimed at preventing pan-Turkish Islamism and a British presence on its border (Xue 2008), betraying a prioritization of its own national interest over the ideologically correct movement of national liberation. The point was not lost on the CCP. On the northwestern front, the Japanese had set up a "Greater Hui State" by combining Gansu, Qinghai, and Ningxia provinces. Alienated by the KMT, many Mongol and Hui elites here were indifferent to the ongoing anti-Japanese war in interior China and vulnerable to Japanese inducements. In the southwest, the traditional inner peripheral zone, the KMT were unable to dismantle the system of native chieftaincy despite intentions to do so. Instead it had to rely on the system to maintain rule there.

The policies of the Republican regimes, in short, failed to hold off centrifugal tendencies in the three decades since the disintegration of the Qing empire. June Dreyer characterizes the KMT's ethnic policy as "neither very good nor wholly bad," placing blame on political treachery and administrative inexperience on the one hand and foreign meddling on the other (1976: 39–40). In contemporary Chinese scholarship, some analysts make a social class argument, attributing Republican failures to the pampering of ethnic elites and the assimilationist policies that alienated ethnic masses (Li 2004a and 2004b). Others make a nationalistic argument, praising the KMT's promotion of national and territorial integration while explaining away its failures (Zhou 2005). Still others point to the brevity of the KMT's rule, interrupted by two major wars (the Sino-Japanese war and the civil war). From the perspective of this study, the Republican failures were due fundamentally to a lack of an institutional order for nation state building.

Making Social Class Alliance

The KMT's failures thus far made an important impact on the CCP's adjustment of political strategies. They alerted the CCP to the paradox of the doctrine of self-determination: if minorities were not given autonomy, they would be vulnerable to incitation of separatism, yet self-determination would also entail secessionism. To overcome the dilemma, the CCP adjusted its political strategy to emphasize a distinction between secessionist ethnic elites and the oppressed ethnic masses. Class universalism would serve this new strategy by appealing to a broad base of ethnic masses while transcending the party's earlier doctrine of self-determination. Moreover, it would help buttress a new institutional order of ethnic governance.

As movements for self-determination raged in outer peripheral regions in the midst of China's anti-Japanese war, abandoning the concept became imperative for the CCP. As the war drew to a close in the mid-1940s, the prospect of a revolutionary victory changed the CCP's perspective from state destruction to state building. Repudiation of the idea of self-determination was explicitly made in the party's decrees on Inner Mongolia in the 1940s. In instructions to Mongol communists, the CCP urged regional autonomy and advised against independence (MUF 1991: 1034). The party contended that the Mongol independence movements had little to do with the liberation of the Mongol people, but had instead subjected their homeland to Japanese imperialism. Ulanfu, a native of central Inner Mongolia and an early communist activist, played a key role in taming those movements. Among native activists for self-determination, some agitated for high autonomy while others for independence and self-rule, but Ulanfu managed to dissuade the secessionists (Xu and Jin 2008: 69–70). As a political comprise, the Inner Mongolian Autonomous Region was established in May 1947 under Ulanfu's stewardship. Thereupon China's first autonomous region came into being, two years before the founding of the PRC itself. It was a historical solution for a major outer peripheral region that had effectively become an inner peripheral region in the demographic sense, with Mongols as a numerical minority in Inner Mongolia (Table 2.1).

In Xinjiang as well, the CCP also relied on class universalism to diffuse ethnic separatism. In response to Uighur uprisings in the 1930s and 1940s, the CCP downplayed their ethno-national tone and actions, framing Uighur revolts as opposition to the KMT's oppressive rule. In 1944, the tri-region uprising (Yili/Ili, Tacheng/Qoqek, and Aletai/Altay) by the Uighurs began with local wrath at Governor Sheng Shicai's excessive levies and harsh rule, cumulating in the establishment of the second East Turkestan Republic (ETR, 1945–9). Despite the separatist implication of the ETR and its brutal efforts to cleanse the Han people (Wang X. 2003), the CCP characterized the uprising as a social revolution, backed rightfully by the Soviet Union. In recent years, the release of Soviet archives has allowed Chinese scholars to learn about the twists and turns in Soviet motives (Xue 2008). Initially the Soviets supported a Uighur national revolution and a communist Soviet in Xinjiang. But the unfolding of the Uighur uprising led Soviet officials to view it differently. To their dismay, few of the uprising's leaders were true revolutionaries, but were aristocratic and religious elites. Worried about an independent Islamic state on its border, the Soviet Union forced the Uighur rebels to negotiate with the KMT.

TABLE 2.1 *Shares of Han population in five autonomous regions (%)*

Autonomous region	1953	1964	1982	1990	2000	2010
Inner Mongolia	85.6	87.0	84.5	81.6	77.2	79.54
TAR	N/A	2.9	4.9	3.7	2.9	8.17
XUAR	6.9*	31.9	40.4	37.6	39.2	40.1
Ningxia Hui	66.44	69.2	68.1	66.7	65.4	64.58
Guangxi Zhuang	62.1	58.9	61.7	60.9	61.6	62.06

Source: For 1953–2000, see SEAC Economic Bureau (1991: 43–4) and SCCO and SBS (1985: 218) and (2002: 18). For 2010, see www.stats.gov.cn.[4]

* The Han and Hui population was an estimated 30 percent in the early 1800s (Millward 2000: 122–3).

The Soviets' change of mind served [4]both Soviet and CCP interests at the expense of Uighur self-determination. For the Soviet Union, its role in stemming the tri-region rebellion allowed it to pressure the KMT into accepting the independence of Outer Mongolia, according to Shen Zhihua, an independent Chinese scholar who used personal funds to purchase and study Soviet achieves (Shen 1999). The independence of Outer Mongolia, unlike Xinjiang, did not present a religious threat to the Soviet Union. For the CCP, the Soviet retreat from supporting Uighur self-determination conveniently strengthened its version of the Uighur uprising as an anti-KMT movement. It also allowed the CCP to sidestep the question of rebel leaders' political preferences and to emphasize ethnic masses' socioeconomic grievances. Ideological purity would have entailed that the CCP support the Uighur rebellion as a movement for national liberation, not just a social revolution. In recent years, greater academic freedom has allowed Chinese scholars to debate the motives of the tri-region rebellion and to challenge the CCP's characterization of the event as a proletarian uprising against the KMT's oppressive rule. One study characterizes the rebellion and the second ETR as brutal campaigns to cleanse Han residents by massacring them on a massive scale (Wang X. 2003). Another study finds the direct role of the Soviet Union in leading the tri-region revolution, not so much for Uighurs' independence but for greater pressure on the KMT to allow more Soviet influence in Xinjiang (Yang et al. 2019).

The doctrine of self-determination took a further retreat as CCP leaders faced the reality of governing ethnic regions after prevailing in the civil war in 1949. Contrary to the suggestion that Mao never intended to honor the party's commitment to self-determination and downgraded the idea once the CCP

[4] Census data for the autonomous regions are available individually from the official census website. For example, the 2010 census data for Xinjiang are available at *Guojia tongjiju* [State bureau of statistics], "Xinjiang weiwu'er zizhiqu 2010 nian diliuchi renkou pucha zhuyao shuju gongbu" [Announcement of major data from the XUAR's 6th census]. February 28, 2012. www.stats.gov.cn /tjsj./tjgb/rkpcgb/dfrkpcgb/201202/t20120228_30407.html.

came to power (Gladney 1991), Mao and other CCP leaders were undecided initially (Wang 2014: 33–4). The hesitation stemmed from the party's past commitment to self-determination. After all, earlier on the Soviet idea of self-determination had influenced the CCP and served it well during its revolutionary years (Connor 1984: 81–3; Dreyer 1976: 77, 91). More pertinently, the retreat from self-determination may be attributed to the impact of foreign powers on China's borders, where most minority communities were concentrated (Mackerras 1994: 72; Pye 1976). On the eve of the CCP's takeover of China in 1949, Mao consulted Li Weihan, the party's expert on ethnic issues, as to whether China should adopt the Soviet ethno-federal system. Li advised against it after giving a thorough analysis of China's history and realities. Citing Stalin's elaboration of "four degrees of autonomy" – contractual autonomy, greater autonomy, political autonomy, and administrative autonomy – Li recommended the last one, or the lowest form, as the most appropriate for China. Mao and the CCP Central Committee concurred. The retreat from the idea of self-determination marked a key divergence from the Soviet approach, defining the frame of ethnic discourse in China since then.

In the end, the national imperative trumped the CCP's ideological agenda of national liberation, though not its class universalism. In fact, class universalism helped to justify this turnaround. Imperial powers, the CCP contended, were the common enemies of China's oppressed peoples, including those of the borderlands. When Zhou Enlai announced the party's choice of the system of autonomous regions in September 1949, at the first meeting of the CPPCC attended by many minority representatives, he justified the party's retreat from self-determination by citing the forces of "imperialism" in Tibet, Taiwan, and Xinjiang (MUF 1991: 1267). Among these three regions, Tibet and Xinjiang were the only ethnic majority regions and outer peripheral regions. Their political incorporation into the modern Chinese state, which was a daunting task for the Republican regimes, would remain formidable for the People's Republic.

CONSTRUCTING A NEW INSTITUTIONAL ORDER

The system of autonomous regions, an ethno-territorial entity with a higher population of a particular (or titular) minority ethnic group, was the CCP's institutional response to the transition from empire to the modern state. Late Qing and Republican regimes tweaked and adapted in piecemeal ways, but the CCP created a new institutional order of ethnic governance. It transformed the pre-modern methods of diverse and indirect rule in two ways: first, a uniform system across ethnic regions, and second, an alignment of the (titular) ethnic, political, and territorial. It redefined the relationship between the central state and peripheral regions, along with formal prerogatives, obligations, and administrative structures.

Class Universalism and Political Integration

The drive to establish the autonomous system, which lasted from 1949 to 1954, spared no efforts to balance the ideals of autonomy and equality, the realities of multiethnic communities, and the imperative of national integration. The classification project was itself carried out to achieve equality and equity in this process. Class universalism both justified and served the twin goals of integration and equality.

Among the evidence for promoting these twin goals was a number of redistricting efforts. The purpose was to redress the wrongs of the KMT era and to accommodate ethno-territorial demarcations. Several cases were illustrative. First, Mongol areas that were carved into different provinces by the KMT were now remerged with Inner Mongolia. Second, redistricting was done in Ningxia and Gansu to congregate Hui areas into the Ningxia Hui Autonomous Region and Hui autonomous prefectures within the region. Third, Guangxi and Ningxia acquired provincial autonomous status despite being very weak cases. During consultations with local groups leading up to the establishment of those two autonomous regions, some expressed misgivings, because the Huis were a numerical minority in Ningxia while the Zhuangs of Guangxi lacked ethnic distinctness. Zhou Enlai persuaded the doubters that these two groups were large enough to deserve their own autonomous regions, so they could see themselves as full members in the family of the Chinese nation (He 2010).

This assembly of disparate groups with little historical cohesion or aspiration for autonomy, however, raises questions as to whether they obscured the more complex national questions in the other autonomous regions. That is, Tibet, Xinjiang, and to a lesser extent Inner Mongolia, all historically outer peripheral regions. In these three cases, argues a Taiwan-based scholar, highly developed local cultures and histories of self-government entailed sufficient conditions for independent statehood (Wu 2013: 26). In this contention, the autonomous system was designed to achieve "divide and rule," that is, to turn the more separatist regions into just another set of minority regions (Wu 2009: 1–2). This reading of the CCP's intent contrasts interestingly with that of Zhou Enlai's critics in contemporary China, who blame Zhou's good intentions and naivety for the (unnecessary) creation of the Zhuang and Hui autonomous regions. Zhou's stated intention was to "pay debts" for past discrimination suffered by minority groups. However, to his critics the Han majority too suffered from oppression under the Republican regimes, so that past sufferings should not be ethnicized.[5] Zhou's intentions, in the context of the CCP's early rule in the 1950s, was likely driven by revolutionary idealism or equality for the ethnic proletariat. Indeed, the redistricting done to congregate Mongol and Hui areas represented strategies of "combine and rule," rather than "divide and rule." Centrifugal forces were strong in Mongol and Huis areas during the Republican

[5] This is a frequent point I have heard in private conversations with Chinese scholars in the field of ethnic studies.

period, but both received enhanced ethno-territorial units under the CCP, not diminished ones. But the Taiwanese scholar raised a valid point that the creation of autonomous regions was only necessary in the three historical outer peripheral regions.

Institutionally, the autonomous system incorporated China's three-tier topography in a uniform way as never before in Chinese history. After the first autonomous system was founded in Inner Mongolia in 1947, three more were established at the provincial level in the 1950s: Guangxi, Ningxia, and Xinjiang. Tibet would come in 1965. By the end of 1958, eighty-seven autonomous territorial units were established in fifteen provinces, including four provincial-level autonomous regions, twenty-nine autonomous prefectures, and fifty-four autonomous counties or banners. A total of thirty-five ethnic groups were represented in titular autonomous units. The autonomous units were recognized in the Chinese Constitution and legally granted a range of powers and rights not accorded to the rest of the country. These rights included the protection of ethnic languages, customs, and religion as well as demands on the central state to aid the development of ethnic regions. In the reform era, one more autonomous prefecture and sixty-six more autonomous counties or banners were established in the early 1980s.

Politically the new system incorporated China's three-tier topography in a centralizing way never before attempted. It has behooved that all autonomous areas accept the institutional frameworks and public policies under the PRC's unitary political system. Most importantly, the autonomous regions, like all other administrative units in CCP-led China, must follow the "centralized leadership of the party." This entailed that a party apparatus system would be superimposed on the state bureaucratic one, the head of the party would be superior to the head of the state at the same level, party directives would set the direction of any national and local policy, and all officials at the subnational levels would be appointed by the party apparatus at a higher level.

Together, the new institutional order completed China's transition from empire to the modern state. But it also departed from pre-modern legacies of ethnic rule, resulting in built-in institutional tensions. These tensions, as in the classification project, derived from the mix of political centralization and ethnic particularism, again with unintended consequences for ethnic mobilization, especially for the remaining outer peripheral regions, Tibet and Xinjiang.

Uniformity and Its Discontents

Above all, the creation of the autonomous system across all ethnic regions deviated from the pre-modern legacy of administrative diversity. Most important was the blurring of the historical differentiation between the inner and outer peripheral zones. Wide differences existed among ethnic communities in these two zones, rendering it questionable as a uniform form of political incorporation. This uniformity reduced the autonomy of outer peripheries more than for inner peripheries, inhering the built-in tensions of the autonomous system: excessive centralization tempered by ethnic particularism to offset its centralizing tendencies.

The five autonomous provinces had very different relationships with the central state in Chinese history. Guangxi and Ningxia had attained the status of en-route provinces seven centuries earlier, under Mongol rule. This contrasted with Xinjiang, with just seven decades of provincial status since 1884. Inner Mongolia had been under provincial administration for less than half of Xinjiang's length, though its ties to Sinic areas varied across Mongol communities that spanned several provinces. In both Xinjiang and Inner Mongolia, separatist impulses were checked by the CCP's class alliance with the ethnic proletariat. Tibet presented a yet more challenging case. The core of modern-day Tibet, the traditional Ü-Tsang area, had never been under provincial administration. Not surprisingly, its political status remains controversial and epitomizes the flaws of uniform incorporation.

The exact nature of the so-called patron–priest relationship between Mongol rulers and the Tibetan theocracy remains contentious. Of the two imperial dynasties with the closest relationship with old Tibet, the Mongol and the Manchu dynasties, both used a special central agency to deal with it.[6] Among Tibetan exiles, a typical argument contends that Mongol dominance was "indirect" and that their occasional military interventions were "external," notwithstanding the Mongols' political clout and a "Tibetan-Mongolian diarchic structure" (Norbu 2001: 139). In China's official view, the establishment of the central agency to manage Tibetan affairs marked the first time that the Chinese state administered Tibet, hence the latter's formal incorporation into China (State Council of the PRC 1992). The Mongols' garrisoning of permanent troops in Ü-Tsang is cited as additional evidence.

Under the Manchus, the Qing dynasty also used a special central agency, *Lifan Yuan*, to administer the outlying regions.[7] The agency's jurisdiction covered Inner, Outer, and Western Mongolia, Muslim Xinjiang, Manchu banners, Ü-Tsang, and western Sichuan (Kham) (Xu and Jin 2008: 43). Except for Kham, the Qing court referred to these areas as *waifan*, or outer peripheral regions: Mongolia, Ü-Tsang, and Xinjiang. But Qing also distinguished them from foreign countries by treating them as internal *waifan* rather than external *waifan*. Annual pilgrimages by native chiefs were mandatory for the internal *waifan*, while tribute from the external *waifan* was voluntary (Zhang S. 2010: 106–14). The requirement signified an obligatory albeit loose relationship between the imperial court and the internal *waifan* areas.

[6] Under the Mongols, a special central agency called *Xuanzheng Yuan* (Bureau of Buddhist and Tibetan Affairs) managed Mongol rulers' relations with Ü-Tsang, through the power of executive appointment and supervision (Wylie 1977: 104; Norbu 2001: 139).

[7] Its rendering in the Manchu language, Office for Managing Affairs of Outer Provinces, provided the most accurate meaning of *Lifan Yuan* (Zhang 2004: 26).

Of those *waifan* areas, Ü-Tsang, or Tibet, had the most distant relationship with the central government during imperial times. China's formal assertion of sovereignty over the region came as late as 1951, when the 17-Point Agreement for the Peaceful Liberation of Tibet was reached between Mao's new China and the envoys of the fourteenth Dalai Lama. As the dissident scholar Wang Lixiong writes, "For China the 17 Point Agreement means that the nature of the relationship between China and Tibet has changed from one based on 'rites' to one based on legalistic sovereignty. The agreement entails that Tibet acknowledges for the first time that it belongs to China, making it the only legal document to that effect" (Wang 2001). Importantly, although this agreement sanctified Tibet's incorporation, it also pledged to preserve the "existing political system in Tibet." Beijing would not alter "the established status, functions and powers of the Dalai Lama" and other leading personnel of Tibet; it would not compel social reforms in Tibet or change the lamas' income; and it would protect the Tibetan ruling strata and monasteries. In other words, Tibet was to retain high autonomy.

Tibet was rendered even more different by the flight of the Dalai Lama and his entourage in 1959. This has rendered contentious the validity of the agreement and Tibet's legal status. After fleeing to India in March, the Dalai Lama explicitly repudiated the agreement in June. For Beijing's part, the agreement remains a legal contract affirming Chinese sovereignty. But its own failure to honor the agreement in its entirety – namely high autonomy – has also helped to render hollow Beijing's commitment to the agreement. The creation of the TAR in 1965 did not formally resolve the issue of its sovereign status. In fact, Ü-Tsang's tenuous ties with interior China were taken into consideration from the beginning. The TAR was constituted from historical Ü-Tsang and two areas of western Kham from the Republican era, Chamdo and Nyingchi. These two areas, being adjacent to inland provinces, had undergone bureaucratization reforms during the late Qing period. Some local cadre reportedly did not want to lose these two areas to the TAR but were persuaded to concede by central authorities, who wanted to strengthen Ü-Tsang's ties with interior China.[8] With the flight of Ü-Tsang's old ruling class, the CCP relied on solidarity with former Tibetan serfs to justify its governance and social transformation of Tibet.

As in Xinjiang and Inner Mongolia, social class alliances helped to achieve political incorporation and regime consolidation in Tibet's case. For these regions, the uniformity of the new system inhered a built-in structural tension: its stability and rationale would be put to question once class universalism waned.

[8] Conversations with Chinese and Tibetan scholars at the China Tibetology Research Center in Beijing, summer 2011 and fall 2013; and at Sichuan University, summers 2015 and 2017.

Titular Status and Its Discontents

The creation of titular ethnic groups – that is, naming territorial units after the appellation of its main inhabitants – deviated from pre-modern practices of ethnic neutrality. But this bumped up against the historical reality of multiethnic communities in a majority of China's ethnic regions. Thus the state was forced to apply a compromised definition of an autonomous unit: it would be a territorial governance division with a higher population of a particular minority group (SEAC 2007b). That is, a plurality among various local minority groups. By aligning the (titular) ethnic, political, and territorial, the titular status also contributed to the built-in tensions of the autonomous system: political integration by associating a titular group with territorial governance, yet parcellation of groups to pit them against one another, thus undermining cohesion and inclusiveness.

Nationally the titular stipulation appeared to diffuse the importance of major groups in the outer peripheral regions. In population shares, as Table 2.1 shows, Tibet and Xinjiang were ethnic majority regions at the provincial level. Even by the plurality principle, a majority of the autonomous units established at all levels did not have over 50 percent of minority populations; and among the rest, just two-thirds of them had an ethnic population of over 60 percent (Tian 2010: 14). Most of these, moreover, were in Tibetan regions, Xinjiang, and pastoral Inner Mongolia. This suggests that the creation of autonomous regions, indeed, may not have been necessary in areas outside the three regions with highly developed local cultures and histories of self-government. Yet the plurality principle elevated many groups in inner peripheral regions to titular status, on a par with the major historical groups of Mongols, Uighurs, and Tibetans. This equalization would have significant impacts on the representation of titular ethnic groups in political institutions at the national level, namely, by diffusing the weight of the large outer peripheral groups. The overrepresentation of inner peripheral groups would entail policy priorities that may not always suit the outer peripheral groups.

Another effect of the titular principle was to pit groups against one another within an ethno-territorial unit. This was so even in the outer peripheral regions with ethnic majorities at the provincial and local levels. In Xinjiang's case, Uighur Marxists trained in the Soviet Union played a key role in promoting an Uighurstan, to be modeled after Soviet ethno-federalism. But the leaders of this group died in Soviet space while flying to Beijing in 1949. The remaining Uighur Marxists still pressed for the name Uighurstan during their discussions with Beijing about an autonomous region in Xinjiang. But representatives of Xinjiang's smaller minority groups opposed the idea, arguing that they were entitled to parts of Xinjiang's territory, especially northern and western Xinjiang. Although Uighurs made up 70 percent of Xinjiang's population at the time, over 90 percent of them resided in southern Xinjiang. It was not the Uighurs but the western Mongols, under the Dzungar state, who had been the "predominant power" in Xinjiang since at least 1670s, before their elimination by the Manchu Qing dynasty in the mid-nineteenth century (Millward and Perdue 2004: 50, 54).

Dzungaria or northern Xinjiang, the areas depopulated by the Dzungars, were filled by various groups of settlers. Brought in by the Qing court to repopulate the area, they included Han Chinese peasants, Manchu bannermen, settlers from Turkestani oases, Huis, and others (Perdue 2005: 285; Millward and Perdue 2004: 59). Mass Kazakh migrants from the Kazakh Khanates were also among the peoples who moved into the depopulated Dzungaria.[9] The settler descendants, who formed the smaller minority groups of Xinjiang, felt as entitled as the Uighurs to Xinjiang because their forefathers had safeguarded the frontiers for the Qing empire.[10] Zhou Enlai thus explained the eventual compromise:

> When we were establishing the Xinjiang Uighur Autonomous Region, we did not agree to using the name Uighurstan. Xinjiang did not just have one ethnicity, but there are twelve others. We cannot have thirteen "stans" (land) for all thirteen minority groups. The party and government in the end decided to establish the Xinjiang Uighur Autonomous Region, and comrades from Xinjiang consented to this. The region's title still has the word Uighur in it, because the Uighurs are the main ethnic group in Xinjiang, comprising over 70% of its population; but the title is shared with the other ethnic groups. … Tibet and Inner Mongolia's names have double meanings, one geographical and one ethnic. A name in itself seems to be of secondary importance, but on the issue of China's autonomous regions, it is very important, because it carries the connotations of interethnic cooperation. (Zhou 1957b)

The retention of Xinjiang as part of the province's new name, the Xinjiang Uighur Autonomous Region (XUAR), was thus intended to be more inclusive. It was implicit in Zhou's passage that Xinjiang's smaller minority groups resisted the dominance of the demographically weighty Uighurs. But it was also the CCP's effort to territorialize ethnicity that effectively pitted minority groups against one another. Bovingdon argues that the system of territorial parcellization dilutes the already meager influence of the Uighurs and gives other groups disproportionate power in the system (2004: 28). Yet small groups had strong incentives to secure their autonomous status against the perceived threats of bigger groups. This could explain why Xinjiang's Mongols, despite being a numerical minority locally, secured two autonomous areas. Alternatively, Bovingdon views this as an intentional design to counterbalance the Uighurs (2010: 46, 47). However, nationwide such parcellation was common: a majority of the newly created autonomous areas contained titular minorities that were not numerical majorities locally.

[9] See Anar Smagulova, "Xviii–Xix Centuries: In the Manuscripts of the Kazakhs of China." East Kazakhstan State University. Date unknown.

[10] Conversations heard from local Mongol, Kazakh, Sibe, Daur, and Han participants at an academic forum in Urumqi, July 2011.

For Tibetan regions, the CCP also faced difficult balancing acts between the ideal of titular autonomy and the reality of ethnic diversity among those who were classified as Tibetans. Initially there were proposals for one autonomous region to combine all Tibetan concentrated areas. Such a project would have required combining regions that had been historically, linguistically, culturally, and religiously divided. Among the three historically Tibetan regions, Kham and Amdo had not been ruled by Lhasa (Ü-Tsang) since the Tibetan Empire (sixth–ninth century) fell apart in the ninth century. Political control since then alternated between Tibetan, Mongol, Han, Manchu, and other rulers (Yeh 2003; Petech 1990; Pirie 2005), along with the influx of non-Tibetan soldiers, administrators, merchants, and other immigrants. The fourteenth Dalai Lama himself was born in a hamlet of Qinghai province in the 1930s, which was then under the control of the Muslim warlord Ma Bufang. He was not released to assume the official title until Beijing made compensation to secure him.

Given such complexities, the CCP rejected suggestions for one autonomous region to combine all Tibetan-inhabited areas. Instead, emphasizing the needs of economic development and national integration, Beijing decided to set up Tibetan autonomous prefectures and counties in four surrounding provinces, with which Amdo and Kham had historically shared ties: Qinghai, Gansu, Yunnan, and Sichuan. These provinces were wealthier than the TAR during the Mao era. The economic justification for separate Tibetan autonomous units continues to be emphasized by leftist defenders of the autonomous system in China today (Wang X. 2009: 6). However, because the TAR has received massive state aid in the reform era, it is the Tibetan regions in the surrounding provinces that now feel disadvantaged.

For Mongol groups, historical scattering made it difficult to place disparate communities of the same ethnicity into one titular autonomous unit at the provincial level or local levels. This effectively reduced the political weight and policy prerogatives of those who did not reside in a titular territorial unit. Despite a number of redistricting actions during the establishment of autonomous units, it was impossible to include all Mongol members in their respective titular territories. While two-thirds of the Mongols were included in their titular province of Inner Mongolia, amounting to about a million in the early 1950s, the remaining third were scattered around the country, including small Mongol communities in the Muslim northwest (Xinjiang and Qinghai), the Tungusic northeast (Liaoning, Jilin, and Heilongjiang), and even the Daic and Mon-Khmer southwest (Yunnan). Although some of these communities also acquired their autonomous prefectures or counties, others had to share the titular status with another group or did not have a titular status at all.

For the remaining two autonomous regions, Ningxia and Guangxi, the titular status correspondingly elevated their political weight and policy prerogatives. The Huis were only concentrated in a number of counties in Ningxia and a numerical minority overall in the province, accounting for just a third of its population in the 1950s (Table 2.1). Moreover, Ningxia's Hui population represented only a fraction of the Hui population nationwide, or about one-seventh of the 3.5 million Huis in China at the time. Unlike the three large outer peripheral groups, the Huis' roots were relatively recent in Ningxia and in several local subunits in Qinghai and Gansu that named the Hui as the titular group. These territories were largely coextensive with the West Xia dynasty (1038–1227 CE), established by the Tanguts. When the Mongol conquest annihilated West Xia in the thirteenth century, large numbers of Mongols, Turks, Iranians, and other Central Asians arrived in the region. The end of Mongol rule allowed other migrants from areas west of the region to come. These diverse sources of population became the ethnogenesis of the Muslim Hui in the northwest (Dillon 1999; Lipman 1998). What remained of the Tanguts may have been pushed to Tibetan regions further west. In Guangxi's case, Han representatives objected to a Zhuang titular province during their discussions with central authorities, out of concerns for the privileged position of the titular group and the diminished weight of Han residents once the autonomous region was established. Their objection was strong enough that they asked for a territorial division of Guangxi into a Zhuang autonomous region and a regular province for Han residents. Central authorities rejected such a division, citing the benefit of integration for economic development (Zhou 1957b).

Associating a titular group with territorial governance and privileges continues to create ethnic bickering in autonomous regions that are multiethnic. The titular group is institutionalized to play a key role in local public policy decisions and resource allocation, which may adversely affect smaller minority groups and local Han residents. Geographic and demographic factors would limit the options of the smaller ethnic groups in any event, but the imposition of such options by the state politicizes their resentment.

Titular Status and Ethno-nationalism

Another consequence of titular status is to strengthen the titular group's proprietary claim. In outer peripheral regions, this claim can be significant as it fuels ethno-nationalism that undermines the state's intended goal of integration. Bovingdon writes of the Uighur case: "formalizing the boundaries of Xinjiang and naming it the Uighur Autonomous Region gave a convenient territorial shape to Uighur political imaginings" (2010: 43). Shakya writes of the Tibetan case: the typological fixity given to "Tibetanness," by the CCP's classification of the people across the Tibetan plateau, has now come to form the basis of contemporary Tibetan ethno-nationalism and concept of territoriality (2012: 24).

This proprietary sense pits the titular group against smaller minorities as well as the Han majority over territorial entitlements. Whether these entitlements are legitimate is beside the point, for it was not among the original aims of the autonomous region. In the words of Zhou Enlai in 1957, the establishment of the autonomous regions was to serve "ethnic autonomy on the one hand, and interethnic cooperation and mutual assistance on the other" (1957b). Yet the effect of the system was more centrifugal than centripetal. Ronald Suny's observations from the Soviet case fit the Chinese case closely:

> Related to the process of nativization during the Soviet period was the territorialization of ethnicity. Formerly, many ethnic and religious communities had much greater loyalty to and identity with either the area in which they lived or, in the case of many Muslims, the worldwide Islamic community (the 'umma). Supranational and subnational loyalties competed with the more specifically national ones. For certain ethnicities, most notable those of Central Asia, the establishment of territorial administrative units on the basis of nationality in the early 1920s was unprecedented and provided clear political and territorial identities as alternatives to earlier religious and tribal solidarities. Following Stalin's own definition of nation, Soviet authorities promoted an idea of nation fixed to territory. (1993: 110)

While territorial proprietorship based on indignity may be persuasive, historical details tell a complex story. In the case of the Uighurs, their ancestors were migrants to Xinjiang, following a famine and a civil war at the end of the Uighur Khanate (744–840) based in Mongolia. They settled in the Tarim Basin in the ninth century, eventually displacing and assimilating the earlier settlers of Xinjiang, the Tocharians and Kushans. Uighurs established a series of oases-based kingdoms and statelets, each with distinctive identities, until the Mongol empire brought the area under its control in the thirteenth century CE. Only after Qing armies annihilated the Dzungars and massively massacred the western Mongols in the late 1750s, did the Uighurs have an opportunity to fill in the power vacuum. Until the Qing conquest the whole region embraced in the borders of XUAR "rarely constituted a unified political entity" (Millward and Perdue 2004: 27). The demise of the Buddhist Dzungars in Xinjiang also allowed Islam to become the dominant faith, to which Uighurs had converted in recent centuries. In the standard Chinese account, the territory was named Xinjiang by the Qing emperor Qianlong to signify the "recovery of former territories" or *gutu xingui.* But this did not capture the history of a region where "parts were controlled either by oases rulers of southern Xinjiang or by outside forces based to the north, northwest, east, or the south" (Millward and Perdue 2004: 28). Indeed, a large part of Xinjiang was once under the control of the Han and Tang dynasties, and the history of Xinjiang, as Bovingdon (2010: 27–39) deftly puts, is complex enough that competing territorial claims can all founder on some historical evidence. A related problem was the patterns of ethnic distribution on the ground. The vast majority of Uighurs were concentrated in southern Xinjiang when the autonomous system was established. The second largest ethnic group, the Kazakhs, was concentrated in northern Xinjiang. The Mongols had a history of ruling Xinjiang since the thirteenth century CE, especially the eastern and northern parts. The Sibe people, dispatched to Xinjiang by the Qing court in 1764, played a special role in defending the frontier region. In various conversations with local minority scholars during my field trips in Xinjiang, all of these groups spoke of their unique claims to Xinjiang.

Two groups of ancient inhabitants have also become sources for asserting claims about original settlement as a way to undermine Uighur claims. Known as the Rouzhi and Diqiang, the two groups were first chronicled in Chinese historical texts of the Han dynasty (206–220 BCE). In a book series on Xinjiang's history, a senior historian at Xinjiang University links the Rouzhi to the ancient Tocharians and the modern-day Tajiks of Xinjiang, a people of eastern Iranian origin. The Diqiang, on the other hand, is linked to the ancient Qiangic people (Liu W. 2010 and 2011: 27, 28). Recent DNA research corroborates the two groups' early settlement (Zhao et al. 2011). Nevertheless, all this does not invalidate Uighurs' claim to settlement in recent centuries. Mindful of the sensitive subject, university officials seemed unenthusiastic about providing financial support for this book series, though the initial publication was reported in the local media and celebrated in a small symposium (field observations, July 2011). Interestingly, if a Uighur scholar were to write a book disputing the above claims, he or she would likely be accused of separatism and the book would be banned.

Even for groups without indigenous roots, the titular status may fuel ethno-nationalism. Most members of the Korean communities were recent immigrants to northeastern China when the Yanbian Korean autonomous area was established in 1952 (as an autonomous prefecture in 1955). Koreans crossed the Yalu and Tumen rivers to the Chinese side during the 1850–1945 period, particularly from the 1910s to the 1930s, when Chinese border controls were weak and Japan ruled Korea. They came to escape famine, to resist Japanese colonial rule in Korea, or were induced by Japan's migration policy in the late 1930s. Due to geographic concentration and social insulation, many Koreans had not fully assimilated by the early 1950s. By all evidence, the establishment of the Korean autonomous prefecture served to protect and prolong the insulation and isolation of Korean communities. Six decades later, "a major debate" still rages among China's Korean intellectuals as to the "real identity" of ethnic Koreans in China, as both ordinary and elite Koreans remain ambivalent about it (Kim 2003: 121).

Both research studies and field observations confirm this ambivalence. Based on survey data, researchers from the Minzu University of China report that ethnic Chinese Koreans routinely identify with South Korea's cultural and economic influences. However, when they work in South Korea as immigrant workers and encounter discrimination their Chinese identity is strengthened (Li 2009: 99–134). This was corroborated by my conversations with ethnic Koreans who worked in South Korea.[11] During my visit on the

[11] Conversations with five ethnic Koreans who were returning from South Korea, Capital Airport, Beijing, fall 2013. Conversations with five salespersons who worked in gift shops and restaurants catering to Chinese tourists, Seoul, June 2015.

campus of Yanbian University, non-Korean faculty members complained about an atmosphere of strong Korean identity that routinely disadvantaged non-Korean faculty in appointment and promotion matters.[12] Key positions at the university, as well as in the Yanbian prefecture as a whole, have been held by Korean ethnics.[13] A campus award ceremony, which I attended, was held in the Korean language, something that would become a political issue on a Tibetan or Uighur campus. There are more bilingual street signs in Yanbian than I have encountered in other ethnic regions.

There is a growing interest among ethnic Korean intellectuals to rediscover and reconstruct history, especially Korean claims to the Goguryeo kingdom (37 BCE–668 CE). The demise of this ancient kingdom had led its territory to be divided among two other Korean kingdoms and China's Tang dynasty (Li 2009: 116–17). The rising nativism among China's ethnic Koreans has led some analysts in China to worry that a unification of the two Koreas will prompt ethnic Koreans to join Yanbian with a united Korea. In this view, the autonomous system has nurtured a sense of proprietorship that serves as its own gravedigger. Meanwhile, the sentiment among ethnic Koreans seems to be one of continued ambivalence, wavering between "not sure" about a united Korea to "genuine autonomy would be good."[14]

SUMMARY

This chapter focuses on changing approaches to ethnic governance in China's transition to a modern nation state. I have argued that pre-modern methods of rule differentiated a three-tiered topography, but the ancient approach could not withstand the challenge of the concept of the sovereign nation state in modern times; yet, late Qing and Republican failures opened the way for the triumph of the system of autonomous regions under the CCP. This new system helped to complete China's incorporation of ethnic territories as sovereign land of the new nation state, but it also built institutional dynamics for ethnic discords in the long run.

Historical legacies and modern strategies of nation state building impacted patterns of transition and their unintended consequences in two major ways. First, the pre-modern structure of three-tiered rule entailed great challenges for incorporation of the outer peripheral regions in modern times. Under imperial dynasties, the three-tiered approach recognized the graded levels of center–peripheral relationships and corresponding prerogatives, obligations, and administrative structures. Most ethnic groups lived as tribal groupings in

[12] Conversations with five non-Korean faculty members on Yanbian University campus, fall 2013. Conversations with two local SEAC officials, January 2018.

[13] Conversations with three local officials (including a deputy mayor of Korean descent) and five university faculty members, Yanbian, fall 2013.

[14] Conversations with a SEAC official, Beijing, January 2018.

loosely defined communities and fluid territorial units. Local autonomy was maintained through negative rights – that is, internal autonomy as long as they did not pose security threats to the imperial state – and it was achieved through a variety of institutional arrangements, depending on geographical and cultural distance. There was greater political integration in the inner peripheries, as they were gradually incorporated into the state bureaucratic system through native chieftaincy. The outer peripheral regions, spanning the Eurasian frontiers of Manchuria, Mongolia, Xinjiang, and Tibet, were left with a variety of alliance- and rite-based arrangements. The prevailing historical patterns survived well into the late Qing.

Those informal arrangements were not conducive to a transition to a modern nation state, as they ill fitted the concept of the nation state. The idea of sovereign state entails the full rights and power of the central governing body over its constituent parts, which did not accurately describe the relationship between the imperial state and the peripheral regions. Late Qing and Republican attempts to increase administrative incorporation bumped up against ethnic separatism in flux. Their policies of frontier farming did increase the incorporation of Manchuria and Inner Mongolia in a demographical and cultural sense, but Xinjiang and Tibet remained the peripheral holdouts. This modern legacy entailed that these regions would remain challenges for nation state building in contemporary times.

Qing and Republican failures paved the way for the CCP to embrace the Soviet doctrine of ethno-nations. This idea had as its corollary the equality of ethno-nations and a linkage of the ethnic to the political. These ideas, too, did not accurately describe the core–frontier relations in pre-modern China. Yet they were initially embraced, largely by virtue of being perceived as viable responses to historical imperatives at the time; that is, to rally minority support against the KMT and to counteract ethnic separatism. Only a retreat from the idea of self-determination and greater reliance on class universalism tempered the CCP's full adoption of the Soviet model. This was a legacy that made a difference in the new institutional order created by the CCP: the system of autonomous regions adopted the Soviet model of ethno-territorial units, without the stipulation of self-determination.

Second, the autonomous system helped to complete China's transition to the modern state, but it also inhered a number of institutional dynamics for ethnic strife in contemporary times. Those dynamics stemmed from two key features of the autonomous system: political uniformity and ethnic titularity. Uniform governing structures were implemented across minority regions, in a dramatic departure from pre-modern legacies of diverse and indirect rule. It also demarcated ethno-territorial units by making an explicit alignment of the (titular) ethnic, political, and territorial, in a dramatic departure from pre-modern legacies of loose and de-ethnicized rule. This new institutional design reoriented the way the sovereign status of ethnic regions would be defined and their territorial domains would be governed. Rather than loose constituents of a "minimalist state" in the imperial times, ethnic regions became nominally equal members of the modern (multi)nation state under the centralized leadership of the party.

A paradox of centralization and ethnicization characterizes the built-in institutional tensions of the new system. On the one hand, political uniformity brought to fruition the new state's leadership over the political direction and policy platforms of ethnic regions, hence political integration. On the other hand, the titular status, on which autonomous units were based, strengthened ethno-territorial identities and claims, contrary to the goals of national integration. These tensions were further heightened by the failure of the new system to accommodate historical diversity in China's three-tiered topography. The inner peripheral regions, historically more integrated, posed few problems for the new state's assertion of sovereignty. But Tibet and Xinjiang posed significant problems, as their local autonomy had been considerably reduced.

3

Changing Approaches to Policy Instruments

From Elite Co-optation to Egalitarian Strategies

This chapter focuses on the transformation of policy instruments for dealing with minority groups in China's transition from empire to the modern state. That is, how and why Chinese approaches evolved from elite co-optation aimed at maintenance and pacification in pre-modern times to a mix of elite co-optation and mass assimilation in Republican times and finally to transformative strategies aimed at egalitarianism in the socialist era.

The socialist strategies, I argue in this chapter, departed from China's historical patterns and created a third set of institutional dynamics for ethnic tensions in contemporary times. In pre-modern times, elite co-optation, focusing on outer peripheral regions, distinguished imperial courts' policy instruments for ethnic maintenance. This approach was practical for the minimalist imperial state with limited infrastructural and resource capacity. With the collapse of the Qing dynasty, the Republican regimes maintained a precarious hold on the imperial methods of elite appeasement, while attempting a strategy of cultural assimilation, both to little avail. The CCP, by contrast, turned pre-modern methods upside down by repudiating traditional ethnic elites and penetrating ethnic regions with preferential policies. The new approach again contained inherent contradictions – promoting political incorporation but also ethnicized policies to fit that goal. These contradictions would be a source of institutional tensions during the radical years of the Mao era and an intensified one in the market economy of the post-Mao era.

The chapter covers the following topics: (1) relevant legacies of China's pre-modern approaches to frontier co-optation, (2) relevant legacies of China's transition to the modern state during the late Qing and Republican periods, and (3) socialist strategies in the Mao era.

PRE-MODERN FRONTIER CO-OPTATION

For China's transition to the modern state, most relevant were the legacies of hegemonic strategies for co-optation of ethnic elites, applied largely to outer peripheral regions. Such strategies entailed the use of soft power to attract and co-opt, rather than hard power to coerce and conquer. They mainly comprised four methods: kinship alliances, conferral of imperial titles, tribute and trade, and Confucian education.

Pre-modern empires, scholars have noted, were constrained by their limited infrastructural capacity to rule over extensive domains. Michael Mann argues that because of this constraint, pre-modern empires needed "compulsory cooperation" of their subjects (1986: ch. 5). Patricia Crone characterizes the pre-industrial state as a "minimalist state" that did not do much, because of limited agricultural resources and infrastructural capacity (1989: 47). In the Chinese case, Dingxin Zhao suggests, most dynasties after Qin (221–6 BCE) came closer than Qin to Crone's minimalist state, even while Qin had given China a very strong state tradition (2015: 195). This strong state, as shown in Chapter 2, pertained largely to the Central Plains or agrarian regions. Imperial dynasties also had more control over inner peripheral regions through administrative measures. But to gain and maintain control or the cooperation of nomadic polities in the outer peripheries, China's agrarian empires were inclined to adopt "hegemonic strategies." This is because rulers of the settled world, in contrast to nomadic rulers, were "much less interested in the barren land of the steppes apart from their security concerns"; and Chinese emperors, in particular, were constrained by the Confucian bureaucracy, whose learned elites were more interested in employing diplomacy than military affairs (Zhao 2015: 324).

Kinship Alliances

Almost all Chinese dynasties, but especially those faced with vast outer peripheries and large nomadic threats, engaged in "kinship alliances" (*heqin*) or "peace marriages." That is, imperial rulers married off princesses, usually members of minor branches of the royal family, to "barbarian" chieftains. The motive, as meticulously documented by Wang Tongling, a notable historian in the Republican era, was never cultural expansion but security interests, namely to discourage nomadic raids (Wang 1934). The power and wealth of the Chinese dynasties, including their settled lifestyles and cultural practices, provided incentives for surrounding communities to accept that "compulsory cooperation." By one account, 81.6 percent of royal "peace marriages" in Chinese history, from the Han to the Qing dynasty, were clearly related to frontier warfare (Chen 1994: 248).

Marriage alliances made by major Chinese dynasties confirmed this pattern of co-opting nomadic tribes. The Han dynasty (206 BCE–220 CE) formally started the policy of kinship alliances after prolonged and difficult battles with the Xiongnu, who were powerful nomadic tribes from the northern steppes (Di Cosmo 2002: 193). At least eight princesses and seven other ladies of the Han court were married off to Xiongnu khans (Zhang 1990: 431). The Sui dynasty (581–618 CE), itself of mixed lineage, placated aggressive raiders from western frontiers by marrying off four princesses to Turkic khans and maintained alliances on northern steppes by marrying off five princesses to Xianbei chieftains (Wang T. 2010: 321). The Tang dynasty (618–907 CE), the height of imperial China's power and reach, employed marriage alliances as a major strategy to maintain its vast empire. Of mixed lineage itself, the Tang court actively and widely established kinship ties, resulting in fifty royal intermarriages with leading ethnic families, including frontier Tibetan, Turkic, Tuyuhun, Khitan, Xi, Huige, and Nanzhao groups (Wang T. 2010: 322–6).

Chinese dynasties under nomadic rulers, despite martial prowess, still relied on peace marriages to balance security interests on the frontiers, mainly the outer peripheral regions. Under the Yuan dynasty (1271–1368), Mongol rulers established kinship alliances with the ruling families of Uighur, Wak (a Kazakh branch), Korean, Tibetan, Jurchen, Tangut, and Dali groups, marrying off a total of thirty-five Mongol princesses (Wang T. 2010: 443–5). Under the Qing dynasty (1644–1912 CE), Manchu rulers used extensive military and marriage alliances to co-opt their leading rival camp, the Mongols. Together, thirty-two Manchu princesses were married off to Mongol chieftains; multiple Mongol princesses were married into the Manchu royal family; and overall more than ninety intermarriages resulted between the Manchu royal family and leading ethnic families during the Manchu dynasty (Wang T. 2010: 536–55). By contrast, the only royal courts since the Han dynasty that did not engage in kinship alliances were Sinic dynasties in significant territorial retreat: Song (960–1279 CE) and Ming (1368–1644 CE). These two dynasties were largely confined to the Sinic territories of agrarian regions.

Conferral of Imperial Titles

The second imperial strategy of ethnic co-optation was the conferral of imperial titles, applied to both inner and outer peripheral regions but with differentiated approaches. In the former, imperial designations were conferred to tribal leaders who then ruled their domains in their official titles (*ye chen ye zhi*). In the outer peripheral regions, official titles were conferred upon nomadic chieftains without such indirect rule by the imperial court (*chen er bu zhi*).

These two types of conferral signified different strengths of the central state vis-à-vis various frontier regions, or the degree of cooperation the center could compel on those regions. "Conferring titles and indirect rule" represented the general pattern in inner peripheral regions, where imperial authorities created administrative units mirroring regular ones and turned tribal leaders into centrally appointed officials. This pattern occurred under the Han, Tang, Yuan, Ming, and Qing dynasties. The second type, "conferring titles without ruling," delineated the general pattern in outer peripheral regions when central influence was relatively strong, such as during the Han, Tang, Yuan, and Qing dynasties. It was also used in inner peripheral regions during times when central presence was weak, such as the periods of Nanzhao (738–937 CE) and Dali (937–1095 and 1096–1253 CE) kingdoms in Yunnan. Sinic dynasties in territorial retreat, namely the Song and Ming dynasties, did not have loose rein over outer peripheral regions, thus conferring no imperial titles to their rulers (*bu chen bu zhi*) (Li Y. 2006: 40).

The circumstances for each type of conferral shed light on the varying nature of core–periphery relationships. Conferral of official titles without ruling was extensively used by imperial dynasties that had surrendered large nomadic tribes. Conferral here served as mechanisms of coalition and co-optation, not integration or incorporation. Thus the Han dynasty actively employed the strategy to deal with the nomadic Xiongnu threats, bestowing a significant number of princely titles to surrendered Xiongnu chieftains. The Tang dynasty, with its expansive loose rein territories, conferred an array of imperial titles upon frontier ethnic elites, especially the submitted Turkic khans. These conferrals differed from Tang's appointment of many ethnic members to the powerful civilian and military offices within or under the Tang court. Of the 369 prime ministers during the Tang dynasty, thirty-six (10 percent) were of nomadic lineage; while among the military ranks, various steppe groups – Turkic, Sogdian, Khitan, Xi, Korean, and the Shatuo Turkic – dominated Tang's multiethnic army (Ho 1998: 134). In the Qing dynasty, different imperial titles were granted to submitted Mongol khans and chieftains in accordance with the size of their tribes and how powerful they were. Such conferrals differed from the extensive appointment of Mongols within the Manchu military and government, which was due to the Manchu–Mongol political alliances.

Contemporary Chinese historiography emphasizes the role that imperial conferrals played in signifying relationships between central authorities and frontier ethnic regimes. If this is intended to assert ancient Chinese sovereignty, imperial conferrals alone were insufficient to support that claim in the outer peripheral regions.

Tribute and Trade

In yet another method of ethnic co-optation, imperial dynasties sanctioned tribute missions and trade rights from frontier groups. But imperial practices differed with regard to the inner and outer peripheral regions. For the former, tribute obligations to the imperial court were required as a symbolic submission, and they became unnecessary over time as administrative incorporation strengthened. For outer peripheral regions, tribute exchange and trade rights were used by the imperial court to co-opt the threatening nomadic neighbors.

In the inner peripheries, mainly the south and the southwest, tribute obligations had been formally required of submitted tribes since the Han dynasty. Tribal chieftains were also obliged to participate in imperial military expeditions. Their formalistic subservience and modest tributes were compensated for by a conferral of imperial titles and gifts, hence the stability of the system for millennia. Over time, however, the financial and physical drain of the tribute institution became burdensome for the imperial court. Moreover, elite co-optation did not necessarily ensure internal order and peace within the tribes. Unruly chieftains and popular discontent were among the reasons why the Qing court carried out reforms to bureaucratize the native chieftaincy (*gaitu guiliu*) since Emperor Yongzheng (reign 1722–35) (Took 2005: 229–32). During his reign, localities already under the native chieftaincy were mostly transformed into regular administrative units, leading to the demise of the tribute system for inner peripheral regions (Huang and Wu 2001: 34). In other words, it was no longer necessary to express the subordination of inner peripheral regions through the tribute system.

In the outer peripheral regions, pressure for tribute exchange often came from the other direction, namely nomadic tribes in the north and northwest. Here the imperial court's permission or rejection of tribute missions was used as an inducement to limit nomadic raids and military confrontation. Typically, tributes from nomadic missions paled in comparison with those brought by inner peripheral tribes. But nomadic missions received in return lavish gifts and benefits that far outweighed their symbolic tributes. For the Han dynasty, which started this tradition, chronic raiding from the Xiongnu had taught Han rulers that military battles alone could not solve the problem of frontier incursions. These incursions were driven by seasonal shortages on the steppes that military battles alone could not deter. By contrast, generous imperial gifts to the Xiongnu served as military mollification as well as economic relief for the "needy nomad" (Xu and Jin 2008: 51). Likewise, the Tang and Qing dynasties, with their overextended empires, sanctioned extensive tribute missions from surrounding nomadic tribes. For Sinic dynasties in territorial retreat, the Song, and sometimes the Ming dynasties, it was the nomadic dynasties in the north and northwest that extorted lavish tributes and gifts from them.

Trading rights were a related strategy to co-opt the nomadic neighbors. Conventional Chinese historiography cites moral justification for trading with the "barbarians." However, contemporary Chinese studies concede that security concerns played a key role in reality (Guan K. 2007; Peng 2004). The steppe communities, while dependent on their agrarian neighbors for grains, salt, tea, and silk, produced horses needed by China's imperial armies and draft animals needed by its agrarian communities. China's dynastic rulers and counselors were well aware of the economic dynamics behind the periodic nomadic raids. They used tribute and trading rights for appeasement purposes, and a withdrawal of those rights for punitive purposes. Dynasties since the Han had set up frontier market fairs (*hushi*) with nomadic communities on the northern and western frontiers. The practice became formalized during the Tang dynasty, the height of the imperial loose rein system. Bustling trade went on with an array of Turkic, Tibetan, Tungusic, Tangut, and Qiangic domains, along all of China's nomadic frontiers (Guan Y. 2007: 85–6). Even Sinic dynasties in territorial retreat, namely Song and Ming, pursued the tea–horse trade on the Sino-Tibetan frontiers to secure border security and warhorses.

Confucian Education

Education also served as a vehicle of elite co-optation, as it was a scarce good in both Han and minority regions. As in Sinic areas, imperial courts offered Confucian education to the children of tribal rulers on the assumption that it provided proper training for official service. For cultural and geographic reasons, this education was usually available to inner peripheral regions on a voluntary basis, but expansive dynasties also extended it to outer peripheral regions.

The Tang and Qing dynasties offered prime examples of such expansive dynasties. For inner peripheral areas, Tang authorized the establishment of schools for children of native chieftains in nearby urban centers, such as Chengdu. For outer peripheral areas, Tang established schools of higher learning in the imperial capital and opened them up to children of nomadic chieftains, including those from Turpan (Turkic) and Tibetan domains (Chen 1994: 248). The Qing court, although a minority dynasty, strengthened Tang's policy of educating tribal successors in the Chinese classics. Emperor Shunzhi (1644–61) employed Han teachers for his own children and mandated Chinese education for offspring of imperial Manchu elites and ethnic offspring slated to inherit the title of native chieftaincy. In Manchu and Mongol areas in northeastern and northern China, the Manchu court established schools for children of local ethnic elites. It also established schools in Beijing for Mongol and Tibetan elite youths to receive education in the capital city. To facilitate Manchu and Mongol successes in the imperial civil service exam, the Manchu court set up separate testing sites and qualifying quotas for Manchu and Mongol candidates (Yu 2003: 41). In the south and the southwest, where the native chieftaincy system had already helped to bring down cultural and linguistic barriers, the Qing court established government-funded schools and promoted privately funded and free schools for Confucian education. The court also encouraged minority students to participate in the civil service exams by increasing admission quotas for ethnic regions (Xu and Jin 2008: 51–2).

As methods of co-optation, the hegemonic strategies entailed that they were effective as long as the Chinese dynasties had soft power and offered appealing incentives for cooperation, especially for nomadic rulers in outer peripheral regions. Once that soft power declined, however, the elusive core–peripheral relationships would also weaken.

TRANSITION TO THE MODERN STATE

The establishment of the Republican government since 1911 rendered obsolete two of the pre-modern methods of frontier co-optation: the kinship alliance and the tribute system. The other two methods, conferral of central titles and education of ethnic elites, continued with a focus on the outer peripheral regions and their ethnic elites. This strategy of elite appeasement, combined with assimilationist policies, nevertheless did little to incorporate those regions or their elites into the post-imperial state.

Elite Appeasement and Mass Assimilation

The early Republican regime (Beiyang, 1912–28) carried out a semi-loose rein policy of elite co-optation in the historical outer peripheral areas. It aggressively courted the Mongol and Tibetan upper strata by guaranteeing traditional prerogatives, central titles, and material rewards. It created the Commission on Mongolia and Tibet in 1912 to maintain political liaison with local aristocracy and elite lamas. It ran a guesthouse in the capital to receive visiting Mongol and Tibetan elites. Any Mongol lama who came to the capital to express loyalty to the new regime would be given central titles. In 1912 President Yuan Shikai restored the central title for the Dalai Lama and then the Panchen Lama. In 1913 Yuan issued decrees to guarantee Tibet's traditional polity and other prerogatives (Yan et al. 2012: 3).

The Beiyang regime continued the policy of educating minority elites in the capital, with paradoxical results. In 1913 it founded the Mongol and Tibetan School and a school of higher learning for frontier affairs, both to train ethnic officials for their homelands. Tuition was provided by the government, as were transportation costs to Beijing. Abandoning Confucian classics, the new curriculum included more practical subjects such as politics and finance. In recognition of rising ethno-nationalism, the language, literature, history, and geography of those two regions were added to the curriculum. But the gathering of educated ethnic youths helped to nurture the first generation of minority communists in the mid-1920s. Studying in Beijing, Mongol students became influenced by the May Fourth Movement of 1921 and supported the herdsmen who came to the capital to petition against frontier farming. Mongol student activism caught the attention of Li Dazhao, an early communist leader, who helped to set up the first communist branch for minority members. Among the Mongol students was Ulanfu, who would become the highest-ranking official of Mongol descent in the Mao era. The Mongol and Tibetan School came to be known as the "cradle of revolution" for Inner Mongolia.

Beyond minority elites, the Beiyang regime promoted assimilationist policies at the mass level. It promoted assimilation in language and customs, issuing a decree in 1912 to encourage intermarriages among the five co-nations of the new Republic (Yan et al. 2012: 3). After consolidating power, it reneged on an earlier promise to halt frontier farming and provincial administration in Mongol regions. It colluded with Mongol aristocrats to reap huge profits from frontier farming, collecting dues from land claimants while allowing Mongol elites to profit from state compensation for local herdsmen. Enticed by these gains, corrupt Mongol elites forced herdsmen onto remote and desertified pastureland, enabling many Han merchants, rural gentry, officials, and warlords to become large land owners (Li 2004b). These realities helped to draw educated Mongol youths to the CCP.

The KMT regime (1928–49) continued with the Beiyang's mixed policy of elite appeasement and mass assimilation. Politically, the KMT intensified co-optation of the Mongol and Tibetan aristocracy, preserving their traditional privileges and appointing them to central and local state offices. It established the Mongol Local Autonomy Political Affairs Committee in 1933, parallel to the provincial system created earlier in Mongol areas. Mongol princes were appointed to the new committee, with Prince Yun as the chairman. In Tibetan regions of Qinghai, the KMT relied on Muslim warlords to deter British encroachments and restrain Tibetan separatists. To this end the KMT courted the Panchen Lama, based in historical Amdo or Qinghai, by granting him central titles, annual stipends, and other central insignias. Throughout the 1930s the KMT sought to show reverence to the institution of the Dalai Lama (Zhang 2003: 50–1).

The KMT continued the policy of educating minority youths from outer peripheral regions, with a more assimilationist drive. Under its platform of "one national race," education was now the chief vehicle for assimilation of frontier minorities (Dreyer 1976: 18). It kept the Beiyang's Mongol and Tibetan School and established the Mongol and Tibetan Department under the Ministry of Education in 1930. A range of measures was decreed to broaden education locally and nationally for Mongol and Tibetan students as well as for students from Xinjiang and Kham (a Tibetan area), including preferential admission and free or cheaper tuition (Zhang 2003: 52). After the anti-Japanese war began in the late 1930s, the relocation of government and cultural institutions to southwestern provinces increased attention on the hitherto neglected minorities in the inner peripheral regions. Whereas there was just one school for border education before the war under the Ministry of Education, forty-four frontier schools of various grades were established or taken over by the ministry after 1938 (Dreyer 1976: 32). These schools were intended to provide instruction in modern education, citizenship, Chinese language, technical and vocational skills, hygiene, and the Chinese nation. However, most measures were not implemented due to domestic turmoil in the 1930s and 1940s. Heavy levies to finance minority education, moreover, alienated local ethnic populations who already lived on the margins of subsistence and found little appeal in assimilation through education.

Other areas of the KMT's minority policy also alienated ethnic masses without winning over ethnic elites. In Mongol areas, it continued Beiyang's policy of frontier farming by Han immigrants, allowing provincial administrations and regional warlords to further promote and abuse it (Li 2004a: 85–6). Although frontier farming benefited Mongol elites who collected fees from land claims, it hurt local herdsmen who lost pastureland. Excessive frontier farming was accompanied by other unpopular policies in Mongol areas, including heavy levies on local herdsmen, central decrees to eliminate the lama system, and prohibition of headscarves worn by Mongol women. In inner peripheral regions, the KMT banned minority languages in urban centers and encouraged minority identification with Han culture. But the influx of Han presence, including arrogant government workers, tax collectors, and absentee Han landlords, did not endear local minorities to Han culture. During the anti-Japanese War period (1937–46), heavy levies and compulsory military conscription led to popular rebellions against the KMT in both inner and outer peripheral regions, including Inner Mongolia, Gansu, Hunan, Hubei, Guizhou, Guangxi, Yunnan, and Xinjiang (Zhang 2003: 52; Yan et al. 2012: 5).

The KMT's unpopular policies allowed the CCP to characterize them as class oppression. The main legacy of Republican policies, thus, was to pave the way for the CCP's minority policy based on class universalism. This was professedly to compensate for the oppression that minority communities had suffered under the KMT.

MINORITY POLICIES IN THE MAO ERA

The hegemonic strategies of imperial China to co-opt frontier regions aimed at little more than securing compulsory cooperation. As June Dreyer notes:

> Abstention from aggression and vague commitment of loyalty to the emperor and the Confucian values he embodied were sufficient to attain this level of integration. Traditional customs, languages, and governing systems were not interfered with so long as they did not pose a threat to the Chinese state. Barring the rise of a major threat . . . most officials had little further interest in the events of these areas. (1976: 12–13)

The Republican regimes' mix of elite co-optation and mass assimilation made little headway in terms of nation state building.

The CCP's policy instruments of egalitarianism departed from pre-modern methods in three critical ways. First, it was intended to encompass and penetrate ethnic communities as a whole, rather than allying with ethnic elites at the top. Second, it was designed to transform minority societies socioeconomically, not just their external relations with the central government. Third, it made little distinction between inner and outer peripheral regions, except in the initial years. Class universalism buttressed the CCP's egalitarian strategies, bridging developmental gaps for the ethnic proletariat in the "backward" regions. Specific strategies, thus, focused on developing regional economies, minority populations, the education and training of professionals, and minority languages.

Promoting Developmental Equality

In contrast to pre-modern practices of tribute and trade, which did not involve the internal affairs of minority areas, the new state emphasized active involvement in developing minority economies during the Mao era. In contrast to historical practices whereby the inner peripheries paid partial taxes while the outer peripheries were exempted, now state subsidies and tax relief were provided to both inner and outer peripheral regions. These financial allowances went far beyond the imperial gifts offered to tribal chieftains during imperial dynasties.

Preferential economic policies included a variety of state subsidies and tax relief for various socioeconomic sectors since the early 1950s. They ranged from large transfers of investment and professional talent to construction of modern industries and infrastructure, including heavy industries, railways, roads, power stations, and irrigation projects to energy and forest industries (Tables 3.1 and 3.2). In a departure from historical practices, the new state transplanted the

TABLE 3.1 *Financial subsidies for autonomous regions in the Mao era*

Period	Type of subsidy	Details
Since 1951	"Subsidy for Educational Development of Ethnic Regions"	Extra funding for elementary and middle schools in ethnic regions
Since 1955	"Subsidies for Ethnic Regions"	For special needs of ethnic regions; for production, healthcare, social welfare, and interest-free loans; shortfalls to be filled by additional funds
Since 1964	"Capital Reserve for Autonomous Regions"	5% of the previous year's fiscal expenditure, excluding infrastructure and floating capital
Since 1964	Capital Reserve (including Yunnan and Qinghai)	5% of fiscal expenditure (3% for regular provinces); 4% for autonomous prefectures (2% for regular districts); 3% for autonomous counties (1% for regular counties)
1964–88	Local retention of surplus revenues	Demised with the end of central planning

Source: Xu and Jin (2008: 80–1); State Council of the PRC (2009b).

TABLE 3.2 *Tax relief for minority regions in the Mao era*

Period	Type of relief
1953–93	Relief of commercial and industrial taxes
Since 1953	Light taxes on agriculture and animal husbandry
Since 1958	Relief of agricultural taxes on poor minority households
Since 1950s	Tax reduction for border trade

Source: Xu and Jin (2008: 81); Zhang W. (2010: 28–9).

developmental model of interior regions to the peripheries. That is, to extend the socialist economy to minority regions, with the intended objective to prevent them from "falling further behind" interior regions. In the early years of the CCP's rule in the early 1950s, the socialist economy was implemented in moderate ways so as to avoid jolting ethnic communities. While interior provinces undertook land reforms and organized rural cooperatives during 1950–3, a majority of rural areas in minority regions did not do so until the late 1950s, when the collectivization drive swept the country during the Great Leap Forward (1958).

In the early years of the CCP's rule, the central authorities made a point of distinguishing inner and outer peripheral regions. The impulse for imposing the socialist economy was held in check in Xinjiang and Tibet, two regions with more distinct features, to avoid jolting ethnic elites. In 1951, Wang Zhen – then Xinjiang's party chief and deputy military commander – tried to crack down on Uighur aristocracy and to implement land reforms, but central leaders rebuffed his initiative. Li Weihan, the party's expert on minorities, rallied the central leadership to stop Wang. Vice President Liu Shaoqi, who chaired the party's meeting to criticize Wang, summed up the party's position this way: "It is a mistake to transplant mechanically the experiences of agrarian regions to pastoral regions" (Xiaohe 2007). Wang Zhen was removed from Xinjiang in 1953.

In Tibet's case, the impulse to transplant socialism was initially curbed by the 17-Point Agreement with the Dalai Lama reached in 1951. The treaty allowed his theocracy to coexist with the CCP's interim government in Lhasa, known as the Work Committee. When members of the committee were anxious to implement socialist reforms in tandem with the rest of the country, the central leadership repeatedly tamed their "leftist excesses" (Jin 2010a: 54–6). But the flight of the Dalai Lama and his entourage in 1959 opened the way for the socialist economy to be transplanted in Tibet thereafter. Its consequences are discussed in Chapter 7.

Another area in which Xinjiang and Tibet received different policy treatment was the infusion of professional talent. College graduates and professionals from interior provinces were assigned to lead the development of modern sectors. They served as modern bureaucrats, educators, medical workers, scientists, and engineers in the newly built modern professions. During the Mao era (1949–76), Xinjiang received over 50,000 of such assigned professionals, while Tibet received about 30,000 (Zhao 2012: 55). The new assignees were required to receive training in ethnic languages and cultures at the beginning of their local careers, and were urged to respect local minorities and customs. This practice served as a gesture of solidarity with ethnic communities, in contrast to the patronizing attitudes of the government workers and professionals sent down by the KMT in the 1930s and 1940s (Dreyer 1976: 33). In southern Xinjiang and Tibetan regions, the early assignees needed to learn the local languages themselves so they could effectively teach their Uighur or Tibetan students.

In another measure of frontier development and integration, frontier farms were established in Xinjiang in the 1950s. Known as "production and construction corps" (PCC, or *Bingtuan*), the practice drew from the traditional *tuntian* system since the Western Han dynasty (206 BCE–9 CE), a strategy of stationing troops to cultivate and guard frontier areas as an important state policy for developing border areas and consolidating frontier defense. The PCCs began in Xinjiang with the settlement of 175,451 demobilized soldiers in 1954 and further expanded in the radical decade of the 1960s, reaching a total population of 1.4854 million and 158 farms by 1966 (State Council of the PRC 2014). In contrast to frontier farming in the late Qing and Republican eras, when pastureland was seized from herdsmen, the PCCs were established on wasteland away from minority populated areas. The measure reflected CCP concerns for national integration (or defense) as well as equality (development). The PCCs would further expand in Xinjiang and other minority regions during the radical years of the 1960s.

As part of socioeconomic development, the demographic growth of minority populations was promoted as a hallmark of developmental equality. From 1951 to 1980, state policies sought to increase minority populations, especially small minority groups. To raise birthrates and reduce mortality rates, modern health facilities were built and health professionals from interior areas were assigned to minority regions, down to remote villages. Minority groups classified as "relatively small" (*jiaoxiao minzu*), or numbering under 10,000 individuals in size, received special protection and assistance. By the mid-1960s, the long trend of low or negative birthrates in minority regions was reversed (Tables 3.3 and 3.4).

Minority members were exempt from family planning policies in the first decade of their implementation in the 1970s, or the last decade of the Mao era. After those policies were written into the post-Mao Chinese Constitution in 1982, autonomous regions could still use their autonomous power to decide the size of families, as well as the minimum legal age for marriage, especially in the two sensitive regions of Tibet and Xinjiang. Since 1985, the TAR has encouraged urban Tibetans to have two children, but has not dictated family planning for Tibetans living in rural and pastoral areas, who comprise 77.4 percent of Tibet's population. In Xinjiang, the one-child policy began to

TABLE 3.3 *Han vs. minority population: annual growth rates*

Population/year	1953–64	1964–82	1982–90	1990–2000	2000–10
Nationwide	1.64	2.09	1.50	1.07	0.57
Han	1.67	2.04	1.31	0.97	0.555
Minorities	1.46	2.88	3.95	1.57	0.67

Source: National Bureau of Statistics of China.[1]

TABLE 3.4 *Han vs. minority in total population in five national censuses*

Year	Total population	Han	Minority	% of minority
1953	576,837,838	547,283,057	34,013,785	5.89
1964	691,180,277	651,296,368	39,883,909	5.77
1982	1,003,913,927	936,703,824	66,434,341	6.62
1990	1,130,510,638	1,042,482,187	90,567,245	8.01
2000	1,242,612,226	1,159,400,000	104,490,735	8.41
2010	1,370,536,875	1,225,932,641	113,792,211	8.49

Source: National Bureau of Statistics of China.[2]

apply to all Han residents in 1980, while family planning was "advocated" to ethnic residents since 1983. Xinjiang's local statutes since 1989 "encouraged" ethnic residents in cities to have two children, and ethnic residents in rural areas to have three children. Only in 2006 did Xinjiang's regional statutes change the word "encourage" to "allow," while loosening control for Han households in rural areas by allowing two children.

Promoting Educational Equality

The new government extended education to the minority public, in a departure from imperial practices of educating children of minority elites only. The state founded elementary and secondary public schools in most minority regions and established special colleges for minority students across the country.

Ten colleges for minorities, or *minyuan*, were opened between 1950 and the mid-1960s in Beijing and provincial capitals in or near the five autonomous regions. The purpose was to prepare minority professionals for the modern sectors. The expansion of lower and higher education for minority members

[1] Census data from 1953, 1964, 1982, 1990, 2000, and 2010, www.stats.gov.cn/tjgb/rkpcgb/. Accessed July 11, 2015.

[2] Ibid.

meant that education and related careers were no longer limited to the offspring of ethnic elites. In minority colleges, students could take remedial classes in the Chinese language and specialize in subjects related to their background, such as the history and language of their ethnic group. For those whose command of the Chinese language was insufficient for regular colleges, minority colleges became the best tickets to higher education and professional careers. In college admissions, state policies tried to balance minority enrollment and academic standards, and emphasized remedial courses for enrolled students (Li 2009: 157, 158). Graduates of minority colleges became the first generation of native administrators and professionals in the new nation state.

Regular colleges and trade schools were gradually established in minority regions as well. College graduates from interior provinces, usually Han Chinese, were assigned to teach there. Many were inspired by the government's patriotic campaigns in the early days of post-liberation in the 1950s. Others, being Communist Party members or leaders of their classes, were under pressure to set examples to their peers, thus they answered the party's call to "devote your life to building the frontiers." Still others felt that they had come from a bad social class background as defined by the party, and had to redeem themselves by choosing to go to the frontiers. For young couples among college graduates, the opportunity to be assigned to the same geographical location – often the only opportunity during the Mao era – was a strong incentive to volunteer for frontier professional jobs upon graduation.[3]

For lower grades, ethnic schools were established parallel to regular schools in minority-concentrated regions. Here an ethnic language would be the medium of instruction. Despite enormous shortages in instructional staff and materials, ethnic schools achieved much to alleviate illiteracy among minority communities. As Table 3.5 shows, a majority of individuals among almost all ethnic groups completed elementary and middle schools, a remarkable record that is difficult to achieve for a large, populous, and multiethnic country. Some ethnic groups not only achieved parity with the Han majority but also outperformed them: the Koreans, Mongols, Manchus, and Huis have done so at the college level, as have the Koreans, Manchus, Mongols, and Zhuangs in basic literacy. Illiteracy rates remain highest among the Tibetan and Yi groups, largely due to a lag of available schools and textbooks in the native language (Tenzin and Zhang 1991: 336–9; Ma 2006: 9 and 2007: 17–18).

The system of ethnic schools, nevertheless, has not been the best at balancing equality and quality, a problem obscured during the socialist era but consequential in the post-Mao period. Many schools in this system were plagued by a lack of qualified teachers and teaching materials in ethnic

[3] Extended conversations with five professionals who were originally from Sichuan and were assigned to Xinjiang and Tibetan regions during the Mao era. Two taught in an agricultural school in southern Xinjiang, one taught in a machinery school in northern Xinjiang, and two taught in a teachers' college in Ngawa. They shared their stories and those of their colleagues.

TABLE 3.5 *Educational achievement of fourteen ethnic groups above age 6 (2000)*

Ethnic group	Level of schooling achieved by population (%)								
	No schooling	Literacy class	Primary school	Middle school	High school	Technical school*	College**	Graduate school	Total (%)
Han	7.3	1.7	37.6	37.3	8.8	3.4	3.8	0.1	100.0
Zhuang	6.0	1.7	46.4	34.7	5.7	3.4	2.0	0.0	100.0
Manchu	4.6	0.5	37.5	40.4	8.5	3.6	4.7	0.1	100.0
Hui	15.6	2.7	36.8	29.0	8.3	3.5	4.0	0.1	100.0
Miao	17.1	3.4	50.9	21.5	3.3	2.3	1.4	0.0	100.0
Uighur	8.8	2.8	53.1	24.6	4.3	3.6	2.7	0.0	100.0
Yi	21.2	4.8	51.6	16.4	2.6	2.2	1.1	0.0	100.0
Tujia	9.9	1.3	47.6	29.9	5.7	3.3	2.3	0.0	100.0
Mongol	7.2	0.7	37.3	34.7	10.2	4.6	5.1	0.1	100.0
Tibetan	45.5	6.1	35.2	7.7	1.7	2.5	1.3	0.0	100.0
Dong	9.1	3.0	49.8	28.4	4.4	3.3	2.1	0.0	100.0
Bouyei	20.3	2.5	50.7	20.3	2.4	2.5	1.3	0.0	100.0
Yao	8.2	2.5	52.3	27.7	4.6	2.8	1.9	0.0	100.0
Korean	2.8	0.5	20.4	43.1	19.8	4.9	8.4	0.2	100.0
Total	7.7	1.8	38.2	36.5	8.6	3.4	3.7	0.1	100.0

* This refers to specialized training schools (three-year program) after middle school.
** This includes both four-year and two-year colleges.
Source: SCCO and SBS (2002: 563–7); Ma (2006: 8).

languages. Because of their remote locations and dispersed habitats, most minority groups did not have access to modern schools before the 1950s. In outer peripheral areas in particular, monasteries and mosques offered the usual avenues to traditional education. During the 1950s and 1960s, the central state expended enormous resources to recruit minority youths to special training programs and to groom the first generation of minority teachers. By 1991, teachers of Tibetan descent still made up just 24 percent of the faculty in middle schools across the TAR and only 2.7 percent in its high schools (Ma 1996: 364). Because of their short history, moreover, the academic and pedagogical skills of ethnic schools lagged considerably behind regular schools, especially in the areas of math and science.

A major challenge was a lack of native-speaking educators in the early years, especially in the outer peripheral regions. When Han teachers were first sent there in the 1950s and 1960s, many had to learn the native language in order to teach the native students. They were burdened further by the difficulty of translating technical terms into the native languages. The lack of minority teachers in the math and science subjects was compounded by the academic programs when colleges were first established in minority regions in the 1950s. Those programs catered to minority students' cultural interests in the language, literature, and history of their own groups. The common cores required by the state, moreover, were courses in the humanities, such as Marxist philosophy and political economy. Programs in sciences and social sciences were not founded in colleges or taught in the minority languages in some autonomous areas until the 1980s.

As minority students disproportionally majored in the language, religion, history, and literature of their own groups, this perpetuated the shortage of qualified teachers in math and science. In an extreme example from a secondary school in Hotan of southern Xinjiang, as recently as the 2000s a native teacher was observed teaching simple but incorrect arithmetic: 1/2 + 1/2 =1/4. The equivalent class in a regular school would be doing algebra and geometry (Ma 2006: 8). Such cases give ammunition to China's integrationists who have espoused bilingual programs in recent years, on the grounds of facilitating the teaching of science, technology, engineering, and mathematics (STEM) subjects to minority students in Mandarin.

The state devoted enormous efforts to developing textbooks in ethnic languages, effectively for the first time in Chinese history. For most minority regions, the subjects of modern sciences and technology were introduced in the 1950s for the first time. Though the same was true of many remote Han areas, a lack of textbooks in ethnic languages posed greater challenges. These textbooks began to be compiled in the 1950s, mainly through the translation of Chinese textbooks. But the task was daunting not only in terms of human and material costs but also in terms of conceptual and terminological difficulties. It was no easy job to invent or find equivalent terms for the definitions, concepts, phrases, formulas, examples, and interpretations in math and science subjects. New coinages also needed to be tested in the classroom and improved progressively. By 1988, over 1,400 different textbooks were published in minority languages for different subject areas (He 1998: 78). Like the building of ethnic schools, the pace of developing minority textbooks varied with different starting points for different minority groups.

The outer peripheral regions, for obvious reasons, posed greater challenges. In the case of the TAR, modern textbooks began to be compiled from scratch, step by step, beginning with the establishment of a "compilation group" in 1960. By 1963 textbooks were available in Tibetan for the elementary school in a few subjects. From 1972 to 1979, textbooks for every subject area were compiled on the model of those used in Beijing's elementary school system. In 1982 a pilot group for collaborative compilation of instructional materials in the Tibetan language was established, consisting of specialists from five provinces. By 1991 textbooks in Tibetan for every subject area in the primary and middle school were completed, while high-school materials were "basically complete" (Tenzin and Zhang 1991: 336–9). Even for inner peripheral provinces such as Yunnan and Guizhou, textbooks in minority languages remain available only for the elementary or middle schools (Ma 2006: 9). Such problems demonstrated the difficult balancing acts between the pursuit of equality and efficiency.

The Chinese-derived textbooks, moreover, were not always a good fit for all minority students. Written from the Han majority's perspectives and experiences, the historical episodes and social settings referenced in the textbooks could be far removed from the world lived by minority students, especially those in the outer peripheries. These students could find themselves studying a society unfamiliar and unrelated to them (Ma 2006: 9). Interestingly, the issue is not the absence of minority roles or achievements in Chinese history, but a Han indifference to the ethnicity of the movers and shakers. For millennia, minority groups were central to the country's multiethnic evolution and dynastic changes, but the corollary of the prolonged historical processes is a desensitized view of ethnicity, reflected not only in Chinese textbooks but China's public discourse in general. Moreover, the CCP's ideological prism during the Mao era, which viewed historical events through the lens of class struggles, reinforced a de-ethnicized account of history. All this can leave minority students feeling resentful for having to study "dead Han poets," even though many of China's famed ancient poets descended from ethnic lineages. Despite improvements in recent years, resentment still is visible in online chat rooms.

Promoting Language Equality

In another drastic departure from imperial policy instruments, language equality was promoted for all minority groups during the socialist era. The policy has alternatively been characterized as promoting pluralism (Zhou 2003), accommodation (Zhou and Sun 2004), nation state building, and identity construction (Zhou 2012). The last characterization is most pertinent from the perspective of this study: language equality was part of the state's promotion of integration and equality, aimed at nation state building; yet by essentializing an ethno-cultural feature, the process also contributed to identity construction.

Here the state made no distinction between inner and outer peripheral regions, where crucial differences existed in terms of the functional utility or historical realities of the written script. Ideological commitment to equality appeared to override concerns for those differences. For the inner peripheral groups that lived in proximity to Sinic areas, a sizable number of their members already used Chinese on a regular basis (EdB 1986: 554). If their languages did not have a written script or one in wide circulation, it was usually due to the small size of their populations and hence limited usage historically. The newly invented scripts could not resolve this problem of limited circulation or their speakers' access to publications in the widely circulated Mandarin. After all, it would be impossible to make all publications available all ethnic languages, especially those of very small ethnic groups. The invented scripts had been taught in some minority schools before transition to the Chinese script, namely in serving as a transitional tool. But research (Zhou 2012) suggests that the efficacy of this approach remains uncertain.

Just as it overaccommodated inner peripheral languages, the policy of language equality ignored the unique linguistic position of the outer peripheral regions. In the former regions, most groups already used Mandarin as their lingua franca, and their elites could read and write in it. Of the four historical outer peripheral regions, the Manchus regularly used Mandarin except for remote areas of the northeast, while a sizable number of Mongols used Mandarin for regular communication. However, in Xinjiang and Tibetan regions of Sichuan and Qinghai in the 1950s, only a small number of native elites – officials who worked in the local Republican governments and some intellectuals – had a working knowledge of Chinese. In Tibet (Ü-Tsang), Chinese was not in any circulation. Hence these regions needed a different type of attention than inner peripheral groups that already used Chinese for regular communication.

The most dramatic measure to achieve language equality was the state's efforts to create or improve writing systems for minority languages, a daunting task in inner peripheral regions where multitudes of small groups existed or were newly classified. During the 1950s, the government used extensive resources to help those languages without a written script to invent one and to help those without a full written system to develop a complete set. In inner peripheral regions, the government invented written scripts for ten minority groups, including the Zhuang, Yi, Buyei, Miao, Dong, Hani, Lisu, Li, Va, and Nakhi, and reformed scripts for the Daic, Lahu, and Jingpo languages. In outer peripheral regions, the state used Latin letters to design new scripts for Uighur and Kazakh, whose Arabic-based scripts had primarily been used for religious purposes in the past (Ma 1984: 17). The policy of inventing languages was modeled after the Soviet Union, which created scripts for those minorities without writing systems in the 1930s. Besides ideological commitment to equality, the Soviets were motivated to improve native literacy based on the belief that minorities could understand the party's programs better in their native languages.

The principal mechanism to guarantee the equal rights of minority languages was the dual system of public schools, which ironically promoted minority rights at the expense of integration in the long run. In autonomous areas where a minority language was the official language, parallel school systems were established in the 1950s – a regular system and an ethnic system. From kindergarten onward, this would entail regular and ethnic schools as physically and linguistically separate institutions. In regular schools, Mandarin Chinese would be the language of instruction while a foreign language could be taught as a second language. In Xinjiang's case, Han, Hui, and Manchu students mostly enrolled in this system, as did children of other ethnic groups if their parents chose to do so. Minority professionals in the urban centers of the autonomous regions began to send their offspring to regular schools in the mid-1950s. From the beginning, regular schools used more rigorous textbooks and standards than those for ethnic schools (SEC 1995).

In the ethnic school system, the local minority language would be the medium of instruction while Chinese was taught as a second language. In more developed minority regions, a foreign language could be offered as a third language. Minority students in autonomous areas usually attended these schools. Where a minority population was too small for a separate ethnic school, children could enroll in a regular school or an ethnic school established for a larger ethnic group. In multiethnic areas, different ethnic groups may have had their own schools. In Xinjiang's case, Uighur has been the language of instruction in a majority of elementary and middle schools in the ethnic system, while Kazakh, Kyrgyz, Mongol, Sibe (Xibo), and Tajik schools make up the rest. Smaller minorities such as the Tatars have usually attended Uighur schools.

The ethnic schools were established in minority regions from the 1950s at varying paces and with herculean efforts for outer peripheral groups. Historically better educated or integrated groups had good starting points, such as the Koreans and Manchus. Outer peripheral groups, for lack of educational traditions and qualified teachers, had to start from scratch. Traditionally over 95 percent of Tibetans did not have access to education. Here schools had to be built gradually from scratch. The elementary school came first, then the rest one by one. Before schools at all levels were established and staffed, many students had to move from an ethnic school in lower grades to a regular school for advanced grades. Until the 1980s, there was no ethnic school at the high-school level in the TAR. Graduates of Tibetan middle schools would attend regular high schools where Mandarin was used for instruction (Ma 2011d). Xinjiang's ethnic schools were better developed, but not without their own serious problems, as I show in Chapter 8.

Intensified Class Universalism

Preferential policies in the Mao era were moderate compared with those in the post-Mao period. However, although they were aimed at ethnic equality in the name of class universalism, minority-specific policies were still periodically attacked by ideological radicals for contradicting the ideology of class equality and obscuring class struggles in ethnic matters. This radicalism resulted in a greater imposition of inland practices to frontier regions, including an influx of more state resources to outer peripheral regions. Ironically, this influx intensified rather than decreased preferential policies.

The radicalization of ethnic policy was first triggered by local resistance to the collectivization movement during the Great Leap Forward campaign (1958–62). Collectivization was a central part of the campaign, launched by Mao to achieve rapid industrialization and rural communes. But it met with greater resistance in minority regions that had distinct local economies and historically internal autonomy. The independent scholar Li Jianglin (2010) traces the radicalization of ethnic policy to the Xunhua incident of April 1958, when local resistance to collectivization escalated into an armed riot by a pastoral Tibetan village in Xunhua county, Qinghai province. In Li's account, the riot was triggered by local officials' efforts to seclude local elite lamas, ostensibly to prevent them from acting as leaders of local resistance to collectivization. Those lamas, formerly viewed as patriotic allies of the Communist Party, were now seen as class enemies.

Thereafter the party ended its political alliance with former ethnic elites. After Qinghai province submitted an official report on the incident to the central authorities, the CCP Central Committee issued the report to party committees across minority regions, along with this key instruction: "the essence of ethnic issues is class issues" (EdB 1993: 143). Other ethnic provinces quickly followed, namely to elevate policy disagreements with former ethnic elites to the level of class struggle. For example, when Yunnan province issued its official opinions on the reeducation of former ethnic elites in October of 1958, it called for "exposing the true nature" of these elites and "stripping them of their political capital" (EdB 1993: 133).

The idea of class struggle ascended in ethnic policy in the ensuing years. The traditional ethnic elites, hitherto treated as patriotic bourgeoisie and co-opted into government structures, became targets of "rectification" (*zheng feng*) and "anti-rightistism" (*fan you*). Their resistance to collectivization was criticized for promoting sectarian interests and opposing the universal interests of the working class. The party's previous emphasis on the "special characteristics" and "gradual progress" of ethnic regions was now criticized for ethnic particularism. Perceived separatists were labeled "class enemies." Many former ethnic elites were purged or even jailed. Meanwhile, convergence with Han regions was promoted, and minority-specific policies were suspended (EdB 1993: 133–43; see also Dreyer 1976: chs. 6 and 8). This convergence, in contrast to preferential policies promoted by the party before, was now regarded as contributing to social class equality.

Radicalization had a special impact in the cases of Tibet and Xinjiang. In the Kham area of Sichuan during 1956, a historically Tibetan area, local officials launched campaigns to collectivize rural and pastoral land. These drives were attributed to the enthusiasm of grassroots party officials who wanted to emulate the socialist movement in interior regions, despite central caution (Jin 2010a: 56–7). Although Tibetan regions outside Tibet were not covered by the 17-Point Agreement, the collectivization movement in these areas led to local elite opposition and apprehension in other Tibetan regions over threats to their traditional prerogatives. Congregating in Lhasa, Tibetan elites staged a failed rebellion in March 1959, leading to the flight of the Dalai Lama and his entourage from Lhasa to India at the end of March. In Xinjiang as well, in the wake of the Great Leap Forward movement (1958), tens of thousands of Uighurs and Kazakhs fled to Russia in 1962. Rather than curbing left radicalism, however, these cases helped to harden it. For eight months between 1963 and 1964, Li Weihan, the key architect of the CCP's ethnic policy, was attacked as a "revisionist" who downplayed social class issues and surrendered himself to ethnic "serf owners" (Xu and Jin 2008: 75–7).

The triumph of the social class paradigm led to an intensified phase of political and economic transplanting to Tibet, which had earlier been constrained by the 17-Point Agreement. With the flight of Dalai Lama and his repudiation of the agreement, the CCP no longer faced political hurdles to establish its political and economic system there. The party's provisional Work Committee in Lhasa expanded into a full-fledged local government mirroring those in interior regions, while the socialist economy was implemented in full swing after the TAR was established in 1965. The commune system was implemented in most rural areas, and central planning in urban areas. Procurement quotas for agricultural products were issued to pastoral regions, leading to the cultivation of pastureland and the destruction of ecology on which herdsmen depended. State enterprises were set up but consistently generated deficits, except for the 1959–61 period when a chemical factory was opened to supply sodium borate to the Soviet Union. The TAR's state sectors – government, industry, construction, education, culture, and healthcare – became the sources of chronic fiscal dependency on the central state (Ma 2010a: 182–9; Jin 2010a: 81–95). State sponsorship of local industries and agriculture, or tolerance of their deficits, rendered the TAR dependent on state subsidies shortly after it became an autonomous region (Table 3.6). In fact, state subsidies ushered in Tibet's fiscal dependency ever since (see details in Chapter 7).

TABLE 3.6 *Government revenues of the TAR during the Mao era, 1952–85 (in ¥10,000)*

Revenue source	1952	1960	1965	1970	1975	1980	1985
Local state sectors							
Industry	-	3,222	124	−230	122	−537	−2,647
Construction	-	69	−24	−69	−27	74	184
Agriculture	-	43	6	−1,084	476	−1,432	−47
Postal service, transport	-	2,773	−146	−1,844	−2,421	−3,029	−1,816
Grains, trade	-	-	−221	−268	−3,098	−1,904	−6,406
Other	4	35	−83	−390	−174	−1,596	−816
Subtotal	4	6,143	−343	−3,885	−5,122	−8,254	−11,548
Local taxes	137	1,316	1,208	1,187	1,953	2,030	4,544
Other	118	2,360	881	556	184	251	967
Depreciation	-	342	493	-	-	-	-
Local revenue total	258	10,167	2,239	−2,142	−2,985	−5,973	−6,037
State subsidy	1,047	2,725	11,805	18,345	29,179	60,104	105,772
Total revenue of Tibet	1,305	12,886	14,044	16,203	26,194	54,131	99,735
% of state subsidy in total TAR revenue	80.2	21.1	84.1	113.2	111.4	111.0	106.1

Source: SBT (1989: 470–1) and (1999: 101–2).

The "class view" of ethnic issues was brought to its height during the Cultural Revolution, leading to a waning of minority-specific policies. Leftist radicals denied the existence of ethnic differences, denounced ethnic classification as bogus, dismissed ethnic customs as outdated conventions, and condemned scholars who participated in the classification project as reactionaries (Xu and Jin 2008: 76–7). State agencies in charge of ethnic affairs were dissolved, while ethnic policy became a taboo area. Ethnic customs were among the old conventions to be discarded, and the use of ethnic languages was discouraged. Ethnic red guards smashed Tibetan monasteries and Muslim mosques, driven by an ideological crusade against old class vestiges. As Wang Lixiong points out, due to poor transportation and geographical distance, few Han red guards reached the TAR during the Cultural Revolution to wreak damage (2002: 96–7). The same was true of the far-flung region of southern Xinjiang, where Uighurs were concentrated. Some ethnic schools were merged with Han schools, and nearly all minority colleges were closed down. Locally, some autonomous areas were broken up or eliminated, then regrouped into nearby regular administrative districts (Dai 1999: 24). Remaining rights and policies for autonomous regions existed in name only.

The period of radicalism also led to the expansion of PCCs in frontier regions in the 1960s. In Xinjiang, PCCs saw several waves of new influx, including urban "educated youths" from several metropolises and provinces, totaling 126,700 between 1963 and 1966; and rural residents from three interior provinces during 1967–70, totaling about 800,000. In addition, there were "anti-revolutionaries" and felons banished from interior provinces, with felons totaling 123,229 by the mid-1970s (20,856 of these from before 1951) (Xu 2005: 111, 112). In Heilongjiang and Inner Mongolia, PCCs were established in 1968 and 1969 to guard against Soviet border threats, and were mostly settled by educated youths sent down from urban centers. PCCs were also established in other minority-concentrated regions in the late 1960s, including the Lanzhou division (with Gansu, Qinghai, and Ningxia under its wing), Yunnan, and Agricultural Construction Divisions in Guangxi and Tibet. From the 1950s to the 1970s, the provinces with the highest population inflows were all frontier regions, including – by ranking order – Inner Mongolia, Jilin, Xinjiang, Heilongjiang, Liaoning, Qinghai, and Ningxia (Zhang 1997: 376). The total population of PCCs across the country reached 4.8 million in 1971, or 2.42 million excluding family members. Xinjiang's PCCs accounted for 40 percent of this total, or 2,036,086 in 1971 (Xu 2005: 111, 112), while Inner Mongolia's accounted for about 3 percent, or 144,600 in 1971 (including over 5,600 military personnel) (Shu 2017).

It remains a contentious matter in contemporary China whether radical excesses irreparably damaged interethnic relations. The prevailing view is that since the radical excesses were de-ethnicized, that is affecting all groups across the country, they did not cause a permanent rupture in ethnic relations. Han interviewees often express gratitude that their minority colleagues helped to protect them during the Cultural Revolution. Others, however, blame the Cultural Revolution for the breakdown of interpersonal trust, including interethnic trust. Overall, both Han and minority individuals express nostalgia for the old days of mutual respect and interethnic harmony in much of the Mao era (Li 2011b; Qarluq and McMillen 2011: 18; Chen 2012). This is also the general impression one gets from talking with older Han and minority members in the southern Xinjiang and Tibetan regions. Importantly, ethnic conflict was contained in the Mao era because even during the radical episodes, the planned economy helped to integrate minority members into the professional and industrial sectors, through state plans and guaranteed jobs. These plans and jobs did not stand out as ethnically based policies, since the planned economy covered the entire country. Together, the policy instruments of the Mao era contributed importantly to political incorporation of ethnic regions and members through egalitarian strategies. This egalitarianism, nevertheless, was centralizing: it promoted the state goals of economic modernization, land redistribution, frontier defense, population resettlement, and equality in education and language. At the same time, they were centralizing in being minority-specific benefits (i.e., ethnicization). The tensions between centralization and ethnicization were already unraveling during the radical years of the Mao era, as ethnic particularism conflicted with class universalism. Those institutional tensions would prove to be even more problematic in the post-Mao era, when ethnic prerogatives can no longer be protected in the market economy.

SUMMARY

This chapter traces the transformation of policy instruments for dealing with ethnic regions in China's transition to the modern state: how and why hegemonic strategies to secure frontier cooperation became ineffective with the end of imperial rule and the onset of modern times and were eventually replaced by socioeconomic strategies that penetrated minority societies in the socialist era. This transformation departed from pre-modern practices of reliance on soft power, while the new ethnic particularism of the autonomous system clashed with more dogmatic readings of class universalism.

Historical legacies and modern strategies of transition impacted patterns of transition and their unintended consequences in two major ways. First, the hegemonic strategies of imperial dynasties relied on soft power to induce cooperation of rulers in outer peripheral regions. But the demise of imperial soft power reduced the policy tools of late Qing and the Republican regimes. Whereas in pre-modern times, those regions were of interest to the imperial state largely for reasons of border security, hence minimalist strategies were used to secure their cooperation. The imperial state did not reach into ethnic areas, but maintained a ritualistic relationship with them through local elites.

Even for inner peripheral areas, although some were partially taxed as they became increasingly bureaucratized in late imperial times, the imperial state had little interest beyond that. In the transition to a nation state, however, those regions were of great interest to the state for reasons of territorial integration and modern state building. Reduced policy tools, however, limited the successes of the Republican regimes in elite co-optation, although their policy of frontier farming did set in motion the transition of Manchuria and Inner Mongolia into inner peripheral ones.

Second, the CCP's strategy of egalitarianism provided attractive policy tools to win over the ethnic proletariat, but they also fundamentally altered the relationship between the central state and frontier minority regions. In the name of class universalism, the CCP's policy instruments reached entire ethnic communities, through wholesale socioeconomic transformation that encompassed economic, demographic, educational, linguistic, and social spheres. The traditional "minimalist state," hampered by infrastructural capacity, became a maximalist state. Most importantly, in a dramatic reversal of the elite-oriented strategies of pre-modern and modern times, the CCP's transformative strategies displaced former ethnic elites and decimated their traditional power base.

The radical attacks on the autonomous system during the Mao era, ironically, exposed the institutional tensions inherent in the CCP's policy approaches. They pointed to the third set of institutional dynamics creating ethnic discord in the long run: policies based on ethnic particularism contradicted centralizing drives for political integration. The assertion of pure class universalism, since the late 1950s, negated ethnically based policy instruments. In emphasizing equality along social class rather than ethnic lines, the radical approach justified repudiation of former ethnic elites and extension of inland practices to ethnic regions. The corollary of pure class universalism, thus, was to turn upside down the pre-modern approaches of elite co-optation and local autonomy, that is to get rid of local autonomy and ethnic elites. In the post-Mao era, when class universalism was replaced by identity politics and developmentalism, institutional tensions would persist in the party's policy strategies for key autonomous regions. Contradictions would remain between centralizing drives and ethnic particularism, aggravated further by market reforms.

4

The Rise of Identity Politics in Post-Mao China

By the end of the Mao era in 1978, China's minority regions and communities had by and large been incorporated into the system of socialist autonomy. The transformation was most dramatic for Xinjiang and Tibet, even while they remained most distinct. While all minority regions experienced a decimation of the traditional power base, these two regions saw the end of theocratic dominance. While all minority-concentrated areas established ethno-territorial units, only those two regions had ethnic majorities at the provincial and most subprovincial levels and still did at the end of the Mao era. The transition to the modern state, thus, entailed special shocks to the two outer peripheral regions. Not surprisingly, in the early post-Mao campaign to redress the leftist wrongs of the Mao era (*boluan fangzheng*), led by CCP General Secretary Hu Yaobang, the TAR and Xinjiang were the party's primary targets among minority regions.

The campaign to redress leftist wrongs have been well received in Western scholarship. Scholars praise a period of liberalization and "Tibetanization" ushered in by Hu's reform policies in the TAR (Barnett 1994; Shakya 2008a) and acknowledge his policy of openness and accommodation in Xinjiang (Bovingdon 2004: 21; Dillon 2004: 36). Within China, however, the campaign has inflamed debates about minority policy ever since. Whenever ethnic riots broke out in the TAR or Xinjiang, criticisms of Hu's reform policies would fill China's blog sphere and private conservations. "Hu Luanbang" or Hu the wrecker of the country, an epithet originally used by Chen Yonggui to criticize Hu Yaobang in 1979 (*Chinacourt* 2014), has become popular usage among critics of Hu's minority policies (*WYZX* 2013). Chen, a vice premier in 1979, rose from a humble peasant background during the Mao era. Hu's defenders, meanwhile, are no less adamant in calling his critics "leftist hitters" (*zuogun*) (*Tianya luntan* 2015).

This and the following four chapters will argue that the built-in tensions of the autonomous system – centralization and ethnicization – have intensified in China's reform era, fueling key sources of ethnic tensions. The driving force for this intensification has been the twin processes of political and economic liberalization: the decline of class universalism and egalitarianism on the one hand, and the rise of identity politics and/or developmentalism on the other.

This chapter focuses on how this intensification first came about and why it affected the two outer peripheral regions in particular. Policies to redress the leftist excesses of the Mao era, I argue, conceptually as well as materially contributed to the end of class universalism and the rise of identity politics in key minority regions. These policies included the "declassing" of minority policy, rehabilitation of former ethnic elites, exit of Han personnel, revival of religion, and finally, accommodation of ethnic customs in law enforcement. These policies have affected the TAR and Xinjiang in particular because of the central government's greater urgency and efforts to implement those reforms here. Yet the very end of class universalism and the advent of identity politics have also made it much harder for the central state to achieve its goal of better integration. Whereas class universalism was divisive intraethnically, pitting ethnic masses against the small group of ethnic aristocrats, identity politics is divisive interethnically, creating cleavages along ethnic lines.

The rest of the chapter will cover two topics: (1) the "declassing" of minority policy in early post-Mao China, and (2) four areas of reform policy that contributed to the end of class politics and the rise of identity politics, which affected the TAR and Xinjiang in particular.

"DECLASSING" MINORITY POLICY

The campaign to redress leftist wrongs was undertaken from the late 1970s to the mid-1980s across China. The crux of the campaign was to end the social class doctrine that set the party's policy course during the Mao era. The class doctrine had justified radical policies, including the persecution of millions of Chinese citizens as class enemies. However, social class alliance had also served to buttress an interethnic alliance, which facilitated the CCP's incorporation of ethnic regions after it came to power. Abandoning class universalism was thus inherently destabilizing in these regions. Ironically, the declassing of minority policy was more thorough in the outer peripheral regions, for the paradoxical reason that centrifugal forces were stronger here and political integration more imperative.

On first look, abandonment of class politics appeared to undermine centralization, but the state's role in promoting it made centralization a key premise of that abandonment. That is, the state itself undertook measures to declass ethnic politics for its desired goals, which were to repair damaged relations with minority communities and to better integrate them into the Chinese nation. The state's initiative and goals can be seen from the series of party decrees and efforts in the early post-Mao period. In the proceedings of the CCP Work Conference on Tibet in April 1980, the party's goal was declared to be the termination of the divisive role of class politics that damaged "ethnic unity" during the Mao era (CCP 1982: 480, 483). The proceedings were issued along with a CCP notification, pronouncing that Mao's equation of ethnic conflict with class conflict was "completely incompatible with the nature of ethnic relations" after the Chinese revolution of 1949 (CCP 1982: 479). In the proceedings of the CCP Work Conference on United Front Work in January 1982, the party stated that it was imperative to unite all political forces to maximize its "alliances and united front" for the cause of "socialist modernization and national unification" (CCP 1982: 1143–4).

The reversal of "wrongful" cases began in minority regions even before the 3rd plenary session of the 11th Central Committee of the CCP in December 1978, the party conference that officially launched the repudiation of radical policies. Cases where minority members were labeled class enemies and politically persecuted or criminally convicted were formally overturned. Over the next two years, the Central Committee approved at least five central documents decreeing the reversal of wrongful cases in minority regions – cases not only from the period of the Cultural Revolution but also from various political campaigns before that. During this period, Hu Yaobang, the newly appointed CCP party secretary general, convened a series of work symposiums to dissuade opposition from local officialdom to this drastic change, especially opposition in Xinjiang, the TAR, Inner Mongolia, and Yunnan. The minutes from Hu's symposiums became official documents to guide reforms on the ground (see Table 4.1). To remove local opposition to rehabilitation of persecuted personnel, some local officials were dismissed or transferred at Hu's instruction (Gao 2015: 193). Local opposition came not just from Han officials but, more importantly, from minority officials who rose from lower social strata.

Wrongful Cases vs. Real Class Enemies

The epitome of declassing minority policy was the rehabilitation of individuals who were persecuted as class enemies during the Mao era, thus ideologically eliminating intraethnic divisions based on social class lines. But regional divergence in implementation showed that rehabilitation served the state goal of integration where it was most needed. Of the many "class enemies" from the Mao era, three broad categories may be differentiated. They were (1) individuals who were so labeled due to radical excesses (i.e., truly wrongful cases), (2) those who received the label due to their social class backgrounds (i.e., mostly wrongful cases), and (3) those who got the label due to their anti-state activities, such as participation in armed rebellions or separatist movements (i.e., not wrongful cases by the state's definition). Rehabilitation

TABLE 4.1 *Central decrees sanctioning religious revival: early post-Mao China*

Date/agency	Title of document	Key contents
February 1979 CCP/MUF	"Request to remove 'the capitulationism' label from the agencies of united front, ethnic and religious affairs work"	To allow party and state agencies in charge of ethnic and religious affairs to open again
1979/9 CCP/MUF	"Request to the remove the label of local ethno-nationalists"	To disavow the labeling of ethnic nationalists as anti-state and class enemy
April 1980 CCPCC	"Minutes from the Work Conference on Tibet"	Repudiated treating ethnic issues as class politics; emphasized respect for religion
July 1980 CCP Central Committee	"MUF opinion on strengthening united front work toward patriotic minority elites"	To rehabilitate former minority elites
March 1982 CCP Central Committee [1982]19	"Basic principles and policies for religious affairs during our socialist period"	To uphold freedom of religion and to expand political alliance with religious groups

Note: MUP is the Ministry of United Front.
Source: CCP (1982, Vol. 1: 478–94; Vol. 2: 1218–40).

of the first two groups took place in all ethnic regions. But only in the TAR and Xinjiang was the third group of people fully rehabilitated.

The first group, or individuals who were persecuted due to leftist radicalism, were not genuine "class enemies." Hence they should not have been persecuted in the first place, for example minority officials, professionals, and others who were persecuted during various political campaigns of the Mao era. They included (1) those who were labeled "rightists" during the Anti-Rightist Campaign of 1957; (2) those who were labeled "local ethno-nationalists" in the Anti-Rightist Campaign of 1957 and the Four Cleanups Campaign of 1963; and (3) those who were labeled "counter-revolutionaries" and "capitalist roaders" during the Cultural Revolution (EdB 1989: 246–93; Gao 2015: 193–206). In all five autonomous regions and multiethnic provinces such Yunnan, Qinghai, Sichuan, and Jilin, those individuals were all rehabilitated, in tune with the political climate in the rest of the country in the early post-Mao era.

The second type of "class enemies" were classified as members of "exploitative" classes during the 1950s or were regarded as part of the old theocratic ruling class. That is, they were "class enemies" for being members of the traditional upper echelons. The rehabilitation of these individuals began informally in late 1978 as part of the abandonment of Mao's class doctrine. Formally, the 1980 CCP notification – issued with the proceedings of the Work Conference on Tibet on April – repudiated Mao's statement that the "essence of ethnic politics was class politics" (CCP 1982: 479). The revised Chinese Constitution, adopted in 1982, solidifies this stand by stipulating that China has already achieved "socialist ethnic relations of equality, unity and mutual assistance." In other words, there should be no more class enemies under socialism, not even the individuals who were "class enemies" before the socialist era.

The third group of "class enemies" best fitted the official label, at least by the state's definition. Mostly former minority elites and their followers, they were sentenced to jail or labor camps for participation in armed rebellions or separatist movements in the 1950s and 1960s. These activities had occurred in Xinjiang, the TAR, Ningxia, and Qinghai. But only in Xinjiang and the TAR were all participants released during the campaign to redress leftist wrongs in the late 1970s and the early 1980s.

In the TAR's case, all three groups of "class enemies" were released or cleared. First and foremost were the members of the Lhasa armed rebellion of 1959. They numbered several thousand and were part of the old Tibetan ruling class. Stripped of their assets and serfs at the time, they had been in jail since the suppression of the rebellion in 1959. As participants in an anti-state insurgence, they were real "class enemies" in the sense of being the foes of the proletariat. All were released in November 1978, given official treatment as United Front allies, and compensated for their property losses. The second rehabilitated group included members of the so-called "exploitative classes" from old Tibet, such as local chieftains, pastoral headsmen, rich rural or pastoral classes, and urban capitalists. Some of them may have qualified as "class enemies" while others not, but all were cleared of their class labels (EdB 2009: 318). The third restituted group included the monastic clergy, or members of the so-called former theocratic class. Some of the high lamas who owned land and serfs may have qualified as "class enemies," but not the low-level lamas. Again, all were restituted regardless of their former status.

In Xinjiang as well, rehabilitated individuals fell under all three categories, but distinctions were not made as to the real or false "class enemies." First and foremost were the Uighur participants in several armed riots in southern Xinjiang in the 1950s, organized by a local mullah in the name of jihads to establish an Islamic state. All were released from jail in the late 1970s and the early 1980.[1] The second group included the "exploitative classes" or landlords and rich peasants. All of them saw their labels revoked (Han 2015: 14). The third group included the Islamic clergy. All of them, too, were rehabilitated. Many were also given nominal government posts or administrative ranks upon

[1] There were four reported armed riots in Hotan during the 1950s. See Qi (2000: 43).

rehabilitation. Of these three groups, the first could be "class enemies" if defined by activities against the proletarian state. Members of the second and third groups could only have qualified as "class enemies" if defined in terms of property ownership.

In addition, there were groups of minority members in Xinjiang who definitely did not qualify as "class enemies." But they were so labeled for their perceived "separatist" sentiments. One group of individuals were labeled "local ethno-nationalists" during the Anti-Rightist Campaign of 1956, likely for raising the issue of autonomy rights: 94 percent of the individuals in this group, or 1,612 people, had their cases reversed.[2] A second group was associated with several cases of "treasonous cliques" and with "treasonous overseas flees" to the Soviet Union in the 1960s, all of whom were rehabilitated (Zhu 2004: 175–6). These individuals should not have qualified as "class enemies" even by official definitions in the Mao era, since the Soviet Union was a fellow proletarian state.

In other minority regions, rehabilitation involved some or all of the above groups of individuals, but significantly less accommodation than in the TAR and Xinjiang. Most importantly, leaders of armed rebellions in Ningxia and Qinghai were not relieved of their "class enemy" labels. These rebellions, dated to the 1950s, were suppressed for anti-regime resistance rather than separatism. The rebel leaders were associated with the Muslim warlord Ma Bufang, a strong ally of the KMT regime who ruled the northwestern regions before 1949 and had fled to Taiwan with the KMT. Despite renewed emphasis on united front outreach to Taiwan in early post-Mao China, not all of the armed rebels were rehabilitated in the two provinces. In Qinghai, only the lowly ranked KMT officers and officials were released from prison, that is those below the rank of the regiment level in the KMT army and its intelligence apparatus and those below the county magistrate level in the KMT party and state apparatus (Wang Y. 1998: 266). This means that rebel leaders remained classified as "class enemies." In Ningxia, reexamination of convicted cases – including those from eight rebellions during the period 1950–67 – began in 1967 and was largely completed by 1978. About 80 percent of the convictions were reversed, with 5,596 individuals rehabilitated.[3] The rest remained classified as "class enemies" in the post-Mao era.

Moreover, those rehabilitated in minority regions outside the TAR and Xinjiang did not collectively have a new political life. The armed rebels released in Ningxia and Qinghai were not given any united front treatment.

[2] Ninety-five of the 1,612 individuals had already left for the Soviet Union. See Zhu (2004: 175–6).

[3] The officially published reversal rate here was 81.9 percent but included wrongful cases from two separate types of crackdown. One was the 1960 campaign against individuals (mostly Han) who came to the frontier region to assist its development. The other was the campaign against eight minority rebellions during 1950–67. It is likely that the reversal rate for those convicted in the second type of crackdown was significantly lower. See Song (2015).

They mostly returned to their home villages, getting by with compensation accumulated from labor camps, welfare benefits for the rural poor, or meager income from collective communes. For the minority upper classes rehabilitated in Qinghai, Ningxia, Yunnan, Inner Mongolia, and Guangxi, some received united front treatment, but individually and collectively they did not have the political clout stemming from a combination of core ethnic regions and theocratic traditions, as existed in the TAR and Xinjiang.

In short, the end of class ideology in minority regions involved greater accommodation to the outer peripheral regions where political integration remained a contentious issue. Within these regions, political forces with potential threats to integration also received more accommodation. Thus, of the various groups of minority members rehabilitated – wrongful cases, exploitative classes, leaders of armed rebellions, and religious elites – the last two groups (leaders of ethnic causes) were given the most political accommodation. The corollary of ending class universalism, thus, was the rise of ethnic identity politics. A closer look at the specific process of this evolution in the TAR and Xinjiang will further illuminate the advent of identity politics sponsored by the state itself.

THE RISE OF IDENTITY POLITICS

For Beijing, the need to redress leftist wrongs was more acute in the TAR and Xinjiang than in other minority regions due to their unique characteristics. The least assimilated of all minority regions, they were the only ethnic regions to have experienced separatist rebellions and overseas flight during the socialist era. As such they evoked concerns about separatism in a way that other minority regions did not. In redressing the leftist excesses of the Mao era, reform policies began with not only the restoration of former ethnic elites but also reduction of Han presence and revival of ethnic conventions, all of which accommodated ethnic particularism while displacing class universalism.

Relegitimization of Former Elites

The restitution of former ethnic elites, above all, helped to transform class politics into identity politics, and to reconnect the ethnic lower classes to the former upper classes. This restitution was the foremost reform policy associated with the campaign to redress past wrongs in ethnic regions. In the TAR and Xinjiang, this "upper-class tilt," as it came to be known, contributed to changes in the composition of local elites by relegitimizing and reintegrating the former ethnic elites, politically and ideologically.

The TAR and Xinjiang, with entrenched traditional establishments, were at the forefront of the CCP's restitution campaign in the late 1970s and early 1980s. In March 1980, Hu Yaobang presided over the CCP Central Committee's First Work Conference on Tibet in post-Mao China. In July 1980, he presided over two conferences of the CCP Central Secretariat on Xinjiang. The minutes from these conferences were issued as central documents, the only ones of their kind (CCP 1980a and 1980b). These documents repudiated Mao's class conception of ethnic relations, called for restoring autonomy rights, and pledged to pull Han cadre out of the TAR and Xinjiang.

The combination of these new policies entailed serious consequences for the composition of local elites. In Tibet's case, the traditional aristocracy used to be castigated as the theocratic rulers of a serf-owning society. Numbering in a few hundred families, they had exclusive rights to own land and, along with top monks, to receive education. Some were also leaders in the armed rebellion against the Chinese state in 1959. With the rehabilitation of several thousand former elites in the early 1980s, even the dissident writer Wang Lixiong concedes that their prominent religious and socioeconomic status was restored. Monastic land was returned to them and other lost properties were generously compensated (Wang 2002).

In Xinjiang's case, former elites included the hereditary headmen, senior clergy, pastoral chieftains, and serf-owning nobles, who lost their stature and property during the social reform of the 1950s. Some were also leaders or participants in the armed rebellions against the state in the 1950s. Once condemned for excessive levies on poor farmers and herdsmen (Zeng 1936: 657–8, 630–8; Na La 2010: 147–57), they and their offspring were now targets of state restitution and wooing. Between 1979 and 1981, the convictions of 596 members of Xinjiang's old clergy were reexamined and 411 of the cases were overturned (Chen 2014: 11). Together, over 1,500 members of the old clergy have been rehabilitated in Xinjiang since 1979 (Tang 2014). In both the Tibetan and Uighur cases, restituted former elites received United Front treatment, and were placed in political consultative councils at local levels (nominal upper house legislatures), state religious associations, and governing bodies or restored religious institutions. The state also began to pay the clerics a stipend. In Xinjiang the number of clerics who received this stipend was over 3,000 in September 1979 and the amount totaled over ¥100 million annually (Dang and Zhang 2003: 181).

The corps of ethnic cadre nurtured by the CCP itself, meanwhile, comprised the main opponents to the rehabilitation of former ethnic elites. During Mao's socialist era, members of the lower classes were elevated as the masters of their own communities, displacing former ethnic and religious elites. Yet the rehabilitation of these elites castigated Maoist policies as "leftist," leaving the party's ethnic loyalists and activists on the defensive and alienated. The passage below, appearing in the flagship website of the Left, *Wu You Zhi Xiang* (Utopian), is a typical leftist critique of Hu's upper-class tilt at the expense of the party's lower class supporters:

> Hu Yaobang listened to the denunciations of the communist party by the old aristocracy and serf-owners. He granted them their wishes, extending united front policies to them.

He rehabilitated a large number of old aristocrats and serf-owners as well as 802 upper religious figures, released 376 rebels of the Lhasa rebellion who were still serving their sentences, and rehabilitated 600 individuals who were assigned to undergo supervised reformation. Their confiscated properties were returned. Large numbers of former class enemies were invited to serve in the people's congresses, government agencies, political consultation conferences and Buddhist associations at various levels. They were given high offices and salaries but only nominal work, and enjoyed various privileges and favors. By 1988, 2100 members of the old upper class were given government offices. Their offspring were sent to the Minzu University of China or Minzu University of Tibet to study, and assigned government offices upon graduation. The commander of the 1959 rebellion, Latso, spent six years in prison and went back to his home village to engage in farming. But Hu Yaobang invited him out to serve as a deputy chairman of the Political Consultative Conference of the TAR, and his wife to serve as a member of its standing committee, and his son to serve as the deputy head of the religious bureau of the TAR. The old aristocrat was once a ranking official under the Dalai Lama, who also became a deputy chairman of the Political Consultation Conference of the TAR. By contrast, the liberated serf class returned to hell, becoming disadvantaged groups in our society, no longer having guaranteed jobs or income and being reduced to hardship. The party's activists in the old days lost their stature, reduced to the impoverished strata. In this way, the activists who hailed from the lower classes and supported the party were abandoned, while the serf-owners marched back. These restored officials and lamas received financial allocations from the central government. If you were a Tibetan, would you feel grateful to Hu Yaobang? (*WYZX* 2009)[4]

Such sentiments appear to be prevalent in early post-Mao China. During the field trips of a Beijing University research team in 1987, a poignant sense of abandonment was observed everywhere among the party's grassroots Tibetan cadre. They complained mostly about the rehabilitation of the former serf-owners and religious aristocrats, or the very people who had oppressed them before the communist revolution. Some told stories of their family members who were sold off by their serf-owners and were lost forever, and this was why they wholeheartedly supported the Communist Party. They stood with the party during its takeover of Tibet and during the aristocrats' rebellion in 1959. Since then their life had turned around, finally having shelters and means of livelihood. However, the party used to love the serf class but now it loved the old upper class. The lamas used to be the parasitic class and now they were the valued guests of the state. The serf-turned Tibetan cadre, meanwhile, felt sidelined and became targets of local ridicule for having followed the Communist Party.[5] Meanwhile, some monasteries even restored "feudal privileges and economic exploitation" that were abolished during Mao's

[4] Critiques like this also appear on other Chinese websites, such as blogs at baidu.com, people.com, jinbushe.org, or weidb.com.

[5] Conversations with Ma Rong, leader of the research team, in Beijing, July 2011 and December 2013, and in Hangzhou, June 2018.

revolution. This refers to the reemergence of servitude to elite clergymen and monasteries.

From the Tibetan cadre's perspective, Hu Yaobang's reform campaign turned justice upside down. The old aristocrats were invited back and assigned prestigious state positions. Liberated serfs were now asked by the state to vacate their residences and return them to restored aristocrats. Moreover, the state compensated these elites with large sums of money for their confiscated properties, at whatever value they claimed. In one example, one aristocrat received over ¥10 million in compensation from the local government, but a week later he returned to assert that he had forgotten to list a necklace worth ¥1 million. He was instantly reimbursed. In 1994, or a decade after the height of the compensation period, the TAR government still spent ¥310,000 million on such compensation.[6] Such a campaign to "redress past wrongs" was incomprehensible to the Tibetan cadres who had been schooled in the party's paradigm of class struggle.

The social class perspective was common among local Tibetan cadre and professionals who were nurtured in the Mao era. Wang Lixiong, an unabashed dissident, makes similar observations about Tibetan bewilderment over the party's restitution policies in the 1980s. The liberated serfs, fearful of the restored clergy, compensated their fright and guilt for destroying monasteries during the Cultural Revolution with great devotion to the monasteries (Wang 2002: 106–7). In one example, a female Tibetan villager, who had actively participated in the land reform after 1959 and in the destruction of monasteries during the Cultural Revolution, turned overly devout under social pressure, pouring donations and time into monasteries in order to "redeem" her sins. When monastic protests broke out for the first time in Lhasa in 1987, local Tibetan cadre viewed the protests as a matter of social class conflict rather than ethnic conflict (Ma 2013a). This social class divide contrasts with outside analyses that view Tibetan monastic unrest as "Tibetan resistance" (Barnett 1994; Schwartz 1994).

In Xinjiang as well, the rehabilitation of former elites helped to advance their agendas rather than those of the former lower classes. At the suggestion of the restored former elites, Latin script for the Uighur language, which was created in the 1950s to facilitate the literacy of Uighur commoners and taught in public schools, was replaced in September 1982 at a standing committee meeting of the Xinjiang's National People's Congress (NPC). The Arabic script, previously used in mosques only, took its place (Ma 1984: 17). This shift instantly rendered illiterate the corps of Uighur professionals schooled during the Mao era, who came from families of lower classes that were the bedrock of the CCP's support base in the region. The rehabilitation of old elites also boosted the revival of religion, reconnecting local ethnic communities to their theocratic traditions

[6] Ibid. Ma has told of these field findings in some of his writings, speeches, and conversations, for example Ma (2013a).

and heralding the growth of religion in subsequent years. The process also legitimized former theocratic elites as ethnic leaders, with adverse effects for the CCP's own cadre who had risen from lower social classes.

The rehabilitation of former ethnic elites, furthermore, helped to reconnect them to the ethnic masses, through the play of identity politics. Once restored, former elites began to change the tone of public discourse among co-ethnics in the two ethnically concentrated regions, Tibet and Xinjiang. More educated than the lower classes with whom the CCP was aligned, the restored upper echelons appealed to ethnic solidarity along cultural and religious lines. In Xinjiang, they provided an alternative discourse about state presence in their homeland, such as "scrambling for resources" and "exploitation of natives." Co-ethnics who were activists in the Chinese political system and loyal to the central state were chastised, helped in part by the CCP's own censure of the leftist blunders of Han and ethnic officials.[7] In the TAR, ordinary Tibetans who had earlier shifted their loyalty from the monastery to the party were now told by the former ethnic elites that since the Han people no longer believed in their own things like Chairman Mao, Tibetans should no longer believe in Han things. Such rhetoric helped to undermine the authority of those Tibetan officials who had arisen from the serf class but were now forced to compete with the lamas for the allegiance of ordinary Tibetans.[8]

Supporters of Hu Yaobang justify the replacement of class politics with identity politics by citing the TAR's and Xinjiang's special circumstances. He Fang, a rehabilitated official himself from 1978 who headed a research institute at the Chinese Academy of Social Sciences in the 1980s, emphasizes the reality of theocratic legacies. Hu Yaobang was justified in having an upper-class tilt in the TAR, he argues, because "the upper classes and religious circles often have more influence over the local people." And without winning over the traditional upper classes, "it would not be possible to win over a broader spectrum of the minority people" (He 2009). The same rationale applied in the Uighurs' case in Xinjiang. Nevertheless, by the late 1980s, when monastic protests broke out in Tibetan regions and religious fundamentalism surged in Xinjiang, it was evident that Hu Yaobang's campaign to redress past wrongs had failed to gain new allies for the party, even while it weakened its support base among the lower classes.

The various reactions to the rehabilitation of former ethnic elites converged on one point: it replaced class politics with identity politics. The political and ideological abandonment of the lower classes has given former ethnic elites

[7] For example, observations along these lines were made by a veteran official of ethnic and religious affairs in the local government of Kashgar in the aftermath of the Urumqi riot of July 5, 2009, www.wyzxsx.com/Article/Class14/200907/92901.html. Accessed July 5, 2013. The link is no longer accessible to provide more details. WYZXSX (*Wu you zhi xiang sixiang*) is a website known for views that are nostalgic about the Mao era.

[8] In-depth conversations with a prominent Tibetan scholar and official, Chengdu and Beijing, summer 2011 and December 2013.

a major boost in legitimacy and strength, which was further bolstered by the departure of Han officials and professionals.

Changing Local Elite Composition

The Han exit policy, announced by Hu Yaobang at the end of his famed tour in the TAR in May 1980, further reinforced interethnic cleavages and intraethnic coalition. Convening all ranking party officials in the TAR on May 29, 1980, Hu summed up a six-word reform platform for the province: "relieve taxes, open up, and let depart" (Chen 1980; Cheng 2013). "Let depart" referred to the departure of Han personnel from the TAR. These personnel – administrators and professionals from interior regions – had been sent here during the Mao era for the cause of frontier development. Han exit would symbolize the end of an era.

From the perspective of the nation state, the Han exit policy helped to delegitimize central rule by blaming the wrongs of the Mao era on Han rule and on Han personnel who personified that rule. This was clear from the statement of Deng Yingchao, widow of Zhou Enlai, who visited Xinjiang around the same period of Hu's visit to the TAR. During her trip she offered an apology on behalf of the Han people for the excesses of the Cultural Revolution. Her statement instantly polarized the local ethnic and Han communities. While the former group welcomed it, the latter group criticized it for ethnicizing the causes of a tragedy that affected all of China. The effects of Hu Yaobang and Deng Yingchao's gestures in the TAR and Xinjiang was to render Han personnel responsible for the CCP's policy failures. The Han exit policy made them appear only more culpable, thus helping to weaken central rule physically and morally.

More importantly, Han exit embodied the demise of class universalism and ascendance of ethnic identity coalition. Class universalism had earlier buttressed the party's social class alliance with minority masses. But Han exit, along with the restoration of former ethnic elites, entailed a retreat of social class solidarity. Thus Deng Liqun, the senior party official in charge of ideological work at the time, criticized the upper-class tilt in Hu Yaobang's Han exit policy, on the grounds that it hurt the Tibetan lower classes while relegitimizing the old aristocracy. In Deng's view, the policy betrayed Hu Yaobang's naiveté about the separatist impulses of the Tibetan aristocracy and was responsible for breeding social instability in the TAR subsequently (Deng 2006: 313–14). Deng Liqun had served in Xinjiang in the initial years of the CCP's takeover (1949–52) and was the party's leading conservative voice in the 1980s.

The presence of Han personnel was deemed beneficial to the Tibetan lower classes because of their professional and developmental role. By Deng Liqun's account, Hu Yaobang offered two reasons for letting Han personnel leave the TAR. First, native administrators had matured in the past three decades and were now capable of running a modern society. Second, Han departure would reduce economic burdens for Beijing. Deng finds the second reason flawed. Hu Yaobang had learned during his Tibetan tour that 80 percent of the central state's annual allocation to Tibet was spent on Han personnel. This led Hu to decide that 80 percent of the Hans must leave. However, in Deng Liqun's view, Hu Yaobang misunderstood local usage of central funding. The disproportionate spending on Han personnel was justified, Deng argues, because Han professionals were needed to develop Tibet's modern public sectors (Deng 2006: 313, 314). In other words, the TAR's "backwardness" necessitated the presence of Han personnel.

Indeed, the Tibetan cadre nurtured by the party opposed the Han exit policy on social class grounds. Like Deng Liqun, they criticized Hu Yaobang's upper-class tilt in making the Han exit policy, because Hu held exclusive meetings with former Tibetan elites to come up with the decision and because Han exit would entail the ascendance of the former Tibetan elites (Ma 2013a). Rag sdi, who rose from the serf class and served as the party secretary of the TAR from 1977 to 1985, vehemently opposed the party's proposal to appoint the Panchen Lama to the top state office in the TAR.[9] To Tibetan cadre like him, such an appointment would symbolize the return of the formerly oppressive class.

For Han officials and residents, the worry was the political implications of changing ethnic composition for national integration. Their emphasis was on ethnic balance that may offset centrifugal forces and protect secular forces in traditionally religious communities. This was a poignant point that emerged in conversations with over a dozen Han professionals who departed the TAR or Xinjiang in the 1980s and in encounters with individuals in Xinjiang who have not been able to leave.[10] Those who have stayed behind, in particular, lament the departure of Han personnel that served to weaken centripetal forces as well as the quality of public and professional services. During field trips in Hotan, southern Xinjiang, one of the first things heard from older Han officials was the decrease of the local Han population from 8 percent before the Han exit policy to just 3 percent, which was deemed too small to counterbalance the rise of religious radicalism.[11] Among those lucky enough to have left the TAR or Xinjiang, almost all lament having sacrificed their youth for the development of the austere regions, even while they insist that state interests should take precedence.

In Xinjiang's case, the geopolitical location made a massive Han exit highly sensitive. By Deng Liqun's account (2008), Xinjiang's party chief at the time,

[9] Conversation with Ma Rong, Zhejiang University, June 2018.

[10] The returnees included four college professors, six members of Xinjiang's production corps, and four former officials; conversations in summers 2011, 2013, and 2015. Those whom I have encountered at academic conferences and informal gatherings in China are too numerous to count.

[11] For example, conversations with an official of a local SEAC branch in Hotan, fall 2013.

Wang Feng, was worried about the security implications of a Han exodus for the Ili frontier, bordering the Soviet Union. In 1962, over 67,000 border residents in the region fled to the Soviet Union, joined later by over forty ethnic officers from the Chinese army (Chen and Sun 2011). Unlike in the TAR's case, the ethnic cadre in Xinjiang supported the Han exit policy. Hence Wang Feng's misgivings about Han exit upset those Han personnel eager to leave as well as those Uighur officials anxious to take things over. The bickering parties could no longer hold a meeting of Xinjiang's provincial party committee in peace. When representatives of the two groups were called to convene in Beijing, Hu Yaobang sided with the ethnic officials, to the frustration of the Han representatives.

To their greater frustration, Hu introduced a proposal for "high autonomy" that privileged ethnic prerogatives. Under this new autonomy, the central state would retain power in just three areas: defense, diplomacy, and a veto power over the region's internal policy. These ideas came to be officially decreed as the CCP's Document 46 of 1980 (He 2009). If implemented, this proposal would have created a "one country, two systems" model almost two decades before Hong Kong's in 1997. This proposal should fully qualify Hu Yaobang as a liberal autonomist. However, his negation of Han contribution to Xinjiang's development further polarized the Han and Uighur officials. Only at the intervention of Premier Zhao Zhiyang, who asked Deng Liqun to wire a cable affirming Han personnel's contribution to the development of Xinjiang, was the delicate relationship among the local multiethnic cadre restored to some sort of balance (Deng 2008). Such developments reinforced the ethnicizing effects of the Han exit policy, or the replacement of class politics with identity politics. If the inflow of Han personnel during the Mao era was justified by the interethnic goals of nation building and proletarian solidarity, the Han exit policy entailed ethnic dissociation, particularly when the Han displacement was coupled with the restoration of former ethnic elites. Whereas Mao's tenet of class struggle transcended ethnic divisions, the Han exit policy helped to heighten awareness about "Han rule" by making a distinction between outsiders and locals.

Indeed, after Xinjiang's provincial party committee held meetings of provincial and local leaders in August 1980 to implement the Han exit policy, Han cadre's reputation suffered and tensions between ethnic and Han cadre increased. The implementation, aimed at pulling Han cadre out of the rural south where the Uighurs were concentrated, made Han cadre look like problems rather than their self-identities as developers (Han 2015: 16). Although a majority of Uighur cadre supported the Han exit policy, a few did write to the CCP's Central Committee to express their concerns and opposition. Thereafter Wang Zhen, the notoriously tough leader in Xinjiang in the early 1950s, was dispatched to investigate the situation. His advice helped to stop the mandatory exit but failed to sooth the Han cadre. Emotionally hurt by official abandonment, they were eager to leave Xinjiang and return to interior provinces.

Defenders of the Han exit policy support Hu Yaobang's privileging of ethnic prerogatives. They insist that changes in local elite composition were not politically destabilizing. Hu's supporters are found among his former associates (Chen 1980; Cheng 2013), liberal-minded intellectuals such as Zhang Haiyang of the Minzu University of China and minority officials such as Wu Jinghua, a Yi ethnic who held the top party post in Tibet from 1985 to 1988. Wu defends Hu's so-called upper-class tilt, arguing that redressing the wrongs of the past was the right thing to do in itself. As for Hu's alleged naiveté about separatism, Wu argues that Hu's promotion of economic development offered the best measure against separatism. Hu only wanted the non-essential Han personnel to depart but the People's Liberation Army to stay, Wu argues, so Han exit was not as destabilizing as Hu's critics would suggest. Fiscally, Wu insists, Han departure was well justified given the TAR's economic difficulties at the time. In response to Deng Liqun's criticism of Hu's personal and idiosyncratic input in the Han exit policy, Wu Jinghua emphasizes the "instructions from both the central party and Hu Yaobang" (Cheng 2013). Evidence suggests that Hu did have the party's sanction to initiate reforms in the TAR, though not necessarily their exact contours. During his trip to the TAR in May of 1980, Hu Yaobang brought along the party's Document 31, which contained reform proposals.

The Han exit policy prevailed in the end, thanks to the eagerness of the Han personnel to leave and that of the party to reverse the policies of the Mao era. The outflow of Han personnel exploded from frontier regions, especially the TAR and Xinjiang. Between 1980 and 1985, about 50,000 (42 percent) of the Han professionals left the TAR, according to Wang Lixiong (2002: 104). Data from Chinese scholars also suggest a large exodus from Xinjiang. In 1981 alone, over 8,000 Han cadre left, half of them professional and technical personnel (Han 2015: 16). Between 1981 and 1990, over 200,000 Han individuals left Xinjiang's PCCs for interior provinces, and many from outside the PCCs also left (Liu 2007: 112). Earlier, the temporary elimination of the PCCs in 1975 had already sent 572,400 members out of Xinjiang during 1975–6 (Liu and Wang 2008: 99). However, the Han exit policy, like Hu's proposal for high autonomy, did not have a plan for execution. Although nearly half of those who left the TAR were reassigned to interior provinces by the central government (Cheng 2013), others received little help. Those who managed to leave had relatives who could help them find new homes and jobs. Those without resourceful ties remained behind. Like many urban youths who were sent down during the Cultural Revolution, they fought long and hard to be resettled in their native hometowns.

For local ethnic communities, the benefits and costs of Han exit varied in accordance with one's emphasis on identity or class politics. For those who value identity politics, Han exit entailed ethnic dividends, or more opportunities for the party's local ethnic cadre. Zhang Haiyang, an outspoken liberal-minded scholar at the Central Minzu University, cites the Han exit as an indication of the party's political trust in minority officials.[12] Wu Jinghua, the party head of the TAR in the 1980s, lauds the increases in the ethnic composition of local official ranks. In Tibet's case, by the end of 1989 ethnic cadre comprised 72 percent of all officials at the provincial level, 68.1 percent at the prefectural level, and 61.2 percent at the county level. Of these, notably, many Tibetans held leading positions, serving as the party secretary in six of the seven party committees at the prefectural/municipal levels, and sixty-three of the seventy-five party secretaries at the county levels (Cheng 2013). These were major improvements in less than a decade.

For those who value class politics, the departure of Han officials and professionals benefited ethnic cadre and former ethnic elites at the expense of the lower strata of local minorities. During the Mao era, ideological and political incentives induced many professionals from interior provinces – administrators, teachers, doctors, educators, and technical personnel – to work in remote minority regions, especially Tibetan regions and Xinjiang. Regardless of the state's intentions, the personal sacrifices of those individuals made it possible to set up government services, public schools, hospitals, and other modern sectors in the largely agrarian or pastoral societies. Improvements in the well-being of poor minority communities were marked in the areas of socioeconomic equality, education, and healthcare, earning the CCP loyalty among the lower classes in ethnic regions.

The emigration of those professionals has substantially disadvantaged the same lower classes, at least in the short term. As long-term and experienced professionals moved out, schools deteriorated, medical care lapsed, and the quality of public services suffered. Wang Lixiong, no friend of state minority policies, frankly notes such damaging effects of the Han exit policy in Tibetan regions (2002: 104). Rigzin Losel, a prominent Tibetan historian and party official, gave a similar assessment. In ethnic counties where even remote villages had Han doctors from major interior cities during the Mao era, he relates, few college graduates could be found in subsequent years. Despite expanded education for local youths, most would choose to stay in urban areas.[13] Most of all, poor ethnic regions lost generations of professionals who came with idealism and dedication. With expectations of long-term stay, they respected local ethnic customs, learned ethnic languages, and mingled with ethnic colleagues and neighbors.[14] Their personal sacrifices, Losel writes, helped to personify the CCP's proletarian solidarity with the poor and to undercut ethnic

[12] Conversations with Zhang at the Minzu University of China, December 2012.

[13] Conversations in Beijing, fall 2013.

[14] Almost all of the Han professionals I encountered in southern Xinjiang who came during the 1950s and 1960s and who worked in the public sector (excluding PCCs) could speak Uighur, as was the case with their offspring if they were raised during the Mao era.

differences (Losel 2011b: 25, 26). Losel himself hailed from a remote mountain in Garzê and personally benefited from Han teachers who came to teach in rural public schools. Most importantly, the rise of the former ethnic elites competed with the party's ethnic cadre for the allegiance of local ethnic masses.

By exiting the Han personnel and restoring former ethnic elites, in short, changes in the composition of local elites helped to undermine the physical and ideological links between the CCP and local ethnic communities. Nevertheless, these policy changes did not alter the relationship between the central state and the autonomous region. Party dictates were simply formulated in small circles and delivered from the top down. Not surprisingly, the changes in local elite composition did not constitute or contribute to genuine autonomy.

Revival of Religion

Revival of religion, sponsored by the state itself, also served to demarcate interethnic cleavages and consolidate intraethnic cohesion. Compared with the Mao era, the post-Mao state has involved itself in minority religions extensively, in terms of both promoting it in directions it deems desirable and controlling directions it deems undesirable. This has especially been the case in the two outer peripheral regions, where religion looms large as the core of local cultural traditions and identities.

Under Mao, the party's strong ideological orientation contained the religious one. The Marxist view of religion as the opium of the people cast a negative light on religiosity. The overthrow of religious elites as part of the old exploitative class resonated at least partly with members of the lower classes who were eager to shed old social hierarchies. The number of mosques and monasteries decreased significantly, and religion was officially discouraged, although Muslims and Buddhists could observe religious practices in private. Only during the Cultural Revolution was religion formally banned and most places of worship closed for being one of the "Four Old Conventions." In fact, when ethnic scholars censure the "left excesses" of the Cultural Revolution, they condemn the destruction of the party's *correct* policy on religion in the earlier period (Chopel 2005; Ha 2009).

Between the late 1970s and the early 1980s, the central party – under Hu Yaobang's leadership – issued a series of decrees to facilitate religious revival in minority regions. As shown in Table 4.1, the first two documents resulted from two Ministry of the United Front conferences in 1979 to redress leftist wrongs in religious policy. Both emphasized the imperative of uniting "the masses of the faithful and the clergy" in the post-Mao era. The third document, dated to the party conference on Tibet in March 1980, declared an end to the party's class approach to religion. Equating "ethnic issues" with "class issues" was wrong, it stated, as were Mao's words that "ethnic struggles are in essence class struggles" (CCP 1982: 479). In their stead, the document emphasized "interethnic unity" and respect for the "normal religious life" of the devout masses. It also made specific mention of giving Tibetan lamas proper treatment as well as protecting and renovating monasteries.

Finally, the party's Document 19 of 1982 lay down the principles and policies for religion in the post-Mao era. These had to be formally stipulated because the previous central decrees to promote religious revival had met with resistance among local cadre. The drafting of the document was chaired directly by Hu Yaobang and carried out by the secretariat under his wing. The document promulgated three key tenets: abandoning the idea of the "class origins of religion," consolidating and expanding the party's "political alliances in the religious front," and winning over the cleric personnel as the primary objective of official religious policy (Duan 2012). The idea of "freedom of religion" was also codified into the Chinese Constitution adopted later in the year on December 4, 1982.

Official policy paid special attention to religious revival in Tibetan areas and Xinjiang, two regions where religion constituted core civilizational identities. Apart from its work conference on the TAR in 1980, the CCP also held a conference on religious matters for Yunnan in February 1981 (where a Tibetan prefecture exists) and one for Xinjiang in July,1981. Earlier, following the CCP's central decrees from 1979 and 1980, Xinjiang had adopted its own local decrees to restore religious activities (Table 4.2). By early 1981, however, some initial signs of "religious fervor" alerted authorities, such as the rise of religious intervention in local politics, law enforcement, and education (Gong 2003: 21). The tone from the CCP conference on Xinjiang, however, was less stringent. It urged continuing the policy of freedom of religion, as long as religious forces did not intervene in politics and education.

In the late 1970s and the early 1980s, places of worship were allowed to reopen, mushrooming faster than public schools in the TAR and Xinjiang and soon exceeded them. Tibetan monasteries, which were enthusiastically destroyed by members of the former serf class during the Cultural Revolution, were restored and new ones constructed with public funding. The state spent over ¥300 million to renovate major Tibetan monasteries in the 1980s and the 1990s, during the height of state support for religious revival. This was followed by ¥44 million in 2001 from the central state and sixteen provinces, and ¥330 million during 2001–5 from the central state for the renovation of major monasteries (Wang and Dong 2011: 175). The number of Tibetan monasteries exceeded 3,000 by the late 1990s, for a population of over five million Tibetans at the time (State Council of the PRC 1999). This number has now increased to over 3,600 monasteries for the six million Tibetans in the TAR and surrounding provinces.[15] Over the years the state has continued to allocate funding for monastic renovations in Tibetan regions, despite increasing control over monastic activities.

[15] This number was provided by a Tibetan official in the CCP's United Front Department.

TABLE 4.2 *Xinjiang's decrees to promote religious revival: early post-Mao China*

Date/agency	Title of document	Key contents
March 13, 1979 XUAR/MUF Party Com.	"Seriously and completely implement the party's religious policy and strengthen administration of religious activities"	To shift the party's religious work to serving unity and stability
September 20, 1979 XUAR Party Com.	"Notification on speedily resolving the problem of places of worship"	To speedily reopen places of worship that had been closed
September 8, 1980 XUAR Party Com.	"Request to provide living expenses to patriotic personnel"	To provide income for over 3,000 "patriotic clergymen" who had no fixed income

Source: Shi (2012): 87–8.

In Xinjiang as well, places of worship grew greater in number in per capita terms at the sanction of the state. Those damaged during the Cultural Revolution were restored and new ones proliferated at state expense. Mosques increased from 2,000 in 1979 to 12,000 after restoration in the early 1980s and to 24,800 in 2008, while the Islamic clergy grew from over 3,000 individuals to 290,000 from 1979 to 2008 (State Council of the PRC 2009a). In Hotan, the southernmost prefecture of Xinjiang with the highest concentration of Uighurs (96.3 percent in the 2010 census), 90 percent of its two million residents were practicing Muslims in 2009, with over 4,000 mosques, or about one mosque for every 400 believers (Liu 2009a: 55). In Kashgar, the westernmost prefecture of Xinjiang with the second highest concentration of Uighurs (90.97 percent in 1998),[16] there were over 9,600 mosques in 1996, or one for over 300 believers (Zhang X. 2009). The high ratio of mosques in Xinjiang's rural Uighur areas, cited as four per village (Min 2014), has become a contentious issue in recent years (see Chapter 6).

Politically and intellectually the revival of religion was boosted by the restoration of the former clergy. In the Tibetan case, hundreds of religious elites were given special "United Front" treatment after their rehabilitation since the late 1970s and early 1980s, and placed in local people's congresses, state agencies, and Buddhist associations (Chopel 2005). By Wang Lixiong's account, the number of Tibetan monks and nuns increased to 46,000 by 1994, or 2 percent of the Tibetan population at the time (2002). Those who were associated with major monasteries began (and continue) to receive a salary from the government, along with fringe benefits and professional ranks. In Xinjiang's

[16] The data are from *Xingzheng huaqu wang*, "Keshi diqu lishi yange" [Historical evolution of Kashgar Prefecture]. November 14, 2014. www.xzqh.org/html/show/xj/21340.html.

case, thousands of former religious elites were restituted with similar treatment from the state (Tang 2014). In subsequent years, Xinjiang's "patriotic clergy" have received income subsidies, with ever-increasing rates and coverage to placate them as well as to ensure their compliance (Li 2013c).

The period of state sponsorship – from the late 1970s to the mid-1980s – also helped to reconnect the local communities to their theocratic traditions, heralding the growth of religion in directions undesired by the state. In Tibetan regions, religious practices were soon revived to a level comparable to pre-1959 days, barring only the restoration of the former monastic economy and theocracy. The few remaining restrictions on religious practices applied mainly to clerical organizations, as Wang Lixiong writes, and even these were largely nominal; and there was little interference in the religious practices of the laity (2002). Contact with the clergy and the Dalai Lama's Tibetan government-in-exile in India are formally banned but informally carried out (Shakya 2008b). Delegations were welcomed into Tibetan regions and given tours at the escort of various state agencies. Religious masters were welcomed back to help with religious revival and reconstruction, or to give lectures. Resettlement offices were set up to welcome Tibetan exiles who wanted to return.[17] In Xinjiang as well, foreign religious delegations were welcomed in the spirit of "reform and opening," to help with religious restoration, including funding and lecturing. Foreign religious organizations, mainly from Saudi Arabia, provided more than $3 million to build 3,000 mosques (Wang Z. 2003: 271). These developments would later be blamed for the infiltration of "Wahhabi" influences.

Whether and how much the state sponsorship of religious revival helped to enhance identity politics remains a matter of contention in contemporary China. Critics of state policy contend that the state-engineered revival played a legitimizing and enabling role, strengthened religious forces, undermined modernizing or secular forces, and facilitated the spread of religious extremism in the long run. Most prominent among such critics is Zhu Weiqun, former deputy head of the CCP's United Front Department who now heads the Committee on Ethnic and Religious Affairs in China's nominal upper house. Zhu blames the rise of religious fundamentalism and radicalism, in part, on the excessive encouragement of mosques by the state in the early reform era (Wang 2013). This is a common perspective in Chinese scholarly and policy circles, which view the proliferation of mosques as a key factor in spreading and strengthening religious influence and identities.

Defenders of Hu Yaobang disagree that the state has overplayed its hand. Tibetan scholars justify the large number of monasteries on the grounds that the inhospitable plateaus make it difficult for believers to travel afar for worship.[18]

[17] Conversations with two county-level Tibetan officials in charge of United Front Affairs, Ngawa, summer 2015.

[18] Conversations with two Tibetan researchers in Chengdu, summer 2015, and two researchers of the China Tibetology Center in Beijing, January 2018.

For this reason the presence of a monastery tends to coincide with a natural village on the plateau. For Xinjiang, Min Yuan – an alias for Hu Yaobang's son Hu Deping – argues that the per capita rate of mosques for the local Muslim population is comparable to the rates for Muslim communities in Ningxia and Gansu, or about one mosque for every 550 believers. Moreover, he argues, the number of natural villages in Xinjiang is greater than the number of administrative villages so that the actual number of mosques for natural villages is reasonable, or about one per natural village (Min 2014). Bovingdon concurs, arguing that the current number of mosques in Xinjiang has merely returned to historical levels, which stood at over 20,000 in 1950. Moreover, the Uighur population grew dramatically in the same period, so that number of mosques per capita was still far below historical levels. In addition, because different mosques have different functions, the total number of mosques is not excessive.[19]

Nevertheless, the ethnicizing effects of the growth of places of worship are readily observed. As Rudelson notes, a majority of Uighur intellectuals consider China's liberalization of religious policy to be "detrimental to the future of Uighur people," as the resurgence of Islam would cause the Uighur peasantry to retreat into cultural isolation and religious fervor – or what Uighur peasantry view as tradition (1997: 121, 122). Tursun, a Uighur researcher formerly at the Xinjiang Academy of Social Sciences, writes that by 1989 the number of mosques in Xinjiang exceeded any country in the Middle East, and this has had a "major impact" on the evolution of Uighur–Han relations in subsequent years (2013: 38). That is, the growth of mosques contributed symbolically and physically to the distancing of the two groups as different communities, or the religious versus the secular.

Indeed, Han analysts worry about the crowding out of the secular by the religious. One reason is the numeric dominance of mosques over secular schools of public education: the total number of mosques in Xinjiang is 5.3 times the total number of schools and colleges in the province, namely over 24,000 mosques versus less than 5,000 schools and colleges. Another is the much higher ratio of mosques to Muslim populations in Xinjiang than in the Middle East, namely one mosque for every 500 Muslims in Xinjiang compared with an average rate of one mosque for every 1,200 Muslims in the Middle East, every 2,500 in Egypt, and every 11,000 in Iran. Within Xinjiang, the number of mosques also exceeds that of natural villages: the total of 8,921 natural villages have an average of 2.7 mosques per village.[20]

At the very least, the state-sponsored revival of religion helped to reverse the secular trends nurtured in the socialist era. Over time the state would prove to

[19] Electronic communications, February 23 and June 19, 2014.

[20] There are many Chinese analyses to this effect. A representative one is Tang (2014), a local Xinjiang scholar.

be incapable of curtailing the direction of religious revival in Xinjiang or the TAR, where religion entails both cultural practices and identities.

Legal Accommodation

The policy of dual legal standards, instituted in 1984, was another reform measure that helped to end class universalism and enhance identity politics. It was designed to allow ethnic customs in law enforcement matters, thus relieving minority communities from standards of national law enforcement. During the socialist era, ethnic customs in penal matters were regarded as instruments of the upper classes to oppress the lower classes. But the end of class politics relegitimated old ethnic customs.

The policy of dual legal standards was stipulated in a central decree known as the CCP Document 5 of 1984. It was issued as a central opinion on the "tough crackdown" (*yanda*) of 1983, a campaign against crimes that had been rising since the onset of the reform era in the late 1970s. During the first phase of the crackdown, from late 1983 to early 1984, most arrests involved homicide, arson, robbery, rape, and indecency, resulting in the arrest of 1.027 million individuals, convictions for 860,000 individuals, and capital punishments for 24,000 individuals (Cheng 2014c). In the second phase, Document 5 instructed, a policy of "less arrest and less death sentence" should be applied to three categories of offenders: members of "minority groups, democratic parties and religious circles." The policy has been blamed on Hu Yaobang by his leftist critics.[21]

The new policy, moreover, was aimed at tailoring the country's new criminal law to the customs of minority regions. The national criminal law, the first of its kind in the PRC, was adopted in 1979 as part of post-Mao efforts to correct the arbitrary rule of the Mao era and to institutionalize criminal codes. During the crackdown campaign of 1983–4, conflicts between national criminal codes and local ethnic conventions were manifest. For example, rape, rape of juveniles, and indecent assaults were criminal under the national law and subject to capital punishment, but they were not considered criminal in Tibetan, Mongol, and Tu customs, where the victim would be at fault. If perpetrators were punished according to the national law, local communities would blame the victims for bringing down the perpetrators. Polygamy and polyandry were criminal under the national law, but still existed as local practices in some Tibetan, Tu, and Hui communities (Xia 2001). In such instances, applying the national criminal law to the letter would run counter to local ethnic customs.

Dispute settlement also works differently in some minority traditions, further requiring the national criminal law to compromise. Communal disputes and violence over resources, such as water, grazing land and territorial boundaries, had historically plagued ethnic communities. Physical brawls among Tibetan

[21] Cheng (2014c) is a rebuttal of the leading leftist critics on the issue, Sima Nan and Xian Yan.

herdsmen, often with knives and firearms, frequently resulted in injuries or deaths, yet victims preferred communal ways of settlement, such as reparations in livestock or cash payments.[22] (Carrying knives and firearms remain legal for pastoral communities.) If such compensations were paid for the "price of blood" (*xuejia*) or "price of life" (*minjia*), victims would not want to seek legal punishment. Local communities objected to law enforcement in such instances, viewing it as a violation of their customs. Even if punishments were issued by state courts, they could be ineffective, as the victims' side would still seek conventional ways of justice such as "blood revenge" (*xueqing fuchou*) and "divine judgment" (*shen pan*). With the rise of household farming and pastoral grazing in the reform era, communal disputes over resources have intensified.

The application of the national criminal law was thus to be tempered in minority regions. After Document 5 of 1984 proclaiming dual legal standards, the CCP followed with Document 6 of 1984 to highlight their application to minority regions. It instructed that "a policy of less arrest and less death penalty must be upheld for minority offenders" and that "minority convicts should receive more lax punishment. ... Law enforcement should be especially cautious in Tibetan regions" (Hu and Cheng 2016: 82). These decrees came to be summed as the policy of "two less and one lax" (*liangshao yikuan*), becoming a general practice to accommodate ethnic customs that do not regard offenses defined as criminal in the Chinese national law (Wu D. 2005; Sakhon 2010: 109) or do not regard punishments decreed by Chinese law as effective. Xiao Yang, writing as China's minister of justice in 1996, confirms that after the tough crackdown of 1983, law enforcement agencies in minority regions have maintained the dual legal standards, and have come up with specific ways to implement them in accordance with local conditions in different minority regions (Xiao 1996: 262, 263).

Further boosting identity politics, the dual legal standards became ethnic prerogatives not only in *intraethnic* criminal cases but more importantly in *interethnic* ones. As originally intended, the dual standards were aimed at transgressions within the same ethnic groups, not those among different ethnic groups. But the distinction was often neglected in practice during the heyday of its application from the mid-1980s to the late 2000s. Law enforcement officers in outer peripheral regions, in particular, were wary of touching off disputes so they preferred to err on the safe side by treating minority offenders leniently regardless of the ethnicity of their victims. Over time double standards of justice became de facto practices in these regions.

[22] Conversations with three Tibetan officials and scholars from western Sichuan, summers 2015 and 2017. See also blog discussion at "Liangshao yikuan: ta daodi shi shenmo?" [Two less and one lax: what is it really about]. Undated, http://blog.renren.com/share/402385140/17103736159/1. Accessed June 6, 2017.

The dual legal standards mattered more in Tibetan and Uighur regions because of local ethnic majorities and language factors. Local majorities entailed the prevalence of local customs and a relative weakness of national law. They also entailed a greater ethnic presence in law enforcement ranks. For cultural and linguistic reasons, minority officers usually handled offenders of the same ethnicity, and vice versa for Han offenders. Thus for the same crime a minority offender may receive drastically milder punishment than a Han offender, for example the death sentence for a Han convicted of murder but a ten-year sentence for an ethnic offender convicted of the same crime. Han residents in Xinjiang frequently complained about this disparity in private conversations.[23] The Uighur scholar Tursun concedes that Uighurs "prevailed" over Han residents in the 1980s (2013). The political atmosphere began to change after the violence of Baren village in April 1990, officially called the first terrorist act in Xinjiang, during which local police was unable to fire at violent attackers without official authorization.

In another legacy that enhances identity politics, dual legal standards have helped to nurture – at least in public perception – an attitude of being "above the law" among those who have become used to legal laxity. Guan Kai, a Manchu scholar at the Central Minzu University, writes that he has seen "individuals with distinct minority appearances" refusing to pay bus fares on the claim that they were "minorities" (2007: 303). Yao Xinyong, a Xinjiang-born Han scholar, recalls that Han residents often attributed common crimes on Xinjiang's streets to disparate justice, which fostered a sense of lawlessness among some native youths (2012). In interior provinces, "Xinjiang criminal groups" became urban legends in the reform era, but law enforcement agencies were often at a loss as to how to handle them. Until recent years, they usually released them after some verbal scolding, thus allowing offenders to return to their gang groups and activities. Meanwhile, innocent Uighurs suffer from the stereotyping of Uighurs as potential criminals (and in recent years, as terrorists). Even for top Uighur students selected to study in high schools in interior provinces, they endure routine discrimination, and easily taken as members of criminal gangs and harassed by security guards or pedestrians (Huang 2011). Even before the current climate of counter-terrorism, Uighur college graduates complained about being shunned by potential employers, who viewed them as above the law and difficult to manage.[24]

Over time, loose enforcement of law and a propensity for law breaking feed one another. This became a particular problem in the reform era when

[23] Conversation with one former police officer, one current police officer, and eight long-time residents from Hotan, Xinjiang, fall 2013 in Hotan and summers 2015 and 2017 in Chongqing. One cousin of this author, a migrant in Hotan, received a long sentence for taking part in a brawl that resulted in a death.

[24] Conversations with seven Uighur students on a college campus in Kashgar, southern Xinjiang, summer 2011.

interethnic interactions grow more common, due to two-way migration in the market economy. Some Uighur migrants, as one Uighur scholar concedes, have done "unlawful" things in interior cities, from theft, scuffles, and public disturbances to robbery, abduction, and drug trafficking (Tulak 2013: 12–14). Such transgressions may be blamed on a lack of social constraints or legitimate job opportunities in new urban settings. But they create an image of "troublemakers" in the minds of local Han residents, rendering it harder for Uighur migrants to rent housing, check into hotels, hail taxis, or seek services from employment agencies (Tulak 2013: 14).[25] Likewise, Yi and Tibetan migrants also suffer from a somewhat negative reputation in Chengdu, the urban metropolis closet to Tibetan and Yi regions, for petty crimes and car theft. One county in Ngawa prefecture of Sichuan province has even become known as the local capital of "second-hand cars," for selling stolen cars from Chengdu.[26] In all of the above cases, local police may be handicapped by a lack of language or dietary accommodation and wariness about touching off sensitive issues, resulting in a cycle of lax law enforcement and law breaking.

Such laxity can also spill over to other areas of law enforcement, becoming a wider ethnic prerogative. Corruption among ethnic officials is no less serious than among Han officials, based on local conversations and encounters as well as offenses exposed through Xi Jinping's anti-corruption campaign from late 2012. Yet it was seldom prosecuted in sensitive ethnic regions, thanks to state reluctance to prosecute intraethnic offenses. In Tibetan regions, the sustained supply of generous state aid has provided ample opportunities for misuse and embezzlement of state funds, so that state benefits do not always reach the bottom in full. Because ethnic officials usually serve at the grassroots levels in Tibetan regions, offenders would also be more likely to be Tibetan officials.[27] In Xinjiang as well, government policies may be generous but specific benefits did not always arrive or arrive fully for ethnic residents. In rural areas these may range from rural subsidies to compensation for resettlement. In urban areas, some local residents attributed conflicts over the demolishing of old Uighur towns to the corruption of ethnic officials, who allegedly undercompensated former residents by personally pocketing state funds. Because they spoke the ethnic tongue, more ethnic officials were involved in persuading former residents to relocate and in negotiating compensation deals. Until Xi Jinping's anti-graft campaign, local authorities adopted an ambivalent attitude toward

[25] Also conversations with six Uighur farmers who had been migrants in interior cities; southern Xinjiang, October 2013 and Suzhou, summers 2015 and 2018.

[26] Conversations with two scholars of Sichuan University, one Han and one Tibetan, summer 2017.

[27] See typical examples of Tibetan cadre's corruption, exposed during Xi Jinping's anti-graft campaign: "Xizang tongbao siqi fupin lingyu fubai he zuofeng wenti dianxing anli" [Xizang announces four typical cases of corruption and transgression in the area of anti-poverty]. *People's Daily*, October 16, 2018. http://fanfu.people.com.cn/n1/2018/1016/c64371-30343039.html.

corruption. The wrongdoings of ethnic officials may be overlooked to avoid outcries about discrimination, although corruption of Han officials may also be downplayed to avoid associating corruption with Han Chinese rule.

Paradoxically, as an ethnic prerogative, dual legal standards may induce both positive and negative discrimination. As the country's political climate has moved away from accommodation to vigilance in recent years, dual legal standards increasingly entail negative discrimination. During the Beijing Olympics in 2008, Uighur and Tibetan migrants were asked to leave the city to avoid potential troublemaking, while other migrant workers and minority groups were not singled out. In Chengdu, which is a popular destination for Tibetans from western Sichuan, some taxi companies instructed their drivers not to take Tibetan riders during the Beijing Olympics. Taxi drivers on their own may sometimes refuse to take Tibetan riders, citing the long knives carried by them, a Tibetan custom allowed by the state. Despite state decrees to ban local discriminatory practices, there are few enforcement mechanisms. A senior Tibetan official in the CCP's United Front Department, himself responsible for crafting those bans, has sometimes had a hard time with airport security personnel due to the ethnicity on his ID card.[28] Even before the enforcement of extreme security measures in Xinjiang since late 2016, Uighurs in Xinjiang had to go through complex and lengthy processes to apply for passports. Designed to curb local Muslims from joining extremist activities overseas, the policy evokes much resentment for treating Uighurs differently.

With the rise of ethnic violence since the 1990s, especially after the Urumqi riots of 2009, the negative effects of dual legal standards are increasingly recognized. By encouraging lawlessness among some minority youths, legal disparity helps to damage group reputation, especially among the Uighurs (Lin 2009; Zhang L. 2010: 99). By inciting public resentment over double standards, the policy helps to damage interethnic trust. By preventing police from responding to rioters in a timely manner, during numerous violent episodes in Xinjiang, the policy helped to cause an undue amount of civilian deaths. As a legal principle, dual legal standards also lack procedural legitimacy, since they came from the party rather than the national legislature. As such, they were political dictates that may go from one extreme to the other when political imperatives require. Even defenders of the policy concede that it was obsolete. Cheng Min, editor of the Hu Yaobang Archives website[29] and a strong defender of Hu, admits that the decree was appropriate in the early post-Mao period when minority crimes were largely intraethnic and rarely occurred outside minority regions (2014a). The free flow of population since market reforms has made interethnic interactions more common, hence the inequity of dual legal standards in adjudicating crimes involving different ethnic groups.

[28] Conversations with the official, Beijing, fall 2013.
[29] www.hybsl.cn/.

Moderate changes came a year after the Urumqi riots of 2009, but the ethnic prerogative lingers overall. A year after the riot, three agencies of the CCP Central Committee and the State Council issued a joint opinion, calling for the "rule of law" in dealing with all offenders regardless of ethnicity.[30] But the document makes just one mention of "equality of everyone before law," while its overall emphasis is on "ethnic harmony." This emphasis is unsurprising, since some minority conventions, especially communal settlement of disputes and offenses, have been revived in the reform era. Moreover, as an advisory opinion from three agencies unrelated to law enforcement, the idea of "equality before law" has little meaning in reality. Indeed, in the state's ongoing war on terrorism, it is now the Uighurs who complain about double legal standards, from severe security measures to strict religious bans. In a street brawl between a Uighur and Han on Xinjiang streets, it is now the Uighurs who are likely to get into trouble regardless of the nature of the dispute, in contrast to police reactions before the anti-terror climate.[31] Such political swings say much about the paradox of ethnic prerogatives.

During the CCP's anti-corruption campaign since 2013, the rule of law initially took a backseat to ethnic considerations. Of thirty-two senior officials brought down in Xinjiang as of January 2016, just four officials were Uighur (*Dute wang* 2017). According to local reporters, this low ratio seems improbable because there is a high ratio of Uighur officials in local state agencies due to the quota system in personnel appointment. Moreover, Uighur officials do have channels to stash assets – in the Middle East, in contrast to corrupt Han officials who prefer private channels in Western countries. One fallen Uighur official, Adeli Nurmehmet, mayor of Hotan city from 2009 to 2014, is reputed to hold assets in Dubai (*Guancha* 2015). Likewise, of seven high-level officials who have fallen in the anti-corruption campaign in the TAR, just one was Tibetan as of mid-2016.[32] This too seems improbable, because of the even higher ratio of Tibetan cadre in the TAR's officialdom and large financial windfalls from state assistance programs. Nevertheless, the fact that the anti-corruption campaign has reached the outer peripheral regions is a sign of change.

The arrival of Chen Quanguo, who became the top party leader in Xinjiang in August 2016, has turned the dual legal standards upside down. In an array of new policy measures to fight religious radicalism, it is now Uighurs who are adversely affected by double legal standards. Prominent Uighur officials,

[30] CCP Publicity Department, CCP United Front Department and State Ethnic Affairs Commission, "Opinions on improving ethnic harmony and progress," July 9, 2010. www.gov.cn/gzdt/2010-07/09/content_1649933.htm.

[31] Conversations with two local officials and one local reporter from southern Xinjiang, summer 2015; and conversation with two Uighur students studying in the USA, fall 2015.

[32] He is the former deputy commissioner of Nagqu Prefecture, www.zaojianxinwen.net/xizang/cc. Accessed July 11, 2016. The link is no longer available to provide details. More of the fallen officials at lower levels are Tibetan, probably because more officials at these levels are Tibetan.

including a former head of Xinjiang's Department of Education and a former governor who later headed the State Bureau of Energy, have been brought down by politically related or corruption charges. These developments, as will be discussed in more detail in Chapter 6, amount to a revenge of identity politics promoted by the state itself.

SUMMARY

This chapter has discussed the post-Mao campaign to redress leftist wrongs that ushered in the second historical transition of China's ethnic governance. The crux of this transition was the abandonment of class universalism and the rise of identity politics, manifested through four major areas of reform. In the two outer peripheral regions, they included the restitution of former ethnic elites and other "class enemies" of the Mao era, withdrawal of Han personnel, state sponsorship of religious revival, and accommodation of ethnic conventions in law enforcement. These policies departed from the Maoist approaches of class solidarity across ethnic groups, and strengthened ethnic particularism by removing the social class justification of interethnic equality and replacing it with an identity justification. Together these policies strengthened interethnic demarcations while weakening intraethnic ones.

Hailed as a movement of liberalization, the campaign to redress past wrongs – as carried out in the key minority regions – was liberalization with a twist. The campaign was driven more by a reaction against the excesses of Mao's radical years than a fundamental rethinking of socialist autonomy. During the Mao era, ethnic particularism was justified yet also conditioned by class universalism. Thus preferential policies could be compatible with an influx of Han personnel, displacement of former ethnic elites, and censure of ethnic religions and conventions. In launching the campaign to repudiate the radicalism of the Mao era, the CCP did not develop a new fundamental framework to define the relationship between the central state and minority regions, in particular the outer peripheral regions. Hu Yaobang had the right instinct by promoting more ethnic autonomy, but fell short of a broader consultation with local communities about a new type of autonomy. Unable to defend his idea of "high autonomy," his reform platform fell back on ethnic prerogatives. It did so by ethnicizing the remedies for the party's past mistakes: restoring ethnic elites and conventions while reducing Han presence. These reforms enhanced ethnic particularism without granting more political autonomy. That is, they were still dictated from the center.

Ultimately, I argue in this chapter, the built-in tensions of the autonomous system have been strengthened by the demise of class universalism and the rise of identity politics. That is, the tensions between centralization and ethnicization. If those tensions were mitigated by class universalism during the Mao era, the demise of this universalism delegitimized the ideological and political underpinning that had earlier helped to neutralize ethnicity and connect the majority and minority communities. It followed that the post-Mao state would compensate for past mistakes by granting more minority-specific prerogatives, effectively replacing class politics with identity politics. In the process, the party ideologically and politically abandoned its former allies – the lower social strata – especially in the outer peripheral regions where these allies were crucial during the first transition. Meanwhile the party also relegitimated former ethnic elites and traditions that buttressed traditional political and cultural institutions. These developments would have long-term consequences for political integration and stability. Given the built-in tensions of the autonomous system, the ascent of identity politics foreshadowed the imperative of centralization to offset its centrifugal tendencies.

5

Ethnic Autonomy and Its Discontents

Following the campaign to redress the leftist wrongs of the Mao era, the CCP made a series of efforts to reinstitutionalize the system of ethnic autonomy. As part of the early post-Mao course of political liberalization, those efforts were intended to better accommodate ethnic communities, thus better integrating them. However, rather than alleviating the tensions between centralization and ethnicization, they intensified them. This intensification has fueled discontent among contending Chinese groups as to the adequacy of the autonomous system, and whether its institutional design is an important source of increased ethnic discontent.

In the Western literature, scholars universally emphasize the large discrepancy between the promise of autonomy and the realities in the Chinese case. The reasons include a dearth of genuine autonomy, a lack of checks against state intrusion on autonomy, subordination to state interests, presence of less autonomy than in regular provinces, and a nearly complete lack of independence of action (Bovingdon 2004 and 2010; Dillon 2004; Starr 2004 and 2003; Moneyhon 2002; Yash 2000; Heberer 1989). At the very least, limits on autonomy result from the marketization of the Chinese economy (Sautman 1999) or a complex system of formal and informal incentives (Hillman 2016). Existing scholarship has also identified an emerging consensus among leading public intellectuals and some party officials in China for policy reform, in the direction of strengthening national integration at the expense of ethnic autonomy and supporting the "melting pot" concept (Leibold 2013). This chapter, however, will show that it is the opponents of the "melting pot" approach who have prevailed politically thanks to their embrace of the institutional compromise of the autonomous system.

In this chapter I continue with the book's argument that the built-in tensions of the autonomous system – at once centralization and ethnicization – have intensified in the reform era, enhancing the institutional dynamics for ethnic tensions. The driving force has been the demise of class universalism and the advent of identity politics. On the one hand, these two developments have made political centralization less justifiable but also more urgent, thanks to the centrifugal tendencies of identity politics, which are now unconstrained by class universalism. On the other hand, the demise of class universalism and the advent of identity politics have made autonomy rights more urgent but also more polarizing, as they are now instrumental to rights assertion and interethnic competition in a new market economy.

I will illustrate these institutional dynamics with three contending perspectives from within China. This contention revolves around the opposing tendencies of centralization and ethnicization in the autonomous system. The liberal autonomists criticize political centralization, which undermine autonomy rights. The integrationists criticize ethnicization, which undermines national integration. The socialist autonomists, meanwhile, embrace the grand bargain of compromised autonomy but ethnic prerogatives. From different angles, the three contending schools help to highlight the institutional sources that contribute to increased ethnic tensions in the reform era, in minority regions in general and in Xinjiang and Tibet in particular.

This chapter covers two topics: (1) post-Mao reforms to reinstitutionalize the system of ethnic autonomy; and (2) the built-in tensions between centralization and ethnicization, as reflected in three contending assessments among leading analysts of minority policy within China.

REINSTITUTIONALIZING AUTONOMY

The reinstitutionalization of the autonomous system, occurring in the late 1970s and the early 1980s, aimed to restore and strengthen the system of ethnic governance. This effort included reinstating the SEAC in 1978, restoring the autonomous system from 1978 to the early 1980s, reopening the ethnic classification project in 1979 (with the Jinuo recognized as the fifty-fifth minority group), convening the first post-Mao CCP work symposium on minority policy in 1980 (institutionalized since 1984), and adopting of the Law on Autonomy of Ethnic Regions in 1984.

A number of changes quickly followed on the ground, but all contributed to the strengthening of the ethnic rather than autonomy per se. This was so because most of the changes brought more preferential policies. Inner peripheral groups prized them more than autonomy. One change was the creation of more autonomous territorial units. In Mongol areas, this was done to reverse radical efforts that de-ethnicized territorial units. During the Cultural Revolution several Mongol prefectures and banners were assigned across five provinces, but were returned to Inner Mongolia in 1979. In the remaining cases, however, new autonomous units were established in inner peripheral regions for groups with little distinctive features. The motive, as widely understood in the Chinese context, was to cash in on the preferential policies that were expanding in the reform era (see Tables 7.1 to 7.3). Two new autonomous prefectures were established in Hubei and Guizhou provinces. Eleven new Manchu autonomous counties were established in northeastern provinces and Hebei province. Forty-one other autonomous counties were created across minority regions. These new counties, fifty-two in all, accounted for 43.3 percent of the total number of 120 autonomous counties that now exist. A number of autonomous townships were also established in rural areas, as were some ethnic districts (*minzu qu*) in urban areas.

A second change was the adoption of new preferential policies. At the individual level, most important were the preferential admission policy after college entrance exams were resumed in 1977 and the policy of exemption from family planning after the one-child policy was introduced in 1978 and formally launched in 1980. These two areas of preferential policies – college admissions and family planning – motivated millions of people to change their ethnic status.

Nationally the most enduring reform legacy was the passage of the Law on Autonomy of Ethnic Regions in 1984. Drafting of the law first began in 1954 under the leadership of Li Weihan, the party's expert on minority issues. It had undergone eight drafts by 1966, before all legislative work came to a halt due to the Cultural Revolution. Against the backdrop of redressing past wrongs, Ulanfu and Ngapoi Ngawang Jigme, the highest ranked Mongol and Tibetan leaders respectively, were tasked with leading the effort to complete the autonomy law. This was finally accomplished at the 6th Congress of the NPC in 1984, which formally adopted the Law on Autonomy of Ethnic Regions (LAER). The law was updated and amended in 2001.

Statutorily, the autonomy law grants more rights to the autonomous regions than their provincial counterparts. First, while the Chinese Constitution grants the autonomous regions the same executive and legislative powers as regular provinces (Constitution 2004, Art. 115), the autonomy law provides additional legal powers for autonomous units to adopt their own "autonomous statutes" (*zizhi tiaoli*) and "locally exclusive statutes" (*danxing tiaoli*). Central approval for local legislation is required *only* in situations where the autonomous regions seek to change or reject central decrees because they do not suit local conditions (LAER, Article 19 and 20). In addition, compared with regular provinces, LAER allows extra legislative and executive prerogatives in six broad areas: personnel matters; economic development; fiscal matters and taxation; resources and environment; cultural and educational policies; and social policies such as law and order, migration, family planning, minority customs, and religious freedom. Finally, the autonomy law mandates that the chief executive at every level of the local government in the autonomous regions be a member of the titular ethnic group locally.

The autonomy law helps to entrench the autonomous system institutionally in several ways. At the legal level, ethnic autonomy is formally codified, making autonomous status and minority policies a legal requirement. At the doctrinal level, the autonomy law provides the master law (*mufa*) for other national and local statutes involving ethnic issues. Subsequent national laws, from civil to criminal, contain provisions for minorities in accordance with the autonomy law. At the local level, a majority of autonomous prefectures and counties began to adopt their own statutes on autonomy (Dai 1999: 25–6). But no autonomy statutes have been adopted by the five autonomous regions at the provincial level, due to the difficulty of defining their relationship with the central government. In the updated version of the autonomy law in 2001, residues of the planned economy in the 1984 version were removed and more preferential policies for economic development are granted for minority regions.

Statutorily at least, the rights granted in LAER compare well with two of the three other governance units that are accorded legislative powers in China: the so-called "major cities"[1] and the Special Economic Zones. This leaves the Special Administrative Regions (SARs), or Hong Kong and Macao, as the only territorial units with greater autonomy than the autonomous regions. The SARs have far more macro-level power in choosing their local political systems and laws. By comparison, the autonomy of the autonomous regions lies largely in local flexibility to interpret, adapt, and apply central laws and policies that affect the interests of local minority communities (Huang 2008: 1–8). This local flexibility, on the ground, often comes in the form of enacting ethnic prerogatives for local ethnic communities, particularly the titular ethnic group. In a range of local policy areas, local governments have decision-making power over practical issues affecting daily lives locally, such as school admissions, family planning, language and education, law enforcement and social policies, and personnel appointment and promotion in the public sector.

To take one example, the local government in the Yanbian Korean Prefecture allocates 50 percent more funding per student to local Korean ethnic schools than to Han schools. The rationale is that because the student body is shrinking in many Korean schools, due to emigration to South Korea and to China's urban centers, their overall funding has shrunk. Hence ethnic Korean schools need a higher per capita allocation of state funds. In one Korean school the number of students is smaller than forty plus faculty and staff that remain on the school's payroll.[2] The dominance of the titular minority group in local autonomous areas makes such allocation possible.

In reality, thus, the autonomous system may provide little genuine autonomy in terms of procedural rights in political choices. But it can provide plenty of ethnic prerogatives in terms of developmental and distributional benefits. The institutional bias may have posed few problems for inner peripheral regions

[1] These include the provincial capitals, the five centrally administered metropolises, and eighteen other cities approved by the State Council as "major cities."

[2] Field observations in Yanbian Korean prefecture, including conversations with two ethnic officials of the local SEAC, two ethnic school principals, and several teachers, fall 2013. Conversations with a SEAC official, Beijing, January 2018.

where development is the priority, but for outer peripheral regions it has proved to be quite problematic.

CONTENDING ASSESSMENT OF ETHNIC AUTONOMY

The problems of China's system of ethnic autonomy are well reflected in three contending perspectives on ethnic policy within China: the liberal autonomists, the integrationists, and the socialist autonomists. The first two groups offer opposing critiques that reflect the enduring tensions of centralization and ethnicization in the autonomous system. The third school acknowledge the practical barriers to autonomy in the Chinese context but accept the trade-off between autonomy and ethnic prerogatives. Importantly, the angle from which the three groups look at the autonomous system differs. The liberal autonomists assess the system from the viewpoint of outer peripheral regions, while the socialist autonomists usually do so from that of inner peripheral regions. The integrationists disparage the particularism of both groups.

Excesses of Centralization

Liberal autonomists focus on the core institutional issue in the autonomous system: the distribution of authority between the central state and the local. Viewing things from the perspective of the two outer peripheral regions, they emphasize political and cultural rights as the essence of autonomy. Thus they reject the official pact of a trade-off between autonomy and ethnic particularism, or a compromise of the former, although they do not forsake the latter. Their critique of the autonomous system echoes the scholarly literature on the structural limits of Soviet ethno-federalism, namely, political centralization renders meaningless the formal system of ethnic autonomy. Needless to say, this view is politically untenable in China's political context.

Through their writings, liberal autonomists are influential in the sense of being the only robust critique of socialist autonomy from outside the official discourse. For the most outspoken among them, their works may be formally restricted but informally available through private channels, and their views are well known to ethnic studies circles and minority dissidents within China. Occasionally their views were solicited by the authorities, as in the case of Ilham Tohti who wrote an internal report for the authorities in 2011 (Tohti 2014). He was formerly a Uighur lecturer at the Minzu University of China. Another leading representative is Wang Lixiong, an independent scholar and dissident writer.

Considered as security threats by the authorities, their views and activities are treated as politically subversive or separatist. Tohti was briefly detained after the Urumqi riots of July 2009. The website he founded in 2006, Uighurbiz .net, was blamed for spreading rumors that helped to incite the Urumqi riots. In September 2014 he was sentenced to life in prison on separatism related charges. His website ceased updating after his arrest in January 2014. Wang Lixiong was imprisoned in 1999 for activities related to his Xinjiang research and faced house arrest during times of sensitive events in China. Among moderate liberal autonomists, Zhang Haiyang's critical views on autonomy appeared on 21ccom.net, a popular liberal website that was closed down in late 2016; and He Fang's writings have appeared on hybsl.cn, the website devoted to Hu Yaobang's legacy. Zhang is a professor at Minzu University of China and He Fang is a rehabilitated official who headed the Japan Institute at the Chinese Academy of Social Sciences in the 1980s.

Liberal autonomists highlight institutional barriers to autonomy, putting them in the unenvious position of challenging the foundations of the Chinese political system. The foremost mechanism that undermines autonomy, they argue, is the centralized leadership of the Communist Party. Although the end of class universalism has weakened its ideological foundation, the party's supremacy remains the same as in the pre-reform era. In this political structure, the party secretary at the provincial level is appointed by and responsible to the CCP above, not the local communities below; he must follow all commands of the central party, and his commands must be followed in turn by the party hierarchy below him (He 2009). The precedence of centralization over autonomy thus negates the very idea of autonomy, rendering it "pseudo autonomy" (Wang 2007 and 2009; Zhang 2014a; Hao et al. 2013). If Hu Yaobang's idea of high autonomy was heeded, Zhang Haiyang asserts, China would not be facing the kind of ethnic tensions it is experiencing in present times.[3] In the reform era, centralization has been strengthened by what Tohti refers to as a "double jeopardy," or the primacy of the party over the state and the appointment of Han officials to the top party posts (Tohti 2009). Needless to say, the end of class universalism and the rise of identity politics have made the ethnicity of official appointees a sensitive matter.

The party's official ideology is another centralizing mechanism that constrains autonomy, especially for the two regions with core religious traditions. During the socialist era, religion and the clergy were delegitimated as instruments of class oppression, a position ideologically coherent to the ethnic proletariat. In the Chinese Constitution adopted in the reform era (1982 and 2004), however, the idea of freedom of religion is stipulated but coexists with the Four Cardinal Principles. These four principles refer to "the socialist path, the dictatorship of the proletariat, the party's leadership, and Marxism and Mao Zedong Thought." Being "cardinal" principles, they render subordinate the idea of freedom of religion. As Tohti writes, by excluding alternative belief systems, official atheism deals "major blows" to the Uighur culture and religion (Tohti 2009).

Indeed, as early as the 1930s the party's own expert on minority affairs understood the centrality of religion in Islamic communities. Based on his

[3] Conversation with Zhang at Minzu University of China, December 2012.

research on Hui Muslims, Li Weihan concluded that more than just being a religion, Islam was the linchpin to the Huis' way of life and their identity as a people (Mo 1996: 1–2). Li's point should apply even more to the Uighur and Tibetan people, since they have not become sinified culturally and linguistically like the Hui people. He Fang criticizes the party's earlier treatment of the ethnic clergy as a "parasitic class," pointing to the deep reverence that their co-ethnic disciples held for them (He 2009). This refers particularly to the reverence of the Tibetan masses for their lamas, whose seemingly idle life was attacked as "parasitic" in the Mao era.

Third, the party's monopoly over official appointments is a key centralizing mechanism for constraining autonomy, especially the appointment of Han cadre to the top official post. During the Mao era, class universalism obscured the issue of the ethnicity of top office holders in minority regions. But the end of that universalism makes the issue more prominent in the post-Mao era. Because the party prevails over the state, the (Han) party secretary's power thus prevails over that of the top state office-holder at the parallel level. The latter always comes from the titular minority group, as required by the autonomy law. This is known as the "double jeopardy" problem, or the party's monopoly over official appointments and its appointment of Han officials at the top in Xinjiang and to a lesser extent the TAR.

The sources of the "double jeopardy" are contentious, revolving around whether they are ethnically based or driven by the rise of identity politics. Liberal autonomists tend to blame the former, citing the party's longstanding lack of trust in minority officials. For example, early Tibetan communists participated in the Long March in the 1930s and in revolutionary activities in Tibetan regions in the 1940s, but there was just one Tibetan, Phun tshogs dbang rgyal, in the party's five-member leadership committee when the Chinese Liberation Army took over Lhasa in 1950; moreover, when the party's provisional government was established in Lhasa in 1958, he was still the sole Tibetan in the eleven-member party committee (He 2009). Even this individual, known as the "red Tibetan" who led the Red Army into Tibet, was suspected of separatism in 1960 and sentenced to prison as a "counter-revolutionary," then released eighteen years later after Mao's death. Educated in Han cities in the 1930s, Phun tshogs was well read in Marxist classics, founded the Kham Tibetan Communist Party, and served as the interpreter during the negotiations between Beijing and the Dalai Lama's representatives in 1951 and in Mao's meeting with the Dalai Lama and the Panchen Lama in 1954. In other words, this was not an individual lacking in social class solidarity or intellectual credentials.

Other examples of "mistrust" involve the dearth of titular minorities appointed to top official posts in autonomous regions. Just two such members have served at the helm at the provincial level, Ulanfu in Inner Mongolia (late 1940s–1966) and Säypidin Äzizi in Xinjiang (1972–8), both during the Mao era. Instead, prominent minority officials were placed away from their native lands. This refers to the appointment of legendary minority officials – in both stature and accomplishments – to nominally high positions in Beijing, for example the tenth Panchen Lama, Nga phod Ngag dbang 'jigs med, Burhan Shehidi, and Säypidin Äzizi (He 2009). Notably these examples all involved outer peripheral regions. The Panchen Lama is the highest ranked lama after the Dalai Lama in the Gelupha school of Tibetan Buddhism. Nga phod Ngag dbang 'jigs med headed the Tibetan delegation to the Beijing peace negotiations in 1951, where he signed the 17-Point Agreement on behalf of the Dalai Lama. Burhan Shehidi, a Tartar who served in the Republican government in Xinjiang and helped to surrender the province to Mao's army in 1949, chaired Xinjiang's provincial government upon the CCP's takeover, and in 1952 headed the preparatory committee to create the XUAR. Säypidin Äzizi, was a former leader of the East Turkistan Republic and the first chairman of XUAR. For some liberal autonomists, these individuals were not appropriately placed to lead their native regions (He 2009).

However, the Mao era actually had a better record of titular minority members serving at the helm. Class versus identity politics may have made the difference. In the Mao era, the bond of social class alliance contributed to the CCP's faith in minority officials, leading to more titular officials at the top in autonomous regions. Even Ilham Tohti, a fierce critic of China's Xinjiang policy, conceded that the party had trust in the Uighur leadership during the Mao era, citing Säypidin Äzizi's top post in Xinjiang during the turbulent period of the Cultural Revolution.[4] Besides Äzizi and Ulanfu, the Hui official Yang Jingren served at the helm in Ningxia and the Zhuang official Wei Guoqing did so in Guangxi, both in the 1960s. Wei also served in the top post of Guangdong province in the 1970s. The better record of the Mao era may be credited to Mao's confidence in the loyalty of minority officials and regions, in contrast to the post-Mao leadership (Yao 2014a). That confidence, argues the prominent Mongol scholar Hao Siyuan, came from the credentials earned by those minority leaders during the revolutionary years.[5] Moreover, the placement of prominent minority leaders in Beijing during the Mao era may not have been a sign of mistrust. Rather, they served as symbols of national unity.

By contrast, the rise of identity politics in the post-Mao era results, ironically, in a dearth of titular minority officials at the helm. Extrapolating the argument about "confidence" in minority officials at the top, the identity politics promoted in post-Mao China helps to weaken universalist bonds based on social class alliance, and along with that, the regime's confidence in minority officials in sensitive regions. Indeed, just two minority members served briefly in the top office of autonomous regions in the post-Mao era: Wu Jinghua in the TAR (1985–8) and Tömür Dawamät in Xinjiang (1984–5). Wu, a Yi ethnic, was not a titular member or a native of the TAR.

[4] Conversations with Tohti at Minzu University of China, December 2012.

[5] Q&A section at the People's University forum on Tibet, July 2010.

In at least two cases involving these two sensitive regions, appointment of titular officials to the top was derailed by apprehension about identity politics. Upon his rehabilitation in the early post-Mao period, the CCP wanted to appoint the Panchen Lama to the top state office in the TAR, but the effort failed due to the objection of Tibetan officials who rose from the serf class and opposed the appointment of former aristocrats.[6] In Xinjiang's case, in the mid-1980s hundreds of Uighurs agitated in the streets for the promotion of Ismail Amat, then Xinjiang's governor (1979–85), to the top party post in Xinjiang, against the CCP's intended appointee, Tömür Dawamet. Due to concerns about Ismail Amat's "separatist tendencies," he was assigned away to Beijing and served as the director of the SEAC from 1986 to 1998.[7] Tömür Dawamet served briefly as Xinjiang's party secretary (1984–5) and succeeded Ismail Amat as Xinjiang's governor from 1985 to 1993.

Within the five provincial autonomous regions, the problem seems to stand out in Xinjiang and to some extent the TAR. That is, the two outer peripheral regions. In an internal report written for the higher authorities in 2011, Tohti (2014) complains that within Xinjiang few Uighur officials hold high-level offices in agencies with substantive power, such as treasury, public assets, finance, and public security, or in state enterprises. At the national level, he laments the size of the Uighur presence relative to that of the Han and other ethnic groups in the country's top political institutions. Moderate Uighur scholars echo such sentiments. Tursun suggests that even when a Uighur holds the top state position, he may still feel marginalized because wherever a Uighur is the county magistrate, a Han official serves as the executive vice magistrate in all counties and may wield more executive power (2013: 29). Both scholars imply that there is a problem of "mistrust" regarding Uighur officials.

The complaint about mistrust may be partly fueled by identity politics. Non-Uighur officials and staff members tend to emphasize universalist rather than ethnic markers, such as gaps in skills and language proficiency. Han staff members who worked or work in different offices of a prefectural government in southern Xinjiang, for example, cited difficulties for Uighurs' officials to "write good reports in Chinese" and their reliance on Han staff for such matters.[8] Differences in political leadership also render it unclear if the appointment of Han officials to the top post is a structural or arbitrary outcome. Zhang Chunxian, who became Xinjiang's party secretary after the Urumqi riots of 2009 (April 2010–August 2016), personally made a difference by actively promoting Uighur party secretaries. Zhang was reportedly surprised

[6] Conversations with Ma Rong and a scholar of the Minzu University of China in Hangzhou, June 2018.

[7] Conversations with a former researcher of the SEAC in New York, March 2012. See also Deng Liqun's memoir (2008).

[8] Conversations with five former or current employees of local state agencies in Hotan prefecture, fall 2013 and summer 2015. Two worked in local bureaus of commerce, two worked in local bureaus of agriculture, and one worked in a logistics office.

to see the small number of Uighurs present at the meetings he held with ranking officials when he first assumed office.[9] His successor, Chen Quanguo, appears less interested in the issue. Since assuming power in August 2016, Chen has focused on tough security measures to stem religious extremism and violence.

The "technical" explanation seems to hold out in the TAR's case, which undermines the identity argument. Here Beijing can draw on a good supply of Mandarin-speaking and educated Tibetans from Tibetan regions outside the TAR to serve in the top posts. Out of nearly eighty administrative units at the county, municipal, and prefectural levels in the TAR, a Tibetan holds the top post of the party secretary in over a quarter of them, including Lhasa. As of July 2013, a Tibetan served in the top party post in five out of seven prefecture-level administrations (*CE* 2013). Below the county level, the Tibetan presence at the helm is even more common, thanks to a lack of longtime Han residents and a lack of unrest beyond the monasteries. There are few if any Han officials at the township and village levels. A few civil servants with mixed Han-Tibetan parentage may be present, but they are often eager to leave when opportunities arise.[10]

The problem of ethnic imbalance in top political appointments is all the more distinct in Xinjiang because it is not a significant issue in the TAR or a distinct one in other ethnic regions. This is even true of Inner Mongolia and the Yanbian Korean Prefecture, two regions that face highly nationalistic co-ethnics across the borders. In fact, Yanbian's party and state agencies are dominated by ethnic Koreans and most of the prefecture's party secretaries have been ethnic Koreans.[11] In encounters at Yanbian University, it was the Han faculty members who complained about being discriminated against in promotion and other professional matters. In Inner Mongolia as well, individual credentials matter more in political and bureaucratic promotions while ethnicity does not usually arise an issue.[12] Needless to say, in Korean and Mongol regions, physical and religious differences between the Han and local minorities are negligible, in contrast to the situation in Xinjiang or the TAR.

Even in Xinjiang, ethnic officials appear to be well represented besides the office of the party secretary. Over half of all officials in Xinjiang are minority members; a titular member holds the top position of the executive, legislative, judicial, and prosecutorial branches at all prefectural and county levels;

[9] Information from a well-placed staff member of a prefectural government, who had worked in a variety of local offices, October 2013.

[10] Field observations in two prefectures of western Sichuan and three prefectures of the TAR, summers 2014, 2015, and 2017.

[11] Conversations with local officials in Yanji, capital city of Yanbian prefecture, including a deputy mayor, an official of the city's SEAC office, two university officials, and at least five scholars, October 2013. Conversations with a minority affairs official of Korean descent, Beijing, January 2018.

[12] Conversations with two scholars of Mongol descent, from the Chinese Academy of Social Sciences and the Minzu University of China respectively, Beijing, fall 2013.

a minority member holds the top state office in most of the prefectures, municipalities, and counties; and many minority members hold the top position in the various departments of the provincial government (Tursun 2012a). Moreover, Zhang Chunxiang's promotion of Uighur officials has had some effects. More Uighurs serve as party secretaries at the county level, and during his tenure in Xinjiang one Uighur became the party secretary of Tacheng (Qoqek) prefecture and a Kazakh secured the post in Changji/Sanji prefecture (*CE* 2019).

However, even liberal-minded Han scholars question the identity politics implicit in the arguments for "ethnic balance" in political appointments. Because of legitimate concerns over ethnic particularism, they argue, it is preferable to have someone at the top who is above particularistic interests and is accepted by all ethnic groups. This is particularly necessary in light of that fact that what many Uighurs object to is not so much the arbitrary nature of the current system of power wielding. Rather, they simply ask for a quota-based distribution of power in the existing political structure. Even if Uighurs were to hold the top party offices at all levels, critics argue, it does not mean that the Uighur people would be well served (Yao 2012). This implies that rampant corruption and bureaucratic indifference afflict Han as well as minority ranks in Xinjiang's officialdom. This point is valid yet perhaps unfair, since Uighur scholars would feel more constrained in criticizing the deeper problems of China's political system. Moreover, as Zhang Haiyang argues, it is unfair to suggest that Uighurs may not treat smaller minority groups equitably (Zhang 2014b). One example was Uighurs' compromise to allow Ghulja to be the capital city for a Kazakh autonomous prefecture, even though Kazakhs were concentrated in pastoral areas outside the city.

Based on field research, the real problem is indeed not so much the ethnicity of the top political appointees but the types of individuals appointed. In Xinjiang's case, Han professionals readily complain about the servicemen turned officials (*jun zhuan gan*) who have a hold on official power in southern Xinjiang. Two factors make these ex-servicemen politically dominant here. One is the mandate for local governments to absorb a number of discharged servicemen, who usually end up in the local party and state apparatus. Another is the weight of political and security considerations in official appointments in southern Xinjiang. But the ex-servicemen, with their combat mentality and military style of command and compliance, help to shape a high-handed style of governance.[13] This style is often brusque and authoritarian, mixed with simplistic perspectives and ubiquitous obedience to higher authorities. As Ilham Tohti notes (2014), this style was shocking even to officials in northern Xinjiang, when a large number of officials from southern

[13] In the fall of 2013, one of the homes where I stayed during my visit to southern Xinjiang was in the residential compound of a prefectural government. This allowed close-up observations of local officials and local offices that were open to the public.

Xinjiang arrived in Urumqi after the riots of July 2009 to help maintain law and order.

Long-term Han residents and professionals find the ex-servicemen destabilizing. They contend that the problem with Han officials is not so much Han dominance per se, but the dominance of ex-servicemen in important party and state offices in southern Xinjiang. As low-level officers discharged from the military, they usually hail from poor interior provinces and have only secondary education. Their service background makes them politically trusted, and with some training in party schools they are assigned to key posts in party and state agencies as well as media and cultural institutions. Their hold on local power, along with the corrupt networks it breeds, frustrates Uighurs as much as Han Chinese born and raised locally. These Han Chinese have local knowledge, care about local communities, and often speak Uighur if they were born before the reform era. They feel that if the government has to appoint Han members to key political posts, at least individuals like them would be more suitable.[14]

By contrast, the ex-servicemen have little knowledge of or ties to civilian society, even less to Uighur communities. While Uighur officials and professionals are reluctant to openly complain, their Han counterparts routinely grumble that professionals are led by the "reds" who know nothing. Cronyism among the network of the ex-servicemen officials is frequent, as they help with one another's careers and relatives. These relatives often come from poor interior regions to land public projects in Xinjiang. In fact Wang Lequan, Xinjiang's party secretary at the time of the Urumqi riots of 2009, was widely resented for this type of corruption – helping contractors from his native province of Shandong to win public projects in Xinjiang. Wang was not one of the ex-servicemen, but like them he came from a rural area of an interior province, and like them he was unpopular with both Han and Uighur residents in Xinjiang. Inopportunely, the servicemen-turned-officials have become the de facto face of Han rule in southern Xinjiang. Here the miniscule size of the Han population in rural counties, unfortunately, can make Uighur experience with these officials their main impression of Han Chinese rule.

The situation is different in the TAR for a number of reasons. The harsh plateau is not attractive for ex-servicemen to stay for long-term employment, and the permanent Han population is negligible in rural and pastoral areas. A small number of Han officials is assigned to the TAR on a rotating basis. Many come to serve for a few years for reasons of personal or career adjustment, or for the generous early retirement packages. Many come from neighboring provinces of Sichuan or Chongqing, where people are said to be tough and willing to endure the harsh terrain in the TAR. The more receptive

[14] Conversations with seven individuals from local state offices, fall 2013 and summer 2015. They worked in the local state offices of agriculture, poverty relief, commerce, land assets, and media administration.

attitudes toward Han officials can be discerned by the jokes and anecdotes that Tibetan scholars and officials casually tell, in contrast to the guarded atmosphere at gatherings with their Uighur counterparts. Take one wisecrack from a Tibetan scholar in a casual conversation: our folks in the countryside are clear headed; they thank their commander-in-chief the Dalai Lama for making Beijing bring us good policy benefits; they prefer Tibetan officials to serve faraway, because they can bring more benefits; they prefer Han officials to serve locally, because they can get things done and they don't wear big robes like Tibetans (meaning they are not as corrupt as those who wear big robes to hide bribes).[15]

In Xinjiang's case, it would be fair to ask longtime Han residents in the south how they would feel about Uighur officials serving in the top post of local government offices and public sectors. After all, they would have most at stake in this Uighur-concentrated region. Their answers are surprisingly fair and practical, based on field conversations. Several young professionals employed in local state agencies said that their Uighur superiors had promoted them, and that these superiors were not calculating like some Han officials, for they did not mind their subordinates doing better than themselves.[16] Some private entrepreneurs also felt that it was easier to deal with Uighur officials. One Han contractor who hatched baby chickens for a village government (to be given freely to Uighur villagers to raise and market) told this author: "When I try to get reimbursement from the village government this year, this [Han] official keeps saying tomorrow. I have made three trips already and still have not got my payment." He continued, "last year, the Uighur fellow happily did my reimbursement after I gave him a couple of thousand Yuan. He even remembered to send me a greeting for the Chinese New Year." When asked why he did not offer the same bribe to the Han official, the contractor explained, "he may think this amount is not worth taking the risk; he may pretend he doesn't want it. He may be using the tens of thousands of Yuan the village owes me for other purposes. You never know. The Uighurs are simpler."[17]

When asked if local Han residents would feel comfortable if Uighurs were to serve in the top party position in local government agencies, few ostensibly objected despite obvious hesitation. Han residents comprise just 3 percent of the population in Hotan prefecture and are concentrated in urban centers. Still, local residents and migrants felt that as long as the CCP was in power, things would be under control. Asked if southern Xinjiang should become a high

[15] Conversation with a Tibetan scholar at Sichuan University, Chengdu, summer 2015.

[16] Conversations with four individuals who worked in local state agencies in southern Xinjiang, fall 2013 and summer 2015. They included those of agriculture, poverty relief, commerce, and land assets.

[17] I went with this contractor on one of his reimbursement trips in November 2013 and conversed with him extensively during the trip. More conversations in the summers of 2015 and 2017 about the issue.

autonomy like Hong Kong, with Uighurs taking charge, older Han residents felt that the right timing had already passed. It would have been possible over a decade ago, they opined, but radical religious groups have now become too dominant and could overpower secular Uighur officials. Younger Han residents, on the other hand, wanted a significant pay raise as an incentive to stay in a Uighur-dominated political environment.[18]

In short, the structural barriers to genuine autonomy are aptly highlighted by liberal autonomists and linked to the Chinese political system. This perspective articulates what critically minded minority members feel, especially those from outer peripheral regions. Their stifled voices serve as a powerful reminder that all things are not harmonious. Nevertheless, liberal autonomists avoid discussing the other end of the trade-off in China's autonomous system, namely ethnic particularism. Thus they are not entirely impartial or realistic.

Excesses of Ethnicization

The integrationists, by contrast, emphasize the ethnicizing effects of the autonomous system in the reform era. That is, the prevalence of identity politics and preferential policies that undermines national integration. Those effects are such, they argue, that they make up the reality of ethnic autonomy in China: that is, an institutionalization of ethnic and ethno-territorial identities through preferential policies. This perspective echoes the key insights from scholarly analyses of Soviet ethno-federalism. It also presents an influential critique that resonates with the general Chinese public. The national orientation of the integrationists has put central authorities as well as the minority establishment on the defensive. The potency of the integrationist view was fully attested by Xi Jinping's public rebuke of it at a party conference on ethnic policy in 2014. But its nationalistic stance makes the integrationist view politically safe, if sidelined for now.

The integrationists subdivide into two groups. The first may be called the liberal integrationists, who criticize ethnic prerogatives for undermining equal citizen rights and a civic national identity. This school is represented by the Hui scholar Ma Rong of Beijing University, whose educational background in America leads him to advocate the American model of multiculturalism and the melting pot. The second group may be called the statist integrationists, who criticize ethnic prerogatives for undermining state rights and interests. This school is represented by Hu Angang (Hu and Hu 2010 and 2011) and Zhu Weiqun (Zhu 2012 and 2015; Wang 2013). Hu is a public intellectual and a professor at Qinghua University, while Zhu is a former deputy head of the

[18] Conversations with five Han residents born and raised in Xinjiang, fall 2013 and summer 2015, southern Xinjiang; with five Han individuals who went to Xinjiang during the Mao era and have returned to their hometowns in Sichuan province, summers 2017 and 2019 in Chongqing; and with four Han individuals born and raised in Xinjiang, summer 2019 in Chongqing.

CCP's Department of United Front and now director of the Committee on Ethnic and Religious Affairs in the CPPCC. The integrationist views are also common among scholars of frontier studies (Zhou 2008a, 2008b, 2008c, and 2010; Wu 2005 and 2011) and among the Han population insofar as Tibet and Xinjiang are concerned.

The liberal integrationists attack the ideological foundation of the autonomous system by tracing it to the Soviet theory and practice of ethno-federalism. Ma Rong started a national debate with this argument in an article in 2004. It contends that Stalin's faulty conception of ethnic groups as "nations with national rights" remains dominant in China and serves as the basis of an entire academic discipline as well as official theory and policy. Confined by Stalin's theory, ethnicity is thus essentialized in China's public and policy discourse, with ethnicity taken as primordial, unchanging, and an object of separate public policy. With the rise of identity politics, preferential policies have not only intensified in the reform era but also become individually and group based, in contrast to group and regionally based preferential policies in the socialist era (Ma 2004). A system designed to achieve national integration has itself become a centrifugal force, a Manchu scholar notes, citing the Manchus' repoliticization as the latest example of ethnic movements driven by the desire to qualify for preferential policies (Guan 2013: 32; 2011: 27). Indeed, although Manchus are now indistinguishable from Han people, many Manchu communities in northeastern and northern China have reignited cultural markers to gain developmental projects and opportunities.[19] However, while the integrationists may be on target here about the unnecessarily ethnicizing effects of preferential policies, they do not make a distinction between the different needs of inner and outer peripheral minority groups.

Unlike liberal autonomists, who assess the state of autonomy from the statutory requirements of the autonomy law, integrationists do so on the basis of what happens on the ground. In mundane issues that impact people's lives directly, Ma argues, autonomy rights are real and politicizing in the era of market competition. Most notable are preferential policies in school admissions, family planning, personnel appointment and promotion, language and education, law enforcement, and social policies.[20] Here local governments have decision-making power over important practical issues. Integrationists see such particularistic use of public resources as a substantive exercise of autonomy rights. Moreover, they view such exercise of autonomy as

[19] Conversations with an official of a local SEAC branch from a northeastern province, October 2013; with a central SEAC researcher and a graduate student from northern China doing a research project on the subject, Beijing, January 2018.

[20] Ma Rong has written extensively on these issues. For a partial list, see the bibliography at the end of the book under both Chinese and English entries. I mainly use interviews here to present his views not expressed explicitly in his writings. His major writings are archived at www.aisixiang.com/data/69296-2.html.

enhancing ethnic identity and undermining national cohesion. They question why ethnicity itself should be a unit of special government treatment and why this service should be supplied to all minority members (Guan 2013). For example, minority students in urban areas go to the same schools as everyone else, but they should receive bonus points in college admissions and be beneficiaries of preferential policies. As such, preferential policies have simply become social capital, used instrumentally in intraethnic and interethnic competition for scarce public goods and in the market economy.

Integrationists, liberal or statist, endorse the government's discourse of national unity and developmentalism, which has replaced class universalism of the Mao era. Ma Rong is explicit about defending what he sees as the larger public interest, which makes his stance politically safe despite his fierce attacks on Marxist and Stalinist doctrine (Ma 2008a). Ma's extensive field research and solid scholarship make him well respected and often difficult to refute.[21] In a three-way debate organized by the independent magazine *Lingdao Zhe* (Leaders) in August 2013,[22] Ma faced the Mongol scholar Hao Shiyuan from the left and the liberal Han scholar Zhang Haiyang from the right. But Ma handily overwhelmed both (Hao et al. 2013). An entire book has been devoted to debating his views, with Ma taking on a host of established Chinese ethnologists (Xie 2010). Ma is singled out for criticism by Ilham Tohti, for negating the autonomous system (Tohti 2009 and 2013). Ma's views make him a lightning rod in academic and policy debates, shunned by some conference organizers and college campuses as a speaker, including the Central Minzu University, for fear of alienating some minority members. He cites just two scholars who openly endorse his views,[23] though many share his views in private. Debates between Ma and defenders of the autonomous system can become so intense that they are sometimes said to bang on the conference table.

The rise of identity politics and its harmful impact, needless to say, are major targets of criticism for the integrationists. The appointment of Han officials to the top posts, they argue, is not an intentional bias but the result of an appointment process based precisely on identity politics. No legal statute mandates that Han officials serve as the party secretary at any level of the autonomous region, Ma Rong argues. Rather, it is because the autonomy law requires that a member of the titular ethnic group be appointed to the top executive position at all levels of the local government. As a result, a member of a different ethnicity is usually appointed to the top party post for political and ethnic balance. This argument of course does not square with the fact that this is

[21] I had extended conversations with Ma during a field trip in Xinjiang in the summer of 2011, during conferences in August and December 2012, October 2013, and June 2018, and in continuous electronic communications.

[22] *Lingdaozhe* (Leaders) was registered in Hong Kong and had more leeway in terms of uncensored speech.

[23] They are Pan Zhiping, director of Central Asian Studies at Xinjiang Academy of Social Sciences, and Xie Zhizhong, professor of sociology at Beijing University.

not a problem in minority regions other than Xinjiang and the TAR. Furthermore, integrationists argue that the appointment of Han officials to the top party post does not automatically curtail autonomy. On the contrary, Han officials, wary of being accused of chauvinism, often defer to particularistic ethnic interests. This assessment may have stemmed from Ma's experiences with officials at the provincial level in outer peripheral regions, where leadership styles may be more refined. Below the county levels and in far-flung regions, things can be different.

Integrationists also blame the appointment of Han officials at the helm on the ethno-territorial system itself. Here the non-titular minority groups often resent the titular group for its numeric dominance over the political process. In conversations with Ma and other integrationists, they attribute this dominance to the autonomous regions' right to have leeway in preferential policies and ethnically based allocation, which fuel conflict among ethnic groups over who gets what. Take Xinjiang as an example. Membership of its legislature is allocated according to the size of local ethnic groups. Thus the titular group can often prevail in the design and implementation of local public policies. In language policy, Uighur is dictated as the language of instruction in most ethnic schools. However, Kazakh, Tajik, Kyrgyz, and other small minorities often prefer the nationally used Mandarin, but have little legislative power to overrule the titular majority. The appointment of Han officials at the top is thus said to help maintain a balance of power among the disparate ethnic groups. This argument, of course, can be easily turned around: as the largest ethnic group in China, the Han majority gets to decide the hegemony of Mandarin for the entire country.

Another practice that irks the integrationists is the quota system in appointment and promotion decisions in the public sectors of the autonomous regions. This system disadvantages qualified individuals whose group quotas are used up, so high-achieving but non-titular groups can feel especially frustrated. Ma Rong cites a case from a college in Urumqi as a typical example. Here a well-qualified minority scholar was considered for the position of the college's vice presidency, but the position required an individual from Xinjiang's titular ethnic group, Uighur. The candidate was of mixed Kazakh and Uighur parentage, but his Kazakh lineage was listed in the official registry and was thus disqualified for the position. He attempted to change his ethnic status to "Uighur," which upset his allies on the Kazakh side. The ethnic factor eventually derailed his appointment. After a long delay, an official of the titular group with lesser credentials was picked to fill the position.[24]

Rather than seeing such compromises as politically necessary, integrationists view them as undermining meritocracy and fairness. Their point is not that minority members are less qualified. Rather, it is that the minority track – in

[24] Conversations with this scholar occurred on two occasions, in Urumqi, summer 2011 and in Yanbian, fall 2013.

schooling, hiring, and promotion – has cocooned minority professionals and officials, limiting their personal growth and career opportunities. Indeed, Ma Rong is a strong advocate of admitting minority students to China's top colleges, rather than channeling them to the minority colleges and the minority track. For integrationists, more opportunities for minority members come from mainstreaming, such as those who have served in the top party post in regular provinces in the post-Mao era: Hui Liangyu (a Hui) in Anhui (1998–9) and Jiangsu (1999–2002), and Bayanqolu (a Mongol) in Jilin (2014–present). Nevertheless, integrationists rarely question if the Han officials – invariably appointed to the top party posts in Xinjiang and Tibet – always meet the standard of meritocracy or fairness.

Another integrationist argument is that autonomy rights are often used or abused to serve the special interests of the already privileged. In Xinjiang, Ma Rong's call for changing preferential policies for college admissions – from ethnic criteria to regional/economic criteria – has met with resistance from top Uighur officials. Ma argues that the regional criterion would not affect the number of overall Uighur admissions, since Xinjiang's poorest regions are populated by rural Uighurs and should thus benefit from his proposal. By contrast, the ethnic criterion favors urban Uighur children in northern Xinjiang, who receive better education and often come from professional families. Ma chastises such preferential policies for serving the interests of ethnic elites at the detriment of those who really need them. Nevertheless, while the regional/poverty criterion is sensible in principle, it is likely to affect the overall number of minority students who get into top colleges.

In another policy arena, the system of minority colleges, integrationists fault the minority establishment for playing identity politics to resist their integration with regular colleges. The system of eighteen minority colleges, Ma argues, has outlived its usefulness and ill serves minority as well as majority students by separating ethnic studies from regular colleges and separating the educational experiences of both Han and minority students. The system continues to exist, Ma and others argue, not because it is good for minority students but because the SEAC retains a portion of the state funding allocated for minority colleges. For example, the central government funds the Minzu University of China at a rate of 130 percent more than regular colleges. The SEAC, however, passes the funding to the university at the regular rate while keeping the extra 30 percent for itself.[25]

The funding mechanism for boarding schools for minority students in Tibet and Xinjiang is cited as another example. Here the best Tibetan and Uighur students are recruited to attend high schools in interior provinces so that they can receive a better education and qualify for better colleges. As a mechanism of

[25] Conversations with Ma, and with an ethnic official of the SEAC and an ethnic official of the CCP's United Front Department, fall 2013. Conversation with two ethnic officials of a central agency in Beijing, January 2018.

integration, this boarding school program exists only for these two regions. However, rather than placing the ethnic students in regular classes in their new schools in interior provinces, they are grouped together in classes separate from regular students. The reason for this arrangement, integrationists argue, lies in the politics of funding. In the case of Tibet, its provincial educational bureau receives no funding from the central government if Tibetan students are placed in a regular class in interior high schools, but the bureau would receive ¥10,000 per student annually from the central government if they are placed in a separate class. The same goes for Xinjiang. The result is that ethnic students from these regions are brought to interior China only to be placed in minority-only classes. With few chances to study and mingle with other students, their experiences away from home can be lonely and unproductive. Yet the funding incentive motivates local educational bureaus to send more students to such classes. Integrationists worry about the psychological impact of their social isolation, arguing that it may enhance ethnic identity rather than integration.

The integrationists' critique of identity politics is most vividly illustrated by the fate of a tiny ethnic group, the Bonans. When first designated a "nationality" in 1952, they had about 4,000 members and loosely identified with the Hui Muslims. With a population of about 8,000 in 1981, they earned a titular status in a newly created autonomous county, the Bonan, Dongxiang, and Salar Autonomous County. This titular order has since entitled the Bonans to more preferential policies than the other two titular groups in the county. All three groups, in turn, qualify for more state benefits than the Huis with whom they used to be associated, since the Huis are not a titular minority in this county. All four groups are Muslims and use the Chinese language. Two decades later, the titular status has transformed the Bonans' identities, personal choices and life chances (Jian 2006). Individual Bonan members make strategic choices in selecting the ethnicity of their marriage partners and children so as to maximize the chances of qualifying for preferential policies, from college admissions to public sector jobs. In particular, the ethnic label is a critical form of political capital for the cadre class, who use it to land government jobs and related benefits for themselves and their offspring (Jian 2006, 2009). The transformation of the Bonans' identity in just two decades epitomizes the politicization of identity, even while this case underrepresents the realities of the autonomous regions as a whole.

The integrationists contribute to the Chinese debate by putting official policy on the defensive and challenging the minority establishment to rise above particularistic interests. They articulate what many ordinary Han Chinese feel about preferential policies, but also what concerns older minority members like Ma himself about the divisive role of rising identity politics in post-Mao China. Nevertheless, the integrationists are no less partial than the liberal autonomists. Much as the liberals avoid discussing the problems of ethnic particularism while blasting centralization, the integrationists evade the problem of limited autonomy while attacking ethnic prerogatives.

Acceptable Trade-Offs

The socialist autonomists, finally, accept the grand bargain of compromised autonomy but ethnic prerogatives. They represent the minority establishment in China. Their spokesmen occupy the three pillars of ethnic policy thinking in China, which also form the institutional base of their influence: the Institute of Ethnology and Anthropology (IEA) at the Chinese Academy of Sciences, the SEAC, and the Minzu University of China. The Tibetology Center of China, based in Beijing and a think tank for the CCP's United Front Department, may be added to the list.

Representatives of the school, not surprisingly, are mostly not from the outer peripheral regions, especially Xinjiang. They include Hao Siyuan, a Mongol ethnologist at IEA; Ming Hao, a researcher and official of Korean descent at the SEAC; and Jin Binghao, a professor of Marxist ethnic theory at the Minzu University of China who is also of Korean descent. Lobsang Dradu, a Tibetan scholar from Garzê who was formerly at the Tibetology Center of China and is now at the Western Development Center of Sichuan University, may be added to the list. They publish in prominent venues and write internal reports, exerting the most influence on official policy thinking. They represent the vested interests noted in the scholarly literature on Soviet ethno-federalism. But Uighur scholars are notably absent from this list.

Instead of political and cultural rights, socialist autonomists emphasize ethnic autonomy implemented as distributional and developmental rights. This is because for minority officials from inner peripheral regions, issues of religious and language rights do not loom large. Such minority groups, moreover, comprise the majority of China's fifty-five ethnic groups, and hence the bulk of minority representation in the political echelons. Their economic priorities are very much in line with Beijing's developmental bias that frames the official policy discourse in the reform era. In conversations with minority officials and scholars about problems in ethnic regions, the most frequent words to emerge from them are the "backwardness" of minority regions and their "need for development." There seems to be little collective will to seek the type of political autonomy espoused by Ilham Tohti. Minority legislators of the NPC, China's nominal legislature, seem to genuinely embrace the bargain that autonomy entails not more political rights but more economic benefits for their homelands. Even moderate liberal autonomists, who cite political rights as being important, would not yield on preferential policies, arguing that they do not amount to "reverse discrimination" (Tursun 2012b).

A series of legislative efforts to amend the LAER is illustrative. Between three sessions of the NPC from 1988 to 1998, minority legislators put forth thirty-two proposals to amend the LAER. Thirty-one of these amendments were passed in 1999. These thirty-one amendments fall into just three areas and all are economically related, according to the NPC's director of legislative proposals (Ao 2001). The first area, involving 75 percent of the thirty-one amendments, mandates more policy benefits for minority regions, including subsidy and investment, infrastructure and development, resource exploration and trade promotion, finance and tax relief, higher education, anti-poverty measures, environmental protection, and compensation for resource extraction and environmental damage. The second area consists of new amendments that mandate "state responsibilities to minority regions." This replaces the softer language of "state guidance and assistance" in the first version of the autonomy law in 1984. The third area contains new mandates that require regular provinces to provide partner assistance to minority regions. In other words, thirty-one of the thirty-two amendments simply ask for more socioeconomic benefits from the state. Rather than complaining about centralizing forces, in other words, socialist autonomists want to utilize them to serve particularistic interests.

Instead of challenging the official system of autonomy, socialist autonomists focus on practical barriers in protecting local economic interests. One frequently noted barrier comes from the competing agendas and interests at various levels of the state. Foremost are the tensions between central priorities and local interests over developmental issues. In the old planned economy, central ministries had jurisdiction over major and strategic resources, including those in ethnic regions. In the reform era, such resources remain under state control as part of the "commanding heights" of the national economy. In a historical reversal of the "needy nomad," it is now the steppe regions – especially Xinjiang and Inner Mongolia – that are rich in the natural resources needed by inland China.

In the resource battle with the state, the autonomy law compromises by urging the autonomous regions to prioritize the "overall interest of the country" (Art. 1: section 7). But the law is silent on why local minority interests should not constitute the "national interest" as well. Taking advantage of this clause, state agencies and state corporations can disregard local interests in the extraction of key resources, such as petroleum, lumber, minerals, and hydraulic power. Compensation to ethnic regions may often be low and not always delivered. Extraction of petroleum by state enterprises, in particular, is a poignant issue for the titular ethnic group in Xinjiang, especially Uighur intellectuals. The appointment of the Uighur official Nur Bekri to head the National Energy Commission (2014–18) was in no small irony in highlighting the "national" nature of Xinjiang's oil reserves.

The prioritization of the national interests here apparently conflicts with the autonomy law's provision that autonomous regions can change or reject central decrees that are ill suited to local conditions. But this provision also has a precondition, namely "prior central approval." This requirement makes it difficult to change or reject central decrees in practice. The autonomy law dictates that after a central agency receives a local request to adjust or abandon a central decree, the central agency must reply in sixty days (Art. 20). However, there is no provision for situations where a central agency does not give approval, does not reply, or does not reply in sixty days (Hu 2011: 18). Moreover, from a local perspective sixty days may be too long to stop projects opposed by local communities, given the fast pace of the developmental frenzy in today's China.

Another barrier to autonomy is local bureaucratic incentives, which can curtail local autonomy over resources. For "major and strategic resources," the autonomy law allows local authorities to negotiate tax rates with companies contracted to extract them. For non-strategic resources, local authorities have the power to choose contractors and the terms of extraction. In both cases, local authorities may be motivated to accept profit-sharing arrangements that benefit the local officialdom but not local communities (Gong 2009: 179).

Local authorities often prefer tax revenues to resource sharing, because tax income helps to defray local administrative costs and deficits. Good performances funded by such income, in turn, enhance local officials' political careers. These officials may also be reluctant to negotiate aggressively on behalf of local communities, for fear of alienating state agencies or deterring outside investors. In their drive to attract outside investment, it is not uncommon for local governments to approve projects that are harmful to local residents. Some sacrifice local traditional means of livelihood, while others force relocation to less desirable locations. Local residents may receive few direct benefits from resource extraction, but suffer long-term economic and environmental consequences. In cases of non-strategic resources, where local officials have decision powers, an additional incentive can be at work: bribery by private developers. Since contractors are usually from Han regions, local resentment over economic exploitation and environmental damage is then directed toward the Han businesses, thus relieving local officials of blame. In Tibetan regions, one may hear complaints about excavating in "sacred mountains," directed at Han miners but not the local officials who approved the projects.[26]

In addition, local officials are inclined to ask the central government for more fiscal assistance, rather than better resource-sharing arrangements that would benefit local residents. This bureaucratic bias results in an odd phenomenon: local governments may be rich with revenues from resource extraction, yet residents may not see real benefits while having to live with the environmental consequences (Xu and Yu 2009: 33). This problem is not unique to ethnic regions, since it afflicts all resource-rich provinces. In fact, as Zheng Yongnian argues, China's ethnic groups enjoy an important "perk" even when deprived of access to local resources: social unrest in Xinjiang gets central attention and assistance. By contrast, local residents in Shanxi enjoy few benefits from private mining companies in their province, and many suffer from bad pollution and dangerous working conditions. Yet they get little redress from the central state (Zheng 2012). This argument is frequently heard at academic forums in China, being made by scholars who are not specialists on ethnic regions. Due to such comparative references, Chinese scholars and officials tend to be dismissive of

[26] Conversations with two villagers in Garzê, Sichuan province, summer 2015.

ethnic grievances. The autonomy part of the autonomy system, and what it entails and why, are usually forgotten.

Local agendas and interests can be curtailed by a lack of financial independence as well. The SEAC has proposed specific statutes (*zizhi fagui*) to govern the autonomy law's implementation at local levels. But these have gone nowhere, due in no small part to a lack of financial, technical, and human capital. Greater resources would be necessary to back up political demands for more independent actions, such as funding local industries, police forces, schools, textbooks, and so on. Party documents reveal that officials from the TAR constantly ask the central state for more financial support and more developmental projects. While giving in to the TAR, central leaders often warn the other autonomous regions not to emulate it (CCP 2005: 470, 473). Such dependence on the central state makes it hard for local authorities to resist central agendas. This argument, however, does not apply to resource-rich regions such as Xinjiang or Inner Mongolia, where local resources should suffice to enable considerable financial independence if they had autonomy over them.

Important incentives are also at work for individual officials. As Hillman notes in his study of Tibetan counties, a complex system of formal and informal incentives deters risk taking and creative policy making among local officials in conflict-afflicted areas. The politicization of unrest and the pressures of political competition compel local officials, especially ethnic officials, to distance themselves from groups associated with protests and to take a tough stand on protesters. This can get in the way of acknowledging protesters' grievances and moving toward policy innovation (Hillman 2016). Within sensitive ethnic regions, a cynical view holds that a level of controllable unrest is useful for getting more resource allocation and for local officials' political report cards, because managing ethnic unrest offers opportunities for political achievement.[27] All of the above incentives appear to exist, based on field observations, but vary with individual circumstances, ambitions, and shrewdness.

Competing agendas and interests can hamper the SEAC itself, an agency designed to protect minority interests. Staffed by a mix of ethnicities, some members may be more ethno-nationally oriented than others. Departmental functions may vary and conflict. The Department of Policy and Law, responsible for drafting state policy and law on ethnic affairs, genuinely seeks to improve and enhance autonomy. Departments overseeing policy implementation or studying grassroots problems may be warier of local interests running amok. Some officials are worried about the "800,000 people" whose ethnic statuses are yet to be identified and who have no access

[27] Conversations with two Tibetan officials from local United Front offices, western Sichuan, fall 2013 and summer 2015; and two Han scholars at Sichuan University, summers 2015 and 2017.

to preferential policies. Others may be critical of official policies in private and sympathize with dissident views。

Beyond the SEAC, autonomy competes with a variety of central and local agendas. The NPC has its own research groups that assess legislative proposals, including those drafted by the SEAC. NPC reluctance has been responsible for the failure to adopt more detailed statutes on autonomy rights.[28] At local levels, the SEAC's authority pales in comparison with regular party and state agencies. Local SEAC offices are supposed to safeguard autonomy rights but when local economic decisions are being made or developmental projects being decided, they are seldom if ever consulted. A big part of the provincial SEAC's job in Xinjiang is to manage pilgrimage trips to Mecca. To avoid overcrowding, Saudi Arabia rations the number of people who can make these trips. Local SEAC offices assign the quotas, maintain waiting lists, screen applicants, and organize pilgrimage tours that are complete with medical personnel. Wary of radical influences on Muslim youths, SEAC agencies now give approval to applicants over fifty years of age with a clean background and a stable income.

Apprehension about centrifugal tendencies is yet another reason for curtailed autonomy, due to overvigilance in sensitive ethnic regions. Thus there is far less space for religious freedom in the TAR or Xinjiang than in other ethnic regions or regular provinces. The works of the Tibetan writer Tsering Woeser, with vague nostalgia for the Dalai Lama and harsh criticisms of the Han people, may be published in an interior province, but banned in the TAR. Xinjiang's campuses strictly ban any sign of the Muslim faith, which is unheard of in regular provinces. The hijab can be worn by performers on musical shows and TV programs in a province outside Xinjiang, which would be inconceivable in Xinjiang. Academic institutions in regular provinces face few restrictions to have international exchanges, but those in Xinjiang or Tibet have a hard time securing official approval. Islamic schools in interior China may operate under the guise of "language schools" for Muslim children, even recruiting students from Xinjiang. But in Xinjiang, Islamic education and worship are strictly banned for those under eighteen years of age.

Such apprehension or vigilance leads back to the sensitive question of "trust" for the less assimilated ethnic groups. Even in the Yanbian Korean Prefecture – a model autonomy where ethnic Koreans dominate all aspects of local society – scholars of Korean descent complain about a lack of trust in them. The local government has sometimes launched campaigns to promote "three correct views," namely, a correct view of history, of the state, and of the nation. Some scholars grumbled bitterly, "Do we not have correct views?"[29] One can only imagine the resentment in Xinjiang and Tibet, where members of the

[28] Conversations with a former SEAC official in Hangzhou, June 2018, and a current SEAC official, Beijing, January 2018.

[29] Field observations at Yanbian University, fall 2013.

titular minority do not routinely serve in the top posts, while anti-separatist campaigns are frequent.

Unlike the integrationists, socialist autonomists take seriously the problem of insufficient minority officials in top political offices. But unlike the liberal autonomists, they do not regard the deficiency as deliberate. Hao Shiyuan, the senior Mongol scholar at IEA, attributes the problem to a lack of experienced minority officials. Hao's wife Fu Ying, a fellow Mongol, was China's only female minority ambassador and now heads the NPC's Foreign Affairs Committee. Yang Minghong, a scholar at Yunnan University, cites a structural constraint: because Tibetan areas are thinly populated, there are simply fewer public offices to which Tibetan officials may be promoted. For similar reasons, an official rank in a Tibetan region weighs less than a similar rank in Han regions, since the size of the population and the complexity of local affairs differ vastly. Due to this gap, Tibetan officials have slim prospects to be promoted to official posts outside Tibetan regions.[30] This point echoes Ma Rong's about the limitations of the minority track for minority professionals.

Yet another barrier to autonomy is attributed to the Han people's patronizing attitude. From bilingual education to developmental projects to community resettlement, decisions are made for local minorities for their own good. Ming Hao, the Korean Chinese researcher at the SEAC, even complains about "Darwinism" (2012). This patronizing attitude is especially common in Xinjiang and Tibet, the two largest recipients of state aid and investment. Baffled by a lack of minority appreciation, local officials have had to promote "gratitude" campaigns after the Lhasa riot of 2008 and the Urumqi riot of 2009. Their bafflement indicates a dearth of official concern for a deeper problem. That is, when local input and participation are absent, the massive dangling of carrots may not earn gratitude. In fact it has left the recipient regions accustomed to state largeness. While Tibetan professionals tend to express sincere gratitude for the tremendous progress in their home villages, Uighur professionals are more grudging due to a lack of local involvement in state aid and investment programs. Even a pro-Beijing Uighur scholar grumbled about a Uighur theme park in their prefecture, donated by a partner province. The park was to be built on the theme of Afanti, a legendary Uighur folk hero familiar to the Han people. But Afanti does not resonate with Uighurs as it represents a Han caricature of Uighur culture.[31] For socialist autonomists, an Afanti-themed park in southern Xinjiang would epitomize Han arrogance or chauvinism. By contrast, liberal autonomists would place blame squarely on a lack of local ethnic autonomy.

The socialist autonomists contribute to the Chinese debate on autonomy by defending the ethnic and the established system. With their main challenge – the

[30] Conversations with Yang during three field trips to Tibetan regions, summers 2014, 2015, and 2017.

[31] Field observations at a college in Kashgar, summer 2011.

integrationists – publicly rebuked by Xi Jinping, they prevail politically and ideologically and safeguard the autonomous system from any fundamental change, at least for now.

SUMMARY

As reflected in three contending perspectives from the Chinese debate on autonomy, institutional tensions in the autonomous system, between centralization and ethnicization, have persisted and intensified in the reform era. The end of class universalism, though aimed at promoting political integration, has undermined the ideological justification for centralization, rendering it a symbol of "Han" rule and even "double jeopardy." The rise of identity politics, though aimed at inducing political loyalty, has enhanced policy mechanisms for ethnicization, rendering it an instrument of ethnic particularism. As the liberal autonomists point out, political centralization constrains autonomy rights in precarious ways, especially for the culturally distinct outer peripheral regions where such rights matter. Yet as the integrationists highlight, ethnic prerogatives undermine the imperative of national cohesion.

Herein lies the crux of the institutional tensions of China's autonomous system: they pull (centralization) and push (ethnicization) at the same time. The autonomy rights asserted by the liberal autonomists are encouraged – if not always legitimated – by the official elevation of identity politics in the reform era; but the ethnicizing effects highlighted by the integrationists are also discouraged – if not always delegitimated – by the centralizing imperative of the Chinese political system. However, when groups at either end refuse to accept the institutional compromises, ethnic discord arises and becomes amplified. That is, the silence of the liberal autonomists on the problems of ethnic particularism entails that they are not likely to be placated by more ethnic prerogatives, as long as centralization persists. This means that the issues of minority rights such as autonomy, religion, and language will likely mobilize those who care about them, and no amount of "carrots" from the state can dissuade them.

At the same time, the silence of the integrationists on the problems of centralization implies that they are not likely to be placated by more centralization, as long as ethnic particularism persists. This means that in the logic of the integrationists, ethnic prerogatives will always politicize those who feel entitled to them, and no amount of centralization can dissuade identity politics. Ethnic discord and conflict will thus be unavoidable in regions where the mix of centralization and ethnicization is most at play, namely Xinjiang and Tibet, because centralization will always constrain autonomy while ethnicization will always fuel ethnic claims.

Opportunely for the state, the prevailing minority opinion tolerates a trade-off between political autonomy and distributional rights. The demise of the socialist redistributive state has made these rights all the more necessary and placatory for those minority members unconcerned about issues of an "ethnonational" nature. Despite practical barriers in implementing the current forms of autonomy, socialist autonomists say little about greater autonomy in terms of self-governance. For the layers of the state apparatus in charge of ethnic affairs or that study the subject, it is bureaucratically rational to remain socialist autonomists and politically expedient to toe the ideologically correct line. Needless to say, some may be genuinely devoted to the idea of ethnic equality and national integration through socialist autonomy. Given their dominance within the officialdom and the ideological legitimacy of their perspective, it is unsurprising that the socialist vision of autonomy – a trade-off between political rights and ethnic prerogatives – would dominate ethnic policy making in the post-Mao era. Nevertheless, this dominance serves to delay confronting the institutional tensions highlighted by liberal autonomists and integrationists.

Ultimately, the nature of autonomy remains fundamentally unchanged in the post-Mao era. That is, autonomy remains defined in terms of the mentality of the Chinese state: substantive rights in development and distribution, rather than procedural rights in political choices and decision-making powers. The nominally procedural rights granted at local levels – by way of local legislative power – are still designed to protect the type of substantive rights defined by the state. These rights – largely developmental and distributional – are intended to serve rather than challenge the central imperatives of interethnic parity and national integration.

6

Religious Revival and Its Discontents

Religion has been a volatile problem in the state's relationship with the two outer peripheral regions, thanks to its crucial linkage to ethnic and cultural identity. This identity, in turn, can be linked to ethno-nationalism and even separatism. This tendency contrasts with inner peripheral regions, where scholars observe an absence of linkage between ethnic identity revival and anti-state sentiments, or between religion and separatism (McCarthy 2009; Wellens 2009).

In the outer peripheral regions, however, strong linkages have been observed. In the late 1980s Tibetan Buddhism became a renewed catalyst for Tibetan nationalism, with monks and nuns leading anti-Chinese or anti-state protests (Barnett 1994). Increased restrictions on religious activities, viewed as suppression of Tibetan nationalism and identity, are largely blamed for the Lhasa riot of March 2008 (Barnett 2009: 17; Topgyal 2011). Or it is claimed that religion – particularly involving loyalty to the Dalai Lama – fueled the 2008 riot (Shakya 2008b) and self-immolation since 2009 (Shakya 2012). In Xinjiang as well, studies suggest links between religion and ethnicity (Mackerras 2018), or that religious practices have been revived with new nationalistic meanings (Harris 2008) and served as a focus for Uighur resistance to Chinese rule (Bulard 2009), while restrictions on religious practices are a major target of Uighur protesters (Bovingdon 2004; Dillon 2004; Fuller and Lipman 2004). However, existing studies have not examined the specific dynamics of how state policies and religious revival/resistance have interacted.

This chapter will continue with the argument that the built-in tensions of the autonomous system, namely centralization and ethnicization, have intensified in the reform era. The driving force has been the rise of identity politics and the state's curtailment of its unwanted growths. The heightened institutional tensions, in the cases of Tibet and Xinjiang, have contributed directly or indirectly to ethnic conflict and violence. Here ethnicization came first, in the form of state facilitation of religious revival and its unintended consequences, as part of political liberalization and ethnic accommodation in early post-Mao China. Centralization ensued, in the form of state curtailment of unsanctioned religious growths. The alternatively facilitating and constraining roles of the state have intensified centralization as well as ethnicization in the religious development of the two outer peripheral regions.

The following topics will be covered in this chapter: (1) the Chinese state and religion, (2) two cycles of state facilitation and curtailment of religion in Xinjiang's case, and (3) the Tibetan case.

THE CHINESE STATE AND RELIGION

Historically, the facilitating and constraining role of the Chinese state toward religion was determined by the hegemonic status of the official ideology, Confucianism. Hegemony entailed the security and confidence of the institutionally dominant ideology, which tolerated the growth of major religions such as Buddhism and Daoism as well as minor faiths such as folk or popular religions (Zhao 2015: 342–4). At the same time, the state also placed limits on religions, requiring them to accept Confucian orthodoxy, banning those sects and cults that were ethnically problematic as judged by Confucian morals, and repressing those that appeared to become political or breed social unrest (Zhao 2015: 345). In other words, the state tolerated religion when its official orthodoxy was secure but did not tolerate those religious elements that deviated from or threatened the state ideology. This historical relationship between state and religion finds parallels in contemporary times.

The contemporary Chinese state has also played a contradictory role in the growth of major and minor religions, facilitating in some ways and constraining in others. In a study on the rise of Protestantism, Yanfei Sun argues that the Chinese state has been the most powerful actor in creating and shaping the sociological context in which religion is situated (2017: 1708). That is, "state actors, out of ideological and practical concerns, constrained and facilitated by state capacity, directly and indirectly create an environment that religious organizations can tap into or are compelled to wrestle with" (2017: 1674). The constraining role of the state includes regulations that set narrow limits on the activities of sanctioned religious organizations, a regulatory regime in the Religious Affairs Bureau (RAB) that enforces religious policies and regulations and cracks down on deviant religious groups (Sun 2017: 1695–6).

At the same time, the state's regulatory power over religion is itself constrained by limited state capacity. As Sun shows, local state agencies are not always capable of enforcing religious policy and frequently sidelined by local economic priorities (2017: 1697–8). The RAB occupies an insignificant place in the local state hierarchy, with few resources and usually understaffed and headed by officials close to retirement. Local branches of the RAB are appointed and funded by local governments, and thus subordinated to their agendas and whims. All this helps to create an "interstitial social space" for religious organizations and groups (Sun 2017: 1714), an outcome of state incapacity on the one hand and contestations between the state and religious actors on the other.

The above insights, from historical and contemporary times, offer a useful framework for understanding the contradictory role of the Chinese state in the religious development of the TAR and Xinjiang. On the one hand, the early post-Mao state promoted religious revival as part of the campaign to "redress the leftist wrongs" of the Mao era. The revival was not viewed as a challenge to official ideology but instead as safeguarding it by contributing to the official reform platform. Meanwhile, the weakness of the state regulatory regime at this stage created the "interstitial social space" for religious actors to grow in unsanctioned ways. Once such growths became political and bred social unrest, the state would curtail them. These constraining efforts would lead to cycles of backlash in the TAR and Xinjiang.

Limited state capacity also manifests itself beyond the religious regulatory regime. In both the TAR and Xinjiang, religion finds its strongest base in the countryside where the state finds its weakest reach. Of the five administrative levels of the Chinese state, the rural township (*xiangzhen*) government is the lowest. But this level of the local state has been rendered hollow after the agricultural tax reform of the early 2000s, which began partially in 2000 and eliminated all agrarian taxes by 2006. The reform has been so transformative that it is considered the third agrarian revolution of the CCP, after the land reform of the 1950s and the household production system of the early 1980s. With agrarian taxes eliminated, the township government lost its power to collect taxes from rural enterprises and households, which used to pay for rural public services, including schools, family planning, distribution of financial incentives, militia training, road construction, and other public projects.

Fiscal resources would now be allocated from the state, but to the county-level government, or the administrative level above rural townships. This transformation renders the local state a tier removed from the grassroots, weakens individual incentives to serve as village officials (who are not on the state payroll), and undermines local state capacity at the village level as well as the reach of the state into the village. As Juan Wang documents, administrative changes following the agricultural tax reform have undermined the extractive, coercive, and responsive capacity of the local state and the fundamental components of a capable government – a coherent and robust local leadership that enables the functioning of the local state (Wang 2017). In fact, village governance has so deteriorated that the CCP's first central decree of 2018 concerns strengthening rural governance and combating organized criminal groups (CCP 2018). These groups have filled in the vacuum left by the decline of the state in the countryside.

The cycles of state facilitation and curtailment comprise the key dynamic of religious development in the two sensitive ethnic regions. By contrast, as in ethnic regions where a perceived linkage between religion and separatism is absent, such as in Yunnan, the space for religious freedom becomes substantially larger and cultural diversity is not viewed as a threat to state security (Wellens 2009). In this sense, Yanfei Sun is right to credit the state as the most powerful actor in shaping the sociological context of religion in China (2017: 1708). This view of the state offers a more useful analytical framework than Fenggang Yang's model of triple religious markets. Yang's model assumes a rational choice understanding of religious affiliation and treats the state as an exogenous and secondary factor (Yang 2006 and 2012). In Yang's model, heavy state regulation will not change religious demand, but will change the structure of religious supply, that is the rise of a black and a gray market besides the (state-sanctioned) red market. But as Sun points out, the assumption of a constant demand for religious products in a given society is unwarranted, and so is the implication that the gray and black markets may provide better religious supply than the red market (2017: 1713, 1714). A state-centered model better explains the cycles of religious development in Xinjiang and the TAR.

THE CASE OF XINJIANG

The 1980s saw the first cycle of state facilitation of religion in post-Mao China, both directly and indirectly. Direct facilitation was driven by the party's imperative to end class politics and to repair ethnic relations damaged during the radical years of the Mao era. In the late 1970s and the early 1980s, a series of central decrees were issued to repudiate the party's class ideology in minority policy, rehabilitate ethnic religious elites, and promote religious revival. Indirect facilitation of religion also ensued from the state's limited capacity to manage the direction of this revival. The specific ordinances and policy measures promoting religious revival are detailed in Chapter 4 (the section "Revival of Religion" and Table 4.1). Many of the policy measures, alone or in combination with other reform measures, were specific to the TAR and Xinjiang.

Facilitating Religion: The 1980s

It is worth reiterating the key policy measures for religious revival and their ethnicizing effects in Xinjiang. First, state sponsorship and funding contributed to the restoration and proliferation of places of worship. This included welcoming foreign religious groups to help restore mosques, heralding religious growth unwanted by the state. As many Uighur intellectuals worried at the time, the resurgence of Islam stifled progress in secular education and modernization (Rudelson 1997: 121). Their fears have proved to be well founded, as religious institutions have become ideological and organizational competitors to secular and modernizing forces. Second, rehabilitation of former religious elite, coupled with the exit of Han professionals, further boosted religious revival politically and intellectually, while undermining the party's secular cadre. The strengthening of religious forces, in turn, eroded the class solidarity that once rallied ethnic masses around the Communist Party, thus weakening the foundation of the interethnic alliance during the socialist era. Third, religious revival helped to shift a class identity to an ethno-religious identity. It reconnected ethnic masses to the former religious clergy, who were no longer class enemies but ethnic leaders and spokesmen.

The immediate effects of religious revival in Xinjiang were the rise of private madrassas and young attendees. The state's initial concern was the impact on secular and public education, as an increasing number of children deserted public schools. Limited state capacity, however, contributed to ineffective responses, thus further facilitating private madrassas. The early response came from the Ministry of Education in early 1983, in a decree on religious interference in public school education in minority regions. It named five provinces – with Xinjiang being the first – where Islam, Tibetan Buddhism, and Theravada Buddhism were intruding into schools or luring a significant number of school children to private madrassas or monasteries. According to the decree, the number of children in Kashgar of Xinjiang who abandoned public schools for private madrassas increased from 4,000 to 18,000 in just six month from March 1981 (MOE 1983) A greater percentage of children were lured away in the Hui county of Gansu and the Dai county of Yunnan (38.8 percent and 30 percent respectively), but Xinjiang's situation was more alarming to authorities because the absolute number was much greater and because four Uighur riots occurred in southern Xinjiang between April 1980 and October 1981 (Shan 2013).

While the Ministry of Education decree signified the seriousness of the issue, its substance attested to the state's lack of familiarity with new religious developments at this time. The main point of the decree was to admonish the large numbers of children abandoning public schools, but the proposed remedy relied on the party's cliché: to strengthen ideological and patriotic education at public schools. The document took a tougher stand on local calls for Arabic classes in public schools, avowing no tolerance for restoring religious teaching in the name of language classes. Local responses in Xinjiang were in line with the state's overall promotion of religious revival at the time: to fight private madrassas with officially sanctioned religious schools. Following the Ministry of Education decree in 1983, Xinjiang adopted local measures to provide authorized channels for religious education: opening at least five Islamic schools at the secondary level in five Uighur-concentrated regions in the 1980s, opening the Xinjiang Islamic College in 1987, and granting permission for local religious elites – members in the standing committee of Xinjiang's Islamic Association and above – to recruit two or three private students over the age of eighteen years old (Li 2013b: 35). These official channels for Islamic teaching were too few to meet local needs and placed age limits on enrollees, but they represented the state's overall support for religious revival.

Imported Islam

By the mid-1980s, the state's inexperience indirectly facilitated a new religious development: imported Islamic influences. The driving forces included a growing number of local Muslims who returned from Hajj trips, overseas religious studies, and business travels, as well as an influx of visiting religious delegations from overseas (Li 2016: 3). In the political climate of "reform and opening" in early post-Mao China, two-way international exchanges were encouraged in religious affairs. The Middle East and South Asia were the main sources of overseas influences, especially the Wahhabi sect. Unfamiliar with imported Islam and its sects, local authorities initially viewed the differences between local and imported sects as intrafaith and unworthy of intervention (Li 2013b). Official indifference and inaction allowed imported Islam to grow unchecked.

What authorities failed to recognize was the threat that imported Islam posed to local Islam, and by extension the latter's legitimacy and indigenized traditions. In the initial years of their arrival in the early 1980s, Wahhabism clashed with Xinjiang's traditional Islamic sects to win believers and authority. Local sects rejected Wahhabism for their strict codes and deviation from Islamic tenets and traditions. But the native imams, trained before the reform era, were often advanced in age, seemingly outdated in their spiritual messages, and unable to prevail over young talibs trained overseas or in local private madrassas. Uighur communities have been predominantly Sunni, which reduced entry barriers for Wahhabism, also of the Sunni sect. Since the mid-1980s, Wahhabism mushroomed locally through existing and new private madrassas, winning converts through simplified rituals, exemption of dues, science learning, and anti-poverty measures. Its reform agenda, according to a local researcher, allowed it to make headway even among some intellectuals, government officials, and businessmen. As a member of Xinjiang's RAB concedes, the excessive religiosity but deep ignorance of the Uighur masses about Islam were a major reason why they embraced the new teachings blindly; moreover, the tradition of relying on imams for dissemination of Islamic precepts added to the blind acceptance (Niyaz 2004: 16). Any dissemination from the Arab world, moreover, was regarded as more authoritative and authentic.

The entry of Wahhabism presented special challenges, not only because of its fundamentalist appeal but more importantly due to its global and political nature. Conflicts between indigenized Islamic sects and the newly arrived sects are not new in China – they had been a phenomenon in the Qing dynasty and the patterns of sectarian rivalry are similar to a degree. However, contemporary changes have greatly empowered external sects in this rivalry, especially porous and shrinking borders due to modern means of transportation and communication. Thus the Uighur scholar Tursun (2014) traced the influx of Wahhabism to an earlier period, that is the Iranian revolution and the Soviet invasion of Afghanistan in the late 1970s. This was particularly true of Xinjiang's westernmost prefecture, Kashgar, bordering Afghanistan and Pakistan. Much as in the Iranian and Taliban movements, local followers in Xinjiang diverged between the religiously conservative and the politically radical: the former observed strict Islamic codes, while the latter espoused violence and political Islam.

Yet these distinctions have not always been clear, posing challenges for adequate responses. In general Wahhabism distinguishes itself from Xinjiang's traditional Sunni Islam by claiming the supremacy of Allah and for politicized Wahhabism, the jihad against the secular state. From the beginning, Chinese officials were unable to neatly distinguish non-political and political Wahhabism, frequently lumping them together and underreacting in the initial years (and overreacting in later years). Among informed analysts, such as those at the Xinjiang Academy of Social Sciences and reporters for the Hong Kong-based *Phoenix* magazine, an emphatic distinction is made between indigenized Islam and imported Wahhabism and between cultural and political Wahhabism (Li 2013a, 2013b, and 2016; Tursun 2014; Zhang 2013b and 2014; Huang 2013 and 2014). While blaming imported Wahhabism for the spread of private madrassas, they pinpoint political Wahhabism for the spread of extremism and violence. Even Ilham Tohti admits to the spread of "extremist religious influences" (2014). The distinctions were less clear to the local authorities or outside observers. In his testimony before a subcommittee of the US Congress, Dru Gladney made a point of noting that Uighurs' Sunni practices were anathema to the strict Wahhabi-inspired Islamic codes (2009: 7). Bovingdon dismisses the spread of Wahhabism as rumor (2004: 36). Understandably, conservative Islam and Wahhabism may not always be distinguishable.

Indeed, most local "Wahhabi" teachers and talibs (religious students) had had only a hotchpotch of exposure to Wahhabism and disseminated its most superficial elements. As of 1992, there were a total of 130 local individuals in Xinjiang who had Islamic training overseas, including Pakistan, India, Saudi Arabia, Egypt, and Turkey, according to a local official report.[1] Instead of a uniform sect of Islam or Wahhabism, different versions were brought back and their local dissemination was haphazard. Rather than any deep understanding, local followers simply professed a symbolic way of identification and belonging. Since the mid-1980s, the niqab for women, in black color and covering the entire face and body except the eyes, began to spread in southern Xinjiang, as did the Muslim beard for men. Traditionally

[1] The data are from XUAR Commission on Ethnic and Religious Affairs, "Xinjiang yisilan gongzuo qingkuan" [Work Report on Islam in Xinjiang]. 1992. Cited in Li (2016: 3).

Uighur women wore colorful headscarves and dresses, and the few old women who veiled their faces used white or brown colors rather than black.

The less educated youths dominated the talib demographics, attesting to the shallow yet ominous infiltration of imported Islam. These talibs ranged from students from secondary school to unemployed or self-employed youths with just secondary education. Some had quit public school for madrassas, others escaped public school for half a day or devoted evenings to madrasas (Li 2013b: 35). In Hotan prefecture, Wahhabi believers grew from a few thousand in the early 1990s to about 100,000 by 1997, or 10–15 percent of Muslim believers in the prefecture, while Kashgar prefecture had over 30,000.[2] But these may represent various conservative or fundamentalist forms of Islam, rather than genuine Wahhabism. Between 1996 and 2000, the number of new enrollees in private madrassas increased 8.84 times in Kashgar prefecture, 90 percent of them public school children and some as young as three years old (CCP 2001a: 270).

With official restrictions on homegrown private madrasas since 1983, the so-called Wahhabi sects filled in the void. According to a local official investigation, the number of private madrasas was 938 in Xinjiang in 1990, with 10,742 talibs; Kashgar prefecture topped the list with 350 private madrasas and the largest number of talibs (about 4,000) (Ma 2002: 13–14; Li 2013b: 35). These numbers, however, did not differ significantly from those cited by a local researcher for the year 1981 (Wu 2001), when local private madrasas first flourished. This could mean that the scale of private madrasas remained stable, contrary to authorities' concerns. It could also mean that the earlier official bans simply resulted in temporary closedowns and reopening in different local areas. Since 1990 over a thousand private madrasas were reportedly closed down each year throughout the 1990s (Ma P. 2003: 74). But this number also approximated the reported 938 madrasas that existed in Xinjiang in 1990. Thus it is unclear if the same madrasas were closed down and reopened later under different individuals.

By the late 1980s, official responses were stepped up against the new rounds of private madrasas. However, new regulations still focused on the impact of private madrassas on public education, rather than the larger political challenge of Wahhabism. In 1988 and 1990, Xinjiang's provincial party issued new policies on such madrassas, using the tougher language of "strict prohibition." In 1990, the Ministry of Education of the central state issued two decrees banning religion in educational institutions. Despite the new regulations, implementation fell short due to official ambivalence. Other

[2] The 1997 dataset is the only one I can find about the size of Wahhabis in any religion of Xinjiang. See "Guanyu woqu wahabipai wenti de diaocha baogao" [An investigative report about the Wahhabi problem in our region], a joint report by the Investigative Group for Religious Problems, the Department of United Front and the Commission on Religious Affairs of the Xinjiang Uighur Autonomous Region, 1997.

than threats to public education, local authorities saw the growth of Wahhabi talibs as a sectarian matter from which the state should stay away. Local state actors, from RABs and police to social organizations and public schools, would not and could not intervene in the spread of Wahhabism, since the talibs' activities were technically beyond their jurisdiction (Li 2013b: 36–7). The prevalence of ethnic cadre in rural areas, where private madrasas thrived, also made it more difficult for them to intervene. Being part of local communities, they faced pressure from relatives and neighbors for not being Muslim enough.[3] All this resulted in local state reluctance to regulate religion.

This incapacity, throughout the 1980s, can be attributed largely to the central state's lack of understanding of religious revivalism on the one hand and local states' ambivalence on the other. The aspirations of conservative Islamic movements – to return to the earliest Islamic sources of the Quran and Hadith – provided the ideology and direction that was missing in the official sponsorship of religious revival. The rise of religious fundamentalism could easily take on political significance for those who viewed the Chinese state as both secular and alien.

Ethnicizing Effects: 1990s

The surge of unsanctioned religion in the 1980s produced unintended consequences in the following decade, that is ethnic violence and "terrorism" in the 1990s (Tables 6.1 and 6.2). These may be conceived of as the ethnicizing effects of religious revival for a critical reason: religious revival enabled the rise of private madrassas and talibs as the ideological and organizational base for ethnic mobilization.

Above all, talibs were responsible for rising violence in the 1990s. In particular, authoritative accounts trace it to the talibs trained by former ethnic elites who were rehabilitated after the Mao era.[4] The most notable case involved Ablikim Mehsum, who was sentenced to twenty years in prison in 1957 for being a member of the separatist East Turkestan party. He was released in 1977 at an opportune time, on the eve of the post-Mao era. Rehabilitated in the early 1980s, he became the imam of a major mosque in Kargilik county of Kashgar and a deputy chair of the county's CPPCC. In 1987 Mehsum opened his own madrassas, accounting for 61 percent of the private madrassas in the county during the late 1980s and the early 1990s. Together he trained over 800 talibs from across Xinjiang. Kashgar is a historical hub of Uighur culture and borders two countries plagued by religious radicalism,

[3] Conversations with a police officer in a Hotan county, who was a Uighur neighbor of one of my relatives, fall 2013. Conversations with a former police officer of Hotan, summer 2015.

[4] For example, Wu (2001) and Li (2012b and 2013b), from the Xinjiang Academy of Social Sciences; Zhang (2009), a former party secretary of Xinjiang's Commission on Politics and Law. See also Li Y. (2013), a Hong Kong-based reporter.

TABLE 6.1 *Onset of violence in Xinjiang: the early 1990s*

Year	Location	What happened	Casualties
April 5, 1990	Baren village, Akto county, Kiziksu Kirghiz	Village government attacked; police vehicles bombed; jihadist slogans; called for East Turkestan (ET) Islamic Republic	6 police and 2 paramilitary officers dead; 9 assailants dead and 7 captured
February 28, 1991	Kuqa/Kuche county, Aksu prefecture	Time bomb set off at bus station; in the name of ET Islamic Reform Party	1 civilian dead and13 injured
February 5, 1992	Urumqi city	2 public buses bombed; bombs placed in other public places, in the name of ET Islamic Reform Party	3 civilians dead and 20 injured (9 severely)
June–September, 1993	Kashgar and Hotan; Yarkant and Kargilik	15 bombing incidents in public facilities claimed by ET Islamic Reform Party	2 civilians dead and over 30 injured
February 5, 1997	Ghulja/Yining city Ili prefecture	Protesters rioted, shouting "expel Hans" and "Islamic state" on Lunar New Year's Day; lasted two days, as police had no order to respond; blamed on ET Islamic Allah Party	7 Han civilians and 9 officers killed; over 200 injured; 39 vehicles and many stores destroyed
February 25, 1997	Urumqi city	Bombing of 3 public buses, on the day of Deng Xiaoping's memorial service	9 civilians dead, mostly minorities, 68 injured

Source: Xjass (2010); Cheng (2014b); NFZM (2007).

TABLE 6.2 *Assassination of Uighur officials and imams: the 1990s*

Place		Target of assassination	Causalities
August 24, 1993	Kargilik/Yecheng county, Kashgar	Mawla Abliz, imam of county's chief mosque, member of county CPPCC	Target severely injured
March 22, 1996	Toqsu/Xinhe county, Aksu prefecture	Akmusdik Haji, respected imam, for testifying in court	Target killed
April 29, 1996	Kuqa/Kuche county, Aksu prefecture	Qawal Toka, village party secretary, member of Xinjiang People's Congress and National CPPCC	4 family members of target killed; target and wife critically injured
May 12, 1996	Kashgar city, Kashgar prefecture	Aronhan'aji, Xinjiang's highest ranked imam, of China's largest mosque	Target and son critically injured
March 23, 1997	PCC Frontier Farm, Aksu	Emerjan, PCC party secretary; in the name of the East Turkestan party, led by Tursun Todi	Target and wife killed
July 30, 1997	Awat county, Aksu Prefecture	Turniyaz, party secretary of Baishenyuerike township	Target and wife killed
November 6, 1997	Baicheng county, Aksu Prefecture	Mawla Yunus Sidik, head of Aksu's Islamic Association	Target killed
January 27, 1998	Karjilik/Yecheng county, Kashgar	Abuliz Haji, imam of chief county mosque, senior county CPPCC member	Target killed
August 23, 1999	Bosika township, Poskam/Zepu, Kashgar	Hudabayer Tohti, political director of township police station; 38 stabs	Target and son killed, target's wife injured

Source: Xjass (2010); Cheng (2014b).

Afghanistan and Pakistan, as well as two newly independent countries, Kyrgyzstan and Tajikistan. Mehsum had allegedly told his talibs to prepare for decades of struggle to bring about Islamic rule in Xinjiang and to achieve East Turkestan through nurturing religious forces via madrassas (Ma and Xu 2006: 123). According to local authoritative accounts, all of the assailants arrested for violence in Xinjiang in the first half of the 1990s were Mehsum's talibs (Wu 2001; Zhang X. 2009: 48; Li 2013b: 37).

Second, a common thread among the assailants was an invocation of religion and East Turkestan, or a linkage of the religious and the political. This mix was presumably more effective than a purely political or separatist call for East Turkestan. The first episode of violence occurred in Baren village in southern Xinjiang on April 5, 1990 (Table 6.1). As the worst armed riot in the history of the PRC at the time, it finally alerted local authorities to the dangers of radical Islam. Many of the participants had studied with Mehsum (Li Y. 2013; Li 2013b: 35). The organizer, Zeddin Yusup, was a talib who returned from Kashgar to establish the East Turkestan Islamic Party in 1990. In preparing for the attack, Yusup's team urged villagers to donate money and manpower in the name of Islam and jihad. Authorities would later characterize the violent incident as the first episode of terrorism in the history of the PRC. Nevertheless, in private conversations some Uighur officials dismissed the official labeling, calling the incident a sectarian battle among Islamic factions, namely, local Islamic and imported Wahhabi sects (Chen 2012). However, insofar as the Wahhabi groups called on jihadist struggles against the secular state, it was not always easy to distinguish between the secular state and the Chinese state. Thus one Uighur writer, in writing about Mehsum's talibs, places blame on human rights abuses in China, refers to Xinjiang as East Turkestan, and calls the Chinese state an "invading power" (Ilhati 2015). It is unclear if East Turkestan means a Uighur state under Islamic rule or non-Chinese rule, or if the distinction makes much difference.

Third, the religious revival of Islam also helped to create a receptive audience for radical Islam, after the fall of the Soviet Union and the breakaway of its Muslim republics in the early 1990s. The revival of Islam in these states spilled over Xinjiang's porous borders, strengthening the fundamentalist appeal (Huang 2013) and independence aspiration (Bulard 2009), or a conflation of the two (Niyaz 2004: 17). Bolstered by the Chechen War in Russia and by weapons smuggled from Central Asian states, East Turkestan parties, private madrassas, and militant training bases sprang up in Xinjiang throughout the 1990s, along with the rise of violent attacks. The Baren incident of 1990 was followed by a series of violence in the name of the East Turkistan Islamic Reform Party (Table 6.1). In 1992, this group attacked Urumqi – Xinjiang's capital with a majority Han population – the day after the Chinese New Year. Escaping back to southern Xinjiang, they carried out fifteen more bombings in public places in 1993. Local authorities alleged that prior to these attacks the group established Xinjiang's first terrorist base in a Kargilik village, funded by money they had robbed from a cash transport van. At half a million RMB, it was the largest case of its kind in the history of the PRC at the time (*NFZM* 2007).

In another indication of mixed religious and political motives, the next East Turkestan group targeted pro-Beijing Uighur elites. Calling itself the East Turkestan Islamic Opposition Party, the group was assembled from a dozen talibs in late 1993. Their plan of action was to kill Uighur religious and secular leaders who opposed political Islam and cooperated with Beijing, with a goal of "burning bridges" between the Chinese state and Uighur communities. The group reportedly drew up a list of twenty-four Uighurs to be killed. Table 6.2 shows the reported casualties of this project. In the most dramatic incident, Aronhan'aji, the senior imam of Xinjiang's largest mosque, located in Kashgar, was stabbed multiple times on May 12, 1996. He escaped death when the assailant could not bring himself to deliver the fatal stab to the most respected Muslim leader in Xinjiang (*NFZM* 2007). However, in private conversations some Uighur officials dismissed the incident as another case of "sectarian strife" rather than one of separatism (Chen 2012). In this interpretation, the incident was an intra-Uighur conflict over local versus imported Islam. Nevertheless, insofar as the two versions of Islam represented different visions for Xinjiang's future, the targeted killings were more than a sectarian conflict. Moreover, additional pro-Beijing Uighur officials allegedly suffered mysterious deaths during this period.[5] It is unclear if they were on the list of twenty-four targeted Uighurs.

In yet another ethnicizing effect of religious revival, religious fundamentalism served as a counter discourse to the modernization drive launched by the Chinese state. From 1992 to 1995, Mehsum's talibs promoted the new *meshrep* – a gathering with religious meanings – as a form of religious cleansing and ethno-political awakening. As economic liberalization deepened after 1992, a significant number of Uighurs became victims of factory downsizing, market competition, unemployment, economic disparities, and social decay. In this context, Ablikim Mehsum may be seen as playing the role of a local "Khomeini" (Huang 2013): his advocacy of a purified Islamic and moral society appealed to a Uighur society thrust into the turbulent transitions of China's reform era. Stripped of its religious form and vocabulary, fundamentalism offers many similar remedies that have appealed to non-Western civilizations in their arduous transitions to the modern world, including cultural revival.

Traditionally the *meshrep* was a secular event, an occasion when Uighur males gathered to celebrate the harvest. The religiosity of the new *meshrep* attracted many members in the 1990s. As they read passages from the Quran and followed a strict code of Islamic conduct in their daily lives, practitioners

[5] Conversations with Ma Rong and another scholar at Zhejiang University, in Hangzhou, June 17, 2018. Examples of "mysterious deaths" included suspicious heart attacks, automobile accidents, and alcohol-related deaths.

found the religious tenets and practices appealing as a critique of modernity. Islamic fundamentalism, not unlike modern China's embrace of Marxism, is a product in response to the modern West. The remedies it offered included elements of socialism and Maoism familiar to the Chinese public, Uighurs included. As such, pure Islam is persuasive to those most affected by economic liberalization, namely the poor and unemployed. With Uighurs being principal victims in Xinjiang's transition to the market, pure Islam offered a path for collective self-salvation.

In this context, reconstruction of moral values and social justice entailed not only religious but also ethno-national revival. Leading talibs saw themselves as soul mates who sought Islamic cultural enlightenment to save Uighur youths rendered "ignorant and hopeless" by official atheism. They revived the *meshrep* with not only religious but also nationalistic meanings (Harris 2008: 104–6). As such it served as a focus for resistance to Chinese rule (Bulard 2009). The traveling talibs, who hailed mainly from Kashgar and Hotan, organized the *meshrep* across Xinjiang, along with a grassroots campaign urging Uighurs to burn their government-issued ID cards and licenses (*NFZM* 2007). It was a way to boycott the Chinese state.

The *meshrep* cumulated in the Ghulja/Yining riot on February 5, 1997 (Table 6.1). Launched on the Lunar New Year's Day, the riot was in response to local official crackdowns on the *meshrep* and talibs in the city. Located in eastern Xinjiang, Ghulja did not seem to be the kind of locale vulnerable to talib influence, being far more modern and secular than rural southern Xinjiang. However, economic liberalization had by then created disparate Uighur societies: a wealthy one thanks to border trade, and a deprived one thanks to factory closures. For different reasons, both groups became afflicted by alcoholism, drug abuse, gambling, and the worst AIDS epidemic in Xinjiang. Not surprisingly, when Mehsum's talibs came to Ghulja in the mid-1990s, they found a receptive audience for the *meshrep*.

Local leaders belatedly recognized the state's counterproductive role in Xinjiang's religious revival. Wang Enmao, party secretary of the province during 1981–5, summed up two lessons from the 1980s. First, the retreat of the state in the countryside allowed radical religious forces to fill in the vacuum. Second, unconditional restitution of former rebels and clergymen allowed the "unrepentant and resentful" to run madrasas (Wang 1997: 502, 585). Indeed, the role of those released and rehabilitated in the early post-Mao era – at least some of them – seemed critical, as their trainees became key members of "radical religious forces" in the 1990s. As Table 6.2 shows, the violence of the 1990s exhibited characteristics of terrorism in the sense of the intentional creation of "terror" and an invocation to East Turkestan. This contrasted with attackers in recent years who exhibited little understanding of the concept of terror or political objectives.

Curtailing Unsanctioned Religion: The 1990s

The violence since the Baren riot of 1990 posed serious challenges to the state's intended goals for religious revival. After the Baren riot, official focus shifted to curtailing unsanctioned religion in the 1990s, in contrast to the previous emphasis on freedom of religion. But the effort was belated and tenuous.

Local and central authorities issued a number of decrees to outlaw underground religious practices and sites. They targeted private madrasas, cross-regional proselytizing, and imported sects (Tables 6.3 and 6.4). The central decree on oversight of religious affairs ([1991]6, Table 6.4) allowed local authorities to utilize an earlier document ([1982]19, Table 4.1) to enforce religious bans. The 1982 document stipulated freedom *of* religion as well as freedom *from* religion. The latter provision forbids anyone from "compelling anyone, especially children under 18, to have a religious faith, become a monk or study religious scriptures." Local interpretations of this stipulation turned it into a ban on religious practices for children under 18. That is, before they could exercise their will freely. In another unprecedented move, Xinjiang's legislature adopted regulations in July 1994 (Table 6.3) banning proselytizing or organizing religious activities by nonlocals.

The escalation of violence in the 1990s, especially the assassination of Uighur imams and officials, led to central and local authorities to crack down the so-called "three forces." The phrase refers to "religious radicalism, terrorism and separatism," thereby linking the religious, the violent and the political. In the most important central decree on this issue in the 1990s, Document [1996]7 (Table 6.4) cited "underground" religious activities and separatism as the "principal threats" to Xinjiang's stability. It also highlighted the paralysis of village governance due to the influence of religious forces.

TABLE 6.3 *Xinjiang's decrees to curtail illegal religious activities: the 1990s*

Year	Decree	Key contents
November 9, 1988	"Temporary regulations for managing places of religious activities in XUAR"	Defines religious activities outside authorized mosques and private homes as illegal
July 16, 1994	"Regulations for the administration of religious affairs"	Bans proselytizing or organizing religious activities by nonlocals
1997 [1]	"Opinions on defining illegal religious activities"	23 demarcations made
1999	"Opinions on organizing patriotic Islamic clergy to train talibs"	Requiring official approval for opening madrasas to train religious students

Source: XUAR (1988, 1994, 1997); Li (2013a), 24.

TABLE 6.4 *Central decrees to curtail illegal religious activities: the 1990s*

Year	Decree	Key contents
1991 CCP[6] February 5	"CCP Central Committee and State Council On Improving Religious Work" (CCPCC and the State Council)	To crack down on criminal activities in the name of religion; to resist infiltration of foreign hostile religious forces
1994 SC[144]	"PRC Regulations of Religious Activities by Foreign Individuals in China" (State Council)	To curb infiltration of foreign religious personnel and activities
1994 SC[145]	"Regulations for Places of Worship" (State Council)	To curb unauthorized private madrassas
1996 CCP[7]	CCP Central Committee [1996]7 "The principal threats to Xinjiang's stability are ethnic separatism and illegal religious activities" (CCPCC)	To strengthen village governance in Xinjiang

Source: The CCP and the State Council (1991); State Council of the PRC (1994a, 1994b); Li (2013a), 25.

To strengthen village governance, the central government initiated a program that was to become routine and massive in the mid-2010s. In early 1997 the central government dispatched work-teams-in-residence, consisting of 203 provincial cadre and 340 village cadre – to thirty-two villages most affected by radical religious forces. Locally, the central document [1996]7 led to a provincial decree in Xinjiang in 1997 (Tables 6.3 and 6.4) to demarcate legal and illegal religious activities, the latter referring to private madrassas, foreign religious personnel, and unauthorized religious materials. To dampen the religious atmosphere, the decree led to policies banning members of the public sector from practicing religion, including party members, government officials, public sector employees, and school students. Local schools issued religious bans on campus, from headscarves, long gowns, and religious insignias to observance of religious holidays and conventions (Guliyan 2010). Since 1997, the provincial government also devoted several years to cracking down on underground madrassas in the most affected regions (Li 2004). In 1999 it renewed a decree, first issued in 1994, to require official approval for the opening of private madrassas.

Official efforts to contain radical religious activities were frequently complicated by a conflation of the so-called three forces. As a US-based report sums up, the root causes of the "three forces" are a complex mix of history, ethnicity, and religion, fueled by poverty, unemployment, social disparities, and political grievances as well as Turkey's unofficial support, Muslim funding, and militant training from abroad (Van Wie Davis 2008). According to local police investigations, underground religious sites played a key role in rallying activists, operating training bases, organizing anti-state attacks, and advocating East Turkestan (Li 2012b and 2013b). Xinjiang's police confiscated over a million copies of printed literature as well as over a million videos and tapes with "jihadist" themes in the second half of the 1990s (Wu 2001). In 1998, local police cracked a series of cases involving the shipment of weapons from Central Asia, self-made bombs, and militant training sites (*NFZM* 2007).

However, the linkages or distinctions between religious agitation and anti-Chinese resistance were not always easy to determine. At best, imported Wahhabism and jihadist literature served to rally the domestically discontented. Ilham Tohti (2014) argues that religion has suffered a huge setback in Xinjiang since official offensives against the three forces in 1997, because local officials often failed to distinguish between fundamentalism and traditional Islamic practices. Draconian restrictions alienated ordinary practitioners of the Islamic faith and were often viewed as anti-Uighur.

For local and central authorities, new restrictions were already too late. Many madrassas had already sprung up, new channels of foreign influences and communication mediums had opened, and religious sites were turning into sanctuaries for the socially disaffected. By 1997, Xinjiang's authorities concluded from their investigations that major episodes of local violence in recent years were all to do with the Wahhabi sects and members, though the term "Wahhabi" tended to be conflated with "radical" and "extremist" (Li 2016: 2). Illegal religious activities were also found among Xinjiang's traditional clergy, such as the private teaching of Islam, but they espoused no political objectives and violence (Li 2012b: 5–6). For Wahhabi sects, the official crackdown simply made private madrassas more covert, dispersed, and digital. In Kashgar, the hub of Uighur traditions, the number of new enrollees in private madrassas increased 8.84 fold between 1996 and 2000, 90 percent of them being public school children and some as young as three years old (CCP 2001a: 270). Meanwhile, the work teams dispatched in 1997 could only temporarily improve law and order in rural areas, as their departure was followed by the return of religious forces. In 1999, Xinjiang dispatched additional work teams – consisting of 13,800 officials from provincial government agencies – to 584 villages and ninety-nine public schools in five Uighur-majority prefectures (Li X. 2017: 30).

The crackdowns since 1997 appeared to have diminished the talibs nurtured by the dissident clergy in the early post-Mao era. But things remained daunting for the state. Of 2000 Uighur clergymen from across Xinjiang who participated in official training classes in 2001, most were poorly educated in religion or otherwise: just 3 percent had associated degrees and above, 12 percent had graduated from high school, a whopping 83 percent had only graduated from middle school and primary school (42.9 percent and 40.1 percent respectively), and 2 percent were illiterate. Moreover, 90.1 percent had studied Islam privately or in unofficial madrassas (Niyaz 2004: 16, 17). If this represented the educational background of the officially approved Islamic clergy in Xinjiang, the background of unauthorized clergymen may be even more questionable. Yet they presented formidable challenges to the state in winning over the hearts and minds of rural and less educated Uighurs.

Facilitating Religion: The 2000s

The 2000s saw the second cycle of state facilitation of religion, indirectly this time. Nationwide, the agrarian tax reform of 2000–6 achieved the intended goal of administrative streamlining and rural relief, but resulted in weakened local state capacity and the rise of criminal forces in the countryside (CCP 2018). In Xinjiang, weakened village governance created new "interstitial space" for religion in the new millennium.

A major consequence of tax elimination was a fiscal shortage for village councils to perform their functions. Fiscal allocation from the state, now the main or only source of village revenues, was insufficient to cover public services, debt burdens, and other financial needs of village governance. Many village councils, after losing tax revenues, had no alternative incomes of their own. In 2005, nearly a third (28.7 percent) of the administrative villages in Xinjiang, totaling 9,183, had no revenues of their own, while nearly half of them had just ¥50,000 in revenues for the year. In 2006, village councils in Xinjiang owed a total of ¥3.1 billion in debts, or an average of ¥320,000 for each village (*TS* 2006). Fiscal shortages, in turn, led to a reduction in public servants and services at the village level. Based on incomplete data, in 2004 Xinjiang saw the merger of 375 administrative villages with others, the downsizing of 25,000 village cadre, the closedown of 907 primary and secondary village schools, and the discharge of 4,095 school teachers (*Sohu* 2004). To save costs, the positions of the village party secretary and the village chief were combined in one person. The job became overwhelming while oversight of village governance became difficult.

Weakened village governance created a political vacuum for religious forces to fill. These forces included former or current instructors and talibs from private madrassas, often located in private homes within villages; imams who were not regarded as "red" or close to local authorities; local religious activists; and hajis, or those who had made pilgrimage trips to Mecca. Their financial resources may have come from local jade and other traders, or from overseas. The overseas sources may have been donations and earnings raised by pilgrims in Mecca, according to a local woman of mixed Han and Uighur parentage who worked privately to assist hajis in their financial dealings.[6] As social services

[6] Conversations with this woman in Hotan, October 2013, and one of her employers in summer 2015. Because of her bilingual skills and knowledge of banking procedures, she helped hajis with money transfers.

dwindled from the village council, those religious forces filled in by bringing money, mutton, and other necessities to Uighur households, enhancing their presence and influence in the process. This was a ground that the state voluntarily yielded.

Rise of *Hizb ut-Tahrir* and *Hijrat*

Limited state capacity, in the form of poor local knowledge and safeguards, allowed room for new religious movements in the late 1990s and the early 2000s. Identified in Chinese accounts as the *Hizb ut-Tahrir* and *Hijrat*, they drew different groups of young Uighurs.

The *Hizb ut-Tahrir*, an international pan-Islamic political organization, made its entry to Xinjiang around 1999. As a transnational movement, originally founded by the Palestinian Taki al-DinNabhani al-Falastini in Jordan in 1953, it serves as an ideological vanguard for radical Sunni Islamism. Its stated aim is the unification of all Muslim nations over time in a unitary Islamic state or caliphate, headed by an elected caliph (*Hizb ut-Tahri* 1998). In post-Soviet Central Asia, *Hizb ut-Tahrir* filled the ideological and socioeconomic void left by the retreat of socialism and the rise of unemployment, with a special appeal among youths. The organization declared the American-led war in Afghanistan from 2001 as a war against "Muslims and Islam." Despite its stated stand against violence, the organization's association with violence in reality has led Central Asian states and Russia to crack down on its cells.

As with Wahhabism, the overseas origin of *Hizb ut-Tahrir* helped it to evade state attention in the beginning. In rural areas of Xinjiang, *Hizb ut-Tahrir* arrived from across the mountains of Afghanistan and the Fergana Valley of Central Asia (Li Y. 2013). In urban centers, its arrival was attributed to Ihrahim Usman, a graduate of Xinjiang Engineering College in 1990. In 1995 he went to study in Turkey and returned two years later to develop *Hizb ut-Tahrir* in Xinjiang, growing cells and members through private forums such as "Arabic classes" (Wu 2001). Its advocacy of "pan-Islamism" and "Islamic fundamentalism," according to local Uighur scholars, effectively compete for young Uighur minds on Xinjiang's college campuses and secondary schools (Kuximake and Wufuli 2008: 81–2). But these scholars, like the state itself, showed little clue as to why imported Islamic influences have a special appeal among Uighur youths, but not Xinjiang's other Muslim groups. The answer may lie in pan-Islamism's role as a rallying and motivating force for the titular ethnic group, who feel greater claims to ethno-national identity and autonomy in Xinjiang.

Hizb ut-Tahrir, like Wahhabism before it, offered an organizational and ideological rallying point for disgruntled members of Xinjiang's titular ethnic group. Specifically, its pan-Islamism serves to implore the supremacy of Islam to reject anything provided by the Chinese state, from government jobs and benefits to business licenses and marriage certificates. Manuals seized from local cells reveal strict mechanisms of control and command, including punishment for deviances. Members pay 10 percent of their personal income as religious dues or must engage in illegal activities to raise the funds. In other words, it would take strong motivations to be cell members. By 2000, *Hizb ut-Tahrir* cells had reportedly trained nearly 3,000 individuals, mainly Uighur youths. They relied on a number of channels to spread their messages, such as private religious settings, "Talibik" forums (religious lectures), special communal occasions (weddings, funerals, circumcision parties), electronic venues, and distribution of translated materials from overseas websites (Zhang Y. 2009: 60–2). In 2005, over forty graduating seniors in three colleges of Xinjiang were found to have been *Hizb ut-Tahrir* members (Liu 2014: 149). By local police accounts, *Hizb ut-Tahrir* cells stayed under the official radar from the late 1990s till the Urumqi riot of 2009 (Zhang Y. 2009: 63–4).

Subsequent state attention to *Hizb ut-Tahrir* activities continued to betray limited state capacity in dealing with unauthorized religious groups. Many perpetrators of violence in the 2000s reportedly had *Hizb ut-Tahrir* membership. Offenses linked to them included poisoning plots and violence in Urumqi, killings in Shandong and Hebei during 2003, threats against pro-Beijing religious leaders in Xinjiang, riots and violence in various localities within Xinjiang, and distribution of bomb-making and poison-making techniques in the months leading up to the Beijing Olympics in 2008 (Zhang Y. 2009: 63–4). In line with its appeal among educated youths, violence in the early 2000s involved more such youths. In Moyu county, a rural area known for breeding religious violence, fifty-four public sector employees were apprehended by local police for violence and illegal religious activities around 2000, half of them public school teachers. In March 2006, forty-six Uighur students engaged in a violent scuffle that wounded twenty-three Han Chinese in Kuerle county (Liu 2014: 150). In another reflection of the more educated background of *Hizb ut-Tahrir* members, violent assaults in the 2000s targeted law enforcement officers and agencies (Table 6.5). *Hizb ut-Tahrir* members, according to a Hong Kong journalist, were also key players in the Urumqi riot of July 5, 2009 (Li Y. 2013). Their ideological and organizational strength may have accounted for the scale and intensity of violence in that event.

The state did no better in averting or confronting another underground movement, the *Hijrat*, which became known in Xinjiang by 2005. The term, meaning the traveling jihadist, originally referred to Mohammad's migration or journey. The movement espouses leaving behind one's earthly possessions and traveling around to engage in the jihad, hence the traveling jihadist. The *Hijrat* came to the attention of local authorities after its members committed violent acts in Kashgar in 2005, but was taken seriously only after *Hijrat* followers hijacked a commercial flight from Hotan to Urumqi in June 2012. Since then the term was included in local official documents on fighting extremism. According to these documents, the *Hijrat* is not as organized as the East Turkistan

TABLE 6.5 *Spread of violence in Xinjiang: the 2000s*

Time	Place	What happened	Casualties
October 24, 1999	Saili village of Poskam/Zepu county, Kashgar prefecture	Attacks on village police station with Molotov cocktails, bombs, and shooting; officer Atawulla Korqawulla killed	1 police officer and 1 civilian dead; 10 rooms and 2 vehicles burned
February 3, 2001	Konasheher/Shufu county, Kashgar	Stabbing of Mammatjan Yakup, county court official, 38 times in his home	Yakup and 1 Han killed; Yakup's wife injured
May 27, 2002	Poskam/Zepu county, Kashgar prefecture	Killing of Yima village police head, Yasheng Mamuti and 2 other officers	3 Uighur officers killed
February 27, 2005	Moyu county, Hotan prefecture	Village party secretary Musali Khan murdered, security chief injured	1 official dead; 1 seriously injured
March 7, 2008	Flight from Urumqi to Beijing	Uighur female tried to set off explosives on flight	Attempt aborted
August 4, 2008	Kashgar city, Kashgar prefecture	Truck into police officers; guns, bombs, and jihadist literature on truck	17 police officers killed and 15 injured
August 10, 2008	Kuqa/Kuche county, Aksu prefecture	Motorcycle carrying explosives driven into Kuqa's county police station	None reported
July 5, 2009	Döngkövrük/Er'daoqiao section, Urumqi city	Hundreds of Uighurs protested Shaoguan incident, escalating into worst violence in Xinjiang under PRC; Han counter-protests July 7 and September 3 2009	134 Han, 11 Hui, 10 Uighur, and 1 Manchu civilians killed; 198 total deaths; 1,721 injured

Source: Xjass (2010); Cheng (2014b).

movement; it advocates violence and assembles militants comprising less educated youths from rural areas, including underage recruits in private madrassas. After official crackdowns on Wahhabi sites in the 1990s and on *Hizb ut-Tahrir* cells in the late 2000s, *Hijrat* groups are largely blamed for violence in Xinjiang since the late 2000s (Zhang 2014). But the official literature offers few details about the *Hijrat* groups, suggesting the movement's disorganized, random, and transitory nature.

As with Wahhabism earlier, limited state capacity had allowed space for *Hizb ut-Tahrir* and *Hijrat* groups to grow in the gray areas of law. Over time, pan-Islamism in these movements blurred the line between resisting the secular state and the Chinese state, so that it would take their violent activities to elicit responses from the state. Although overdue, state responses did not always address the root causes of their appeal among Uighur youths.

A Failed Society

Among the root causes is the increasing breakdown of Uighur society since the 1990s. This lay at the core of the expansion of Uighur radicalism and violence. Yet limited state capacity, as a corollary of unbridled market forces and weakened governance, facilitated that expansion by neglecting the deterioration of Uighur communities.

The signs of a "failed" Uighur society were visible to Uighur and Han observers by the late 2000s, and even to a careful visitor. Ilham Tohti (2013 and 2014) points to surging crimes, disintegration of the social and moral fabric of Uighur communities, rising cultural conservatism, religious fundamentalism, growing hatred of the Han people, and increased relative impoverishment. Huang Zhangjing cites epidemics of drugs, crime, AIDS, and violence (2012: 42). In the early and mid-2010s, it was plain to a field observer like myself that two decades of economic liberalization had taken a heavy toll on Uighur society. Crowds of idle young men filled the streets of southern Xinjiang day and night, looking for opportunities to make quick money but not necessarily a real job. They filled the video arcades that had proliferated in urban centers, bankrupting their parents by using their income to play video games. These parents pleaded with local state agencies to close down the arcades, and many of them survived on government assistance themselves.

Divergent diagnoses of this failed society, however, reveal that limited state capacity is not merely due to material factors. More importantly, it is due to cognitive ones. To Uighur analysts, their frustrated society is in dire need of spiritual sanctuary, so its conservative turn is understandable. This frustration stems from a series of generally recognized factors: a loss of trust in Uighurs from the state and the Chinese public, masses of downsized workers and unemployed youths, demonization and discrimination of Uighurs by the general public, competition from new migrants and finally, and deterioration of Han–Uighur relations (Tursun 2013: 38). However, Tohti singles out a highly controversial factor for blame: bilingual education. He rejects the typical Chinese view that Mandarin is key to Uighurs' economic advancement. On the contrary, he views Mandarin dominance as the source of Uighurs' predicament: bilingual education embodies a threat to Uighurs' cultural and linguistic survival, but a lack of Mandarin proficiency hinders their entry into the job market and the modern world, while cultural isolation leaves uneducated Uighurs in a state of "ignorance, backwardness, narrow and close mindedness, savageness and desperation" (Tohti 2014). A lack of Uighur-language publications in official venues, easily discernible by a quick walk through local bookstores, further limits Uighur access to modern information. These problems produce receptive audiences for the "three forces" of radicalism, terrorism, and separatism.

Rather than religion, Tohti's argument suggests, language is critical in the battle against the three forces. Indeed, a lack of Mandarin proficiency has made it difficult for the government's messages of modernization to reach villagers, especially in the rural south. Available publications in Uighur do no better in reaching those who do not read Chinese. In local Xinhua bookstores, a causal visitor like myself was surprised to find few publications for the general Uighur reader, though school textbooks were plentiful for Uighur children. The scarcity of Uighur publications may be due to a lack of qualified bilingual inspectors as well as apprehension about nationalistic writings (Wu 2001). Such a genre did emerge in the 1980s, penned by newly released political prisoners. They gained sympathetic audiences on Xinjiang's college campuses, triggering alarm among local authorities. The ensuing restriction of Uighur-language publications has created a different set of problems: a culturally barren land for those youths who cannot read or understand Chinese or are averse to it, thus driving them to private madrassas and jihadist websites.

Han Chinese responses, official or otherwise, tend to emphasize linkages between religion and the "failed" Uighur society. Even the most sympathetic account calls out the deeper, psychological barriers to modernization on the part of Uighur communities. That is, if the Han people had long learned to take modernization for granted, Uighur society still agonizes over modernization's threats to its identity, hence the religious root of Uighur frustration (Huang 2013). Typical of a Muslim society, this line of argument goes, Uighur society tends to counterpoise modernization and religion, and to shield the onslaught of the former under the cover of the latter. Put in this light, rising fundamentalism is not just a consequence of Uighur frustration, but a cause of Uighur stagnation. This is a rather common sentiment among Han officials and publics inside and outside Xinjiang. Needless to say, Han society tends to forget that it had taken them a painful century to adapt to the challenges of modernization. And as in China's case a century ago, modernization is imposed from outside, making it hard for Uighurs to accept.

This outsider role is often ignored by the Chinese leadership and public, who take the imperative of development for granted. During the Mao era, egalitarianism shielded ethnic groups from economic competition, easing the imposition of economic practices to Uighur society by the central state. But this is no longer the case in post-Mao China, when economic liberalization was imposed on Uighur and other ethnic regions with little regard for its social consequences. The debilitating impacts of economic liberalization on Uighur society are discussed in Chapter 7, as concrete evidence for the root cause of the failed Uighur society.

Ethnicizing Effects: The 2000s

The pent-up frustration of Uighur society found some temporary release in the Urumqi riot of July 5, 2009 (Table 6.5), but the event did little to resolve the deeper dilemmas faced by Uighur communities. The riot pushed more members into a retreat to religion, further away from reconciling the tensions between identity and modernization. Initiated as a student protest, the Urumqi riot was the first incidence of violence that was not blamed on talibs or madrassas by local and central authorities. In official media and private conversations, blame was placed on migrant youths from southern Xinjiang, who usually congregated in the Döngkövrük section of Urumqi. Regardless, the bloody rampage ruptured Han–Uighur relations.

In this context, religion emerged as the cultural symbol to demarcate the "Other." The ethnic rupture made Uighurs more receptive to pan-ethnic pressure to conform to conservative religious mores, ostensibly to intensify defiance and solidarity. In a culture keen on communal gatherings, extended families and local communities became the main avenues of conservative pressure. "Are you not a Uighur?" is the usual phrase used to pressure young women to dress conservatively and young men to behave piously.[7] Most visible was the "Arabianization" of Uighur costumes and mores after July 2009, especially for women in southern Xinjiang. Black niqabs contrasted sharply with the colorful headscarves conventionally worn by Uighur women. Those dressed in modern clothing, such as short-sleeved shirts and skirts, may encounter verbal and physical threats on the streets, even in the secular and modern city of Urumqi. Female college graduates from the south, who left off their headscarves as local campus rules required, faced pressure to put them on in order to find marriage prospects back home. In elementary schools, teachers saw a sudden surge in female children wearing headscarves after the Urumqi riot, in defiance of school bans. One secondary school student noted, "we

7 Information in this paragraph is based on observations in three cities of southern Xinjiang, summer 2011, and in five counties of Hotan, fall 2013. These included conversations with local residents in Uighur bazaars and college campuses.

suddenly remember we used to have the head scarves and made a point of finding them and putting them on."[8]

For Uighur men, behavioral changes became even more visible, especially among the younger generation in the rural south. Mosques experienced a dramatic surge in prayer attendance by young men after the Urumqi riots. The outpouring of tears during prayers, immediately after the Urumqi riots, sent disturbing signals for both Uighur and Han observers (Tohti 2014; Huang 2013). More young men chose to wear the Islamic beard. Even more of them refused to drink or smoke so as to observe Islamic codes. More restaurants banned alcohol. Stores selling alcohol and cigarettes risked being attacked. Prayer posture changed from the traditional Uighur way to the Arab way. More men pressured their wives to wear the burka (covering the entire body and face) and to quit their jobs because it was not "Muslim" to work away from home. The loss of income and independence for Uighur women, in turn, has led to increased domestic abuse in rural households. In another setback for Uighur women's rights, religious officiating of marriages has reappeared, meaning the return of polygamy among conservative Uighurs.[9]

The conservative surge may be seen as religiously and politically driven. As often asserted by online posts at Tohti's Uighurbiz.net, the religious surge amounted to a form of anti-state resistance. In reality, the line between boycotting the Chinese state, the secular world, and traditional Uighur customs may not be always clear. This was manifest in the conservative efforts to impose what was Muslim and not Muslim interethnically and intraethnically. Some stores, restaurants, foods, or even bottled water came to be labeled "un-Muslim," an understandable form of protectionism or cultural demarcation. Anything supplied by the state – from business and marriage licenses to anti-quake housing – were also labeled "un-Muslim," another understandable form of political resistance. However, in a trend that is troubling to many Uighur intellectuals, even traditional Uighur dances, music, paintings, sculpture, and other art forms came to be labeled "un-Muslim." Expression of emotions on special occasions, such as festive sentiments at weddings or sad feelings at funerals, were also discouraged by neo-conservatives as "un-Muslim" practices.[10]

In another sign of rising fundamentalism, its linkage to separatism became more ambiguous. Although Chinese authorities often accuse extremist groups of utilizing religion to promote separatism, local radical groups do not necessarily identify with the separatist but nonfundamentalist World Uighur

8 Ibid. and conversations with eight female students at a Kashgar college and three female students on an Urumqi college campus, summer 2011, and conversations with five teachers at a public school in southern Xinjiang, fall 2013 and two in summer 2015.

9 Ibid. and conversations with four members of work-in-residence teams, Hotan, summer 2015 and electronically, 2017 and 2018.

10 Observations in Yutian county, Hotan, fall 2013. Conversations with three Uighur jade traders in Suzhou, summer 2017 and 2018.

Congress (WUC), according to a Uighur professional who monitors online forums in southern Xinjiang (Zhang 2014). Rather, they vow to fight a war with WUC leader Rabiye Qadir in the future. In other words, the line between fighting the Chinese state and the secular state seems blurred, as the fight is both religious and political. Not surprisingly, educated Uighurs are torn – they are genuinely worried about fundamentalism but also uncomfortable with state intervention in Uighurs' identity expression and religious practices. Many establishment intellectuals did join with the state by writing commentaries in local newspapers, urging Uighur women not to cover "their beautiful face."[11]

In a growing "cultural barren land" for those Uighur youths who cannot read Chinese, pan-Islamic and jihadist electronic media filled in the gap. In the rooms of many Uighur youths in southern Xinjiang, pictures of armed Taliban soldiers were hung on the wall and idolized as heroes. In their smartphones were videos and websites of foreign imams delivering fiery religious messages in Uighur, Turkic, and Kazakh tongues, dotted with references to oppression suffered by Uighurs and the brotherhood of all Muslims, and with bearded and black-wrapped men standing in the background, holding guns and the Koran (Zhang 2013b and 2014). Uighur professionals blame the flourishing of such influences on a lack of positive guidance for the youths, because the foreign sources' mediums of transmission are highly popular with local youths.[12] The imams in the electronic venues may be reputable figures from the global Muslim world, including the Middle East. Cheap and counterfeit smartphones have facilitated transmission. The problem is severe enough that local authorities shut off the internet in sensitive times and ban certain apps. But some of these efforts may be rendered ineffective by locally available VPN vendors.

In the post-riot context, suicidal martyrdom became worshiped among some rural youths in southern Xinjiang. A sense of alienation prevailed among those plagued by a lack of education and employment. According to a Uighur lawyer who worked on cases involving jihadist violence, his clients were largely young Uighurs, 90 percent of them illiterate. The extremist videos and websites also impacted Uighur youths more generally. A young professor in Urumqi notes that, increasingly, it was the well-regarded students who became "problems cases" – those who aspired to achieve something, and to carry out the dream of their people and religion. "To become THAT kind of person, even to sacrifice oneself, seems a glorious thing" (Zhang 2014). Parents of these youths, raised in the secular years of the Mao era, were perplexed by the transformation of their children, who may even refuse to eat the food prepared by their parents for being un-"Halal."

11 Observations in Hotan, fall 2013. I skimmed through a whole year's local newspapers, up to the end of October 2013.

12 Conversations with two Uighur police officers in Hotan county, Hotan prefecture, fall 2013.

Extremism divides Uighurs in other ways. Its supporters hailed the assailants who killed three Uighur community workers (e.g., the April 23 Bachu incident of 2013, Table 6.7). Village elders assigned to keep vigilance over their neighborhood were fearful of reporting suspicious activities to local authorities (Li 2012c). Private madrasas were as much an attraction as a tragedy for Uighur parents, as child abuse was increasingly uncovered. Three cases in a short span of time in 2012 offer telling examples (Li 2013b: 32–3). In April, a Uighur child unable to recite religious texts was beaten to death at an Urumqi private madrassa. In May, another child was beaten to death by madrasa staff in Korla city. In June, local police raided a private madrassa run from an apartment of a residential building in Hotan city. Local media reported that fifty-four children were freed from the site. Based on my observation of the building in 2013, it would have been impossible for the neighbors not to notice a group of this size in one apartment, but no resident apparently wanted or dared to alert the authorities.

Combating Religious Extremism: Phase I

Faced with the array of challenges after the Urumqi riots of 2009, the central and provincial governments launched campaigns to combat the tide of radical Islam. The first phase lasted from April 2010 to May 2014, or from Zhang Chunxian's arrival as Xinjiang's new party secretary to the Urumqi market attack that killed thirty-two civilians. Zhang emphasized a "gentle approach" to governing Xinjiang (*yi rou zhi jiang*), with a view to winning over Uighur communities through good deeds and improved ethnic relations. Under his rein, anti-extremism measures included cultural construction projects, deradicalization campaigns, rural vigilance and ideological education. Though targeted at fundamentalist and radical Islam, those strategies had unintended ethnicizing effects, while achieving limited success.

The cultural construction projects have attempted to fill in the intellectually barren land in rural Xinjiang. That is, to bring modern and secular messages to Uighur villagers. Since mid-2010, various central agencies have donated large volumes of visual, audio, and printed materials to rural libraries, township cultural stations, and village service centers, which were set up in every village. Mobile bookstores and libraries, media equipment, and media rooms have also been donated. Mobile movie teams have been dispatched to show movies to villagers, while radios, TV sets, and reception equipment was provided free of charge to every rural household. These efforts are intended to ease the isolation and insulation suffered by rural communities, but their effects are often limited thanks to a lack of local interest or social pressures to avoid them. Free newspapers may be left unopened, and the monthly movie shows sparsely attended. Villagers may be deterred from watching TV programs and movies by radicals who label them un-Muslim, or the programming may not appeal to them because urban and modern themes seem alien.

TABLE 6.6 *Xinjiang's decrees to define illegal religious activities: early 2010s*

Year	Decree	Key contents
[2011]1	"Opinions on defining illegal religious activities"	Defining 26 demarcations
2013, May [2013]11	"Guiding opinions on further tackling illegal religious activities and curtailing the infiltration of religious extremism"	Spelling out illegal religious activities and how citizens should fight them

Source: XUAR (2011 and 2013).

Deradicalization campaigns also began under Zhang's leadership, though in moderate forms compared with recent years. Between April 2010 and May 2014, the provincial government issued two decrees to delineate the distinctions among ethnic customs, normal religious practices, and extremist displays of Islam (Table 6.6). The extremist forms, imposed by religious radicals as authentic Islam, were singled out for crackdown. Earlier, local authorities who tried to curb them were accused of engaging in unlawful acts (Chen 2015). With the new statutes, some localities began to ban individuals who wore the burka and long beards from entering state agencies, state-owned enterprises (SOEs), public buses, banks, and hospitals. Other localities penalized defiant individuals by withdrawing public assistance. Many localities launched the "lift your beautiful face" campaign to dissuade women from wearing the niqab. The new statutes, however, did not solve the problem of over-reaching by local states. In state agencies and public schools, even the traditional Uighur headscarf was discouraged. Some schools enforced the religious ban on campus to the point of intervening in students' fasting rituals and religious holidays, with dubious effects. Students may defy the bans, and ethnic schools may play a cat-and-mouse game with local inspectors who came to check on the religious ban.

A third area of anti-extremism measures during Zhang's rein targeted the rural south, the source of many vagabond and violent youths. Respected elders and community workers were assigned as watchmen in village neighborhoods and paid with the government's "stability funds," although they did not always want to report on fellow villagers or were afraid to do so. Income subsidies were increased for officially sanctioned imams, but only to make them lose credibility in the eyes of those who distrusted "red imams" (Li 2012b). In early 2014, Xinjiang expanded the work-teams-in-residence program, which began in 1997 with 543 cadres and increased to 13,800 in 1999. Now it dispatched 200,000 cadres from local state agencies to the countryside, on a one-year rotation for the next three years. The first group was sent down in March 2014 and included more than 70,000 cadres in over 11,000 work teams. As part of Zhang's "gentle approach" to governing Xinjiang, their mission was to "learn about local conditions, improve living standards and win over hearts" (*Chinanews* 2014). But as outsiders, those work teams were no rival to the covert strongholds of religious radicals in the countryside.

Ideological education was yet another area of anti-extremism measures under Zhang's governorship, intended to promote an alternative discourse and worldview. In state agencies and public sectors, employees were required to memorize the latest official literature on combating religious extremism, to take quizzes on it, and to write self-criticisms about negligent attitudes toward manifestations of extremism. These measures often seemed formalistic, although Han interviewees tended to view them as useful in demarcating boundaries for state and public employees, whose participation in religious activities would send signals of state concession to religious radicals. In public schools and colleges, classes on political ideology added sections on Marxist theory of ethnic relations, or new classes were created on "interethnic harmony." In rural areas, cultural activities aimed at ideological education were held every Friday, though their attendance may be formalistic and their effects dubious.

Most of all, the various anti-extremism measures only reached sectors and individuals that the state could reach, not the talibs in private madrassas or the vagabond youths responsible for violence. Even for those within the state's reach, official educational materials may often be unappealing. Textbooks for political ideology classes remain dry and out of touch with reality. The sight of Uighur students trying strenuously to memorize Marxist tenets from Chinese texts, which would be formidable enough for native speakers of Mandarin, can easily elicit bafflement about the futility of official textbooks. An elementary teacher at a rural Xinjiang school, whom I met on a train ride in southern Xinjiang in 2013, conceded that his pupils had little interest in or understanding of the "Marxist views of ethnicity" that he was teaching in a class called "Ethnic Harmony." When pressed, he himself had a hard time explaining what those Marxist views were. As another tiresome formality, the state's ideological platform is not likely to offer an effective alternative to religion as a source of identity and worldview.

Indeed, the various policy measures did little to stem the violence during the four years of Zhang Chunxian's "gentle approach" to governing Xinjiang in 2010–14. On the contrary, local state intervention in religious activities appeared to have triggered violence. The violent incidents on June 26, June 28, and October 28, 2013 (Table 6.7) support this point. Moreover, violence continued to target the arms of the state – police stations, paramilitary posts, and Uighur community workers. Increasingly, violence was also aimed at large civilian crowds, cumulating in the Kunming Rail Station attacks that killed twenty-nine pedestrians on March 1, 2014 and the Urumqi market massacre that killed thirty-nine civilians on May 22, 2014 (Table 6.7). As these attacks were often carried

TABLE 6.7 *Escalation of violence in Xinjiang, late 2009 to mid-2014*

Date	Location	What happened	Casualties
August 19, 2010	Kuqa/Kuche county, Aksu prefecture	Motorcycle drove into a paramilitary post in Yiganqi township, with explosives	6 dead (5 Uighurs), 15 Uighurs injured
July 18, 2011	Hotan city, Hotan prefecture	Knife/bomb attacks on police station by 18 Kashgar men;[13] jihadist slogans against veil ban; links to Pakistani group[14]	2 Han female hostages, 1 Han officer, and 1 Uighur paramilitary killed
July 30–1, 2011	Kashgar city, Kashgar prefecture	Truck driven into crowds and explosives set off, both downtown; Pakistan training[15]	13 civilians killed; 40 civilians injured
February 28, 2012	Kargilik/Yecheng county, Kashgar	Knife and axe attacks on crowds in pedestrian district	15 civilians, 1 officer, and 8 assailants killed
June 29, 2012	Flight GS 7,554 Hotan to Urumqi	Six assailants tried to storm cockpit door and ignite explosives; subdued	Several hijackers, crew, and passengers injured
April 23, 2013	Selibuya township, Maralbishi/ Bachu, Kashgar prefecture	3 Uighur community workers killed when inspecting madrassa site; 12 officers burned alive or killed[16]	15 civilians and officers killed (10 Uighurs); 6 assailants killed

(*continued*)

[13] The WUC blames police clash with protesters, but local Han and Uighur residents indicated no occurrence of such protests. See Kathrin Hille, "Tense mood prevails after Xinjiang attack." Financial Times, July 21, 2011. Web.

[14] Ananth Krishnan, "Analysts see Pakistan terror links to Xinjiang attack." *The Hindu*, July 21, 2011. Web.

[15] Ananth Krishnan, "Terrorists trained in Pak. camps behind Xinjiang attack: China." *The Hindu*, August 1, 2011. Web.

[16] For the WUC version, see "China's oppressive policy causes the Bachu violent incident." BBC, April 24, 2013. Web.

TABLE 6.7 (*continued*)

Date	Location	What happened	Casualties
June 21, 2013	Kargilik/Yecheng county, Kashgar	Assailants drove vehicle into county police station, setting off explosives	13 assailants dead
June 26, 2013	Lukqun township Piqan, Turpan	Retaliation for police arrest of suspect who prepared attacks over beard/niqab ban	24 officers and civilians and 11 assailants dead
June 28, 2013	Hanerik township Hotan prefecture	Large group stormed into Hotan city upset over change of imam at mosque[17]	6 protesters killed;[18] many possibly injured
October 28, 2013	Tiananmen Square, Beijing	SUV drove into crowd on Tiananmen, possibly to avenge mosque demolition[19]	2 pedestrians and 3 in SUV killed; 38 injured
November 16, 2013	Selibuya township, Bachu, Kashgar	Knife and axe attacks on township police; assailants 17 to 23 years in age[20]	2 paramilitary officers and 9 assailants killed
December 15, 2013	Sayibage township, Konasheher/ Shufu county, Kashgar	During year-end inspection, police found suspicious gathering at rural house; officers killed; weapons found in house	2 police officers killed; 14 assailants killed and 6 captured

(*continued*)

[17] The previous imam was possibly arrested. BBC, "Chinese leaders are concerned with escalating violence." September 1, 2013. Web.

[18] This author's observation of public circular of the Public Security Bureau of the Hotan Prefecture, dated July 9, 2013.

[19] Andrew Jacobs, "Tiananmen xijizhe yiwei baofu qingzhensi beichai" [Tiananmen attacker possibly retaliated at mosque demolition]. *New York Times* (Chinese) November 8, 2013. http://cn.nytimes.com/china/20131108/c08xinjiang/.

[20] Radio Free Asia, "Bachu xiean xiqji shijian bei shisha, zuixiao shiqisui" [Shot in the Bachu incident, youngest was 17]. November 18, 2013. www.rfa.org/mandarin/yataibaodao/shaoshu-minzu/ql2-11182013100507.html.

TABLE 6.7 (*continued*)

Date	Location	What happened	Casualties
December 30, 2013	Yarkant/Sache county, Kashgar prefecture	Attacks on county police station with explosives; police vehicles set on fire	8 assailants dead; 1 injured
January 24, 2014	Toqsu/Xinhe county, Aksu prefecture	Assailants tried to drive vehicle into pedestrian street; exchanged fire with police; explosions followed	12 assailants killed; 5 captured; 1 officer injured; nearby stores damaged
February 14, 2014	Uqturpan county, Aksu prefecture	Police vehicles attacked, 5 vehicles destroyed	11 assailants killed; 4 others injured
March 01, 2014	Kunming Railway Station, Yunnan	Knife-slashing attacks on passengers inside rail station; young assailant revealed plans to join jihads overseas[21]	29 civilians killed and 143 injured; 4 assailants killed; 1 or more captured
April 30, 2014	Urumqi Railway Station, Xinjiang	Knife-slashing attacks at Urumqi rail station; explosives also ignited	1 civilian and 2 assailants killed; 79 injured
May 22, 2014	Urumqi city	Two SUVs stormed into crowded market, followed by explosions	39 civilians and 4 assailants dead; 94 injured

Source: Oriental Daily (Hong Kong), *The Telegraph*, Reuters, and BBC.[22]

out by poorly educated Uighur youths, even teenagers, the absence of proper education – religious or otherwise – became a more visible problem. With little understanding of the concepts of political violence or separatism, the young assailants were simply incited by calls to jihad by co-ethnics who operated private madrassas or *Hijrat* cells.

[21] Yunnan's party secretary reported this confession by a sixteen-year-old female captive on March 4, but this version of events disappeared from the Chinese media after Beijing blamed the event on separatist forces. *Nanfang Daily*'s report of the earlier confession is no longer available online (original link: http://news.nfdaily.cn/content/2014–03/05/content_94008996.htm).

[22] The news sources, too numerous to list here, are available upon request.

Combating Religious Extremism: Phase II

On May 23, 2014, one day after the Urumqi market massacre, Xinjiang escalated its anti-extremism campaign by launching a year-long "strike hard special operation." It would include a crackdown on perpetrators and promoters of extremism and a more aggressive deradicalization program, both with mixed effects.

The crackdown part of the special operation claimed initial successes. Of those on the state's most wanted list, 334 suspects were apprehended and 117 groups were hunted down during the second half of 2014. Of the targeted transmitters of extremism, 171 private madrassas were closed, 238 individuals who taught or provided sites for such madrassas were arrested, and 757 talibs were freed from these sites; religious intervention in marriages was curbed in 219 cases involving 519 individuals (referring to religious officiating of polygamy), over 23,000 items of "illegal propaganda materials" were confiscated, and forty-four cases of online dissemination of bomb-making technologies and 294 cases of online violent videos were dealt with (*Guancha* 2014a; RFA 2014). Uighur rights groups, based overseas, rightly question the nontransparent and hasty manner in which the crackdowns and convections took place (RFA 2014).

The deradicalization part of the "strike hard" operation, from mid-May 2014 to 2015, claimed initial success as well. Experiments were carried out to deradicalize inmates convicted of violent or violence-related crimes, with some promising results. Abuduwayiti Saidiwakasi, vice chairman of the Islamic Association of Xinjiang, served as the head of the Deradicalization Expert Group for Xinjiang's Prison Administration and its lead religious counselor. According to him, most of the inmates did not understand their culpabilities, nor did they show remorse or recognize the legitimacy of the secular state or state laws. They only identified with Islam as they understood it. Religious counseling – through talking and debating about Islam – offered the only effective way to deradicalize them (Chen 2015; Zhou 2017). For individuals who participated in extremist activities but were not criminally charged, local authorities resorted to community correction centers (*shehui jiaozhi zhongxin*), the beginning of what would become the notorious "re-education camps." Dozens of experienced Muslim officials were dispatched to these centers, who took turns living and working with inmates (Chen 2015). When the internees experienced a catharsis after they realized the folly of religious extremism, deradicalization would then be deemed successful.

The community correction program was not a Xinjiang invention but a formal nationwide program that had been operational since 2012. After initial experiments in six major cities/provinces in 2003, it went through a second round of experiments in twelve provinces/cities and a third round across the country in 2009, before it was codified into the 8th edition of China's criminal law in 2011. Its stated purpose is to keep felons convicted of light crime out of jail and leave them with local communities, with supervision, reeducation, and assistance from local governments, communities, and family members (*Hualv* 2012). Private lawyers in China praise the program as humanistic (Li W. 2012; Dong 2019). However, what makes it different in Xinjiang is that the enrollees are apparently not criminally charged or convicted; nor are they left with local communities or sentenced to a definitive term in the program. Its legality is also unclear. It resembles the cadre reeducation schools during the Cultural Revolution, with more ideological education and no labor. Like the cadre schools, it is unclear if the program will be a source of collective resentment or genuine redemption.

Deradicalization strategies appeared less effective with the general public at this stage. In late 2014 Xinjiang issued new decrees to distinguish and restrict "extremist" religious practices, including online speeches, attire, and beards (Table 6.8). However, the state mainly reached urban and state sectors, rather than the rural and private sectors susceptible to "extremist" influences. In the latter sectors, banning "unusual religious practices" (Figure 6.1) was hard to enforce unless offenders walked into state facilities (a welfare office, a hospital, etc.). In public sectors, after earlier bans on the practice of religion, observance of fasting during Ramadan was banned in mid-2014 for party members, youth league members, government employees, and public school teachers and students. The official justification was to dampen an atmosphere that boosted religious conservatism, but the ban violated the local state's own decrees (Table 6.6) that differentiated between ethnic customs, normal religious practices, and extremist displays of Islam.

TABLE 6.8 *Xinjiang's decrees to combat religious extremism: mid-2010s*

Year	Decree	Key contents
November 2014	"XUAR's Regulations on Religious Affairs"	Granting more power to restrict certain religious practices, to censor online speeches, and to ban extremist attire and beards
November 2014	"Basic knowledge for distinguishing extremist religious activities"	Identifying 75 extremist manifestations of religion
2014 [28]	"Opinions on Further Strengthening and Improving Work Regarding Islam"	Supplementing Document No. 11 of 2013 (see Table 6.6)
August 2016	"XUAR Provisions for Implementing the Counter-Terrorism Law of the PRC"	Supplementing the country's Counter-Terrorism Law (December 27, 2015) with local provisions

Source: XUAR (2014a, 2014b, and 2014c) and *China Daily* (2016).

FIGURE 6.1: Poster: "Five Unusual Practices" banned in public facilities
Top left: "The burqa is banned for females of all age groups." Top right: "The hijab is banned for juvenile, young and middle-aged females." Center left: "The niqab is banned for females of all ages." Center right: "The beard is banned for young males." Bottom: "Clothing with the star and moon symbol is banned for all."
Source: Guancha (2014b).

In this context, the deradicalization campaign was made at once complicated and simplistic by the conflation of religious and ethnic identity. On the one hand, the growth of conservative Islam has affected not just Xinjiang but also other Muslim concentrated provinces, such as those in Qinghai, Ningxia, and Gansu. The absence of separatism and violence in these other regions suggests the assertion of religious identity is at work. On the other hand, strict restrictions in Xinjiang also point to identity assertion as a backlash against state control. Indeed, other than violence and jihadist mobilization, local officials in Xinjiang have not had a good idea as to what constitutes "religious extremism," so that outward forms are often targeted – Arabianized appearances, madrassa attendance, forced abstinence, prohibition of native or modern customs, boycotting of government services, and excessive Halal observance.

However, those who follow these practices are often poor rural Uighur youths with little idea about Islamic teachings, let alone Islamic fundamentalism. As official media concede, the young and uneducated offenders captured for terrorist attacks, including female teenagers, were often goaded into violent activities by (male) relatives (*Zhongguo ribao wang* 2014). Moreover, those who do not find success in the secular world may seek solidarity through the religious world, by donning more in-group "Islamic" practices, leading to a conflation of ethnic and religious identity on their part. Overvigilance against those practices may drive moderates to become radical and radicals to become extremist.

The restriction of electronic communications, another measure to combat extremism, has also been stringent, with mixed effects. The purpose was to control the spread of jihadist messages by blocking access to many international websites and domestic social media sites. Yet the bans annoyed Uighur and Han residents alike without deterring the more determined and resourceful, who could use VPN programs to access blocked apps and websites. Popular resentment at such inconveniences, moreover, overshadowed official efforts to make Islam more available, through authorized magazines and websites. In fact, the provincial government has been increasing efforts in this direction since 2001 (Luo 2016: 169), including sending dozens of Islamic clergymen overseas to study in Islamic institutions of higher education, sponsoring eight groups of Islamic clergymen annually to visit interior Chinese provinces, organizing 3,000 local Muslims to make the pilgrim trip in Mecca each year, and sponsoring publication of religious books and the Koran in local Muslim languages.

The "work teams in-residence" program gained special importance during the "strike hard" campaign. In early 2015, the second group of work teams since early 2014, involving over 74,000 cadres, was dispatched to rural Xinjiang. The third group of a similar size was sent down in early 2016. The team members, assigned on a yearly rotation basis, lived in temporary housing constructed on the edges of assigned villages and stepped up efforts to solve real problems for villagers. Different teams had different approaches to tackling the tasks, depending on their institutional resources. Teams from commerce bureaus can help villagers obtain business licenses and find business projects. Teams from state banks can help bring in credit and loans for local investment. Teams from public health agencies can help improve local healthcare access. Teams from educational and cultural sectors run educational and recreational programs for villagers. Teams from media organizations can help promote village products. Often, work teams had to take on these tasks because village councils were not functioning or trusted by villagers. Work teams filled in the void by improving governance and connecting villagers to the modern world.[23] Overall their work helped to soften the harshness of official crackdowns.

The role of the work teams in combating extremism was tentative during this period, depending on each team's approach. Programs to promote literacy and secularism, waged as a battle of ideas against conservative influences, certainly did not hurt. Chinese reports have rosy stories of how village councils have become popular places for villagers and children to visit, after initial indifference toward the work teams. At the same time, some work teams may overreach and produce unintended consequences. For example, some work teams made home visits to account for the whereabouts of young male villagers. However, while such visits helped village households to exert pressure on their young male members to stay away from trouble, this deterred those who wished to be migrant workers elsewhere. Driven by similar pressures to keep their locales free of incidents, various local administrators adopted a tactic of sending away young Uighur migrants who did not hold regular jobs. Those leaving one locality may find themselves unwelcome in another. Work teams were unable to solve the fundamental problem of poorly educated rural youths.

Security measures and police powers, which expanded during Zhang's "strike hard" campaign, also created a considerable backlash. Measures such as ubiquitous checkpoints, patrol officers, inspection of ID cards (especially of randomly gathered young Uighur males), and greater police leeway to shoot suspects, resulted in more instances of Uighur noncooperation or direct confrontation, leading to more police shootings and fatal casualties on both sides (Table 6.9). Fatal attacks on the symbols of state power and Han presence continued, most notably in the carnage of July 28, 2014 and September 18, 2015 (Table 6.9). Outside Xinjiang, attempted attacks by Uighurs were reported in five interior provinces during 2015.[24] In three of the five cases, some suspects were shot dead during confrontations with police, suggesting that

[23] Conversations with two officials and one professional of southern Xinjiang who were members of work teams in the rural south, summer 2015. Electronic conversations with two scholars in Beijing who were on work teams to southern Xinjiang, 2018.

[24] These included Shijiazhuang, early 2015; Shenyang, July 13; Wenzhou, July 23; Zhengzhou, September 7; and Shanxi, December. Sources for these cases are available at https://zh.wikipedia.org/wiki/2015年新疆系列袭击案.

TABLE 6.9 *Escalation of violence in Xinjiang: mid-2014 to 2015*

Date	Location	What happened	Casualties
June 21, 2014	Kargilik, Kashgar	Vehicle driven into police station	13 assailants killed
July 28, 2014	Yarkant/Sache county Kashgar Prefecture	Clashed with police for carrying explosives to Kashgar Trade Fair; retreated to attack township offices, security posts, and passing vehicles	37 civilians and 59 assailants dead; 13 injured; 31 vehicles damaged
July 30, 2014	Hëytgah Meschiti Kashgar city	Assassination of Jüme Tahir, pro-Beijing Mullah at Xinjiang's largest mosque	1 civilian dead; 2 assailants killed
September 21, 2014	Bügür/Luntai county, Bayingolin	Bombs set off at markets and police station	6 pedestrians, 4 officers, and dozens of attackers dead
October 10, 2014	Pishan county Hotan Prefecture	2 assailants stabbed Uighur police officer to death near police station	1 police officer 2-months pregnant
October 12, 2014	Bachu county Kashgar Prefecture	Knife and bomb attacks at open market	22 civilians and 4 assailants dead
November 28, 2014	Sache county Kashgar	Home-made bombs and axe-waving attacks on pedestrians on gourmet street	4 civilians dead and 14 injured; 11 assailants killed
January 28, 2015	Yutian county Hotan	3 refused to stop truck at checkpoint; stabbed 3 security officers	2 assailants killed and 11 arrested (age 17, 18, 16)
February 13 and 16, 2015	Pishan and Moyu counties, Hotan	Pishan set off bomb killing 8 officers and injuring over	8 police officers and 1 civilian/ assailant dead;

(*continued*)

TABLE 6.9 (*continued*)

Date	Location	What happened	Casualties
		30; Moyu man stabbed patrol officer, was then killed	over 30 officers injured
February 17, 2015	Baicheng county Kashgar	4 security officers were stabbed to death when trying to stop suspicious gathering	4 security officers and 9 assailants killed
March 8–12, 2015	Sache and Kashgar city, Kashgar	7 men killed Sache's head of armed 4 assailants killed; 8 injured in game room	2 officers, 2 civilians and forces, his 2 family members and security guard; Kashgar group attacked game room
March 12, 2015	Moyu county Hotan	Man stabbed police officer to death who was checking ID cards of street drifters	1 officer killed
April 19, 2015	Yutian county Hotan	6 killed by police inside a house suspected of planning terrorist attacks; bombs found	6 suspects killed (aged 17–25)
May 11 and 25, 2015	Luopu and Moyu counties, Hotan	Home-made bombs thrown at police at checkpoint, killing two officers; attempts to throw bombs at patrol police	2 police officers and 2 assailants killed; assailants aged 18–26
June 2015	Shule, Kashgar	Police officer at checkpoint stabbed by 4	2 assailants dead
June 10, 2015	Pishan, Hotan	Police raided suspicious gathering	8 suspects dead

(*continued*)

TABLE 6.9 (*continued*)

Date	Location	What happened	Casualties
June 22, 2015	Kashgar outskirts	Police checkpoint attacked	15 attackers, 3 others dead
August 18, 2015	Hotan outskirts Hotan	Man arrested for unauthorized teaching of religion, shot 7 officers before escaping	Unknown
September 18, 2015	Baicheng county Aksu	Group attacked coalmine dorms, killing miners who were asleep	Over 40 miners and 5 police officers killed

Source: For 2014, *Oriental Daily*, *ifeng*; for 2015, RFA.[25]

police outside Xinjiang have also been authorized to shoot in cases of terror suspects. However, as Uighur rights groups complain, when an explosion is set off by non-Uighur Chinese, it is not treated as a terror case.

In early March in 2016, Zhang Chunxian declared his strike hard campaign a success at the 4th plenary of the 12th NPC. But the duration of the campaign, from mid-2014 to late 2015, witnessed at least seventeen reported cases of violence, one of which resulted in the death of more than forty mining workers and five police officers on September 18, 2015 (Table 6.9).

Combating Religious Extremism: Phase III

When Chen Quanguo replaced Zhang as Xinjiang's party secretary on August 29, 2016, he became the first senior official in the history of the PRC to have been appointed to the top post of both sensitive ethnic regions. Serving at the helm in the TAR during 2011–16, Chen was known for "innovative management" of Tibetan monasteries and communities that maintained "social stability." In contrast to previous official strategies, Chen does not regard economic development as the solution to religious extremism. Rather, "tough crackdowns" (*yanda*) are just as important. Since his appointment, Chen has adopted draconian measures to counter extremism, even by Xinjiang's standards.

First, existing approaches were quickly strengthened. On October 12, 2016, barely two months into Chen's new post, Xinjiang's legislature passed two laws

[25] The news sources, too numerous to list here, are available upon request.

aimed at curbing the human supply for violent activities, that is underage youths (Table 6.10). The new laws allow local officials to stop adults from taking children out of public high schools and sending them to private madrassas and extremist groups. On March 29, 2017, Xinjiang issued a decree to broaden previous bans on "extremist manifestations of religion" (Table 6.9), including more than two dozen "overly religious" baby names, such as Islam, Quran, Mecca, Jihad, Imam, Hajj, Medina, Muhammad, Arafat, Mujahid, and Saddam. The new decree allows local authorities to lawfully use administrative measures to penalize those who defy official bans, for example by withholding child welfare and child healthcare benefits for violators. As of 2017, Xinjiang's minimum income allowance (welfare benefits) per individual is ¥750/month for urban residents and ¥3,840 /year for rural residents, while a basic healthcare insurance is fully provided to poor households in urban areas and subsidized for poor households in rural areas (*Hualv* 2019; State Council of the PRC 2017b). Additional subsidies are available for poor households to apply for in case of illness so that eventual medical costs are minimal for them. Basic health insurance costs ¥290 (about $42) a year for Xinjiang's rural residents (*Xinnonghe* 2013; *Dajia bao* 2016).

To strengthen interethnic ties, the work-in-residence teams were supplemented by a new "paired kinship" program from late October 2016. Every employee at public sector institutions must "adopt" one rural and ethnic family as kinship. A minority professional must do the same with a rural Han family. One must visit one's adopted family a few times a year like a family member, bring along ¥200 in gifts for each trip, talk about the party's latest political message, chat about family matters, have at least one meal together, and stay at least one night in the ethnic family's home. The ethnic family is invited to visit their new urban relatives in return. Employees from all public sectors are required to take part in the kinship program. Ethnic cadre are paired with a rural Han family. Teachers may be paired with a student's family. At most, one may need to spend as many as three nights during each visit and a combined total of two months annually with a rural kinship family. For officials and professionals in northern Xinjiang, this may mean a few hours of air travel for each trip, plus a few hours of driving to the countryside.[26] Many complain about the onerous and superficial nature of this program, but supporters point to the de facto result of interethnic interaction, even if compelled by the state.

Among Chen Quanguo's groundbreaking approaches to fighting extremism, foremost is the targeting of so-called "double-faced individuals" (*liangmian ren*) in the local officialdom. This refers to officials who are guilty of covert collusion, indulgence, and negligence as well as corrupt governance that facilitate religious extremism. They can be both ethnic and Han cadre. Days after the first violent

[26] For one example, see "Xinjiang Wulumuqi: 'jieleqin jiushi yibeizi de qinqi" [Xinjiang Urumqi: Kinship for life]. December 6, 2016. www.chinapeace.gov.cn/zixun/2016–12/06/content_11384659.htm.

TABLE 6.10 *Xinjiang's decrees to combat radicalization: late 2010s*

Year	Decree	Key contents
October 12, 2016 XUAR Legislature	"XUAR Laws to Prevent Crime by Juveniles"	Forbidding adults, parents, relatives, and guardians from goading, compelling, or indulging juveniles to participate in terrorism, extremist activities, private madrassas, or religious activities or to wear extremist attire and insignias
October 12, 2016	"XUAR Laws on Mandatory High School Education in Southern Xinjiang"	Forbidding any organization or individual to force or lure students to forgo high-school education, or to hinder such education in the name of religion
March 29, 2017	"Regulations for deradicalization in Xinjiang Uighur autonomous region"	Forbidding unusual beards, baby names with religious fervor, niqabs and burkas, insignias of religious radicalism, rejection of public radio and TV programs, use of Halal criteria beyond foods, religious marriage, and divorce without legal procedure

Source: Guancha (2016) and *TS* (2017a).

attack since Chen arrived in Xinjiang, on December 28, 2016 (Table 6.11) in Moyu county of Hotan prefecture, the party secretaries of the county and the prefecture – both Han officials – were dismissed from their posts. Moyu county had been a frequent site of violence and a frequent source of assailants. But the assailants' entry into the county's party headquarters in broad daylight, randomly slashing people inside, did indicate dereliction of duty on the part of county officials. Two months later, six officials came under investigation for the Moyu incident, including those from the prefecture's public security bureau and police as well as from the county's public security bureau (*People's Daily* 2017). Simultaneously, Satar Sawut, the head and deputy party secretary of Xinjiang's Department of Education, came under investigation for three textbooks that had "Pan-Islamic," "Pan-Turkestani," and "de-Sinification" contents.[27] Those textbooks had been in use in Uighur schools for almost a decade preceding his

[27] An example is a suggestive glorification of Uighurs' bloody violence against Qing armies in the nineteenth century. Conversation with a scholar who has read a Chinese translation of the textbooks, at Zhejiang University, June 2018.

TABLE 6.11 *Waning of violence in Xinjiang: late 2016 to 2017*

Date	Location	What happened	Causalities
December 28, 2016	Moyu, Hotan	4 assailants attacked the county party committee compound	4 assailants and 1 civilian killed
February 14, 2017	Pishan, Hotan	3 assailants attacked a residential compound	5 residents killed and 5 seriously injured

Source: Reuters (2016); SCMP (2017).

downfall. In March 2018, the seven officials – all Uighur – received heavy prison sentences, including a suspended death sentence for Sawut.

Two other programs have expanded drastically from previous measures. One is the deradicalization program via re-education centers. While "community correction" was previously intended for individuals who had participated in extremist activities but were not criminally charged, now it expanded to include individuals who had been subject or susceptible to extremist influences. These range from accessing proscribed websites or harboring "strongly religious views" to following conservative or "Arabianized" customs or having been exposed to extremist influences overseas. Tellingly, official emphasis is on rectifying the minds of the "unsettled and violent generation," namely individuals who were born in the post-Mao period and have grown up in an era of identity politics and market competition. Variously known as centers for "reeducation" (*zai jiaoyu*), "transformation" (*zhuanhua*), or job training (*zhiye peixun*), the deradicalization program attempts to inculcate a sense of national identity and a correct worldview as well as to teach Mandarin and job skills. It also allows local authorities to close the loopholes whereby political studies could only reach public employees and students. More importantly, they allow authorities to use the stigma and sanction associated with the centers to deter deviance and compel compliance among local populations.

The political part of the reeducation, including official ideological perspectives, Xi Jinping's thought, and official anti-extremism materials, does not differ fundamentally from mandatory studies required of employees in state and public sectors, as routinely observed in southern Xinjiang during my field trips before Chen Quanguo took power here in 2016. Under Chen, the same measures have been intensified for all public employees, Han or ethnic: more meetings about deradicalization, sessions to study counterextremism pamphlets, quizzes about their contents, and self-criticisms and criticisms about areas where oneself or others have not done enough to fight extremism. Political education for regular citizens is intended to be preventative, it is intended to be as curative at the reeducation centers.

Compared with political education required of ordinary citizens in Xinjiang, the reeducation centers differ in their targets, format, and intensity. First, they are intended for individuals who need "thorough reorientation," especially those without formal institutional affiliations. But public employees and public school students are also sent to the centers if they are found to exhibit problems that cannot be handled by their workplaces or schools. Second, involuntary confinement makes political education here different from that mandated for regular citizens. The reeducation centers are located in specially designated or constructed venues with open or closed programs. The open programs allow attendees to go home at night, while the closed programs do not. Third, the intensity of ideological education is much greater because it is a full-time drill that demands mental transformation. The duration of study is unspecified, since it depends on perceived successful transformation. In a state TV reportage, an example of success was a 29-year-old Uighur male who admitted to the folly of his extremist deeds. He was placed in a center because after the family diner he owned had been visited by radicals, he began to bar non-Muslim customers and refuse to have anything to do with non-Muslim things, including the use of roads, buses, and the Chinese currency (*Guancha* 2019). It is unclear what the overall success rates are from the perspective of local authorities, at what costs in terms of time and resource, and if the holdouts would be kept indefinitely.

The reeducation centers are increasingly referred to as "education and training centers for occupational skills" (*zhiye jiaoyu peixun zhongxin*) or even "boarding schools" (*jisu xuexiao*). Mandarin and vocational classes are now part of the program to enable future job placements for their "*xueyuan*" (students or trainees). For practical purposes, the program's financial sustainability is patently questionable if it is only designed for elusive ideological education. Besides the costs of constructing massive facilities and operating daily maintenance, there are also huge logistics and personnel costs associated with administrative and instructional staff as well as with the "trainees" themselves. While the bulk of the costs are born by stability funds from the state, different localities may have different policies for covering the remaining costs. Some localities charge the internees (or their families) for their own meals. Other localities place them on the state's welfare program. Salaried employees who are sent away to the centers continue to receive their regular paychecks. Yet another huge cost is to create jobs for "trainees" upon completion of their programs, especially when official reports claim a 90 percent employment rate for graduates (*Xinhua* 2019).

Last but not least, the global backlash against the program has put local authorities on the defensive. Occupational training becomes a useful platform to defuse resentment at home and criticisms abroad. Increasingly, official reportage highlights job training and job placements as the key strategies of deradicalization. A major publicity report by CCTV 4, the CCTV's international channel, makes a point of showing delegations from Muslim countries, such as Malaysia and Afghanistan, visiting the centers and praising them for being far different from portrayals by Western media (*Guancha* 2019). But there is no mention of whether China's investments are helping to win their stand on the issue of re-education camps (Perlez 2019). Domestic audiences who watch the report would be left with a strong impression that the centers are saving a large number of uneducated Uighur youths who had been lured into extremist and violent activities.

Another program that has expanded on a draconian scale under Chen Quanguo is the surveillance system, digital or otherwise. Ostensibly to curb potential assailants, its omnipresence and intrusiveness inconveniences minority and Han residents alike. Roads and train stations are guarded by security checkpoints with scanners to check ID cards and smartphones. Movements in and out of public and commercial centers are tracked by facial scanners. Residential compounds have security checkpoints or ID scanners at entrances. Suspicious smartphones are searched by police for encrypted apps and content. Drivers are required to install GPS trackers on their vehicles, and to swipe ID cards and stare into a camera before filling up with gas (as vehicles have frequently been used for attacks). Surveillance cameras and patrol vehicles are ubiquitous. Shopkeepers bear extra costs to install mandatory security equipment in their stores. Chopping knives, often used in previous violent attacks, are now sold with buyers' ID card numbers engraved on them, and chained to tables at fruit and butcher stands. State collection of DNA information from local adults is reputedly in the planning, presumably for crime identification. Needless to say, ethnic and Han residents alike are resentful of the daily inconveniences, Uighurs far more so since they are the presumed targets of surveillance. Ordinary Han residents tend to place primary blame on "terror acts" rather than the government for the extreme measures, even if they may empathize with innocent Uighurs.

Old systems have been revamped with new technologies. The *Baojia* mutual security network was a community-based system of law enforcement and civilian control, dated to the Song dynasty and expanded across China during the Qing dynasty. In its updated form, the "ten-household cooperative self-defense" system (*shihu lianfang*) has been implemented in rural areas of southern Xinjiang since late 2016 and early 2017. The ten adjacent neighbors form a cooperative system of self-defense and mutual monitoring. An electronic alarm device links the ten households, so that any one of them can quickly notify the rest regarding imminent threats and call for instantaneous assistance before the police arrive. In urban sectors of southern Xinjiang, the "ten shop cooperative self-defense" system (*shipu lianfang*) is adopted among business owners. As in the residential case, an electronic alarm system links ten adjacent shops, and if one faces terror threats, the rest are required to come to its assistance in less than a minute. In urban residential communities, local states have stepped up the "grid management" system *(wangge shi guanli)*, which began in the early 2010s (Zhang 2013a). It is a system of small police booths and networks of communities carved in a grid pattern, serving as neighborhood committees to address routine disputes as well as security threats in a timely fashion. Under Chen Quanguo's rein, the TAR has implemented this system, which is also becoming common across China as a mechanism to maintain social stability.

The extreme security measures appear to have been effective, on surface at least. Since Chen's arrival, Xinjiang saw just two violent incidents in the early months of his tenure (Table 6.10). Needless to say, this relative stability has been achieved at tremendous cost. It remains to be seen if those measures can eradicate religious radicalism in the long run, not just violence in the short run. Han intellectuals have long worried about the alienating effects of discriminatory security measures (Zhang 2013a; Yao 2013b), as they have experienced discrimination first hand for being *Xinjiang ren* (Xinjiang locals) in inland provinces. The financial costs, certainly, put into question the sustainability of Chen's security programs, while the moral costs at home and abroad are immeasurable. In fact, one prominent program implemented by Chen during his tenure in Tibet has already been discontinued after his departure: a guaranteed job in the state sector for every college graduate of Tibetan descent and TAR residency. This policy, aimed at placating educated Tibetan youths after the Lhasa riot of 2008, is presumably unsustainable in the age of the market economy.

THE TIBETAN CASE

State facilitation of religion has been more substantive in the Tibetan case than in Xinjiang's in the post-Mao period, thanks to the internationalization of the Tibet issue. The state has made elaborate and generous efforts to restore monasteries, accommodate former religious elites, reconnect ethnic masses to the former elites, and even tolerate exile involvement in the Tibetan religious revival in China (see Chapter 4). As in the Uighur case, official facilitation has led to unsanctioned religious growth and increasing curtailment by the state. Limited state capacity, likewise, has facilitated religious developments in unwanted directions as well as limited the state's efficacy in curtailing them.

Curtailing Religious Growth

In contrast to private madrassas and violence in Xinjiang's case, unsanctioned religious growth in the Tibetan case has mainly involved Tibetan monasteries of the Gelugpa sect and their exiled counterparts in India. The exiled Gelugpa sect, historically the ruling sect headed by the Dalai Lama, embodies the Tibetan theocratic legacy and is a political rival to the CCP. State facilitation and containment of religion, thus, have been more delicate matters in the Tibetan case. Specifically, three episodes of unsanctioned religious growth and state control may be identified here: the late 1980s, the mid-1990s, and from the 2000s to the present.

The first episode, during 1987–9, resulted from the state-sponsored revival of religion a decade earlier. During the height of this revival, contact between local and Tibetan monasteries in exile was tolerated by state authorities. While not formally sanctioned, such contacts were informally carried out. Religious masters in exile were welcomed back to help with the restoration of monasteries and religious instruction (Shakya 2008b). These interactions served to fill the gap left by decades of clerical decline and displacement.

The exiles' religious influence would soon become destabilizing. In September 1987, the Dalai Lama delivered a speech in the US Congress, marking a huge comeback for the exiles since the Sino-US rapprochement in the 1970s. Days after the speech, a group of monks from the Drepung Monastery in Lhasa held public demonstrations, the first of its kind since 1959. As the mother monastery of the Dalai Lamas for centuries, Drepung has been the most important monastery for the Gelugpa sect of Tibetan Buddhism, or the royal sect to which successive Dalai Lamas belonged. Dozens of additional protests by Gelugpa clerics occurred during the remainder of the 1980s. Khedrup Chopel (2005), director of ethnic studies at the Minzu Institute of Tibet in the 1990s, cites the participation of about 400 lamas and their pupils from eleven monasteries, four sutra halls, and one Buddhist school. He blames their involvement on the "poor quality" of low-level clerics who had proliferated due to the "uncontrollable" expansion of monasteries since the early 1980s.

The lamas' protests led to three ordinances from the TAR government, issued in 1987, 1989, and 1991, to check undesired religious growth. The decrees aimed largely at limiting exile influences in Tibetan monasteries within China (Table 6.12). In particular, the 1989 ordinance emphasized educating clerics on anti-separatism and was followed by the dispatch of official work teams to deal with "chaotic" mismanagement at monasteries. This refers to the mismanagement of monastic affairs and personnel, revenues and expenditures, public safety, and cultural relics. These problems were blamed on the "out of control" expansion of monasteries, their personnel, and exile influence. Official work teams moved into sixteen monasteries, sutra halls, and Buddhist schools, expelling some clerics from monasteries (Chopel 2005). The TAR adopted temporary regulations for religious affairs in December 1991 (updated on January 1, 2007), which mandated prior official approval for the construction of new monasteries, recruitment of monastic trainees, convening of major monastic events, participation of exiles in monastic events, and hosting of monastic events by exile lamas (TAR 1991).

TABLE 6.12 *Central and regional decrees to regulate religion in Tibet*

Year	Decree	Key contents
November 9, 1987, TAR regional government	"TAR Regulations for Democratic Management of Buddhist Monasteries" (Implemented in 1996)	To reform elected boards of monastic administrators so as to reduce exile influences
December 29, 1988, CCP Central Committee	"Several Issues Concerning Work in Tibet"	Urging better maintenance of social stability
September 21, 1989, TAR Party Comm't and regional gov't	"Opinions on Strengthening Management of Monasteries and Reforming Monasteries"	To implement patriotic education and send work groups to reform monasteries
December 9, 1991, TAR regional gov't	"TAR Temporary Regulations for Religious Affairs"	Regulations for opening and operating monasteries

Source: TAR (1987 and 1991); Chopel (2005).

Limited state capacity in enforcement, however, allowed exile influences to continue in gray areas. This has especially been true of Tibetan areas outside the TAR, where more leeway has been permitted. According to the Tibetan historian Tsering Shakya (2008b), "[T]he flow of people between historic monasteries in Tibet and newly established ones in India has been constant since the 1980s. There is daily communication via phone and it is not uncommon for monks to spend a few years in India and then return to Tibet. Similarly, monks from Tibet have to come to India for their education." In my field observations, this education in exile monasteries remains normal at least for major Gelugpa monasteries located in Tibetan regions outside the TAR. It is routine for them to send cleric pupils to Dharmsala for training, and it is common to see portraits or photos of the Dalai Lama on display in these monasteries.[28] Although the Karmapa Lama, head of the Karma Kagyu sect of Tibetan Buddhism, is an escapee from China, his lectures are routinely available in audio and visual broadcasts in many monasteries I visited in western Sichuan and the TAR. This was true even when he was an exile in Dharmsala and well before his escape to the USA in 2017.

The reason for official tolerance is a recognition, if reluctantly, of the traditions of Tibetan Buddhism. According to these traditions, because senior lamas who left Tibet in 1959 have established monasteries in India, these places are seen as the legitimate seats of those lamas. Thus, monasteries in Tibetan regions look to the exile monasteries as the source of religious teaching (Shakya

[28] Observations inside the Kīrti monastery, the leading Gelugpa monastery of Kham, and several other monasteries in Ngawa and Garzê, summers 2014 and 2015. Conversations with family members of a monk of the Kīrti monastery, summer 2014.

2008b). Yet the political impact of such monastic ties is inevitable. As two Sichuan scholars put it, "folks in the Gelugpa sect think of power, not just religion. They used to rule, after all."[29] Herein lies the crux of unsanctioned religious growth: exile linkages and yearnings for the Dalai Lama as symbols of the traditional Tibetan order.

The second episode of unsanctioned religious growth and state control, during 1993–6, revolved around the selection of the eleventh Panchen Lama. Rivalry between Beijing and exiles to control the selection process gave rise to agitation among key Gelugpa monasteries in Tibetan regions. Protests picked up in the final stage of Beijing's preparatory work in 1993, but were viewed by local authorities as "exile interference." After the Dalai Lama announced his own choice, Beijing still officiated its pick in late 1995, which led to unrest among key Gelugpa monasteries in the first few months of 1996. By May, local authorities responded with a "patriotic education" campaign to cleanse exile influence, starting with the top three Gelugpa monasteries of Lhasa, the Deprung, Dga'-ldan, and se ra dgon. The campaign put pressure on local lamas to disavow loyalty to the Dalai Lama, which was particularly frustrating for the Gelugpa clergy, to whom the Dalai Lama was the supreme spiritual leader. The patriotic campaign also tried to remove allies of exiles from monastic leadership.

The third episode of unsanctioned religious growth and state control, from the 2000s to the present, may be broadly linked to the cumulative effects of market reforms. The demise of the socialist state has strengthened monasteries as sanctuaries for those who try to escape the forces of the market. These individuals often come from Tibetan regions outside the TAR rather than the TAR itself, which has been better shielded from economic liberalization. In pastoral and rural areas of the TAR, agrarian taxes have been exempted since 1984, well before the nationwide agrarian tax reform in the early 2000s. While those areas experienced a hollowed out local state earlier than the rest of the country, state aid programs and welfare benefits, generously provided since the 1980s, have helped to enhance state presence and policy tools in rural areas of the TAR, thus offsetting the effects of weakened state capacity. This has made rural areas of the TAR more stable in comparison with Xinjiang or Tibetan areas outside the TAR.

In Tibetan regions outside the TAR, agrarian tax reforms were implemented in the early 2000s along with the rest of the country, with similar effects of weakened state capacity. The retreat of the state has allowed monasteries here – often located near natural villages – to fill in the vacuum by providing missing functions, such as welfare services for the poor, medical services through traditional Tibetan medicine and prayers, or even social networks in the secular world. The demise of rural cooperatives and the rise of market

[29] Conversations with a Han scholar and a Tibetan scholar, both of western Sichuan at Sichuan University, July 2018.

competition have led more rural youths to seek refuge in the monasteries.[30] These youths would otherwise become migrants in cities, including Lhasa, but poor education has ill prepared them for the urban job market (Ma and Tenzin 2008). Not surprisingly, they were ready participants in the Lhasa riots of March 2008, which targeted Han businesses and migrant workers for attack. Low-level monks from outside the TAR have also been responsible for most cases of self-immolation committed since early 2009.

In the wake of the Lhasa riots of March 14, 2008, official efforts sought to curtail unwanted religion through two planks. As would be expected, they have involved a mix of ethnicizing and centralizing mechanisms. For the former, official policy has stepped up welfare benefits to compete for the allegiance of rural Tibetans, including low income stipends, medical insurance, healthcare and public health facilities, free public education, and housing projects.[31] These benefit programs also empower village cadre who distribute them, thus providing incentives for individuals to serve as village cadre (who usually receive a small stipend but no formal salary). An added incentive is that for the village cadre in the TAR, there is a quota for one individual to move into the state civil service at a given time. This is a rare opportunity to become a salaried official without taking the civil service exam.

For ethnicizing mechanisms, generous policies were also implemented to induce compliance among lamas. During Chen Quanguo's tenure at the helm in the TAR (2011–16), he instituted two sets of "full coverage" for all monasteries. The first provides healthcare insurance, pensions, low income allowance, and personal injury insurance to all monastic members. The second provides roads, utilities, media services (radio, TV, and newspapers) and communication services to all monasteries (Liu 2014). Since monasteries are often located in remote villages or mountains and provide no formal income to their clerics, the two "full coverages" entail tremendous policy benefits for monastic members. With the first coverage, low-level lamas no longer have to rely on their families for financial help. With the second coverage, clerics are easily connected to the outside world physically and electronically.

For centralizing mechanisms, Chen implemented greater administrative oversight over monastic management. Under his stewardship, regulatory committees for monasteries (*simiao guanli weiyuanhui*) have moved into monasteries, along with the state officials and party branches that staff them. These committees are housed in a small building close to the entrance of

30 In-depth conversations with a Tibetan Rinpoche in western Sichuan, summer 2015. He is also a vice chairman of the county CPPCC.

31 Electronic communications with a senior researcher at the China Tibetology Center and a senior researcher at the Western Development Research Center of Sichuan University, February 2018. I directly observed local officials signing up rural Tibetans for public health insurance in rural areas, the TAR, July 2017.

a monastery. Their regulatory mechanisms are based on a tripartite coordination among monasteries, regulatory committees, and lamas' families. The last element refers to the requirement that officials of a regulatory committee must each befriend at least one lama, visit the family he has left behind, learn about their economic difficulties, and help solve at least one problem for the family. These would become part of Chen's kinship program in Xinjiang.

Although the state provisions may initially induce gratitude, over time they tend to be taken for granted as another set of ethnic prerogatives. Their long-term effects in maintaining monastic allegiance are uncertain, especially when juxtaposed against state controls over monasteries.

Self-Immolation

Self-immolation, mostly by low-level Tibetan monks, emerged less than a year after the Lhasa riots of 2008, in February 2009. By the end of 2018, a total of 155 Tibetans in China had self-immolated, according to the International Campaign for Tibet (ICT 2018). Has this self-directed violence been a result of the same dynamics as in Xinjiang's case? That is, the alternatively facilitating and restraining roles of the state in the religious revival of the two regions.

The existing literature answers in the affirmative. Tsering Shakya suggests that the locational factor in self-immolation cases points to the state's role in facilitating religion. The most frequent site of self-immolation has been Ngawa, western Sichuan, which has enjoyed a more relaxed religious policy as part of eastern Tibet (i.e., outside the TAR). In the early 1980s, many senior lamas in exile were allowed to come back and lecture, including the chief lama of the Kīrti monastery in exile. Eastern Tibetan regions continue to enjoy more freedom to travel to and study in exile monasteries, enabling close ties between them (Shakya 2012: 29, 34). At the same time, the sectarian source of self-immolation points to the state's role in curtailing religion. Self-immolation has occurred primarily among monasteries of the Gelugpa sect, in eastern Tibet, especially the Kīrti monastery of Ngawa, and these monasteries have been mostly involved in protests as well (Shakya 2012: 24, 33, 34). As the leading sect of Tibetan Buddhism, Gelugpa monasteries feel intimately violated by state controls, particularly the pressure to denounce the Dalai Lama and to distance themselves from religious communities in exile (Shakya 2012: 28, 29).

Other studies place key blame on the state's repression of religion. Based on self-immolators' last words, Wang Lixiong finds that their motives stem largely from religious sentiments not permitted by the state. That is, yearning for the Dalai Lama (Wang L. 2012b). This finding rebuts the view of both the Chinese state and the Tibetan exiles that wishing for the Dalai Lama's return is equivalent to calling for Tibetan independence. Han and Paik (2014), through a statistical analysis of the spread and frequency of protests in Tibetan areas, find that those protests are significantly associated with the number of officially registered Tibetan Buddhist sites, as well as the historically dominant religious sects. Andrew Fischer (2012) finds a correlation between the geographic spread of Tibetan protests, self-immolation, and resettlement. Although no self-immolator had come from any resettlement sites, Shakya argues that Tibetan grievances – derived from ethno-nationalistic claims of a homeland – are related to an identity institutionalized by the state, the Tibetan nationality (2012: 24).

My own conversations and observations in various Tibetan regions suggest an intertwining of state roles and local dynamics in breeding self-immolation. In western Sichuan, local officials and scholars acknowledge that sectarian and religious sentiments are aggravated by state policy. Specifically, local communities yearn for the Dalai Lama for religious reasons, while the state refuses to allow his return for political reasons.[32] As they understand tacitly, self-immolation is a form of political pressure on Beijing to allow the return of the Dalai Lama.[33] In contrast to the usual official Chinese rhetoric, that is blaming "Western forces" for inciting this pressure, local dynamics point to exile influences. In one chance encounter I had in a Ngawa village, a rural Tibetan family, whose son was a lama in the Kīrti monastery and received religious training in Dharmsala, casually mentioned that the monastery had received word from Dharmsala to stop self-immolation, because it had not worked.[34] By contrast, another Tibetan family in a Garzê village I visited, whose daughter was a monk at the Sêrtar Monastery, was indifferent to self-immolation or exile influence, since they belonged to the Nyingma sect of Tibetan Buddhism.[35]

Geography and history make a difference in the impact of exile influence and state response. In Diqing, Tibetan prefecture of Yunnan, monastic influences appear modest and require little state interference. Dozens of Tibetan villages share one monastery, a visibly sparse one compared with those in western Sichuan or the TAR. Few families send their offspring away to be monks. The villages look more like those in inland China than pastoral villages on the plateau. The exiles have vied to increase influence by providing a free internet

32 Conversations with two local United Front officials who were in charge of liaison with the Kīrti monastery of Ngawa, a Rinpoche who is a member of the county CPPCC in Ngawa, and three scholars of western region development from Sichuan University, summer 2014. Conversations with a Tibetan rural household in Garzê, and two scholars (one Tibetan) of western region development at Sichuan University, summer 2017.

33 Zhu Xiaoming, former head of the China Tibetology Center who headed Beijing's search for the new Panchen Lama, conceded this point, based on my conversations with a scholar at Sichuan University where Zhu was a visiting scholar, summer 2015.

34 While driving toward Garzê on July 5, 2015, several local scholars and I were stopped by a mud slide. We decided to visit a student of one of the scholars who was from a Ngawa village. We spent hours chatting with the student's family of nine people.

35 This was the family of our Tibetan driver during my trip to Garzê with local scholars in July 2015. This was also an unplanned visit because he offered it when we were driving through his village.

service,[36] but the influence of the Karmapa Lama, who was born and raised in socialist China, seems a modifying force here.[37] Diqing is also the only Tibetan region where no self-immolation has occurred, in contrast to western Sichuan, Qinghai, Gansu, and the TAR. Diqing's historical role as a commercial gateway between interior China and Tibet, moreover, makes it a meeting place of cultures and peoples. Whether out of appearance or genuine gratitude, local officials and villagers praise the CCP for improving their livelihood in a way that harkens back to pre-reform days. They frequently cite their annual stipends from the government, totaling tens of thousands for each household. Party members wear the party badge on their outfit and hang the party flag in front of their homes. Almost all children go to public schools and some make it to college, serving as role models for secular achievements. Village officials proudly name the local children who have attended college and landed jobs in government offices.

By contrast, the high plateau of western Sichuan has a high frequency of monasteries for the convenience of local pastoralists. The power and agitation of monasteries here have forced the state to exert more controls on the Gelugpa sect, while also pouring resources into road construction, utilities, and renovations for the monasteries. Financial sponsorship for individual monasteries and lamas also flows in generously from wealthy Han businessmen of inland provinces, which further strengthen the grandeur and influence of major monasteries and lamas in Garzê and Ngawa. Some elite lamas seem to be hugely enriched by their Han sponsors and by the donations of their parishioners.[38]

Indeed, social class cleavages undercut the ethno-religious sentiments emphasized in the Western literature about self-immolation. It has been mostly the young, poorly educated and lowest-ranking monks who self-immolated. And it is always a pastoral or rural family that sends away its offspring (at least one from each household) to be a lowly monk. Of ninety-two self-immolators in Wang Lixiong's data (2012), nearly a third (31 percent) were under nineteen years old and nearly half (45 percent) were between twenty and thirty years old. By contrast, just 8 percent were between thirty and forty years old, another 8 percent between forty and fifty, and 5 percent over fifty years old. This means that over three quarters, or 76 percent, were younger than thirty years old. Most were low-level monks with some monastic education, while the few laymen who self-immolated had attended middle school. Financial incentives may even play a part, even if unknown to the self-immolators. According to a Taiwanese scholar who has done fieldwork in Dharmsala and western Sichuan, there are linkages between exile fund raising, middlemen, and self-immolators' impoverished family. The

[36] Field observation, Diqing, Yunnan, August 2016.
[37] I thank an anonymous reader for raising this point.
[38] Field observations in Ngawa and Garzê, summers 2014 and 2015.

middleman plays a nefarious role by profiting from the deceased, as he pockets the bulk of the compensation fund while the deceased's family usually receives a small portion of it.[39] In this scenario, the lowly self-immolator is an exploited victim physically and financially.

Social class cleavages also leave a deep chasm between Tibetan elites who have risen within the Chinese system and those in exile. The former's antipathy for the old monastic order stems not only from their preference for local development, but also from their political interests in resisting the return of the old elites, who would compete for the support of Tibetan commoners. Detailed conversations with a prominent Kham native (hereafter Khampa) are illustrative of the views of the CCP's Tibetan cadre. As the descendant of a poor Tibetan household who welcomed the arrival of the Red Army, he has risen from the mountains of western Sichuan to become a researcher and policymaker at the highest level in China.[40] Khampa emphasizes the background of self-immolators as the poorest, least educated, and lowest of the young monks in the monastic hierarchy. Decades earlier, these individuals would have been the CCP's natural allies against the theocratic elites. However, being left behind by economic liberalization, poor young Tibetans have become allies of the monastic upper class and are sacrificed for its political cause. In this perspective, the religious roots of Gelugpa grievances derive from their theocratic aspirations for the return of the old order. Based on his own experience in Garzê, some religious elites have taken advantage of China's negotiations with exiles to spread word of their imminent return. Local commoners, fearing retribution in the event of a regime change, try to protect themselves by answering some lamas' call for noncooperation with Beijing.

In this social class perspective, it is the state's weakened capacity that contributes to the geopolitics of self-immolation. Self-immolators had come from just a handful of the 3,600 plus monasteries across Tibetan regions in China. Most self-immolations, Khampa contends, occurred in northern Kham and southern Amdo, or the "three counties and seven villages" at the junction of Sichuan, Qinghai, and Gansu provinces. Traditionally plagued by intertribal strife, these unruly areas suffered harsh suppression from the Muslim warlord Ma Bufang during the Republican area. In the first three decades of the post-Mao era, these peripheral regions were neglected by local states and left impoverished and marginalized. This contrasts with the better governed and integrated Tibetan area of Diqing, Yunnan, which has seen no protest or self-immolation. In the TAR as well, which has been highly tended by the state, it was largely visiting monks from outside the province who committed the small number of self-immolations there. Renewed state attention to the neglected

[39] Comments at the Q&A section at an internal academic forum of a Chinese university, Hangzhou, June 2018.

[40] He wished to be only identified as "Khampa" so his private views would not be taken as official positions. Conversations in Beijing, fall 2013.

communities of the tri-provincial regions, through the western development program, has led to conflicts among developers, local communities, and the state. Khampa views this as an inevitable part of the developmental process, rather than ethnic battles to be politicized.

Needless to say, self-immolation is unlikely to exert political pressure on "red" Tibetan elites such as Khampa, who abhors the return of exile elites. Based on field observations, this intraelite conflict remains the most important barrier to resolving the Tibet issue.

Traditions that Make a Difference

In contrast to Xinjiang's case, Tibetan traditions make key differences in the nature of unauthorized religious growths and state response. That is, these growths do not foster the type of security threats associated with private madrassas and jihadist ideology, thus allowing more leeway in state response.

First, while rural Uighur parents prefer some religious education for all children, rural Tibetan families usually follow the convention of sending one child to the monastery, thus easing the need for underground religious teaching sites. If contention over private madrasas is a major cause of state control and Uighur violence in Xinjiang's case, the same dynamics are absent in the Tibetan case. Although some state officials are unhappy about the overgrowth of Tibetan monasteries, such growth does not pose the kind of security threats that justify forceful closedowns.

An example is the Sêrtar Monastery. Founded in 1980 in the Larung Valley of western Sichuan by a lama of the Nyingma sect, it received official endorsement and became the world's largest Buddhist academy by the 2000s. Its sprawling presence is astounding: situated at 3,800 meters on the plateau, it consists of a few main buildings and by 2016, tens of thousands of small dormitories spreading across adjacent hills and housing at any given time about 40,000 monks, nuns, disciples, and elderly persons. The uncontrolled growth bothered some state officials, who worried about expanding religious influences. Authorities could try to limit the Sêrtar in a number of legal ways, simply by citing the multitude of safety and sanitation hazards, but they hesitated to take any action for fear of creating a "human rights" crisis.[41]

The rebuilding project eventually began in late 2016 and carried out what may be called streamlining. The Buddhist academy was separated from the monastery, while monastic members were separated from nonmembers by demarcating their dormitories. Elderly people were moved to senior homes built at a cost of ¥1.36 billion. Unlicensed building structures, which were usually makeshift dormitories, were demolished. Tenants who were not from the local area were sent home, both Han and Tibetan. Sewer systems were built for the renovated buildings and structures. Finally, oversight was tightened over

[41] Field observations and conversations, Sêrtar county and Sêrtar Monastery, July 2015.

the size of monastic and academic members.[42] In short, the rebuilding project involved scaling down and reorganization, rather than forced closedown of madrassas as in Xinjiang's case.

Instead of private madrassas, contention over loyalty toward the Dalai Lama is at the center of state intervention in the Tibetan case. Public display of that loyalty is banned as a sign of separatist sentiments. Monasteries are asked to condemn the Dalai Lama as part of their patriotic education. State demonization and the Dalai Lama's failure to return may even be a major cause of self-immolation. However, things can be quite different in private. The Dalai Lama's portraits can be seen hanging in the Kīrti monastery of Ngawa, the major source of self-immolation. They can also be seen in a few other monasteries and some rural families I had visited in Ngawa and Garzê in 2014 and 2015, although I did not see the Dalai's portraits in the monasteries I visited in the TAR in 2017. But Tibetan families can book tours to visit Dharmsala through travel agencies in Lhasa, including a possible visit with the Dalai Lama himself. One Garzê family I chatted with had taken such a trip and met the spiritual leader.

Second, the presence or absence of religious extremism and violent attacks makes a key difference in the Tibetan and Uighur cases. These two factors in Xinjiang put pressure on the state to take drastic actions, but their absence obliterates such pressure in the Tibetan case, thus easing the need for invasive restrictions. There are no equivalents of Wahhabism, jihad, *Hizb ut-Tahrir*, *Hijrat*, and the like in Tibetan Buddhism. Rather, Buddhism has the renowned precepts of nonviolence and no killing. Although the Lhasa riot of 2008 led to the death of eighteen civilians, there have been no "terrorist" attacks in Tibetan areas. Self-immolation has been a form of violence, but is fundamentally different from lethal attacks directed at the general public.

The religious ban for minors applies in Tibetan regions, but the absence of violence here renders it unnecessary for the state to be overly vigilant. Tibetan children are sent into monasteries under various pretexts with ease, from taking care of the uncle to being in need of the uncle's care. The Sêrtar Monastery has students who are toddlers. The inclination of children to stay for the long run varies with their preference for the monastic life or the secular school. For adults, the same religious ban exists in principle for public sector employees and public schoolchildren, but enforcement is not nearly as strict as in Xinjiang, due to different threat perceptions.

Third, the openness of Tibetan Buddhism mitigates threat perceptions and lends itself to better public understanding. The lack of gender, costume, and dietary restrictions makes Tibetan Buddhism accessible to the non-Tibetan public. While women – Muslim or otherwise – cannot enter mosques in Xinjiang, they can enter Tibetan monasteries, become

[42] Electronic communications with a Sichuan scholar who was involved in proposing ideas for the "demolition and rebuilding" project. August 17, 2018.

nuns, or tour as casual visitors. During field trips, I frequently encountered hostility in front of mosques in Xinjiang and was never allowed inside one, but always received a welcome reception inside the Tibetan monasteries I visited (those that require no purchase of tickets to enter). As materialism increasingly consumes China, many Han Chinese are intrigued by Tibetan piety. It has become a fad among some Han nouveau riches to be financial sponsors of Tibetan monasteries and elite lamas. A constant flow of Han Chinese men and women are among the students at the Sêrtar Monastery. Intermarriages have increased thanks to physical mobility in the reform era. According to Ma Rong's (2001) study, Tibetans are among the minority groups in China who have relatively more intermarriages and who demand no religious or other special requirements of their future spouses. By contrast, Muslim groups are the only ethnic minorities that require their marriage partners to have the same faith, resulting in the lowest rate of intermarriages. In fact, if a few Han Chinese men can be found in remote Tibetan villages, it is usually because they have married local Tibetan women.

Finally, the tradition of sending one child to monastic pursuits does not discourage secular schooling in the Tibetan case. As long as one child is in the monastery, rural Tibetan parents usually encourage their children to go to the secular public school. Like rural Uighur parents, pastoral Tibetan households may not always find schooling useful in the practical world, but they are more compliant when it comes to mandatory public education. When some local governments, in order to fulfill the state's mandatory education requirement, assign quotas to each family to send a certain number of their children to the public school, Tibetan parents try to oblige in some way. In cases where extra hands are needed on the pastureland, they may be willing to pay other people to have their children attend school so as to fulfill the quotas assigned to their household. These factors contribute to a far better equilibrium between secular and religious education in the Tibetan case.

In addition, the geopolitical setting differs in the two cases. Islamic extremism spreads not just in Xinjiang but in many of China's neighboring countries along Xinjiang's border in West and Central Asia, especially Pakistan and Afghanistan. By contrast, Tibet's external neighborhood of a Hindu state and several Buddhist statelets poses no extremist or terrorist threats. Thus Xinjiang imposes a much higher geopolitical pressure on China. The absence of this pressure obliterates the need for draconian state responses to control unauthorized religious growth in the Tibetan case.

SUMMARY

This chapter has examined changing religious policy in the post-Mao era as a dynamic of institutional tensions built into the autonomous system. That is, a paradox of centralization and ethnicization, pulling the system in opposite directions. In the early post-Mao era, religious revival was promoted by the state as a mechanism of political integration, to repair damaged relations with key minority communities. This ethnic accommodation, however, encouraged ethnic identity expression that has evolved in directions undesired by the state, periodically challenging and undermining the state's goal of national integration. Religious growth then has had to be curbed in progressively constraining ways, leading to frustrated identity, ethnic mobilization, political resistance, or even violence, and more curtailment from the state.

I have chronicled two cycles of these developments in this chapter: the state's direct and indirect facilitation of religion in the 1980s, leading to ethnicizing effects that compelled state curtailment of religion in the 1990s; and the state's indirect facilitation of religion in the 2000s, resulting in ethnicizing effects that has led to the state's draconian curtailment of religion since the late 2000s.

A key finding of this chapter is that religion or its suppression by the state did not automatically become a focus of anti-state sentiments, as is often implied in the existing literature. Rather, I argue, the state played a crucial role in facilitating religion's position as a focus of ethnic identity expression, namely, religious revival as a mechanism of political integration backfired. Moreover, limited state capacity has exacerbated religious growth unsanctioned by the state. In Xinjiang's case, state failure to differentiate variants of Islam and Islamic groups has resulted in underreaching and overreaching in controlling radical forces, leading to an escalation of radicalism and violence. In the Tibetan case, state failure to differentiate religious and political sentiments has resulted in overreaching in curtailing religious sentiments. In both cases, reform policies helped to make ethnic members who are susceptible to ethno-religious identity politics more vulnerable, by way of weakened rural governance and economic liberalization. The problem will be examined in more detail in Chapter 7.

Despite the broad similarities, four distinctions have contributed to divergent state responses and outcomes in the two cases. First, traditional sectarian variance, in the Tibetan case, makes it difficult for the leading sect to assert influence over all religious communities, unlike the easy entry enjoyed by Wahhabism in traditionally Sunni communities in Xinjiang's case. Second, traditional sectarian variance makes it difficult for the likes of religious fundamentalism or pan-Islamic ideologies to gain ascendance in the Tibetan case, in contrast to Xinjiang's case. Third, a lack of religious radicalism mitigates threat perceptions in the Tibetan case, allowing gray areas of religion to survive. Fourth, a lack of religious restrictions beyond the clergy obliterates pressure across Tibetan communities to observe them, thus further mitigating threat perceptions or strict enforcement of religious bans. All this is not to say that self-immolation is not a serious form of violence or political resistance. But it poses a different threat perception and on a different scale. The four distinctions allow a much less volatile religious climate in the Tibetan case than is the case for Xinjiang.

For these two ethnic regions, religion poses special paradoxes for autonomy. While autonomous regions are granted formal jurisdiction over "minority customs and religious freedom," the revival of religion was itself sponsored by the central state. The state's intention was to salvage minority support damaged by the Cultural Revolution, but it had little understanding of the complexity of religious lineages and sects. When religious revival evolved in directions unintended by the state, religion itself must then be curbed. Herein lies the ultimate irony of socialist autonomy. Finally, religious revival has had the most adverse impact on minority members of the lower classes, since they have become the main perpetrators and victims of ethnic violence associated with religious revival.

7

Economic Modernization and Its Discontents

If class universalism has been replaced by identity politics in key minority regions since the early 1980s, egalitarianism has been replaced by developmentalism across the country since the early 1990s. Developmental policies have demonstrably favored the politically sensitive ethnic regions, first Tibet and then Xinjiang, serving as the state's powerful instruments for national integration. After all, the post-Mao state views economic development as the best way to bridge regional, intraethnic, and interethnic disparities. Why then have developmental policies failed to generate desired outcomes in terms of political loyalty and national integration in the two outer peripheral regions?

Scholars diverge in their assessment of China's developmental policies in minority regions. Some find that anti-poverty programs play an overall positive role, even if they may not always reach those most in need (Bhala and Qiu 2006). Others attribute interethnic income gaps to spatial rather than ethnic reasons, namely minorities tend to live in poorer regions than Han people (Gustafsson and Li 2003). Analyses of the TAR and Xinjiang tend to have a more negative view, often suggesting that the benefits of development are mainly available to Han residents. For example, economic development indicators are much stronger for predominantly Han areas than for predominantly Uighur areas (Becquelin 2000: 68; Moneyhon 2004: 498); Uighurs may be targeted for exclusion (Dillon 2002: 27); land dispossession plays a significant role in catalyzing Uighur protest (Cliff 2016); urban-centered development does not benefit the rural and pastoral areas inhabited by poor Tibetans, resulting in "poverty by design" (Fischer 2002 and 2005); or economic growth with marginalization, polarization, and stratification in urban Tibet (Fischer 2013). At the very least, developmental policies have created dependency in Tibet (Dreyer 2006) or accelerated integration and Sinification in Xinjiang (Becquelin 2004).

These critical analyses are far apart from Beijing's policy intentions. These intentions can be seen from three angles. First, post-Mao economic policies for minority regions started under Hu Yaobang, while he was pulling Han Chinese out of Tibet and Xinjiang. So obviously he did not *intend* for those policies to benefit Han residents only. Second, further expansion of developmental programs has accompanied Beijing's concern for social stability in those two regions, which obviously cannot be served by increasing ethnic disparities. Finally, analysts within China are increasingly critical of the state's developmental programs for those two regions, not for creating exclusionary outcomes but wasteful and dependent ones. Obviously Chinese analysts do want to see minority policies work better. In other words, a distinction may be drawn between the *intentions* of state policies and their *consequences*.

In this chapter I will continue with the argument that the built-in tensions of the autonomous system, or centralization and ethnicization, have intensified in the reform era, fueling key sources of ethnic strife in the TAR and Xinjiang. The driving force has been the state's developmentalism as strategies of development and integration. Here centralization is manifested in top-down developmental models, either planned economy or economic liberalization, while ethnicization is manifested in more state aid and preferential economic policies as well as their ethnicizing consequences. In the TAR's case, state subsidies have sustained an "affirmative action" economy, resulting in dependency and questionable viability. In Xinjiang's case, the undoing of the socialist economy has left behind ethnic members whose ascriptive endowments disadvantage them in the marketplace, resulting in ethnically based grievances. In both cases, developmentalism has pitted local minorities against inland migrants, fueling ethnic conflict. As remedies, the state resorts to heavy aid programs, thus intensifying central drives as well as ethnic prerogatives.

This chapter will cover three topics: (1) preferential economic policies for minority regions in the reform era, (2) developmentalism and dependency in the TAR case, and (3) developmentalism and ethnic marginalization in Xinjiang's case.

DEVELOPMENT AND PREFERENTIAL POLICIES

Preferential economic policies for ethnic regions have greatly expanded during the reform era. The driving force has been state developmentalism: since the late 1970s/early 1980s as part of the post-Mao modernization drive, since the early 1990s as part of market reforms, since the late 1990s as part of the western development program, and finally since the late 2000s as a strategy to address the root cause of the Lhasa riot of 2008 and the Urumqi riot of 2009.

These policies fall into several categories. They include financial subsidies from the central state (Tables 7.1 and 7.5; Figure 7.1), partner assistance from interior provinces, cities, and firms (Table 7.4), anti-poverty assistance

TABLE 7.1 *Fiscal subsidies and modernization drive for ethnic regions: since the late 1970s*

Period	Subsidy category	Usage
Since 1977	"Subsidies for frontier enterprises"	Economic, cultural, and healthcare development
Since 1980	"Funds for ethnic work"	Emergency and sensitive events affecting social stability; ¥5 million in 1980 to ¥50 million in 2006; totaling ¥280 million in 2001–6
1977–88	"Investment aid for frontier construction"	Economic and social development, frontier defense, legacies of frontier wars
1977–88	10% annual increase in state financial subsidies	For five autonomous regions and the multiethnic provinces of Guizhou, Yunnan, and Qinghai
Since 1992	"Developmental fund for ethnic regions"	For improvement of basic services, skills, technologies, traditional crafts, and industries
Since 1995	"Subsidy measures in the transition period"	Regionally based subsidies, at higher rate and amount for ethnic regions; policy-based subsidies for ethnic regions and subject to continuous increase in accordance with state revenue growth
Since 2000	Local retention of taxes	80% of value added taxes

Source: Xu and Jin (2008: 80–1); Zhang W. (2010), 27–8.

(Table 7.3), policies promoting education and employment for minority members (Table 7.2), and myriad tax relief policies for the commercial, industrial, and agricultural activities of minority businesses and individuals (Zhang W. 2010: 29).

Although the above policies apply to all minority regions, the TAR and Xinjiang have received more state attention than the rest. As shown in Figure 7.1, the TAR has received the highest share of state subsidies in recent decades, averaging over 90 percent from 1990 to 2016. Xinjiang's share averaged over 65 percent from 2000 to 2016 and it netted the highest amount of state subsidies after 2013. Despite the state's strenuous efforts, these are the only two ethnic regions where socioeconomic disparities fueled ethnic riots. The reasons help to illustrate the

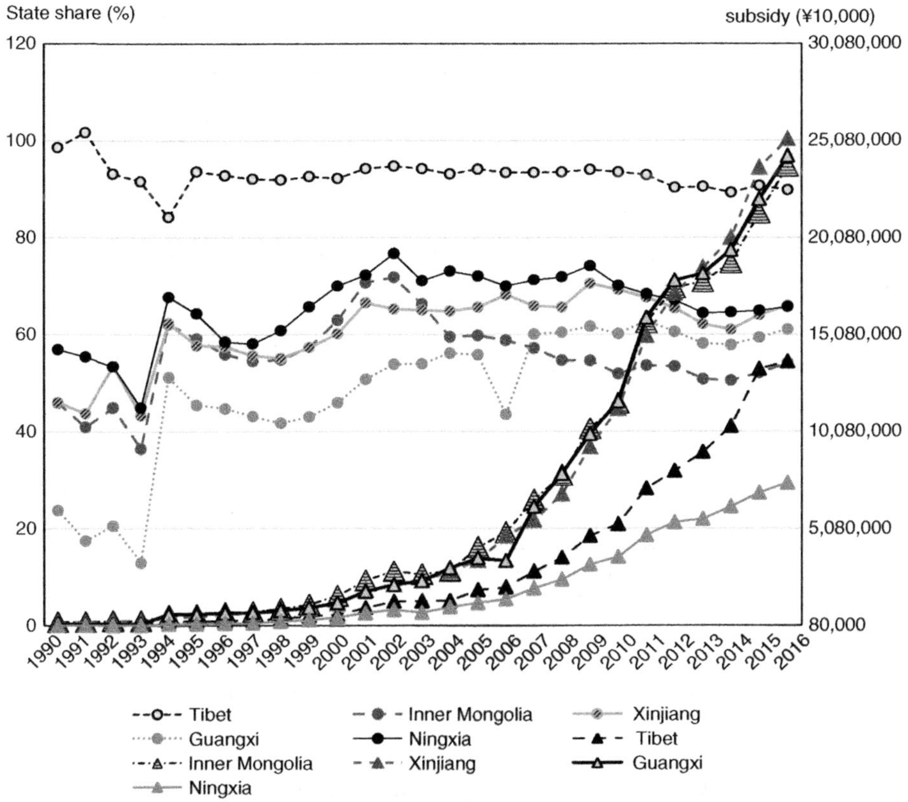

FIGURE 7.1: Share of state subsidy in the total revenues of autonomous regions
Source: SBT (2001: 106; 2003: 258; 2010: 75); SBG (2001: 99; 2010: 197); SBIM (2001: 249; 2003: 204; 2010: 196); SBN (2001: 102; 2010: 213); SBX (1995: 147; 1997: 177; 1999: 185; 2003: 99; 2010: 180); MOF (1993–2017).[1]

excesses of the state's role on the one hand and the faults of market forces on the other.

AN "AFFIRMATIVE ACTION" ECONOMY

Visitors to the TAR will be impressed by the modern streets and infrastructure that make the previously sparse plateau look like another Chinese city. In rural areas, roads, electric grids, and spacious houses look better than those in many rural areas of interior provinces. These achievements are all the more striking because it is so difficult to build

[1] Page numbers for data from the MOF, too numerous to list here, are available upon request.

TABLE 7.2 *Minority education/employment and modernization drive: since the late 1970s*

Period	Policy types
Since 1977	Preferential college admissions; expanded minority enrollment
Since 1979	Policy benefits for education of minorities in mixed communities
Since 1984	Preferential hiring of ethnic members in state sectors
Since 1992	Policy benefits for professional and technical schools in ethnic regions
Since 1997	Policy benefits for education of female children in poor ethnic households
1995–2010	Assistance for public schools in poor ethnic regions

Source: Xu and Jin (2008: 83).

TABLE 7.3 *Anti-poverty and modernization drive for ethnic regions: since the early 1980s*

Period	Type of anti-poverty fund
Since 1982	Developmental funds for underdeveloped regions
Since 1983	Anti-poverty loans
Since 1985	Wavier of tuition and other school costs for children of poor households
Since 1987	Anti-poverty loans with subsidized interests for pastoral areas
Since 1989	Capital allocation at higher rate and amount for poor ethnic regions
Since 1989	Low-interest loans, low taxes, and subsidies for ethnic businesses in poor ethnic regions
Since 1989	Extended periods for loan repayment in ethnic regions
Since 1989	"Basic living standards" projects in ethnic regions
Since 1990	Funds for "basic living standards" in poor ethnic regions
Since 1991	Local retention of fiscal surplus by poor ethnic counties; funds for transportation development in poor ethnic regions
1994–2001	"The 8th Seven-year Plan to Fight Poverty," with focus on ethnic regions
2001–10	Action Plan for "Enriching Frontier Regions and Peoples"
Since 2005	Program of development for small minority groups

Source: Xu and Jin (2008: 81–2); Zhang W. (2010: 27–8).

those projects on high plateaus. Meanwhile, local cadre busily sign up villagers and herdsmen for medical benefits and basic living allowances. Behind such prosperous signs, however, is the TAR's nearly total

TABLE 7.4 *Partner assistance and development of western regions: since the late 1990s*

Recipients (ethnic and multiethnic provinces)	Providers (local states and state firms from inland provinces)	Types and usages
Tibet (since 1984, an exception)	17 provinces and cities, and 17 state enterprises	Donation of 0.2 to 0.6% of the annual revenues of a partner province or city to aid programs; 0.6% for Shanghai and Shenzhen; 0.5% for Zhejiang
Xinjiang (since 1997)	19 provinces and cities	
Inner Mongolia	Beijing	
Qinghai (98% are autonomous areas)	Shandong, Hubei, Liaoning, Wuhan, Shenyang	
Ningxia	Shanghai, Fujian	Matching funds and tax benefits from the central government
Gansu	Tianjin	
Guangxi	Jiangsu, Guangdong	Provision of capital, management, personnel, and execution for developmental projects
Yunnan	Shanghai	
Guizhou	Hebei, Guangdong, Dalian, Qingdao, Shenzhen, Ningbo	
Sichuan	Zhejiang	Creation of jobs, housing, and schools
Shaanxi	Jiangsu	Improvement of education, sciences

Source: Xu and Jin (2008: 82); Gao and Mu (2011: 88–9).

TABLE 7.5 *Development initiatives for western regions: since the late 1990s*

Period	Initiatives
Since 1999	Western Development Strategy; state financing and development of transport infrastructure, ecological protection, support for foreign investment, promotion of education (exemption of tuition and fees since 2005), and retention of talent.
Since 2017	The thirteenth Five-Year Plan for Frontier Development and Enrichment; state financing and development of infrastructure in transportation, energy, communication; urbanization, anti-poverty, housing improvement, social welfare, education, healthcare, entrepreneurship, public and social services, local industries, cross-border trade, and frontier defense; totaling thirty-four projects.

Source: State Council of the PRC (2017a).

dependency on state subsidies and aid programs, making it an unusual case even among the heavily subsidized autonomous regions.

The TAR case illustrates the most dramatic dynamics of centralization and ethnicization in China's system of ethnic governance. Centralization here involves the state promotion of developmentalism, sustained by heavy state outlays and other preferential policies, or ethnicization. Because of state outlays, the TAR has been spared the brunt of economic liberalization that engulfs the rest of the country in the reform era. Two of the three principal sectors of the socialist economy have been preserved in the TAR: the government/public service sector and the state industrial sector. These two sectors have induced Tibet's chronic fiscal dependency on the central state. It is a phenomenon known in the Chinese discourse as "blood transfusion" without the capacity for "blood self-generation." Previously it would take a dissident like Wang Lixiong to assert that state aid to the TAR has created a culture of dependency and that such dependency is unsustainable (2009). Now a professor at the Central Party School, Jin Wei, advances similar arguments, depicting an "aid dependency" in the TAR's case (Jin 2010a, 2010b, and 2016).

The state's own data give a compelling account of a dependent economy. Its history is even longer than that shown in Figure 7.1. In the first five decades of the CCP's rule, from 1952 to 2013, state subsidies accounted for 91.45 percent of Tibet's total revenues and defraying 92.36 percent of its fiscal expenditure, while the local state covered just 8.37 percent of its own expenses, the lowest rate in the country. For the same period, state subsidies increased at an average of 16.02 percent annually, higher than the average annual growth rate of 14.49 percent for Tibet's local fiscal revenues (Jin 2016: 5). In fact, for thirty-three years out of those five decades, state subsidies covered over 100 percent of the TAR's expenditure. In addition, state investment has accounted for the bulk of investment in fixed assets in the region. State share was 59.87 percent in 2005, far exceeding the average of 4.49 percent for all Chinese provinces and the average of 9.32 percent for western provinces excluding the TAR. Nationwide, the provincial average for nonstate investment in 2005 included domestic loans at 17.25 percent, foreign investment at 4.21 percent, and self-financing at 58.26 percent, compared with 2.91 percent, 0.16 percent, and 18.26 percent respectively for the TAR, the lowest in the country (Jin 2010a: 409–16). By 2013, state investment still amounted to 56.59 percent, compared with an average of 4.53 percent for the country (Jin 2016: 8). In yet more forms of special policy benefits, the TAR has received myriad developmental and aid projects since 1984; it has been relieved of rural and pastoral taxes since 1984, two decades before the rest of the country; its college graduates were provided with full employment till 2007, the longest among autonomous regions and almost two decades longer than regular provinces.

Yet the TAR has not graduated to a self-sustaining economy. Why? Arguments about "urban bias" or "ethnic marginalization" may explain the poverty for some Tibetan groups, but they do not explain the TAR's high dependency overall. Nor do arguments about "assimilationist drives" explain this dependency. For purposes of assimilation, the state should have strong incentives to improve economic efficiency. The dynamics of centralization and ethnicization, meanwhile, offer a more plausible explanation, as it underscores a symbiotic relationship between the state's economic models and its preferential policies.

Integration and Dependency

Integration has been the paramount reason for the state to apply its version of development to the TAR. The purpose has been to close developmental gaps so that the TAR would not be susceptible to separatist forces. The phrase "sovereignty anxiety" (Jin 2010a: 64) aptly denotes the source of state motives. In the Mao era as in the post-Mao era, integration has to be achieved at all costs, or whatever preferential policies it would take. Politics trumps economics.

During the Mao era, class universalism justified transplanting the socialist system to Tibet. It was the collectivization movement of 1956 in Kham areas that triggered fear among Tibetan elites, leading to the Lhasa rebellion of 1959. With the flight of traditional elites in 1959, socialism was now to be established and to bring equality to the poor Tibetan masses. The party's provisional Work Committee expanded into a full local government in Lhasa, mirroring interior regions. The planned economy was fully implemented after Tibet formally became an autonomous region in 1965. Communes were set up in most rural areas and central planning in urban areas. Procurement quotas for agricultural products were issued to pastoral regions, leading to the cultivation of pastureland and the destruction of the ecology on which herdsmen depended. Industrial plants were set up but consistently generated deficits, except for the 1959–61 period when a chemical factory was opened to supply sodium borate to the Soviet Union. The planned economy never generated revenues to support the new public sectors in the TAR, including government, industry, construction, education, culture, and healthcare, which became sources of chronic fiscal dependency on the central state (Ma 2010a: 182–9; Jin 2010a: 81–95). In other words, political and economic integration necessitated state subsidies from the beginning. These subsidies would not have been necessary if Tibet's traditional system were left alone.

With the end of the socialist era, a different kind of transplantation to the TAR has intensified: developmentalism. Aside from continued subsidies to the local state and economy, the central state launched partner assistance projects. Started in 1984, these projects expanded significantly after the CCP's third work conference on the TAR in 1994 (Jin 2016: 6, table 1). The reason was a heightened "sovereignty anxiety" (Jin 2010a: 64), thanks to the rise of identity politics at home and the ascendency of the Dalai Lama on the global scene since the late 1980s. Thereafter it has become a political priority to develop the TAR regardless of economic costs. Successive central leaders have pledged unconditional fiscal support, providing Tibetan officials with whatever they requested, to the point of admonishing other autonomous regions to not emulate this (CCP 2005: 447, 465–70, 492, 547, 561, and 568). Therein lies the linkage between the imperative of integration and exceptional preferential policies for the TAR.

This linkage can also be seen from domestic defenders of fiscal infusion to the TAR, who are usually officials and specialists based in the TAR or China's western regions. They adamantly view it as a state responsibility to bring development to the TAR, as the path to national integration and improved human rights. Sun Yong, former head of the Tibet Academy of Social Sciences, denies that Beijing has a "sovereignty anxiety" issue, since Western countries are concerned about Tibetans' human rights, not sovereignty (2015). Wang Daiyuan, researcher at the same academy, defends state outlays for building Tibet's integration with the rest of the country (Wang D. 2012). Pan Jiuyan, a scholar at the Southwest Minzu University, defends those outlays as the responsibility of China's more endowed provinces (2009). In their analysis, extraordinary fiscal allocation is simply a reflection of the TAR's low level of development, and a normal function of the central state to raise this level. If anything, Tibet's high dependency signifies its developmental gap and requires more state assistance to achieve "integration" (*yi ti hua*). Importantly, Chinese officials and analysts, Tibetan Chinese included, view economic development as the best way to improve human rights, so convergence with interior regions is not a violation of Tibetan human rights, but on the contrary, a positive contribution. This line of defense, however, fails to explain why decades of fiscal assistance have failed to develop the TAR, leaving it in a perennially high state of dependency.

Either economic transplantation and state assistance, or both, have been at fault. That is, integration does not necessarily mean a dependent economy, and state assistance may create disincentives for weaning off dependency. However, financial incentives have served to reinforce state subsidies, since those who depend them are most likely to defend them. At most, some analysts may point out the state's arrogant benevolence that views minority regions as "backward" and in need of help from "advanced" regions. This dichotomy, a SEAC researcher writes, is at the root of state transplantation and betrays a social Darwinism (Ming 2012). A Han scholar also calls out the state's normative bias, namely, to equate local divergence from Han regions with "backwardness" (Fan 2011). These are remarkably critical voices in the Chinese context. However, they criticize the state's faulty strategies without questioning its right to do so, nor do they question Tibet's entitlement to special treatment.

The primacy of state rights, in fact, is at the heart of the problem. For the corollary of state primacy is a lack of local autonomy. This has prevented alternative paths of local development, such as indigenous and nonindustrial paths. Beginning with the TAR's transition to socialism in 1965, indigenous merchants – 206 at the time – were labeled "capitalists" to be "transformed." Handicraft industries were labeled "old conventions" to be discarded. Skilled craftsmen were turned into farmers. By a partial calculation, the annual output of local handcrafts industries decreased from ¥8.92 million in 1965 to less than ¥3 million in 1996 (Tseten 1995: 114). Granted, handicraftsmen and merchants comprised a tiny fraction of the old Tibetan society and did not make much difference in Tibet's overall economy. But local specialty products and trade would have represented viable alternatives to industrialization for indigenous growth paths.

By contrast, industrial plants promoted by the state have been the leading source of the TAR's fiscal deficits. State subsidies to sustain them accounted for 40.43 percent of the TAR's total revenues from 1963 to 2005. Moreover, for every unit of increase in those plants' output value, state subsidies nearly tripled (Jin 2010a: 91, 95; Wen 2006: 39, 40, 51). Thus, rather than contributing to the TAR's development, state industries have become its major liabilities.

Industrial Development and Dependency

Why have such liabilities been sustained for so long? The dynamics of centralization and ethnicization have been at work. In the Mao era as in the post-Mao era the central leadership has sponsored Tibet's development with an industrial focus, equating modernization with industrialization and the only way out of poverty. This is evident in an array of leadership statements and central documents (Jin 2010a; CCP 2001b: 208). The same pronouncements also reveal an earnest desire to bring material progress to these regions.

For minority regions, the industrial focus in development often leads to a neglect of resource endowments and ethnic heritages that entail diverse paths of development. The CCP emphasizes "local ethnic characteristics" not to justify a retreat from industrial development but rather greater efforts to push it so that "backward" regions can "catch up" with more advanced ones. Thus, not only were all of the TAR's industries built from scratch by the state, but their share in the local economy has remained the highest in the country: 100 percent in the 1950s, 90 percent in the 1960s, 75 percent in the 1970s, 63.31 percent in 1993, 59.75 percent in 2000, 50 percent in 2004, and 21.94 percent in 2013. This compared with a rate of just 1.84 percent and 1.94 percent for China as a whole in 2004 and 2013 respectively. Moreover, state industries contributed to just 0.17 percent of tax revenues in the TAR, well below the national average of 6.24 percent (Jin 2010a: 149, 201, 424; Jin 2016: 10).

Many factors account for why the TAR remains poorly endowed for industrial development. These include a lack of raw materials and fuel, high costs of transportation, and a limited local pool of skills and consumers. Oblivious to these factors, a whole assortment of industries was built in the

1960s, despite chronic deficits. Even the most useful industries – power plants – have generated scarce revenues due to high costs to produce each unit of electricity, a small consumer base, and free or subsidized access for local consumers. Not surprisingly, many plants have operated at a loss or simply closed to save costs. As a Tibetan analyst puts it, mines have been built but there is no coal to be mined or the coal may be unsuited for use; chemical plants churn out substandard products that no one wants; machinery factories have no buyers for their products; and sugar factories have no raw materials to work with (Tseten 1995: 112). Such plants were kept going because of state subsidies.

In the reform era, state subsidies have disincentivized such firms to close down or improve. Despite the demise of central planning elsewhere, subsidies have persisted in Tibet, sustaining capital inflow to unproductive state firms. These firms also receive support from local bureaus of finance, which supervise local state banks. Loans to unproductive state firms have been the leading source of nonperforming loans for those banks (Wang and Zhu 2005: 25). As of 2004, state firms represented 62.67 percent of the total asset value of all firms in the TAR, the highest in the country. By contrast, state firms accounted for just 1.84 percent of all firms across China in 2004, representing 44.1 percent of the total asset value of all firms nationwide (Jin 2010a: 149, 424). By 2013, SOEs had decreased to 21.94 percent of all firms in the TAR, but this was still above the national average of 1.94 percent. Moreover, state firms contributed just 0.17 percent of the TAR's tax revenues, much lower than the national average of 6.24 percent in 2013. In the same year, 73.4 percent of the investment in fixed assets went to state firms in the TAR, three times the national average of 25.61 percent; 57 percent of that investment came from state funding, compared with the national average of 5 percent. Despite a higher than national average rate in economic growth between 2001 and 2013, 12.36 percent versus 10.03 percent, much of it came from investment in fixed assets from state funding and partner assistance (Jin 2016: 7). In fact, this type of investment exceeded the total volume of the TAR's gross domestic product (GDP) in the decades from 1959 to 2013. In other words, unproductive state firms have persisted well into the reform era, unlike in the rest of the country, thanks to state funding.

The emergence of local companies in recent years has led to greater confidence in the state's industrial strategy. They point to the emergence of twelve publicly listed local companies as evidence the TAR has finally acquired the ability for self-development (Yang 2018). However, a closer look tells a different story, as none of the new companies are in the business of industrial production. Many of them utilize local natural resources – tourism, herbal medicine, mineral water, mineral extraction, and beer – while the rest are in real estate development and motorcycle sales.

Aid Projects and Dependency

The state's development aid programs for the TAR have intensified since 1984, and with each CCP Work Conference on the TAR since then (1984, 1994, and 2001). They have added significantly to the dynamics of centralization and ethnicization, as more state aid begets more dependency. The reasons are similar to the growing criticisms of western aid to Africa, for fostering dependency and corruption without requiring positive changes (Moyo 2010).

State aid programs for the TAR consist of two major types. The first may be called "partial aid" programs, involving developmental and investment projects allocated by the central government. These usually come after each of the CCP's Work Conferences on Tibet or are included in the state's five-year economic plans. These investments added up to 678 large projects between 1984 and 2011, totaling ¥6,070.85 billion. The central state does not consider them to be aid programs, since it makes similar allocations for all provinces. However, the TAR alone is exempted from contributing matching funds to those projects, hence they may be considered as "partial aid" programs from the central state.[2] The second type of state aid programs falls under partner assistance (*duikou yuanzhu*), involving developmental projects donated by central agencies, interior provinces, or cities and large state firms. Mandated by the central government, 7,516 projects were donated to the TAR between 1984 and 2013, totaling ¥26 billion. Unlike the central projects, which are implemented by local states, partner assistance projects are funded and executed by partner agencies, which bring in resources and personnel on-site to work on a one- to three-year rotation.

A breakdown of aid projects in the TAR shows that they are developmentally oriented and not intentionally designed to create dependency. Between 1984 to 2000, central projects comprised 33.21 percent for the energy sector (power plants and grids), 21.84 percent for the rural sector (farming, forestry, animal husbandry, and drinking water), 17 percent for urban development (roads, drinking water, and sewage system), 9.24 percent for social development (new schools, rural health services, and radio and TV antennas), and 6.03 percent for industries. For the period of 1984 to 2005, partner projects consisted of 55.35 percent for transportation (highways and railways), 19.43 percent for rural areas (irrigation and pastureland), nearly 15 percent for energy and for social development, 9.99 percent for postal services and telecommunication, 6.5 percent for local government, and less than 3 percent for state industries (Jin 2010a: 124). Together, the infrastructural and energy sectors received most assistance, which should provide physical foundations for economic development and improved efficiency. Importantly, infrastructural projects provided by partner assistance take a major financial burden off the

[2] I thank Professor Yang Minghong for clarifying the distinctions. Electronic correspondence, July 15, 2018.

TAR's local government, as interior provinces have to finance their infrastructural projects mostly on their own.

In reality, not all aid projects in the TAR play developmental roles. Many may be white elephant ventures that require more outside assistance to be sustainable. The problem was legendary in the TAR's case in the earlier days. Plants were erected but the equipment was too advanced for local skill levels, or there were no raw materials or market prospects for their products. Public squares, roads, or convention centers were constructed, with scanty usage but huge maintenance costs, becoming what Wang Lixiong calls "political showcases" (2009: 409–14). A majority of polled professionals who had worked on partner projects in the TAR were not optimistic about their impact on the local economy (Jin 2010a: 190; 2010b: 68). In fact all of the partner projects that Jin Wei has studied have required additional funding for maintenance and operation, as they are not productive enough to survive on their own (Jin 2016: 11). The more state and partner assistance, thus, begets more dependency.

Driven by political imperatives, aid projects can be misconceived from the beginning. For projects allocated by the central state, influencing peddling by local states is important. The TAR is no exception to the general pattern of "*paobu qianjin*" (frequenting ministries to get funding) that characterizes the funding dynamics between the central and provincial states, except that the TAR is guaranteed more hearing and success because it is the economically most needy or the politically most sensitive. This special status often leads to distorted incentives and wasteful expenditures. There is a "use it or lose it" mindset on the part of local officials (Ma 2013b: 3), hence they do not bother with careful feasibility studies or public input.

Details from partner assistance projects offer insights on the decision process. In the TAR's case, project proposals originate from local state agencies. These agencies, instead of addressing local conditions and needs, usually want to emulate the economic patterns and living standards of the donor provinces (Jin 2008: 15, 16; 2010a: 154). Their proposals then move to central agencies for review and approval, where there is even less knowledge about local needs. Once approved, local states go to partner provinces for financing and execution. The entire decision-making process is devoid of participation from local communities. In addition, a lack of coordination among different partner organizations, which may be subordinate to different central or provincial agencies, can result in redundant or wasteful projects. By contrast, projects funded by foreign foundations and donors, though often miniscule compared with colossal state and partner projects, tend to solicit grassroots participation and address local concerns more productively.

For partner or donor provinces, central imposition is an important reason for implausible projects. Partners invariably take up their role as political and financial burdens. They are mandated to build projects, hand over keys, and spend a scheduled amount of funding in a given period, but without rights in the usage and operation of the projects. Thus, partner teams may be more interested in finishing projects than in their long-term viability. As donors, moreover, they are accountable to themselves, and temporary stays on project sites further dampen a sense of accountability (Pan and Zhou 2010: 64; Yang 2011: 114). Sichuan province managed to back out as a participant by arguing that it had Tibetan regions under its own jurisdiction. Even for rich provinces, project staff can be turned off by a lack of say in the use of the projects they have built and/or the people to be hired. Without vested incentives, partner projects remain sustainable largely through central dictates.

Instead of "poverty by design," as Fischer has argued, "poverty by protection" more accurately characterizes the dynamics of partner assistance and dependency. Because partner assistance comes without hard constraints or accountability, and is free and continuous, local officials are motivated to "wait for, rely on and request" aid from the state and partner provinces. The result – even if not the intention – is "more aid, more poverty" (Jin 2016: 12). In other words, perverted incentives have nurtured a culture of dependency, popularly known as an "anemia complex." That is, the more "transfusion" to the TAR, the worse its "anemia." This means that aid projects are unable to provide localities with the ability to "self-generate blood," that is to be productive on their own. These terms are commonly used in Chinese discussions about state subsidies and partner projects to the TAR and Xinjiang.

As the most assisted province, the TAR offers ample examples. Some poorest counties here chronically depend on state assistance, yet they may spend generously on local officials' entertainment needs – at least before Xi Jinping's anti-corruption campaign. Unconditional aid has fostered a habit of "expecting, relying on and asking for outside assistance" among local officials, farmers, and pastoralists (Sun 2006: 72–9). That is, rural and pastoral people are being dragged to the state's modernization drive, hence their tendency to passively wait for outside aid. Given these problems, there has been an increasing emphasis on overcoming the passive role of aid recipients. In rural villages of the TAR, big posters can be seen on public display with the slogan, "Fight Poverty with Dignity," which implicitly urges villagers to avoid aid dependency.

Geographic and resource limitations compel Tibetan officials and intellectual elites to be pragmatists, placing more value on policy benefits than autonomy. Thus they support continued state assistance. One rationale is that dependency is a trade-off or even necessary condition for economic integration and progress. Another is that problems associated with state subsidies and partner projects are not unique to the TAR.[3] But the trade-off is not only reduced autonomy but

[3] See a summary in Yang Minghong, "Xizang fazhan zhengce yanjiu yu guancha: Guanyu 'duikou yuanzang' wenti yanjiu de xueshu zhengmin" [Developmental policy for Tibet: Debating the "partner assistance program"]. Unpublished paper.

reduced ability to withstand the onslaught of market forces from the rest of the country.

Market Expansion and Ethnic Conflict

While two of the three principal sectors of the socialist economy have been preserved in the TAR, economic liberalization was launched in the third sector, the rural and pastoral. Rural communes were disbanded in 1984 and replaced by individual household production. In urban areas, a nonstate sector emerged, mainly in retail and catering businesses. This economic liberalization may be still conceived of as a centralizing move, being a part of the state's new developmentalism. Market expansion has not favored all Tibetans, for ecological, technical, and ascriptive reasons.

Economic liberalization, above all, compounded demographic and ecological strains that already distressed the TAR. The demise of communes created a large number of unprotected and excess labor. This is an important point because this sector was where most Tibetans were based and remain so. Although the emerging nonstate sector opened up new opportunities, pastoral labor was (and remains) ill prepared for urban jobs and life. While communes absorbed the excess labor, now households and individuals were on their own. In the TAR, as in other minority regions, a number of factors – higher birth rates, lower marriage age, and improved healthcare – had allowed minority populations to grow at faster rates than the Han population. In the three decades since family planning was implemented for Han families, from 1982 to 2010, the Han population grew by 21.43 percent while the minority population grew by 57.28 percent and the Tibetan population by 40.75 percent (Table 7.6). Preferential policy has exempted rural and pastoral households from family planning, but the demise of communes ended the guarantee of a place for everyone in the local economy.

Tibet and other ethnic regions, despite their vast geographic expanse and low population density, are not better endowed with arable and habitable land in per capita terms than Han regions. Covering vast territories in northwestern and western China, they consist mostly of rangeland and/or deserts. Arid land, mountainous terrains, and scarce precipitation characterize the topography of four of the five autonomous regions – Inner Mongolia, Ningxia, Tibet, and Xinjiang – but especially the final two outer peripheral regions. Arable land in the TAR, the province with the lowest population density, is close to the national average of 1.4 *mu* (0.165 acres) per capita. Oases make up just 4.2 percent of Xinjiang's terrain. Even Yunnan, a multiethnic province known for its pleasant climate, is mostly made up of mountains. With high birthrates, arable and grazing land has declined proportionally. This is particularly a problem for frontier regions like the TAR where urbanization rates are low and ethnic members are concentrated in rural and pastoral areas. Constrained by geography, climate, and water resources, it is difficult to rely on arable or

TABLE 7.6 *Population growth of ethnic groups: 1982–2000*

Ethnic group	Total growth (%)	Annual growth rate (%)	Annual growth rate compared to Han	Ethnic group	Total growth (%)	Annual growth rate (%)	Annual growth rate compared to Han
Gelao	969.63	14.07	13.0	Derong	60.28	2.66	2.5x
Monba	682.72	12.11	11.2	Ewenke	57.26	2.55	2.4
Russian	435.10	9.77	9.0x	Blang	57.14	2.54	2.4
Hezhen	211.62	6.52	6.0	Tajik	54.24	2.44	2.3
Qiang	197.69	6.25	5.8	Salar	51.16	2.32	2.1
Tujia	183.00	5.95	5.5	Tuyuhun	51.10	2.32	2.1
Maonan	180.84	5.9	5.5	Lahu	49.12	2.24	2.1
Lhoba	178.14	5.85	5.4	De'ang	45.85	2.12	2.0
Gaoshan	170.36	5.68	5.3	Yi	42.33	1.98	1.8
Manchu	148.14	5.18	4.8	Jingpo	42.13	1.97	1.8
Mulao	129.48	4.72	4.4x	Kyrgyz	41.84	1.96	1.8
Xibe	125.64	4.62	4.3	Shui	41.84	1.96	1.8
Dong	107.54	4.14	3.8	Uighur	40.85	1.92	1.8
Oroqen	99.76	3.92	3.6	Tibetan	40.75	1.92	1.8
She	90.77	3.65	3.4	Li	40.66	1.91	1.8
Yao	86.79	3.53	3.3	Daur	40.66	1.91	1.8
Dongxiang	83.81	3.44	3.2	Bouyei	40.21	1.9	1.8
Bonan	83.04	3.42	3.2	7 groups[1]	30–9	1.7	1.6

(*continued*)

TABLE 7.6 *(continued)*

Ethnic group	Total growth (%)	Annual growth rate (%)	Annual growth rate compared to Han	Ethnic group	Total growth (%)	Annual growth rate (%)	Annual growth rate compared to Han
Miao	78.05	3.26	3.0	4 groups[2]	20–9	1.5	1.4
Jino	74.71	3.15	2.9	Tatar	18.63	0.95	0.9
Gin	71.78	3.05	2.8	2 groups[3]	1–9	0.3	0.3
Mongol	70.43	3.01	2.8	Nationwide	23.78	1.19	1.1
Achang	66.08	2.86	2.6	Han	21.43	1.08	1.0
Bai	64.11	2.79	2.6	Minority	57.28	2.55	2.4

Source: SBS and SEAC (2003: 2, 3).

1. These include the Hui, Hani, Kazakh, Dai, Lisu, Wa, and Pumi groups.
2. These include the Zhuang, Nakhi, Yugur, and another group.
3. These include the Koreans and another group, whose low rates of growth are due to exodus and/or intermarriages.

grazing land to support the increasing population or to raise per capita income. Ecological degradation, such as soil erosion and shrinkage, salinization of lakes, desertification, and deforestation, has worsened the problem. Chinese population experts attribute the principal culprit to overgrazing (Huang 2009: 24–6; Xu 2005: 129–37; Ma 2010a: 94).

The Tibetan countryside, which depends mostly on pastureland, best illustrates the problem of demographic pressure on the land. The TAR enjoys the most favorable tax and aid policies. Farming and pastoral products are entirely at the disposal of rural households, since no rural taxes have been levied since 1984. Urban sectors are heavily subsidized by the central government. For the rural population, there are no extraneous burdens other than contributions to monasteries. Central subsidies and partner assistance, furthermore, help to defray living costs for rural residents by providing inexpensive or free healthcare, education, electricity, drinking water and irrigation water. Still, pastoral and agricultural production has not kept up with the TAR's growing population. While the local population tripled from nearly a million in 1964 to three million in the 2010 census, animal husbandry increased just 50 percent; pastureland was overgrazed by about 40 percent, leading to soil erosion (over 30 percent of pastureland), desertification (over 10 percent of pastureland), damage to the ecological balance, extinction of species, and the spread of pests (Huang 2009: 26). For these reasons, per capita herding by Tibetan herdsmen is now lower than the period before the 1950s (Huang 2009: 26).

Demographic pressure on the agrarian sector is no better. According to Melvyn Goldstein's study of four Tibetan villages in 2000, based on two age groups of married females (50–4 and 55–9), the average of children per woman was 6.9 and 7.1 respectively. Moreover, because of high birthrates, per capita arable land decreased 19.9 percent during 1981–96, which was the leading cause of poverty among the villagers (Goldstein 2006: 205–6). State efforts to halt ecological degradation, through programs such as "retire farming, restore forestry" and "retire livestock, restore pastures," have further reduced arable and pasture land.

Market expansion has added to the local demographic pressure by drawing migration from inland provinces. Unlike in the Mao era, migration is self-initiated in the reform era, driven by economic forces since the 1990s (Howell and Fan 2011). Inland migrants to Tibet are mostly low-skilled farmers from the nearby Sichuan province, while local migrants usually come from rural or pastoral areas within the TAR. According to official data, the Han population in the TAR decreased after Hu Yaobang's Han exit policy but picked up since the western development drive of 2000. Before the Han exit policy, the Tibetan share in the TAR's local population was 92.7 percent in 1980. This share increased to an average of 96.3 percent from 1994 to 2001. Since the western development drive, the Tibetan share decreased to an average of 95.4 percent from 2002 to 2007 and 90.48 percent in 2011, when the Han people accounted for 8.17 percent of the local population (SBT 1989, 1993, 1995, 2008, and

2011). Han migrants are concentrated in urban businesses or traveling hubs along highways, while Hui migrants are concentrated in the yak-slaughtering business and the trading of Tibetan local produce. The Lhasa riot of March 14, 2008 made the TAR the only region other than Xinjiang to have witnessed violent riots against migrants. In both cases, violence during the riot was perpetrated by local ethnic migrants.

As such, the question of why migration fuels conflict is an inflammatory one. Beyond the rhetoric of "population swamping" and "settler colonization," a more realistic assessment is the urban concentration of migrants, which skews economic opportunities in their favor. As Andrew Fischer notes, the "population swamping" thesis "has a basis that is partially valid, but only with respect to the Tibetan urban areas, where Han and Muslim migrants mostly congregate; ... the perception of population swamping is essentially an urban-centric assessment of ethnic shares in the population, even though the Tibetan areas remain some of the most rural in China" (2004: 1). As he argues further, differentials between ethnic groups, such as urbanization rates and education levels, are the critical factors generating social marginalization and fueling ethnic conflict, rather than baseline characteristics such as population shares or poverty levels (Fischer 2002 and 2005). These patterns are corroborated by studies within China (Wu and Song 2014; Zhang and Wu 2017; Ma 2003; Ma et al. 2005; Ma 2009d and 2010a).

The official data, nevertheless, can underestimate migrant presence in several ways, thus underpredicting the migrant issue as a politicizing factor. First, residential registration for Han migrants remains in their native places. Official census data include a category for "regular residents" (*changzhu renkou*), which is different from the category "permanent residents." Census data for "regular residents" are drawn from home visits made by census workers rather than from residential registration. Census workers are supposed to count all residents in their assigned districts whenever they can, that is, if the migrant workers are home when census workers visit. However, many may not be home because they are usually in the TAR between May and October, but census visits are made at the end of the year in December. In one scenario, when a census worker went on vacation, thousands of residents under his jurisdiction were not counted (Ma 2008b: 171). Another missed group is the People's Liberation Army soldiers, whose residential registration remains with their native provinces. This is the situation for People's Liberation Army soldiers across China, but their increasing size in the TAR and Xinjiang poses a serious problem for demographic balance in urban centers where patrol vehicles and squads may seem ubiquitous. Moreover, some of these soldiers stay as ex-servicemen officials after leaving the military.

Ascriptive and technical advantages offer a good explanation for why inland migrants present real competition to local migrant groups. When Robert Barnett (2009) suggests that the Lhasa riot of 2008 involved a wider spectrum of society than the monastic basis of earlier protests, he is right in the sense that most of the rioters were migrants and vagrants from rural and pastoral Tibetan areas outside Lhasa. As the literature on economic modernization and politicized ethnicity suggests, when young men of one ethnic group from the countryside found themselves disadvantaged in the new labor markets on the ground of their ascriptive traits, they became receptive to political mobilization along ethnic lines (Deutsch 1953; Gellner 1983). In a study of six ethnic cities in western regions – including in the TAR and Xinjiang – by Ma Rong's multiethnic research team from Beijing University, the China Tibetology Center, and the Tibetan Academy of Social Sciences (Ma and Tenzin 2008), local Tibetan migrants were found to face greater difficulties than Han and Hui migrants in landing jobs in Lhasa: 20.3 percent of the Tibetan respondents reported difficulties, compared with 4.5 percent of the Han and 8.2 percent of the Hui respondents. However, educational levels made a key difference, as a third of the Tibetan migrants surveyed in the study were illiterate, while half of the Han migrants had completed secondary schools. The Tibetan respondents were also unfamiliar with life and employment in urban settings, or skills suited to the urban job market.

Han and Hui migrants have faced their own barriers, thanks to their cultural disadvantages. In my casual conversations on the streets of Lhasa and Shigatse in the summer of 2017, Han and Hui migrants complained about language barriers as much as did local ethnic migrants, more so the further away from urban areas. Ma and Tenzin (2008) report that Han and Hui migrants complained more about discrimination than did the Tibetan migrants in Lhasa. Illiteracy rates among the Hui migrants are on a par with Tibetan migrants, though this did not usually handicap them. Nevertheless, in the years leading up to the Lhasa riot of 2008, income differentials among the different migrant groups were real: in 2005 Han migrants earned 1.5 times more than Tibetan migrants on average, but in 2008 the differentials increased to 2.2 times for Han migrants and two times for Hui migrants.

A number of cultural assets work in their favor. For Hui migrants it is their intraethnic business ties and business traditions, while for Sichuan migrants the popularity of Sichuan cuisine enables them to dominate in the catering business. Literacy – even if moderate among inland migrants – helps them to land construction jobs, as they are able to follow drawings and measurements. Work habits accrued from intensive agriculture also make a difference. Lobsang Dradu, a Tibetan scholar at Sichuan University, illustrates with a bridge project in a pastoral area of northern Tibet. Initially Tibetan workers were hired at the instruction of the county's party secretary. But the construction fell behind schedule and exceeded the original budget. The party secretary had to give permission to hire Han migrant workers after watching on-site how the two groups handled their jobs (Yang 2014). In Tibetan villages I visited in Ngawa, Garzê, and Diqing during the summers of 2014–16, villagers usually hired Han migrant workers to build their houses, citing better workmanship and timely completion.

Regardless of the underlying causes, income differentials and underlying barriers to economic parity result in ethnicizing consequences. That is, they are conducive to ethnic finger pointing and conflict. Particularly in the decade prior to the Lhasa riot of 2008, when the state provided few protections for local migrants and unemployed youths, local resentment had built up over "Hans coming to our territory, competing for local jobs, earning more than us, and taking away money." Varying versions of this complaint, particularly in Lhasa, were found in Ma and Tenzin's (2008) study on the eve of the Lhasa riot. Such popular sentiments helped to incite rioters to target Han and Hui businesses as well as state agencies and state enterprises for destruction during the violent riot of March 2008 in Lhasa.

True to the dynamics of centralization and ethnicization, the local state ethnicized policy remedies in the wake of the violent riot. It stepped up preferential policies – not so much to help low-skilled Tibetans compete in the market economy, but to provide a more comprehensive "affirmative action" economy. In rural and pastoral regions, new and existing subsidies added up to a dozen kinds for each household by early 2011 (*Xinhua* 2011). These include subsidies for new housing (up to 80 percent of costs), staple crops, farm machinery (30 percent of purchase price), diesel oil, and even household electronics and home furniture; financial rewards for family planning (for families with two children, till eighteen years of age); pensions, social security, and medical insurance (¥20 or $3 a month); and free seed animals (three female yaks or thirty female goats). There is also a subsidy to stop overgrazing, called the "retire livestock and restore pastureland" program, paid to pastoral households by the size of their pastureland. Based on my field observations, this size is often hard to measure on the sprawling plateau, and grazing continues even though households collect subsidies for not doing so.

For the more "destabilizing" forces, an array of policy benefits helps to neutralize ethnic mobilization. Generous subsidies reduce incentives for rural and pastoral youths to do migrant work in cities, thus preempting urban unrest. Welfare and healthcare benefits for monastic members, provided since 2014, induce compliance. From 2011 till Chen Quanguo's departure as Tibet's party secretary, college graduates of Tibetan descent and TAR residency were guaranteed a job assignment in the state sector, and those willing to take job offers outside the state sector or the TAR were given financial incentives to do so. Together, these measures serve to placate the social forces most likely to hold protests. But they also create more aid dependency.

Interestingly, it may be market forces that have done a more effective job of easing in-migration to the TAR. Labor shortages in inland provinces have reduced incentives to seek opportunities on the high plateau. For those who stay, security concerns have led them to add local Tibetans to their staff. For migrants with school-age children, it is more important to return to their hometowns for a better education for their children. For the second generation of migrants who have grown up in the TAR, who are no longer impoverished as their migrant parents were, few are willing to make sacrifices like their parents and spend the rest of their lives on the plateau. In addition, reform of rural subsidies since 2015 has incentivized farmers in inland provinces to stay on their farms. Previously those subsidies were tied to land, so that many farmers would collect subsidies and still head out for migrant jobs. Reform of rural subsidies has now tied subsidies to cultivation, thus motivating farmers to grow crops on their land.[4]

Economic forces, rather than aid dependency, have also done a better job of integrating Tibetan migrants and immigrants in Chengdu, the top destination of Tibetan out-migration. Many well-to-do Tibetans from Ngawa and Garzê prefectures, and even the TAR, purchase houses in the capital city of Sichuan and its nearby counties, either to send their kids to better schools here or to enjoy their retirement in a city known for fertile plains and relaxing teahouses. Tibetans also come to Chengdu for better hospitals, jobs, and business opportunities, thriving in and out of Tibetan towns in a diverse metropolis that attracts a host of other minority groups from surrounding areas. A 2012 study shows that over 30,000 Tibetans have permanent resident status in Chengdu; another 150,000 to 200,000 live there as regular residents without formal registration; and yet another one million Tibetans from Greater Tibet move about the city each year. Tibetan immigrants who are regular residents of Chengdu make up about 5 to 6.675 percent of the total migrant population in the city and 67 percent of the minority migrant population in the city (Losel and Huang 2012: 8). These Tibetans, along with the Yi migrants from the Liangshan area of Sichuan, have become the most visible and routine presence of minority members in Chengdu.

It remains to be seen whether state promotion, through subsidies or the market, can genuinely integrate the TAR's economy with the rest of the country. That is, to build economic ties based on mutual interests and longtime viability, rather than one-sided dependency.

ECONOMIC LIBERALIZATION AND ETHNIC CONFLICT: XINJIANG'S CASE

Xinjiang, which went through economic liberalization like the rest of the country, illustrates the dynamics of centralization and ethnicization in a different way. Centralization has been twofold in Xinjiang's case. The first component is economic liberalization, construed as centralization because Xinjiang did not have the option to resist this national policy or to determine the fate of local workers affected by it. The second component is the state's preservation of two pillars of Xinjiang's planned economy: the "commanding

4 For details of the reform, see "Nongye butie huo xiang zhongliangzhe qingxie, zhengce tiaozheng haiyou houshou" [Agrarian subsidies to lean towards cultivators, policy adjustments will follow]. *Jingji guancha bao*, September 13, 2015.

heights" (energy, transportation, and telecommunications sectors) and PCCs. These two components have had a significant impact on Han-Uighur employment patterns in the reform era, and consequentially on ethnic tensions.

Ethnicization, on the other hand, refers to the mix of market victimization and preferential policies. Both energize identity politics. Xinjiang has experienced perhaps the worst consequences of economic liberalization because it is one of the two autonomous regions where cultural and linguistic endowments create formidable barriers to market competition, yet it does not enjoy the kind of state protection and geographical insulation that shields the TAR.

Market Expansion and Uighur Victimization

Economic liberalization, above all, transformed the socialist employment system and left Uighurs disproportionally affected. Before the reform era, the employment system consisted of three tiers: (1) the government and public service sectors, including local party and state agencies, cultural and educational institutions, and healthcare facilities; (2) SOEs, including large ones owned by the central state and small/medium sized ones owned by the local state; and (3) the rural sector, or agrarian and pastoral communes. Everybody was guaranteed a place in the planned economy, if at meager income levels, which mitigated interethnic competition. Economic liberalization, however, ended the second and third tiers of the local employment system, that is communes and local state enterprises. These changes have had the most adverse impact on Uighurs.

In the top tier (Tier 1), economic liberalization has least affected ethnic balance in employment. During the Mao era, professional jobs existed only in state sectors, assigned through government plans. Minority members, after college education, were assigned jobs in local state agencies, state firms, ethnic public schools, and ethnically related fields such as academies of social sciences, cultural institutions, creative unions of writers and artists, translation and publishing houses, and the like. Much like the Central Asian republics during the Soviet era, the emergence of new middle classes was "state engineered and state supported and can only be partially attributed to the process of modernization" (Zaslavsky 1993: 76). In the 1970s, the government of Xinjiang mandated that at least 30–50 percent of the annual hires in public sectors be minority members (Li 2009b: 177), an impressive ratio given that most minorities had only enrolled in schools for the first time in the preceding two decades. In the early post-Mao era, preferential policies were strengthened, with a 60 percent quota mandated for minority members in state hiring, army recruitment, and college admissions (Wu and Song 2014: 23), slightly above their demographical presence in the local population. Although this mandate has loosened for state firms, the quota system – based on local demographic ratios – has continued for hiring in state agencies and other public service sectors. Studies confirm that controlling all other factors, Uighurs enjoy similar access as local Han residents to these state jobs (Zang 2010) or even better access due to preferential policies (Wu and Song 2014).

In Tier 2, or SOEs, economic liberalization disproportionally impacted those employed in local state enterprises. Large state enterprises owned by the central state, being strategic and more capital intensive, have continued under state ownership. Han settlers from the Mao era, concentrated in the energy sector and PCCs, thus escaped massive layoffs. However, smaller factories owned by the local state, being more labor intensive and nonstrategic, had a different fate. Minority workers were concentrated in such firms. During the socialist era, preferential policies were in place in local SOEs for hiring minority members. For example, they comprised 53 percent of all factory hiring in 1976, 48 percent in 1977, and 27.2 percent in 1978 (Li 2015: 30). However, since partial reforms began in 1979, SOEs openly recruited employees in the job market. Although preferential policy was still maintained, minority hiring decreased. In that first year of reform in 1979, 25 percent of new factory hires were minority members across Xinjiang, with a 34.7 percent in the Uighur-concentrated south (Li 2015: 30).

By the late 1990s, pressure to meet the conditions for China's World Trade Organization (WTO) entry led to the demise of local SOEs. During Zhu Rongji's second term as China's premier, from 1997 to 2002, all local SOEs nationwide – except for the TAR – were ordered to restructure ownership and management. Often, ownership was assumed by former factory managers, their relatives, or private buyers. Workers were laid off after receiving some nominal shares or compensation. In Xinjiang's case, minority workers were affected disproportionately due to their less skilled positions. In the first year of SOE restructuring in 1997, they comprised 25.6 percent of downsized workers in 1998, 5 percent more than the ratio of minority workers employed in local SOEs. Many of the downsized were well before their retirement age and not well educated. Almost half were under thirty-five years old and slightly over half were between thirty-five and forty-six years old, while nearly half were female and just under a third had high-school diplomas or associate degrees and above (Li 2015: 30–1). Few of them, especially the female minority workers, were able to re-enter the industrial workforce.

What became of the defunct local SOEs, moreover, had further ethnicizing effects. Based on field observations and conversations, downsized Han workers – especially female workers – did not fare better than their Uighur counterpart in reentering the workforce. However, downsized Uighurs had more reasons to be resentful because of what and who replaced them. Old factories were often sold off to businesspeople from interior provinces, but new owners were oblivious to local sensitivities and eager to reap profits. They quickly snatched factory sales, turning them into shopping centers and filling them up with vendors from interior provinces. Even if they continued to operate the factories, they replaced old employees with migrant workers from interior provinces and left the displaced local workers unattended. As a Uighur writer complains on Uighurbiz.com, the new market-driven firms, with their preference for Mandarin speakers in hiring, became a key source of Uighur fury (Azad 2010). This is especially so among Uighur youths (Zang 2012). New factory owners prefer migrant workers over minority workers as well as local Han Chinese workers, who are seen as more laidback than migrant workers from inland provinces.

As new types of firms emerge dominant, all are inclined to hire Mandarin and bilingual speakers, thus limiting opportunities for Uighur speakers. First, the commanding heights, or large state firms and strategic industries, are headquartered in interior cities and are nationally oriented. Their local branches follow the operating language and protocols of their parent companies based in interior China. Next are the new firms based on partnerships between local firms and outside investors, the latter often from coastal provinces. Out of operational expediency they use Mandarin, the language of their technical managers, manuals, and equipment. Third, the informal sector is dominated by small businesses owned by inland migrants and local residents, especially downsized workers of both Han and minority backgrounds. Migrant business owners, citing different work habits, religious practices, and language barriers, have few qualms about not hiring local ethnic workers. As small business, they usually find hiring local staff "not worth the additional hassles."[5]

In the new mixed economy, large SOEs have more autonomy in their hiring practices, contributing to another disadvantage for local minorities. Although SOEs are still required to maintain preferential policies, the state no longer has the kind of administrative power for enforcement (Zang 2010). State firms have leeway to give more heed to market considerations than politicized factors such as ethnic status or party membership. This has put at a disadvantage ethnic members whose native language is not Mandarin or whose academic preparation and technical skills are not strong. Even if initially hired, ethnicity alone no longer offers job protection. While large SOEs still maintain preferential minority hiring, all businesses are at liberty to hire from around the country. The decline of the household registration system, paradoxically, has decreased hiring discrimination on the basis of residential status (Wu and Treiman 2004), but increased hiring discrimination based on market dynamics (Wu and Song 2014). After the Urumqi riot of 2009, the state has made elaborate efforts to place more minority college students in large state firms. This is visible on the counters of state banks, telecommunication stores, and other state companies in urban centers of southern Xinjiang. But such hirings do little to change the scenes of idle young males gathered on urban streets or in electronic game rooms, who usually come from the countryside.

[5] Observations and conversations at several bazaars in two cities of southern Xinjiang, fall 2013. Conversations with two migrant business owners in southern Xinjiang, summer 2015.

In rural areas, economic liberalization may have brought more turmoil than opportunities, especially for the surplus labor and the youth. The demise of communes ended a basic safety net for everyone. Land apportioned to rural households has increased incentives to improve production, but high birthrates also put pressure on arable land and irrigation water. Oases make up just 4.2 percent of Xinjiang's expansive terrain, while arid land and scarce precipitation characterize much of its topography. Leasing farmland to migrant farmers brings in incomes, but also loss of potentially greater incomes. Farmers' markets provide opportunities to sell produce and increase income, but also competition from migrant farmers. Many Uighur farmers have fruit and nut trees on their land, but a lack of access to distant markets hinders earning good incomes from them. Some adventurous youths bring local produce to interior provinces to peddle, but logistic costs prevent them from becoming competitive sellers nationwide. The PCCs, by contrast, are equipped to do this nationally and even globally. Cultural and language barriers also limit the options of rural Uighur youths to be migrant workers across China, unlike rural youths elsewhere in the country.[6]

For the less educated and the downsized, in short, the two job avenues where state protection exists is closed off for them. That is, the government/public service sectors and large SOEs. What is left for them are two avenues with the least state protection and most market competition: private enterprises and self-employment. These two sectors not only had low entry barriers but also the only opportunities available to them. Of ten laid-off workers I conversed with in southern Xinjiang, all were reemployed through those two avenues.[7] Two of them, a Han couple, opened a small diner. One female of mixed parentage rented a booth in a bazaar making inexpensive clothes. One female Uighur sold traditional scarves and hats in such a booth. The remaining six workers, all female, including one of mixed parentage, two Hans, and four Uighurs, "watched stores for other people" on a regular or irregular basis. They made a few hundred yuan a month ($60–80), not much worse than before, but now they had to pay into their social security and medical insurance, which used to be free from their factories. Laid-off workers who were not married to a state employee were eligible to stay in the factory housing and collect *dibao*, a minimum living allowance of ¥100 (about $12.50) per person in the late 1990s. This system was mandated by the central state in 1997 to cover laid-off workers from SOEs. Laid-off workers with several children, usually minority members (since Han workers could only have one child), could collect a few

[6] Trips to Hotan, Luopu, Moyu, and Yutian counties, with a former village official, an agrarian contractor, and two downsized workers, including home visits with two rural Uighur families and two Han farmers' families, fall 2013.

[7] Fall 2013, Hotan prefecture. The laid-off workers were from two local silk factories and a concrete factory.

hundred yuan a month, plus a minimal medical plan. This allowed them to get by without taking a job.

Laid-off workers faced competition from migrants from inland provinces if they wanted to reenter the workforce. Some who were self-employed made more money at the beginning, but soon lost to migrant businesses. Self-employers who vended clothing and articles of daily use, for example, could not compete with venders from Wenzhou who had better merchandise from Zhejiang province. In fact, individuals from Wenzhou and Sichuan quickly became dominant as owners of private businesses in urban centers of southern Xinjiang, from hotels to gambling parlors and retail stores.[8] Despite a lack of local ties initially, they have outcompeted local residents, both Han and Uighur. Local residents – both Uighur and Han, refer to recent migrants as "*kouli ren*" (people from inside the pass), a somewhat derogative term historically used by Uighurs and Kazakhs for people from inside the Jade Gate Pass, or the pass that residents of interior China had to go through before entering Xinjiang. As Wu and Song's study (2014) documents, where state intervention is weak, that is private sectors, income differentials between Han and Uighur groups are significant, with Han migrants holding advantages over local Han residents.

Downsized workers came to view things in ethnic terms over time. They initially blamed economic reform for their job loss. The better informed among them blamed Zhu Rongji, who as China's premier pushed for China's entry to the WTO and for the restructuring the SOEs. But as Han and Hui businesses grow increasingly dominant, Han–Uighur cleavages assume more prominence in local public perceptions, regardless of the provincial origins of the new businesses.

Market Expansion and Cultural Clash

Economic liberalization has also caused cultural clashes, thus ethnicizing winners and losers in the new market economy. Much as the state's industrial focus in the TAR, economic liberalization ignored critical local conditions in Xinjiang. That is, local communities whose ascriptive endowments, or gaps in resources and skills, place them at disadvantages in market competition. Although preferential policies exist in college admissions and state hiring, these are not able to address ethnic disadvantages in private and informal sectors. On the contrary, they give the perception that public policies already favor local minorities, thus shifting blame to group traits and heightening identity politics.

Market competition, above all, pits the religious worldview of Uighur commoners against the secular materialism of the state and Han communities. Zhang Haiyang, a liberal autonomist, describes state developmentalism as

[8] Conversations with an official of a local state regulatory agency, Hotan prefecture, fall 2013 and July 2015.

"extremist secularism," a "misfortune from the sky" fallen on minorities in their home turf, forcing involuntary natives into the state's modernization drive (Zhang 2014b). Even Uighur scholars who support this drive view it as "modernization by outside engines," a necessary but compelled process.[9] Pro-modernization Uighurs are known locally as the "14th minority group," meaning they are distinct enough to be a minority group by itself. Officially there are thirteen minority groups in Xinjiang. The "14th minority," a derisive term, suggests that this group is a small and distinct one, with whom the larger Uighur community may not identify. Needless to say, most Han Chinese easily forget that it has taken them over a hundred years to fully accept modernization, with many reform movements and revolutions in between. Peripheral regions such as the TAR and Xinjiang, by contrast, have been swept along rather than being given time to adapt to modernization. If egalitarianism made secular modernism tolerable during the Mao era, market competition made religiosity a defensive mechanism against it in the reform era.

Given this overall divide, other aspects of cultural clash are unsurprising. A key source of Uighur culture, as Qarluq and McMillen suggest, lies in religious traditions: because religious manners and customs have seeped into Uighur culture for over a thousand years, it is difficult to separate "religious sentiment" from "secular pragmatics" (2011: 19, 11). Thus religious customs are dearly held as integral to Uighur culture and not compromisable. However, Han managers and co-workers tend to view those customs through a secular lens, that is in terms of their impact on employee turnout and schedules. Even educated Han employees in professional sectors would subtly grumble about local customs and attitudes: for example, frequent religious observations and kinship celebrations, which put extra burdens on nonobserving colleagues; a mistrust of new technologies, which holds back Uighur farmers; and reluctance to let go traditional practices, which hinders material progress. Such cultural differences mattered little during the socialist era, when the quality of performance made little difference in pay or job retention. But interethnic dynamics have changed in the competitive market. As much as they would like to cling to religion, Uighurs (and Tibetans for that matter) can find themselves bothered by the material success of migrant workers on their home turf.

Fueling another cultural clash, market competition juxtaposes the "take hardship" (*chi ku*) culture of inland migrants against the "laid back" culture of local communities. Qarluq and McMillen describe the latter as "a 'take things as they come' attitude," which tends to leave the Uighur people "satisfied with their status quo and hold back their sense of 'go-aheadism'" (2011: 19, 11). The second generation of Hans, born to settlers from the Mao era, has acculturated into the easygoing attitude to some extent. This element of local culture irks owners of private firms from interior provinces. Despite tax

[9] Remarks by a Uighur scholar during a conference talk at Xinjiang University, July 2011.

incentives to hire rural Uighurs, particularly in rural areas, they cite "high turnover rates," "low skills," and "high costs of training" as the top reasons why they are reluctant to hire local minorities. "Cultural traits" they frown on include a lack of "discipline," "punctuality," "contractual compliance," "sense of efficiency," "longtime planning," "easy contentment with the status quo," "disinclination to improve," and a preference for "spiritual life over material life" (Li 2015: 36). Uighur officials attribute these tendencies to "our people's preference for unconstrained life and flexible ways of making a living" (Li 2015: 36). The Xinjiang-born Han scholar, Yao Xinyong, views those traits as ecologically nurtured and sensible, better suited for Xinjiang's sustainable development than its overdevelopment in recent decades (2013a). Interestingly, private businesses find it reliable to hire middle-aged, married, or divorced Uighur females, who make a stable workforce. This shows that the so-called cultural traits are not intrinsic or immutable.

In rural Xinjiang, market competition has pitted migrant farmers against local Uighur farmers, for cultural as well as policy reasons. Migrant farmers, mostly from poor rural areas of Sichuan and Henan, enjoy cultural advantages as successors to a prolonged agrarian civilization. Forced to strive on their own, they have usually fared well through agrarian skills and social networks rather than state assistance. Many make it by leasing land from Uighur farmers and growing produce for local markets. They do not receive the range of state assistance enjoyed by their ethnic counterparts, such as free seeds, free fertilizers, tax exemptions, and free installation of greenhouses. The only production cost for Uighur farmers is the water for irrigation, a precious resource in arid Xinjiang. Among other things, mistrust of modern methods holds back local farmers. In a Hotan village, one agrarian official told me stories of how he taught Uighur villagers to shield crops from the desert sun with plastic coverings, but dubious villagers would take them off as soon as he left. Migrant farmers, meanwhile, need to pay all their production costs, in addition to ¥800 per mu (0.16 acres) in leasing fees to Uighur landowners annually (about $125 as of the mid-2010s). Their skills and willingness to use modern technology have made them more resourceful than local farmers, who are left with a sense of relative deprivation. Based on my field observations in Aksu and Hotan in the early and mid-2010s, migrant farmers pose visible competition to ethnic farmers at local farmers' markets, in terms of the quantity, quality, and variety of their farm produce.

A contrast with Tibetan regions shows a key difference made by local ecological culture. The high plateaus of Tibet deter immigration of Han farmers, who are unaccustomed to pastoralism at high altitudes. For the few who have delved into rural areas, their survival stories resemble those of migrant farmers in Xinjiang, that is leasing land from local owners to grow commercial crops. However, a lack of religious stricture makes it easier for Han migrants to integrate or marry into Tibetan communities, in contrast to Muslim communities. Based on my field observations, the few Han farmers in Tibetan villages – at most two or three in a village close to interior provinces – have usually married into Tibetan households. Resentment at migrant farmers is rarely seen or felt in rural Tibetan areas.

The problem of the so-called local culture does raise some legitimate issues. It puts into question the demands of the central state for economic convergence, as well as the Han people's expectations that ethnic communities make such progress.

Market Expansion and the Migrant Threat

Migration is another issue where market expansion helps to ethnicize native versus migrant cleavages. Although the scale of Han migration to Xinjiang is often the target of criticism (Becquelin 2000 and 2004; Bovingdon 2004; Seymour 2000), the nature of the migrant threat makes the migration issue more combustible in Xinjiang than in Tibet.

Above all, inland migrants pose wide-ranging competition to native Uighurs in the reform era, in contrast to limited competition in the Tibetan case. In the Tibetan case, Han migrants are concentrated in urban businesses and coal mining, thus presenting little competition to the core of the Tibetan economy in pastoral regions (Huang 2014). Han migrants are also physically unfit for long-term settlement on the high plateau and usually stay on a temporary basis. By contrast, Xinjiang's terrain poses no such prohibition. Even in rural areas, Han migrants buy or rent farmland and grow commercial crops, resulting in reduced farmland for local Uighurs. Water is a major cause of friction between the two groups (Li 2011a: 4), as it is a scarce resource in arid Xinjiang. In urban areas, cultural advantages lead to a competitive edge for Han and Hui migrants, including hometown networks, an early learning curve in the market economy, and Mandarin proficiency. The successes of Wenzhou businesspeople and Sichuan farmers are frequently heard, to the resentment of native Uighurs as well as longtime Han residents. Finally, unlike the Tibetan case, two Han-dominated sectors – PCCs and state petroleum companies – have a formidable presence in Xinjiang's economy. The result is a shrinking of survival space for Uighurs since the 1990s, resulting in intense frustration.

Second, demographic balance is a more volatile issue in Xinjiang than in the TAR, as Uighurs' numerical advantage is more precarious. As of 2014, Uighurs made up 48.53 percent of Xinjiang' population, while Han (37.01 percent) and eleven other minorities made up a small majority overall (*Sohu* 2016). By contrast, Tibetans have held a solid majority at over 90 percent in the Mao and the post-Mao eras. Ethnic spokesmen such as the Dalai Lama and Ilham Tohti famously worry about long-term demographic shifts in favor of the Han, citing trends from the 1950s and blaming these in part for the ethnic riots in recent years. Han residents, by contrast, tend to see the size of the rural Uighur household as the underlying cause of poverty and unemployment. Typical are the arguments made in an online article that appeared days after the Urumqi riot of 2009, about the "population economics" behind the riot (Yi 2009). It argues that preferential policies in family planning have led to higher births among minority families, while those for school admissions have led to lower incentives for minority youths to acquire hard skills for the market, resulting in higher youth unemployment among Uighurs. Unemployed youths, in turn, are easily mobilized for antisocial riots. With the dwindling of older Han immigrants and the temporary stay of new migrants, the article worries about Xinjiang's longtime stability. In rebuttal, critics point out the concentration of Uighurs in rural Xinjiang, hence their lower rates of employment; but supporters of the article blame high birth rates in part for the poverty of the rural south.[10]

Official data confirm the gap in urbanization rates for Han and local minorities. In Xinjiang, the Uighur population remains the majority in the south, where they have been traditionally and rurally concentrated. They account for 81.73 percent of the local population, with the Han population at 18.27 percent. In rural counties, the Uighur population is often over 95 percent. In more developed northern Xinjiang, the Han people constitute 62.66 percent of the population, with minorities at 37.34 percent (Bingtuan 2013). A more fundamental question remains: what role does state policy play in migration patterns? Why has random and temporary migration of the reform era led to serious ethnic tensions, far more than the large-scale migration of the Mao era based in the production corps?

Interethnic competition patterns provide the key answer to this question. Xinjiang received the most varied types of immigrants during the Mao era, from involuntary settlers who came as members of PCCs, to professionals assigned by the state, to economic refugees who came voluntarily. By contrast, other minority regions usually received involuntary settlers, and Tibetan regions received just one type: professionals assigned by the state. In Xinjiang's case, the various groups of settlers show a complex picture of pull and push factors for Han immigration before the post-Mao era.

Most importantly, immigration in the Mao era did not pose competition to local communities in a way that migrants have in the reform era. First, members of PCCs were concentrated in northern Xinjiang, shielded from direct encounters with the hub of Uighur settlements in southern Xinjiang. PCCs did present some resource competition to surrounding local communities, as their massive water use drained local wells and the shipment of their grain and cotton products to interior regions gave the impression of resource flight. The functions of PCCs, officially glorified as frontier defense, evoked a mistrust of local ethnic populations. In addition, official exaltation of PCCs' successes created perceptions of prosperous fortifications in the midst of ethnic homeland. This image of prosperity was

[10] Comments left at "Xinjiang shijian de renkou yinsu" [The demographic economics in the Xinjiang incident]. *Tianya shequ*, November 11, 2012. http://bbs.tianya.cn/post-173-544059-1.shtml.

not true, as Tohti concedes, but it was nevertheless ethnically divisive (2014). However, the state did not emphasize PCCs' role in opposing the "three forces" during the Mao era. An overemphasis on this role in recent years has increased Uighur antipathy toward PCCs.

The second group of immigrants to Xinjiang during the Mao era consisted of professionals assigned to help develop modern sectors. Working alongside native professionals, the small size of this group did not overwhelm the natives linguistically or culturally. The planned economy, with its suppression of competitive mechanisms, helped to obscure differences in credentials and skills, while the official discourse of class universalism helped to de-ethnicize collegial and communal relationships. Their children grew up together in the same housing compounds provided by their workplaces, speaking one another's languages. Across Xinjiang and other minority regions, older natives and settlers remain nostalgic about their warm relations in the socialist era. This is particularly the case in Xinjiang (Li 2011b: 1; Qarluq and McMillen 2011: 23; Xu 2005: 1; Chen 2012), where interethnic relationships have turned distinctly tense. Uighur intellectuals complain about today's ethnic relations marked by discriminatory attitudes and behaviors (Qarluq and McMillen 2011: 23), a sentiment readily observed and heard locally. They lament that the post-Mao generations of locally born Hans, as well as newcomers, do not bother to learn ethnic tongues or respect local cultures, a problem worsened by the commercial housing market in the reform era.

A third group of immigrants during the Mao era came to Xinjiang voluntarily as economic refugees, as it offered loosely controlled household registration and less political turmoil. Several hundred thousand came to escape famine after the Great Leap Forward in the late 1950s (Liu D. 2010: 118), and an untold number of others came for economic and personal opportunities during the Cultural Revolution period. They built a new life by marrying demobilized soldiers and other settlers, using *guanxi* (connections) to secure legal residence in PCCs or in rural areas, or simply doing odd jobs or cultivating wasteland. Ethnic natives were structurally protected in the planned economy during the Mao era, either in rural communes or urban state sectors. The refugee migrants, by contrast, lived on the margins of the new society rather than marginalizing members of local communities.

A fourth group of settlers had already been an entrenched part of local society. They were officials, merchants, farmers, and exiles left from the Qing and Republican eras. When Mao's soldiers and officers arrived and stayed on during the late 1940s and early 1950s, they found marriage partners among their descendants and their ethnic employees.

Did the Mao-era immigration pave the way for voluntary immigration in the post-Mao era? This is a question about whether post-Mao migration is merely a function of market forces or a part of the long-term dynamics of national integration sponsored by the state. In James Seymour's argument, PCCs paralleled British colonial stations, providing a degree of physical and psychological safety for settlers in an otherwise uncongenial environment, and "something to come to" in terms of basic amenities (2000: 188). While this may have been the case in the Mao era, it is no longer so in the post-Mao era. With so many settlers and their offspring already entrenched in local life, new migrants' entry and safety are provided through individual rather than organizational channels. Based on my field observations and conversations, rural migrants from inland provinces have come to join their relatives or home-towners already settled or working in Xinjiang. While the original "seed" settler may have come through formal channels during the Mao era, such as PCCs or state assignments, new migrants come to stay temporarily with a relative or fellow villager until they find a job.

Most importantly, it is the relaxation of household registration in the post-Mao era that has enabled voluntary migration to Xinjiang. During the late 1970s and early 1980s, the possibility of securing household registration in Xinjiang's countryside was a significant factor for voluntary immigration. After central planning ended in the early 1990s, household registration was no longer a hurdle for business people and migrant workers wanting to move, at least for temporary stays and jobs.

Two-Way Migration

Although the state no longer sponsors migration to ethnic regions, state policy can induce "pull" or "push" factors for migration. Ironically, heavy developmental programs for key minority regions stimulate economic opportunities that attract voluntary migrants, while a dearth of such opportunities for other minority regions pushes out-migration. In other words, the state's policy preferences to develop sensitive minority regions can end up creating the migration problem that undermines the state's own goal of stability and integration. At the same time, cultural disadvantages create formidable barriers for Uighur migrants in particular, constraining their out-migration and reinforcing perceptions and realities of one-way migration.

Economic opportunities, created by large outlays of state investment, contribute to important "pull" factors for in-migration. That is, opportunities for migrants to work on developmental projects or to serve project needs. Based on available data for 1995–2000, the autonomous regions with the highest in-migration rates were Xinjiang, Ningxia, Yunnan, and the TAR (Table 7.7). Except for Yunnan, the other three provinces happened to receive the most state investment in per capita terms during that period (Zhang et al. 2006: 96). Critics of Beijing may suspect that such investment was designed to draw Han immigrants. However, analyses of demographic trends in the TAR, from 1991 to 2005, suggest that central developmental policies corresponded with

TABLE 7.7 *Provinces with the highest migration rates: 1995–2000*

Province	Regions within province	Migration rates (%)	Province	Regions within province	Migration rates (%)
Sichuan	Chengdu	5.84	Shaanxi	Xi'an	5.42
	Other localities	-6.36		Other localities	-2.21
Chongqing	Central city	1.88	Ningxia	Yinchuan	8.35
	Other localities	-6.80		Shizuishan	2.30
				Other localities	-1.86
Guangxi	Nanning	8.85	Yunnan	Kunming	9.85
	Liuzhou	6.28		Other localities	-0.45
	Other localities	-5.05			
Guizhou	Guiyang	-6.83	Tibet	Lhasa	7.37
	Other localities	-3.78		Other localities	0.20
Gansu	Lanzhou	6.21	Xinjiang	Urumqi	18.01
	Other localities	-2.98		Karamay	5.01
				Shihezi	17.73
				Other localities	3.50
Qinghai	Xining	0.39	Western regions	18 cities	6.20
	Golmud	6.69		Other localities	-3.52
	Other localities	-3.05			
Inner Mongolia	Hohhot	6.88	Net total for all provinces		-1.90
	Baotou	4.54			
	Other localities	-2.26			

Source: State Council of the PRC (Census Office) (2000).

significant increases as well as decreases in the size of Han residents (Ma 2008b: 169). That is, investment projects only induced temporary immigration. My conversations with migrant workers in southern Xinjiang confirmed this. Many said that they planned to work from project to project where jobs were available or where hometown networks led them.[11] Yunnan is an exception because it attracts in-migration for a different reason. With its pleasant ecology and booming tourism, the province attracts Han and Hui immigrants to operate lodging and catering businesses there. There is resentment over some land purchases and land developments by outsiders, but a minimum of physical,

[11] Conversations with at least ten migrant workers in local markets and construction sites in Hotan, Aksu, and Kashgar, summer 2011 and fall 2013; and with five migrant workers from Hotan, summer 2015. They were mostly from Sichuan and Henan.

linguistic, and cultural distinctions has mitigated escalation into ethnic conflict.

The in-migrants to Xinjiang and the TAR come mostly from rural areas of interior provinces where economic opportunities lag behind. Sichuan, Gansu, and Henan top the list (Ma et al., 2005; Ma and Tenzin 2008; local observations 2013–17). Many toil as temporary laborers on construction projects or in retail and catering services, at considerable cost to their family and personal well-being. China's healthcare reform provides all citizens with medical insurance at low premiums, but coverage is available through hospitals in the province of their permanent household registration. This means migrant workers have to go back to their native hometowns if they suffer serious illness. For them, sacrificing healthcare and time with their family, especially children, is among the many trade-offs they face in their itinerant struggles to make a better living. Many migrants I encountered in southern Xinjiang, usually on construction sites and at farmers' market, said they were there because "it's easier to make money" or "the plains here are easier to grow crops than the hills back home."

At the other end, a key push factor for out-migration of minority members is a lack of economic opportunities at home. This can be seen from the migration patterns of ethnic and multiethnic provinces. As it happens, all of the officially designated twelve "western regions" are ethnic or multiethnic. They include the five autonomous provinces, three multiethnic provinces (Yunnan, Guizhou, and Qinghai), and three provinces with ethnic prefectures or counties (Gansu, Sichuan, and Chongqing). Four of the twelve regions have had net in-migration (ratio of migration to total local population) during the reform era: Xinjiang, Ningxia, Yunnan, and Tibet. The other eight have net out-migration, of which the top four provinces – Sichuan, Chongqing, Guangxi, and Guizhou – are also ranked the highest in out-migration in the entire country (Table 7.7).

Those provinces with the highest rates of out-migration, significantly, correlate with low levels of state investment. They are also multiethnic provinces without threats of ethnic unrest or separatism. Of the top five provinces with the highest out-migration rates, Guizhou, Guangxi, Gansu, Sichuan, and Chongqing also had the lowest level of state investment in per capita terms at the time of the 2000 census. The first three provinces have large ethnic populations, while Sichuan is the home to the largest group of Tibetans outside the TAR, the largest Yi minority group in the country, and the only Qiang-concentrated community in the country. Chongqing has four autonomous counties for the Tujia and Miao. Despite having sizable poor ethnic communities within them, those five provinces did not and do not receive the kind of state investment accorded to politically sensitive Xinjiang and Tibet. In fact, the Tujia, Dong, and Zhuang groups have higher out-migration rates than the Han Chinese in the reform era. Due to such out-migration, the ratio of minority members has been declining in western regions but correspondingly increasing in eastern and central China (Zhang et al. 2006; Wang 2008). Needless to say, minority members who out-migrate usually come from groups that face few language and cultural barriers in interior provinces.

They have flowed, not surprisingly, to the most developed provinces and metropolises. From 2000 and 2010, Zhejiang province experienced the most growth in minority migrants (207.22 percent), followed by Shanghai (167.87 percent) and Guangdong (62.89 percent); provinces and cities with increases of 20–50 percent include Jiangsu, Beijing, Fujian, Tianjin, and Jiangxi; while a number of localities with low state investment and/or poor economies saw negative growths in minority population: Anhui, Liaoning, Chongqing, Henan, Hubei, Guizhou, Shanxi, Jilin, and Heilongjiang (Zheng 2013: 3). Like other migrant workers in China, minority migrants have helped to improve economic conditions back home by sending their earnings home.

Barriers for Uighur Migrants

Uighur migrants, however, have not benefited as much from the two-way migration in the reform era. They have faced unique difficulties in the marketplace, both ascriptive and structural. Besides Tibetans, they are the only group who can be hampered by language barriers in interior China. But Tibetans mostly migrate to Chengdu, where they have sizable co-ethnic communities to mingle with and rely on locally. Many Tibetans, moreover, are fluent in the Sichuan dialect. Uighur migrants, on the other hand, do not have those cultural assets. Their migrant experience shows once again that the market economy victimizes minority groups who are not endowed with competitive ascriptive or technical assets. If Uighur migrants are at the bottom of the job market in Xinjiang, their plight is been worse outside it. Migration experience, which in theory should strengthen their identification with the rest of the country, can ethnicize them by reinforcing their alienation.

State policy initially facilitated economic opportunities that attracted Uighur out-migration. In the early 1980s, Beijing's municipal government welcomed Uighur kabob stands to the capital city. In 1982 a deputy mayor of Beijing went to Urumqi to invite eighteen Uighur families who specialized in mutton kabobs to open businesses Beijing. News of their successes in Beijing inspired hundreds of other Uighurs to follow suit. In 1986, Beijing's city government ordained that each district of the city should have thirty kabob stands, or thirty kabob family business (Abdugheni 2011: 28). Kabob success expanded into larger businesses, from Uighur cuisine and local produce to Uighur artwork and entertainment. In the 1980s and 1990s, the relative ease with which business permits could be obtained facilitated such expansion. A few "Xinjiang villages" (*Xinjiang cun*) became attractions for inexpensive ethnic foods in the nation's capital.[12] Uighur population grew from several hundred in the early 1980s to several thousand around 2010 (Abdugheni 2011: 22). Uighur migrants spread to other major cities in interior provinces from the mid-1980s and to smaller cities in the 1990s, as more of them chased the paths of earlier migrants. The exact scale of Uighur out-migration is difficult to know, since many do not register their temporary residence with local governments. As with Han migrants to Xinjiang, most Uighur migrants come from poor rural areas, especially southern Xinjiang, driven by surplus labor and a lack of economic opportunities at home.[13]

With the growth of Uighur migrants across interior provinces in the 1990s, the problem of language and cultural barriers became more apparent and serious. Due to a lack of language, skills, and other resources, most Uighur migrants have had difficulty landing jobs beyond limited Uighur circles. In their struggle to make a living, it is not uncommon for a few to break law, as Uighur scholars would concede (Tulak 2013: 12–14). The spread of a negative reputation and worsening relations with local Han residents compound the "strangers" status they already face. Language and legal barriers added more injury. Local police in interior provinces could not communicate with apprehended Uighur offenders, and because of the "dual legal standards" ordinance, did not know what to do with them. So they usually released them, thus encouraging more offenses and local resentment at Uighur migrants as a group. In recent years, interior cities with a sizable number of Uighur migrants are assigned Uighur police officers from Xinjiang. This helps to overcome language and cultural barriers in communication, reduce offenses and enhance effectiveness in law enforcement.[14]

A negative reputation of Uighur migrants, since the 1990s, obscures the institutional barriers faced by migrant workers in general and Uighur migrants in particular. For China's migrants in general, the system of household registration is a major hurdle to making a living in another province or even city within one's home province, such that it may be the leading reason for crime committed by migrants (Li W. 2012). The lack of local household registration deprives one of local access to job training programs, welfare and healthcare benefits, and public schools for one's children. This leaves new migrants with little recourse if they cannot find a job right away or have no local ties. Uighur migrants face greater hurdles on both fronts. Aside from language barriers and gaps in skills, some local state

[12] In the early and mid-1980s, I attended graduate school in Beijing close to an emerging "Xinjiang village" in Beijing, Ganjiakou.

[13] Based on casual questions posed to a dozen Uighur migrants or returned migrants in Suzhou, Beijing, and Chongqing. A Uighur scholar's research on Uighur migrants in Beijing confirms this, see Abdugheni (2011: 40, 41).

[14] See an early example of this practice in Shi Po, "Xinjiang jingcha guanzhi Xinjiangji xiaotou" [Xinjiang police officers tackle Xinjiang thieves. *Nanfeng chuang*, March 6, 2008. http://news.sina.com.cn/c/2008-03-06/111915089313.shtml.

agencies may try to avoid "incidents" in their districts by making it difficult for them to stay, such as requiring extra procedures or paperwork for local landlords to accept Uighur tenants or for Uighur migrants to apply for temporary residential status and business permits. The central state has policy guidelines asking hotels in inland provinces not to deny service to minority members from Xinjiang, because only an extremely small group of people are "separatists, religious extremists and terrorists" (SEAC 2002). But there are no enforcement mechanisms or specific legal protections for minority migrants. "Institutional exclusion," as a Uighur scholar puts it (Tulak 2013: 17), makes it hard for Uighur migrants to secure jobs or housing outside Uighur migrant communities.

Uighur migrants also face various forms of social exclusion due to cultural barriers and outright discrimination. Confined to Uighur migrant communities, they are practically left to self-contained ghettos on the margins of a "strangers' society," without a sense of belonging, local friendship, or economic and psychological security (Tulak 2013: 15–20). While other migrants can rely on their hometown networks to find jobs in mainstream society, hometown networks for Uighur migrants remain self-contained within their own migrant communities. The language barrier may be most responsible for this social exclusion, as the highest percentage of surveyed Uighur migrants (72 percent) cite it as the most important obstacle to bridging with local residents (Tulak 2014: 66). It may explain why Hui migrants, who practice Islam but use Mandarin as their native tongue, do not face similar barriers to social inclusion.

The spread of Uighur violence to interior cities, needless to say, has worsened the social exclusion of Uighur migrants. One account from a young Uighur villager, whom I encountered at a fruit stand in Luopu county of Hotan prefecture in November 2013, is illustrative. Just days earlier, he was a migrant in Beijing peddling Xinjiang produce. After a Uighur man ran an SUV into pedestrians on Tiananmen Square on October 28, 2013, he was asked to leave his rented room. No motel would take him in. Police did not allow him to sleep on the street. "Am a citizen of China?" he asked bitterly. He had to return to his home village and sell fruit near the highway. In another encounter in front a mosque in a nearby county during the same field trip, a hostile imam in his thirties told me that he had tried to do business in an interior city but returned to Xinjiang embittered. Their experiences were certainly not isolated cases among Uighur migrants or visitors to interior provinces. Discrimination of Uighurs stands out even among those ethnic groups who suffer from frequent discrimination. Yi and Tibetan migrants suffer from some negative reputation in Chengdu, for petty crime and car theft. But they are treated as rural folks from the outskirts, rather than "strangers" from a troubled province, which is how Uighurs are often made to feel in interior provinces.

However, as with Tibetan migrants to Chengdu, economic forces appear to do a better job of integrating Uighur migrants. The city of Suzhou, site of China's largest jade-carving trade, has attracted several thousand Uighurs to sell raw jade. They bring the precious stone from Hotan, the main source of nephrite jade in China. When they first came in the 1990s, a Uighur trader could make as much as six figures a day in Chinese currency (about $2000). For the more entrepreneurial among them, such earnings have helped to open doors to formalistic inclusion in the city. They purchase homes, which allow their children to go to public schools. A few of them lease trading floors in the jade markets and rent individual stands to Uighur sellers on a daily basis (¥50–100 per day as of 2019, or about $8–15), or buy buildings and turn them into hostels for Uighur migrants to rent on a daily basis (¥50 per day as of 2019). Such hostels provide optimal arrangements for these migrants, since it is difficult for them to rent housing from local residents.

The successful Uighur businessmen in Suzhou also help new arrivals in matters involving the local government. These range from applications for temporary residential status and business permits to dispute settlement and debt collection. They acquire Mandarin proficiency or use translation apps on smartphones. The local carving industry seeks their collaboration while the local government has a welcoming attitude toward their presence. The less well planned among the Uighur traders may have squandered their good earnings and fail to buy homes in the city, and are thus unable to send their children to local public schools. The sight of these children wandering the jade market is a painful reminder of a lack of state policy coordination, for in Xinjiang local schools and teachers would do anything to get all children into the classroom. Yet in Suzhou these Uighur parents are eager to send their children to local public schools but are unable to do so because they do not own local housing. The same policy applies to Han migrants, but they usually reserve savings to send their children to nonpublic schools, which require tuition payments and are less reputable than public schools.

The jade trade has waned since Xi Jinping came to power in 2012, as his anti-corruption campaign has reduced demand for jade products. Because they are extremely expensive, jade products are often purchased for gift giving, or bribe giving before the corruption campaign. Still, even the less successful among the Uighur traders continue to have a stable life in the city, due to their possession of precious stones and the hostels run by fellow Uighurs. Most of all, a lack of negative reputation preempts a vigilant attitude among local residents toward the Uighur migrants. Local residents usually mention "wealthy" and "driving good cars" when asked about Uighur traders in the city. It also helps that a Uighur police officer is stationed in the security office on the trading floor of the major jade market in Suzhou.[15]

Two-way migration, overall, remains particularly asymmetrical in the case of Xinjiang. The resources of Uighur migrants in the marketplace are no match for those of Han migrants in or outside Xinjiang. The disadvantages and

[15] This paragraph is based on observations and conversations on Xiangwang Jade Street in Suzhou, June and August 2017–19.

discrimination they face may foster more alienation than integration, serving as a politicizing symbol of their plight nationwide. In this context, it is unsurprising that it was an incident involving Uighur workers in an interior province, the Shaoguan incident in which two Uighur workers were killed, that triggered the Urumqi riot of 2009.

Partner Assistance as Remedy

After the Urumqi riot of 2009, partner assistance has become the state's principal means to elevate Xinjiang's economy and Uighurs' well-being. As in Tibet, the state relies on top-down developmentalism as the strategy to address the socioeconomic roots of ethnic grievances, with little attention to local initiatives or models of development.

First launched in 1997, the initial program focused on improving the quality of government services and public sectors. Between 1997 and 2010, several hundred professionals from fourteen provinces/cities came on a rotating basis, including administrators, economic managers, technical experts, educators, and medical doctors. In the wake of the 2009 riot, an all-out offensive was launched at its First Work Conference on Partner Assistance to Xinjiang, in March 2010. Nineteen provinces and cities now participated, plus a number of central agencies and large SOEs (Li Y. 2010). The new initiative focused on improving living conditions and creating jobs.

On first look, partner programs and their results are impressive. Before and after 2010, the most resourceful partners, such as Beijing, Zhejiang, Shanghai, Guangdong, and Shenzhen, have been assigned to Uighur-concentrated southern Xinjiang. Kazakh- and Han-concentrated areas in northern Xinjiang, by contrast, are assigned partners from middle-income provinces. Based on Xinjiang's official data, between 2010 and 2016, 7,015 partner projects were implemented, at ¥72.4 billion in partner funding. Another 7,260 projects from outside investors were brought in by partners, with ¥1.138188 trillion already funded. These two types of projects contributed to 23.9 percent of Xinjiang's total fixed assets, which stood at ¥4.957756 trillion in 2017. Seventy-four percent of partner funding went to improving local welfare and livelihood, totaling 4,296 projects; 80 percent of partner funding was spent on rural and pastoral areas; 1.45 million housing units were built or renovated for rural residents and over 88,400 were built for herdsmen's settlements, covering over 600 farmers and herdsmen (*TS* 2017b).

For the same period, or 2010 to 2016, partner assistance was credited for Xinjiang's impressive economic growth. Its total GDP grew from ¥541.881 billion in 2010 to over ¥955 billion in 2016, at an annual growth rate of 9.9 percent, higher than the national average. Its GDP per capita grew from ¥25,034 in 2010 to ¥40,427 in 2006, a 40 percent increase. Its fiscal budget more than doubled from ¥50.058 billion to ¥129.895 billion. The disposable income for urban and rural residents grew respectively from

$13,644 to $28,463 and from $4,643 to $10,183, or more than doubled, a growth rate among the highest in the country (*TS* 2017b). The contribution of partner assistance, in the south and rural areas in particular, is spectacular in appearance: infrastructural constructions, public housing projects, modern schools, hospitals, disease control centers, health clinics, welfare agencies, utility grids, waste management systems, renovated villages, greenhouses, fruit orchards, anti-desertification and drinking water projects, indoor farmers' markets and produce warehouses, forestry and fruit industries, and rural enterprises. Migrants from rural areas of Sichuan and Henan confirmed that they found Xinjiang's infrastructure and public amenities to be much better than those in their home villages, which made their temporary relocation there tolerable.[16]

Nevertheless, a few problems have undermined the effectiveness of partner assistance in the early years of its massive launch in 2010. Foremost was a lack of local job creation. Job creation is of greater urgency in Xinjiang than in Tibet due to the much larger size of surplus rural labor and factory downsizing. However, because project personnel came on a rotation and budget, their priority was to finish the projects efficiently, including hiring experienced contractors and skilled migrant workers from interior provinces.[17] Although the state began to emphasize job creation after 2013, this did not pick up until 2016, after Chen Quanguo's arrival. Another problem is the so-called "hand-over-keys projects," or projects that may not be sustainable or practical in the long term. Modern facilities may be built and keys handed over to local governments, but the skills and resources required for running and maintaining them remain lacking. These facilities can range from hospitals and utilities infrastructure to vegetable cultivation projects in the arid south. Public housing is another example. Because a matching fund is required to buy a public housing unit, even if small by market values, it is still a major hurdle for poor rural and pastoral families (Li 2012a: 25). Utilities and maintenance costs are additional hurdles for these families. The eventual buyers may not be those whom partner assistance intended to assist.

Another problem is the transplantation of developmental models from coastal regions. Partners such as Zhejiang, Guangdong, Shanghai, and Shenzhen have built economic zones or industrial parks, following the coastal model of attracting outside investors. But Xinjiang's inner Asian location is ill suited to the export-oriented manufacturing model of coastal cities. Even if a few businesses opened here, they required skilled workers unavailable locally.[18]

16 Conversations with a group of seven migrants at a barbecue eatery in Cele (Chira) county, Hotan, fall 2013.

17 Observations in Hotan and Yutian counties, fall 2013. Conversation with a commerce bureau official of Hotan, summer 2015.

18 I twice visited an industrial park in Hotan built by Zhejiang province between 2011 and 2015. I also visited a few other partner assistance projects in Hotan's counties, including schools, medical centers, an industrial park, and an irrigation system, fall 2013.

Yet another problem is a lack of coordination among multiple partner organizations and rotating project personnel. Partners from multiple provinces are often assigned to the same prefecture or county within it, but they design and work on their projects independently. Managerial and technical personnel work on a one- to three-year rotation, so that there is not always consistency or continuity among the project staff. The lack of coordination can lead to poor development of land use and the built environment, which includes natural and human resources, public services, and infrastructural networks (Ma 2013b; Liang 2014: 35–6). Together these problems can lead to local apathy toward partner assistance, even complaints such as Tohti's (2013) that partner projects have little to do with the Uighur people.

Top-down developmentalism is at the root of the above problems. Structurally this is reflected in the chain of command in partner assistance programs. The central state is extremely effective in giving marching orders to partner provinces. Between March 2010 and June 2019, the state held seven work conferences on partner assistance to Xinjiang, showing its highest regard for this task. The conference proceedings became official decrees, to be followed by the designated provinces. The first three conferences (2010, 2011, and 2012) focused on improvement of living conditions and anti-poverty, which quickly led to massive funding and construction of public housing and public service projects. The next three conferences (2013, 2015, and 2017), shifted to job creation for local Uighur communities. The 2019 conference places emphasis on dispatching talented personnel and developing enterprises for southern Xinjiang. In a notable new strategy, PCCs would play a greater role as flagship enterprises in this region (*Renmin ribao* 2019), a sign of greater central penetration into the south. The overwhelming role of the state in all of this means that there is little room for local initiatives.

One top-down campaign has been a "million-job" project in the textile and apparel industries since 2014. Policy incentives are offered for investors to come and manufacture for domestic markets and external markets in Eurasia. Partner assistance teams have actively sought investors from their home provinces and cities. By 2016 and 2017, they helped to establish hundreds of plants in industrial parks across the four prefectures in southern Xinjiang, hiring local ethnic workers (*Sohu* 2017 and 2018; CCTV1 2018). Since Chen Quanguo assumed power in Xinjiang in August 2016, the province intensified the drive to create jobs for Uighurs. Free Mandarin training is provided to unemployed and rural Uighurs. For Uighur households below the official poverty line, at least one family member is guaranteed a job in one of the new factories on an industrial park (CCTV1 2018). The top-down approach has yielded fast results.

Important elements of these swift outcomes come from the top-down leadership structure of partner assistance, whereby partner teams play a dominant role. The imperative of immediate remedies, after the riot of 2009, dictated quick execution rather than elaborate deliberation among local agencies, let alone the local public. As recipients of assistance, local state agencies are in a "subordinate" position in the partner relationship (Liang 2014: 35–7). In principle the Commission on Development and Reform (CDR) at each administrative level in Xinjiang's bureaucratic hierarchy is responsible for coordinating with partner teams on projects. However, for effective execution and funding purposes, key members of the partner team are appointed to leading positions in a few key agencies in the recipient local government, for example the party committee, the mayoral office, the CDR, the treasury bureau, and the urban development bureau. The types of appointment vary by location, from the top party post to a deputy executive post, but the outside officials are in a position to play a more important role in decision making and execution of partner projects, since they bring in their managerial and technical teams.

Such arrangements amplify the appearance of state transplantation. Although outside officials have technical competence, they have little familiarity or experience with local ethnic, religious, and social problems, thus giving little heed to these issues when designing and undertaking their projects. Local agencies familiar with these issues, such as the RAB, the Labor and Employment Bureau, the Education Bureau, and the Civilian Affairs Bureau, have no role to play in project planning and execution. The consequences are projects mismatched with realities, resentment of local officials marginalized in the process (Han officials included), and even perceptions of "internal colonialism" (Ma 2013b: 4). At the same time, the appointment of outside officials to the local government can place extra pressure on these individuals, as the burden of developing the local economy falls on their shoulders.

Backlash

Ironically the massive infusion of funds and projects to the TAR and Xinjiang has had an ethnicizing effect on the lesser "important" ethnic groups. A common grievance is that "peaceful minorities do not get rewarded." One popular saying sums up their sentiment: "if Inner Mongolia makes trouble, no money will come; if Xinjiang makes trouble, money will come; and if Tibet makes no trouble, money will still come." If such a sentiment helps to reduce empathy for the recipient group, especially the legitimacy of their grievances, it may even provoke hostility toward the state for playing favoritism.

Within Xinjiang, lesser ethnic groups see a "reverse discrimination" by the state in giving special treatment the titular group. Kazakhs, who are concentrated in pastoral areas in northern Xinjiang, complain about unfair distribution of partner funding and projects (Ma 2013b: 5). Southern Xinjiang, where Uighurs are concentrated, gets richer partner provinces and cities, and receives better funding and projects. Other small groups, such as Mongols and Sibes, also frown on the exceptional policy benefits enjoyed by the titular group. Longtime Han residents complain too, for they are numerically a small minority in southern Xinjiang and live in the same environment as their ethnic neighbors, but do not receive the special loans, tax relief, and subsidies granted to minority businesses and members.

Another perception is a "culture of dependency" fostered by the state. The lesser groups are aware of various aid programs and their impact on the ground. For example, every state agency and public firm in Xinjiang is assigned to donate supplies to a designated number of poor households in southern Xinjiang on a periodic basis. Some households may use up a delivery before the next one and call in for a new donation, while others may sell the donated items and call for new deliveries.[19] In my interactions on Xinjiang's college campuses, Uighur students from rural areas told similar stories. In one student's account, her uncle received poverty aid in the form of four goats, intended for him to raise and breed. He sold three of them for cash and killed the fourth for a feast.[20] For stability's sake, however, local state and aid agencies do not mind distributing more goats. The assignment of work-in-residence teams in recent years has entailed further donations from state agencies and firms. In rural villages in the south, a variety of assistance programs creates the impression that all is taken care of for rural Uighur communities. A local joke goes that "other than your wife, everything is provided for by the government." These perks can range from free building materials for villagers' new housing construction to free TV sets and antennas, and from free baby chickens for one to raise and sell to winter supplies.

In Tibet, a lack of sizable minority groups prevents comparative references, but this does not stop Tibetans and minority groups outside Tibet from making them. Tibetans residing in areas outside the TAR, namely in the four surrounding provinces, complain about being "second-class" Tibetans, for they too live in underdeveloped areas but receive less state benefits than their ethnic brethren in the TAR (Jin 2010a: 239). For example, for an official of the same rank, the monthly salary is a few thousand yuan more in the TAR. Some scholars actively push for the "equalization" of state benefits for other Tibetan regions, from public employee salaries to developmental programs. In Qinghai, where Hui Muslim warlords used to rule over local Tibetans, Hui members wryly joke about Tibetans – including those in Qinghai – being the Han people's favorite children while the Huis are the adopted children.

Such sentiments have also extended to Xinjiang among minority groups outside the region. Typical are remarks by a Guangxi official: "In 2010 Xinjiang received ¥100 billion in state subsidies and ¥200 billion in partner assistance from nineteen provinces and cities, But we get little, even though we sacrificed our economic interests by accepting environmental regulations to ban local lumbering. How is this fair?" Adds a Guangxi scholar, "Is it because we in

[19] Conversation with a bank official and reporter of southern Xinjiang, summer 2015.
[20] Yao (2013a) notes the same behavioral patterns for Kazakh herdsmen.

Guangxi are more compliant so we get little state attention? . . . there are experts studying Xinjiang and Tibet but not Guangxi; and there is a Xinjiang class and a Tibet class at the Central Party School, but nothing for Guangxi" (Jin 2011: 132). Such sentiments, of course, are induced by the state's blurring of inner and outer peripheral groups as equal "nations" in principle, but differentiated treatment in reality.

In minority regions where ethnic groups have few distinctions and coexisted historically, Han residents feel their treatment has been unfair. In Guangxi, Han villagers complain that while roads have been built for Zhuang villages, nothing has been done for Han villages for decades. Ma Rong, who spent a decade in rural Inner Mongolia as a sent-down youth and later a frequent researcher of the region, recounts that the poorest villagers in Inner Mongolia are the Han farmers, since they do not receive state subsidies or tax relief like their ethnic neighbors to buy farm vehicles to grow their businesses.[21] Ironically, lesser state aid may have saved these autonomous regions from immigrant waves in the reform era, while also undercutting a coalition of inner and outer peripheral groups.

Ultimately, assessment of the state's economic strategies in the two sensitive regions comes down to whether it can help overcome economic disparities and grievances or whether they will reinforce dependency. The latter would hamper the local economies' long-term viability and capacity for job creation and for deep – rather than sponsored – integration.

SUMMARY

This chapter has examined how the institutional tensions of the autonomous system, that is the paradox of centralization and ethnicization, have intensified in the post-Mao era. The driving force has been the state's developmentalism as strategies for both development and integration.

The centralizing dynamics (via sponsorship of state economy and market) and ethnicizing dynamics (via more preferential economic policies) have led to economic patterns and consequences not best suited to local development or ethnic advancement. By looking at these patterns and outcomes, I have shown how institutional dynamics help to fuel sources of ethnic strife in the TAR and Xinjiang.

In economic strategy as in other areas of state policy for autonomous regions, genuine autonomy is sacrificed for the cause of integration and substituted by ethnicization. In the TAR's case, subsidy and aid programs have amounted to nearly total state sponsorship of the local economy, inhibiting incentives and mechanisms to come up with locally viably economic models, despite dubious returns on state investment. In the end, state sponsorship has created dependent development, whose viability remains questionable. In the case of Xinjiang,

[21] Conversations with Ma Rong, Beijing, fall 2013.

economic liberalization proceeded without local control over the nature and phasing of this transformation, leaving minority members disproportionally affected while businesses from interior provinces disproportionally advantaged. The process thus ethnicized the outcome of economic reform. Partner assistance programs, designed and executed by provinces from outside, transfer a huge amount of resources without enhancing autonomy.

In both cases examined in this chapter, two-way migration intensifies the effects of economic liberalization, especially interethnic competition. This is all the more politicizing when in-migration to the TAR and Xinjiang is less affected by ascriptive features like language and cultural barriers, while ethnic migrants from these two regions are hindered by ascriptive features and technical skills in urban areas on their own home turf as well as outside it. The result has been to shrink economic opportunities for minority members where ascriptive features and technical skills matter, hamper their socioeconomic progress, weaken their competitiveness against the free movement of labor and business, and ultimately pit minority and migrant groups against one another. These consequences serve to aggravate minority sentiments of discontent when things do not work out in the real world as government policies promise. Meanwhile, those who are not entitled to preferential policies find cause to blame socioeconomic disparities on individual or group failures, further fueling ethnic tensions. Ultimately, these tensions not only impair the state's own immediate goals of economic convergence and development, but also its ultimate goal of national integration.

8

Educational Expansion and Its Discontents

Hours after the Urumqi riots of 2009, some students at Xinjiang University celebrated till the wee hours of the morning. Such reactions, by the best of Xinjiang's educated youths, shocked casual and close observers alike. Why did the largest group of beneficiaries of state educational policies, Uighur college students, seem unconcerned about the violent bloodshed and turn against the state? This chapter will continue to illustrate the built-in tensions of the autonomous system in the reform era, by focusing on of the issues of education and language.

Scholars have observed serious strains in contemporary China's education and language policies for minority groups, especially Tibetans and Uighurs. These policies, they argue, sustain and accelerate assimilationist trends through schooling, leading to language loss, identity disarray, social displacement, and damage to interethnic relations (Beckett and Postiglione 2012: 4; Dwyer 2005; MacPherson and Beckett 2008). Language and education policies are found to drive Tibetan and Uighur worries about cultural and identity loss, fueling their secessionist sentiments (MacPherson and Beckett 2008) and the state's fear of resurgent nationalism (Henry 2016). At the very least, bilingual and trilingual education in Xinjiang and Tibet pose various challenges in balancing unity and diversity (Leibold and Chen 2014). Among the less pessimistic perspectives, Tibetan students are credited with creative educational strategies in the Chinese education system that contributes to the exploration and expression of new forms of "Tibetanness" in contemporary China (Zenz 2013).

This chapter focuses on education and language policies as sources of ethnic conflict in key minority regions in the reform era. These sources, I argue, stem once again from an intensification of the built-in tensions of the autonomous system, or the paradox of centralization and ethnicization. The driving force is the state's developmentalism in minority education. Here centralization inheres in the state's expansion of higher education on the one hand and of bilingual education on the other, while ethnicization is manifest in intensified preferential policies to promote those goals. Specifically, the state pursues an expansion of higher education and bilingual education for minority members for the purposes of economic development and political integration. However, this expansion, especially when aided by preferential policies, has come up against the realities of the new market economy, which favors competitive skills and disadvantages minority students. Both processes – preferential policies for minority access to higher education but disadvantages for minority graduates in the marketplace – enhance ethnicization at the expense of integration. The state responds with intensified bilingual education as remedies, whose draconian nature adds further to ethnic grievances. The case studies for this chapter will be drawn from Xinjiang, where the issues have been most salient.

This chapter will cover the following topics: (1) minority education in the reform era, (2) paradoxes of preferences and protection, and (3) bilingual education as a response and its problems.

MINORITY EDUCATION IN THE REFORM ERA

The era of economic reform has entailed that the established ethnic prerogatives of educational and language rights come up against the realities of the new market economy. During the socialist era, the language and academic gulf produced by ethnic public schools did not matter. Cocooned by the planned economy, graduates of higher education were assigned professional jobs, while graduates of secondary and vocational schools were given factory jobs. Others could return to rural or pastoral communes, which provided a basic social safety net. There was a place for everyone in the planned economy.

All this changed under economic reforms that began in the early 1980s. First the household responsibility system replaced the collective communes, leaving individual households and their members on their own. Then in the mid-1980s, the state bureaucracy began to unload many of its former functions, such as managing the planned economy and many aspects of society and culture. The retreat of the state, along with administrative streamlining and decentralization in general, has reduced the size of the state at all levels. Finally, since the early 1990s, reform of state enterprises allowed them to be sold off or closed down, except for the "commanding heights" of the economy or strategic industries. All of this means that guaranteed jobs in government agencies and public sectors have shrunk or even disappeared in the reform era. When the state officially ended job assignments for regular (or nonethnic) colleges in 1989, student furor became the initial catalyst for the Tiananmen protests of 1989. But the growth of the nonstate economy since 1992 helped to smooth the transitional process in inland China.

In minority regions, where modern sectors were largely created by the state after 1949, the state remained the main source of professional jobs for graduates of higher education. In Xinjiang and Tibet, guaranteed job assignments for college graduates were sustained for the longest period of time: it did not end till 2003 in Xinjiang and in 2007 for Tibet. Because Xinjiang has had a longer period to experience the consequences of education in the market economy, I will largely draw on this case in the remainder of this chapter.

Expansion of Higher Education

Two decades before the Urumqi riot of 2009, the overexpansion of college enrollment during the first decade of reform (1978–88) helped contribute to the Tiananmen protest of 1989. This was so because in China the university is a radical institution and because a disproportionate recruitment of students into the social sciences and humanities unintentionally magnified the political impact of enrollment expansion (Zhao 2001: 80–4). These two factors were further compounded by the end of guaranteed job assignment for regular (i.e., nonethnic) colleges in 1989. The overexpansion of higher education and the end of guaranteed job assignment have had similar impacts in Xinjiang.

Nationwide, the expansion of college enrollment in the 1980s was followed by a major expansion in 1999. It was part of the central state's educational drive for the new millennium (MOE 1998). Total college enrollment grew by 7.85 times in the two decades between 1980 and 2000, from 0.281 million students in 1980 to 2.206 million in 2000. It grew by eighteen times between 1980 and 2005, or 5.045 million students in 2005 (SBS 2006: 800). It has been an era of developmentalism in China and in its higher education, a new "Great Leap Forward."

The waves of enrollment expansion have also affected minority students. In 1950, just 1,300 minority students were enrolled in colleges across China. The number increased to 42,900 in 1980 and 953,200 in 2005 (SEAC and SBS 2007: 517). This amounted to a growth of 22.2 times between 1980 and 2005. Table 8.1 shows the percentage change in higher education enrollment for eighteen minority groups with a population above one million, in the first two decades of the reform era. Except for Koreans, who had already been doing well, the other seventeen groups increased their percentage points more than five times between 1982 and 2000.

Xinjiang has experienced an exceptional expansion of higher education, both because the starting point was lower here and because of preferential policies for minority students. In the late 1970s, less than 8 percent of high-school graduates could go to college. In 1997, one year after colleges officially began to charge tuition, 35.6 percent of the graduates from regular high schools and 40.5 percent of the graduates from ethnic high school entered college. The ratio was higher for ethnic schools thanks to preferential policies in college admissions. Since 2000, one year after the official launch of enrollment expansion, more than 50 percent to nearly 70 percent of high-school graduates have enrolled in college. Between 1980 and 2005, the total number

TABLE 8.1 *Percentage of college graduates in total population over age six by ethnic group*

Ethnic group	1982*	1990	2000	% increase, 1982–2000	Ethnic group	1982*	1990	2000	% increase, 1982–2000
Zhuang	0.26	0.65	2.0	7.7	Dong	0.24	0.70	2.1	8.8
Manchu	0.94	1.91	4.8	5.1	Yao	0.17	0.60	1.9	11.2
Hui	0.80	1.77	4.1	5.1	Korean	2.18	4.82	8.6	3.9
Miao	0.14	0.46	1.4	10.0	Bai	0.48	1.23	2.9	6.0
Uygur	0.39	1.10	2.7	6.9	Hani	0.05	0.20	0.7	14.0
Yi	0.10	0.30	1.1	11.0	Li	0.19	0.56	1.3	6.8
Tujia	0.18	0.82	2.3	12.8	Kazakh	0.56	1.52	4.1	7.3
Mongol	0.95	2.19	5.2	5.5	Dai	0.12	0.34	1.0	8.3
Tibetan	0.24	0.52	1.3	5.4	Han	0.69	1.63	3.9	5.7
Bouyei	0.16	0.45	1.3	8.1	China	0.68	1.58	3.8	5.6

* Data for 1982 includes students who graduated with a degree or without it.
Source: SCCO and SBS (1985: 240–3; 1993: 380–459; 2002: 566–7); Ma et al. (2005: 8).

of enrolled minority students in college increased from 6,455 to 75,744, a jump of 11.7 times in a twenty-five-year period (SBX 2006: 524).

Finally, the proportionality principle, issued by the Ministry of Education and the SEAC in 1980 and incorporated into the autonomy law in 1984, requires that minority college enrollment is not lower than the ratio of corresponding minority populations in autonomous areas. In Xinjiang, this has meant that 60 percent of the admitted must be ethnic members, regardless of differences in test scores. This ratio entails that the overall growth of enrollment also allows proportionally more minority students to be admitted to colleges. By 1997, the number of local students admitted to colleges outside Xinjiang exceeded those admitted to local colleges in Xinjiang, since there are far more colleges outside Xinjiang.

Besides regular enrollment, for-profit college programs have also exploded in the reform era. Short-term certification and continuing education programs have been created for students who fail to enroll through the regular admission process. In addition, many government agencies operate their own training programs, offering degree certificates through affiliation with local vocational schools.

The state drive for expanding minority higher education, however, has entailed two major problems for Xinjiang. One has been the quality of academic preparation and the other a lack of a matching job market. Xinjiang's colleges were allowed to expand enrollment in part because they were no longer confined by mandatory job assignments for graduates after 2003. However, unlike in interior provinces, the new market economy here could not create tens of thousands of new positions annually to accommodate the surge of college graduates. Moreover, preferential admissions since the early 1980s have left another legacy: two different student groups. One is the Mandarin-speaking group who have gone to regular public schools and made it to college through regular entrance exams. The other is the ethnic language speakers who have gone to ethnic public schools and been admitted to college under preferential policies. The latter group would soon find out that preferential policies could not shield them from the new job market.

Sheltered Job Expectations

One of the trade-offs in the socialist era was that despite limited autonomy, there was at least job guarantee. In minority regions, this guarantee had nurtured expectations of a stable job in a government agency or the public sector. Because modern administration was built from scratch in most minority regions after the founding of the PRC, especially in Xinjiang, Inner Mongolia, and Tibet, there was a great need for bureaucratic and professional staffing while college graduates were few.

In the reform era, expectations about government positions have persisted for minority members in these regions, as the very expansion of higher education by the state fosters such expectations. In Xinjiang, local surveys of Uighur college students suggest that a large majority of them – often a combination of over 80 percent – prefer public sector jobs (Li H. 2017: 165; Li et al. 2017: 241; Qi and He 2007: 165–6; Wang 2006: 35). This is confirmed in conversations with Uighur students on Xinjiang's campuses as well as those randomly encountered during my field trips. The same goes for Tibetan college graduates. In a survey conducted by Tibetan students attending boarding schools in interior China, three-quarters of the surveyed students chose state sectors as their top choice of place to work (*Xuezi* 2015). This corresponds well with Adrian Zenz's (2013) finding that a vast majority of Tibetan students in China aspire careers in the state sectors. In Inner Mongolia as well, students of Mongol descent have strong preferences for government jobs, much as Uighur and Kazakh students in Xinjiang (Ma 2006: 17). Hesitant to take a job in the private sector, those students placed hope in the networks of their relatives and friends to land a public sector job eventually. But the civil service exam and professional certification exams, implemented since the mid-2000s, have reduced the utility of such networks while increasing grievances about quota distribution among ethnic groups.

A mix of reasons contributes to minority preferences for jobs in state agencies and public sectors. Foremost is the status associated with being an official, rooted in the Mao era when minority college graduates were few and sorely needed for the new state sectors in minority regions. Expectations for cadre positions linger in the reform era, especially in the outer peripheral regions where the modern state emerged only in the Mao era. In one case that reflects such a mindset, the parents of a Tibetan scholar in Sichuan are unhappy that their son pursued a doctoral degree only to leave his old job as an official of a local state agency for an academic job in a university, with comparable levels of income and job security.[1] Likewise, when Tibetan village cadre told me about the number of village youths who had graduated from college, they were most proud that they became officials in the county seat.[2] Preferential policies in college admissions, which have been greatly expanded in the reform era, entail that more ethnic members are admitted than can meet regular admission standards, yet they are given false hope that they will be getting a public sector job because of their preferential ethnic status.

The security and perks of government and public sector jobs comprise another inducement for public sector jobs. This becomes all the more important because nonstate sectors tend to be more competitive as well as more discriminatory in hiring. Among Uighur students at Xinjiang University, a Uighur professor reports, those who receive their education in an ethnic language particularly lack confidence to land a job on their own. Viewing themselves as less competitive in technical skills and Mandarin, they prefer a job in a state agency or public school that offers job security and protection from market competition (Zulhayat 2009: 123–4). Uighur graduates usually prefer to work near home, close to their social networks and cultural customs, thus further limiting job opportunities (Jia et al. 2006: 55). Some minority graduates are willing to wait in vain for several years for a public sector job. One Uighur student in Urumqi gave me a typical account. Her sister, a graduate of a local teachers' college, had been unemployed since the mid-2000s, and living on a monthly stipend from the local welfare bureau for over seven years. Because she only wanted a teaching job in a local public school, she kept waiting rather than looking for employment in the nonstate sector. The Uighur student was aware of many others like her sister.[3] It took the teachers' certification exams, implemented in 2015, to finally make or break their career dream. Previously, graduates of teachers' colleges received teaching certificates from their colleges, but this did not guarantee a job.[4]

College costs, whether financed by parents or scholarships, add to the minority illusion that the investment will pay off. College was free in the socialist era, along with dormitories and textbooks. Since the early 1990s,

[1] Conversations with a Tibetan scholar at Sichuan University, Chengdu, summer 2015.

[2] Conversations in Xiaodian village, Diqing prefecture, August 2016.

[3] Conversation with a Uighur student at a teacher's college in Urumqi, July 2013.

[4] The issuance of teachers' certificates began in 2002 in Xinjiang, but graduates of teachers' colleges did not need to take certification tests. Since 2015, graduates of all colleges must take the tests to get certified as public school teachers.

colleges in different provinces began to charge tuition at varying paces. The amount was initially small, a few hundred yuan in the mid and late 1990s ($30 to $100). By 2005 it grew to several thousand yuan (around $1,000), a considerable burden for rural families. In Xinjiang, the annual earnings of rural households averaged ¥4,605 in 2005, with net income (after production costs) being only ¥2,482 (SBX 2006: 216). Thus college costs for one student amounted to the annual income of three rural households. Even for urban families, 40.41 percent of the households surveyed in 2005 reported that the annual costs of their children's college education took up over 50 percent of their family income (Wang 2006: 37). Despite the rise of need-based scholarships, some rural and urban families borrow money to pay for their children's college costs. By past experiences, they expect their children to get a government job in cities, complete with fringe benefits. Expanded higher education has given them a seemingly blissful chance of a worthy investment, so they have tolerated the costs, especially in the earlier years of college expansion.

Frustrated expectations, however, give rise to ethnic grievances. When Uighur students cannot find government jobs, they leave their parents feeling that their investment has been in vain and worst yet, they have been ripped off. Because of the financial burdens on their parents, many minority students are eager to see quick returns on their tuition through a well-paid and secure government job. This expectation causes them to be particularly anxious (Wang 2006: 37). By comparison, their Han counterparts in Xinjiang tend to have diverse job expectations, due to less expectations about government jobs, greater social capital, and easier adaptation to the new market economy. Although a large proportion of Hans worked in Xinjiang's public sector during the Mao era, Han graduates are more willing to work in the private sector or temporary jobs with low pay and limited benefits. A lack of religious and dietary considerations also allows flexible relocation. Proficiency in Mandarin gives them an inherent advantage, which is a key complaint of Uighur students. But as Uighur students also concede, Han students acquire a variety of professional certificates, enabling them to find jobs (Zulhayat 2009: 124).

In the first decade after the guaranteed job system ended in 2003, joblessness among a large proportion of Uighur college graduates became the most serious issue among Xinjiang's minority youths and one of the most destabilizing issues in the province. Their expectations for state and public sector jobs, nurtured by expanded higher education and ethnic prerogatives, were mismatched with the realities of the new market economy.

Changing Job Market

While developmentalism has helped to expand higher education for minority members, it has also ushered in competition in the job market. The expansion of higher education after 1999 followed the retreat of socialist job sectors already going on in the 1990s. In Xinjiang's case, the end of state job assignments in 2003 and the onset of qualifying exams for public sector jobs have made entering these sectors yet more challenging for minority graduates. The shift to market and meritocratic criteria has created not only job competition but competition along ethnic lines, especially as perceived the major ethnic group, the Uighurs.

To begin with, public sectors in the post-Mao era are no longer part of a "big rice bowl" system with all its inefficiency and patronage. As in the old system, hiring quotas for state agencies and public sectors are allocated by the local state's personnel budget. These quotas come with not only salaries and fringe benefits but also subsidized housing and lifetime employment. However, as central planning and local SOEs waned by the late 1990s, the scale of the state bureaucracy and public enterprises shrank, as did public sector hiring. Moreover, competitively and professionally based procedures of hiring and promotion, implemented since the mid-2000s, constrain the kind of overstaffing common in the past. Earlier the prevalence of using personal and political connections in the hiring process had already created overstaffing in Xinjiang's public sectors. During my casual visits to local state agencies in southern Xinjiang, it was not uncommon to find roomfuls of staffers idling in their offices. In the public school system, also a popular destination for Uighur college graduates, the problem is compounded by the dwindling of the student population in ethnic schools, especially in the lower grades. In cities and towns, more minority parents tend to send their children to regular schools for the rigorous academic programs. Ironically, ethnic schools offer less rigorous programs in part because the use of connections to land jobs used to be prevalent, so that not all of the teachers hired in the past were necessary, qualified, or equipped with the bilingual skills that are in high demand now. Some of the excess teachers have had to teach courses outside the areas of their specialty, resulting in a cycle of poor instruction. Demands for bilingual teachers have grown dramatically in recent years, but the new openings are usually in remote rural regions unappealing to many job candidates. The civil service exam, implemented since 2004, has created a more transparent but also more competitive process for entry into state agency jobs. This is the job sector most desired by minority graduates. Each year over 100,000 applicants take the exam in Xinjiang for the several thousand job slots in state agencies. In the initial years of the exam, there were no specifications for ethnic requirements (*Meiwen wang* 2017). Qualifying scores were lowered for minority candidates, but the testing itself was perceived as favoring the academically strong Han candidates.

After the Urumqi riot of 2009, a change was implemented between 2012 and 2015 that provoked more Uighur resentment. About 30 percent of the hiring quotas were allocated to candidates who were not entitled to bonus points, which essentially meant Han or other Mandarin-speaking candidates.[5]

[5] See "2015 nian Xinjiang gongwuyuan kaoshi gonggao jiedu" [Explicating the public announcement for Xinjiang's 2015 civil service exam]. *Zhongguo jiaoyu zaixian*, August 12, 2015. Web.

Although the purpose was to strengthen local state agencies in southern Xinjiang, Uighurs perceived discrimination against their group. The dissident website, Uighurbiz.net, complained that for positions in the provincial government in 2012, about half of the openings did not specify ethnic requirements, which favored the academically strong Han applicants; about 30 percent of the spots were designated for those who were not entitled to bonus points, which also favored Han candidates; and the remaining quotas were spread among those who were entitled to bonus points, or minority candidates, whereas for openings at subregional government levels in 2012 a whopping half of the positions asked for Han candidates (Nijatkar 2012). Since 2016, ethnic allotment is no longer specified in official announcements for Xinjiang's civil service exams. Instead, a ten-point bonus, amounting to 8–15 percent of the minimum qualifying scores, is given to ten of Xinjiang's twelve traditional minority groups, or those whose native tongue is not Mandarin (*Zhonggong jiaoyu* 2018; *Gongwuyuan* 2016). This effectively pits Uighurs against Xinjiang's smaller but better integrated minority groups, such as the Mongols, Sibes, and Kazakhs. Hui and Manchu groups do not qualify for bonus points.

From the point of view of local state agencies, the problem stems not so much from discrimination but from the tussle between the demands of integration and ethnic prerogatives. In some years there are more quotas for Han candidates because the hiring quotas for them have not been filled for some local agencies, while the reverse may be true for minority members. Even new minority hiring may simply be due to preferential policies, as ethnic quotas have already been filled up. A related problem is the gap in performance scores in the civil service exams. In principle any minority member is eligible for any position, except he or she cannot receive bonus points on the exam. Hence when the local state did mention ethnic allotment in its job announcements, it listed the share of positions open to minority members as above three-quarters of the total slots.[6]

In southern Xinjiang, local state agencies had for a few years more openings for Han applicants because of a local requirement instituted after the 2009 Urumqi riot. It mandated that a third of the civil servants at county level and below be native Mandarin speakers. This "one-third" requirement was obviously political, since Mandarin speakers do not make up a third of the local population. In fact, among the three Uighur-concentrated prefectures in southern Xinjiang, Han residents comprise just 3 percent of the population in Hotan, less than 10 percent in Kashgar, and less than 30 percent in Aksu. The official rationale was the imperative of national integration, through the use of the national language and improved technical efficiency. More of the Han job candidates have degrees in technical fields, while minority members tend to have degrees in the humanities. In fact, every year some of the official openings draw no applicants, because they require special skills and/or national exams, for

[6] See above, Article 5 of the public announcement for the 2015 civil service exam in Xinjiang.

example openings in the areas of counter-terrorism, such as judges, prosecutors, forensic scientists, cyber detectives, and Arabic and Urdu speakers (*Huatu* 2011). In the initial years of its implementation, the "one-third Han" requirement appeared to undermine integration by aggravating Uighur grievances. A sizable proportion of the young recruits hired under this rule find it economically and culturally inhospitable to stay in southern Xinjiang for the long run. After a couple of years on the job they would try to transfer to a similar civil service job in a different location (civil service jobs are transferrable if another state agency is willing to accept a candidate), or take another civil service exam for a different position elsewhere. Some may try to relocate by bribing their way out. The ongoing rates were said to be fairly stable, around ¥20,000 to ¥30,000 ($3,000–5,000) in 2011–15. To curb the flight of young recruits, since 2015 the provincial government has banned active civil servants and quasi-civil servants from taking the civil service exam.[7] Based on my field observations, Han officials who have remained at the county level and below have usually come from the relatively poor neighboring province of Gansu. The exam ban, after all, does not bar individuals from quitting their jobs and depart for the private sector or a job out of Xinjiang. In 2016, Xinjiang ended ethnic allotment in the civil service exam, which makes the "one-third" rule superfluous. The influx of the "work-in-residence" teams in recent years, moreover, has made the staffing of young recruits, Mandarin speaking or not, a less urgent matter in the local governments of rural and southern Xinjiang.

Since the mid-2000s, the so-called quasi-civil service sectors have also adopted qualifying exams, making entry to these sectors competitive and complex. Known as "*shiye danwei*" or public service entities, they differ from state agencies on the one hand and state enterprises on the other. The quasi-civil service sectors include education, science and technology, culture (entertainment, media, and publishing), healthcare, and a dozen more areas owned and run by the state (*Zhonggong jiaoyu* 2017). These sectors used to require professional degrees but not qualifying exams, so nepotism was common in hiring. Local residents frequently complained that the children of local cadres were able to land jobs while the children of ordinary families had to wait for years for a slot.

Qualifying exams were adopted for these public service sectors at various pace in the 2000s,[8] resulting in a two-track hiring system. In the formal track, those hired through the exams secure lifetime jobs that come with good salaries, professional ranks, and a full range of benefits. In the informal track, new hires

[7] See above, Article 2 of the public announcement for the 2015 civil service exam in Xinjiang. "Quasi-civil servants," or *cangong renyuan*, are professional employees in public sectors that are not state agencies. Although not formally civil servants, they are subject to similar personnel regulations and salary standards.

[8] Locally administered exams for quasi-civil service sectors began in 2006, but not for all sectors at the same time. Xinjiang's healthcare sector began the exam in 2009. Its public schools implemented certification exams for all applicants in 2015.

do not need to take the exams but get a job on a contractual basis, with lower salaries, no professional ranks, and no fringe benefits. This two-track hiring also exists in state agencies but is more common in the public service sectors. Since it is difficult to get official hiring quotas for the formal track, many public entities resort to hiring contractual employees to get things done. Their second-class status leads to low retention rates, but they are still sought-after jobs for those who need a transitional job or work experiences.

The two-track hiring system can be confusing to outsiders and vulnerable to perceptions of nepotism and ethnic resentment. In particular, Han residents are perceived as having more resources to pay bribes to land a public sector job, even if it is just a contractual one. For example, one Han graduate from a medical school landed a job in a local hospital after his mother paid a middleman ¥30,000, almost her entire salary in 2012. However, it was a probationary position that could become formal only after the job holder qualified in the certifying exam. Resenting his second-class treatment, the medical student soon left for a health clinic, though the new position was still on the informal track.[9] Regardless of the circumstances, perceptions of Han resourcefulness at landing public sector jobs is a major source of Uighur resentment, according to several individuals of Han-Uighur mixed parentage in southern Xinjiang. Meanwhile, Han professionals have just as many grievances. The medical student cited above, who twice took the professional exam in Xinjiang but missed the qualifying score by a few points each time, complained about the extra points awarded to minority students (he eventually tool a civil service exam in an inland city and qualified for a position there). In the initial years of the medical certifying exams, the qualifying scores for minority members were considerably lower, but over time the exams and qualifying scores have become unified, except for the certification exams for ethnic medicine.[10]

The shift to market and meritocratic criteria in public sector hiring, in short, has made access to public sector jobs no longer a guarantee for Uighur college graduates. Aggravating the problem is the gap between the expansion of higher education for minority students and their academic preparation for the new job market.

PARADOXES OF PROTECTION AND PREFERENCES

Confined by the developmental discourse of the state, policymakers and mainstream analysts focus on searching for the reasons why Uighur graduates

[9] Conversations with this family in Aksu, fall 2013.

[10] Conversations with a physician from a Hotan hospital, summer 2015, and with a Hotan-based reporter, summer 2019. For differentiated qualifying scores in 2017, see "Xinjiang 2017 nian yishi zige bishi gaoshi chengji chaxun ji fenshuxian" [Checking test scores for Xinjiang's medical certification exam in 2017 and the cutoff scores]. *Xindongfang zaixian*, August 29, 2017. http://yixue.koolearn.com/20170829/648235.html.

fail to be competitive in the marketplace. In this discourse, preferential policies in high-school and college admissions have become a key target of criticism. Instead of ethnic equality, critics argue, they have done much to achieve superficial parity while damaging real progress for minorities. Although minority students receive various ranges of bonus points in college admissions in all minority regions and regular provinces, preferential admission policies in Xinjiang refer to policy benefits for two groups of minority students. They are (1) the *Min Kao Min* (MKM), minority students who attend ethnic schools and take academic tests in an ethnic language and (2) the *Min Kao Han* (MKH), minority students who attend regular schools and take academic tests in Chinese.

These two groups of minority students are found mainly in minority regions where the ethnic tongue is spoken in local communities and the dual school system exists. Besides Xinjiang, other ethnic regions that have these two groups of students include the TAR, Qinghai (for Tibetans), Inner Mongolia, and Jilin (for Koreans). While ethnic schools in Inner Mongol and Korean regions are held as exemplary models that provide quality education, those in Tibetan and Uighur regions have more issues with the quality of education. These issues in turn require more preferential policies in college admissions to make up for their students' lower scores. The lack of well-qualified teachers is an important reason for poor quality, but preferential policies in high-school and college admissions also play a significant role in creating a vicious cycle of low motivation and low performance. The problem appears to be especially serious in Xinjiang.

Triple Protections in Admissions

As part of educational expansion in the post-Mao era, three preferential policies for MKM and MKH students have been in place for high school and college admissions. First, MKM students would take admissions tests in an ethnic language, with easier content than tests for regular students. Second, qualifying admission scores are lowered for MKM and MKH students across the board, though the specific cut-off point differs from group to group and region to region. Third, the proportionality principle essentially compels colleges to admit students on a higher to lower scale, disregarding the official cut-off points for admissions. These triple protections make China's preferential policies far more comprehensive and entrenched than affirmative action policies in America's college admissions. This fact is usually neglected in the literature (e.g., Benson 2004: 196–205; Sautman 1998).

Preferential policies start with the high-school admissions. These are equivalent to pre-college admissions, since the kind of high school one enrolls in will affect the quality of one's preparation for the college entrance exams. High-school admission scores also decide if one goes to a vocational school, with no prospects of going to college. The MKH students go to regular middle schools with native Mandarin speakers so they take the same tests in Chinese. But thanks to preferential admissions, it is much easier for MKH students to qualify for a good high school. In addition, MKH students enjoy a range of bonus points, so the academic gulf between the two groups is even greater than their score differentials may indicate. For the MKM group, academic preparation also pales significantly when compared with those who go to regular middle schools, thanks to the different content of textbooks and the admission tests they must prepare to take. Different admission scores for different groups entail that wide gaps exist in their academic preparation, which in turn lead to different academic performances in high school.

These gaps are then compensated by preferential policies in college admissions. The once-a-year National College Entrance Exams (NCEE) is the sole ticket to higher education for the great majority of students in China. It consists of six half-day exams that test the students' deep knowledge in six subject areas. Nationwide, the lowering of college admission scores for minority students was decreed in 1978, one year after the NCEE resumed in 1977. The proportionality principle followed in 1980, or the idea that minority enrollment should not be lower than the ratio of the corresponding minority populations in a given ethnic region. The decree met with initial resistance from below but was reiterated by the Ministry of Education and the SEAC in 1981. The policy formally became law as part of the LAER adopted in 1984.

In 1981, the Ministry of Education issued a third policy, with far-reaching impacts. This policy exempted MKM students from the translated version of the NCEE. That is, autonomous regions could administer their own tests, in ethnic languages and with easier content. A Chinese-language test would be given but not calculated into one's combined total score. For those applying for admission to colleges with Chinese as the language of instruction, they would take all subjects in translated versions of the NCEE in an ethnic language, plus the Chinese language test. Together, the three policies entailed that minority students could be admitted with lower scores, through easier tests, and in proportion to their population size. But the trade-offs soon would become visible, as students struggled in college. In response, the state issued a series of adjustment between 1980 and 1986, including the requirement of remedial classes (especially in math and science) and the maximum score reduction allowed (Teng and Wang 2002; SEAC 1991).

Xinjiang instituted lower scores and proportionality for minority admissions when the NCEE resumed in the late 1970s. The proportionality principle mandates that colleges from outside Xinjiang admit no less than 50 percent of minorities among all admitted students and the mandated ratio is 60 percent for colleges from within Xinjiang. This means that MKM students are effectively admitted on a scale of higher to lower scores, with no real cut-off point. The early results were distressing: scores on math and science subjects were extremely low for most applicants. Of 4,248 MKM students admitted to math and science programs in 1998, 1.4 percent scored above the passing point of sixty (out of 150) in one of the three science subject exams; 60.2 percent scored just 10–29 points, and 7.5 percent scored between 0 and 9 points (Ren 2003: 30). Moreover, of all MKM students who applied to math or chemistry programs, not one student passed the NCEE in the subject area of their intended major; and of all MKM applicants to physics programs, just one student passed the subject test. In response, in 1999 Xinjiang established a minimum of fifteen points required for college admissions on any single subject test (out of 150 points), and this increased to eighteen points since 2003 (out of 150). However, this requirement remains too low to motivate MKM students to spend time on science subjects. They usually try to raise their combined total scores by doing better on humanities subjects (Li 2009a: 162–5). Here they have stronger academic preparation and can rely more on rote memorization to improve test scores.

Xinjiang has done better in reversing the third preferential policy in college admissions, that is the policy that replaced the NCEE with local tests. To halt the decline in academic standards, Xinjiang began to make a partial return to the NCEE in 1984, when the math and politics tests were reverted to translated versions of the NCEE. By 1995 all subject tests were reverted to translated versions of the NCEE, except the verbal test for the MKM group, which is in a local ethnic language. Graduates of bilingual programs would take the regular math and science tests, but the verbal test in their native language. Since 1997 the central state began a separate Chinese-language test for minority students. Known as *Minzu Han Kao*, it can be taken by minority students as a substitute for the Chinese-language test in the NCEE. Since 2017 the bilingual group is categorized as a separate group from the MKM. They take the regular math and science subjects in the NCEE and Level II subject tests in the Chinese verbal and English tests, which are easier.

Table 8.2 shows the cut-off point for college admissions for different groups of students in Xinjiang from 2002 to 2018. The gap between ethnic students and regular students (those whose native tongue is Chinese, including Hans, Huis, and Manchus) is significant, especially in the math and science subjects. Regular and MKH students both attend regular schools and take the NCEE in Chinese. The gap in their combined scores averaged over 140 points in the 2000s, out of a maximum of 750, and this after the MKH students had already received bonus points (Table 8.3). In a highly competitive admission environment where every point counts, a gap of a hundred or more points is substantial. This gap has narrowed in recent years, but without the bonus points the real gap remains considerable.

These bonus points are blamed as the very reason why MKH students do not perform as well as Han students, despite attending the same schools. A Uighur professor at Xinjiang University observes that the comfort of preferential admissions damps the drive of MKH students to work hard and excel (Zulhayat 2009: 115–16). Her point is supported by the qualifying scores for

TABLE 8.2 *NCEE cut-off points for college admissions in Xinjiang: 2002–19 (maximum score= 750)*

Year	Student group	First-tier colleges: Humanities and social sciences	First-tier colleges: Math and sciences	Second-tier colleges: Humanities and social sciences	Second-tier colleges: Math and sciences
2002	Regular	490	499	436	420
	MKH	330 (16*)	315 (18)	296 (16)	265 (16)
2003	Regular	493	456	450	390
	MKH	333 (18)	307 (18)	288 (18)	265 (18)
2004	Regular	538	522	484	477
	MKH	381 (23)	382	345	352 (23)
2005	Regular	516	507	455	433
	MKH	393 (25)	367 (27)	300 (23)	300 (25)
2006	Regular	517	520	452	448
	MKH	398 (26)	357 (29)	371 (24)	328 (26)
2010	Regular	485	471	433	415
	MKH	432 (29)	364 (33)	409 (28)	342 (32)
2011	Regular	504	473	433	407
	MKH	424 (30)	353 (34)	396 (29)	321 (33)
2012	Regular	493	445	326	390
	MKH	415 (30)	338 (34)	385 (29)	303 (33)
2013	Regular	460	443	394	378
	MKH	425 (30)	342 (35)	392 (29)	300 (34)
2014	Regular	516	475	446	405
	MKH	456 (30)	359 (35)	424 (29)	327 (34)
2015	Regular	485	446	414	381
	MKH	324 (30)	334 (35)	349 (29)	304 (34)
2016	Regular	489	464	415	394
	MKH	442 (30)	344 (35)	403 (29)	308 (34)
2017	Regular	486	437	375	333
	MKH	411	383	333	303
	Bilingual	359	374	325	321
	MKM	429 (30)	325 (33)	374 (28)	270 (29)
2018	Regular	500	467	372	341
	MKH	421	398	353	310
	Bilingual	384	376	350	309
	MKM	418 (31)	327 (35)	369 (29)	271 (32)
2019	Regular	510	450	387	326
	MKH	408	365	338	284
	Bilingual	347	325	314	270
	MKM	345 (31)	295 (35)	302 (29)	240 (32)

Source: For 2002–4, *Edu.sina* (2004); for 2005–6, *Edu.sina* (2006); for 2010–18, EOL (2018); for 2019, Xinjiang ribao (2019).

* The numbers in the brackets in all columns of this table represent the minimum scores required on the math test for each disciplinary area.

the bilingual group in 2017 and 2018. To support bilingual programs, Xinjiang began to list students of these programs as a separate group in the NCEE since 2017, who would receive no bonus points. An adjustment was made in 2018 by which the bilingual group would receive a twenty-point bonus if they are not from the south with at least one minority parent. In both years their net scores were higher than the MKH group when the latter's fifty bonus points are excluded. Notably, the minimum required score for the math subject is established only for the MKM group. It has ranged between sixteen points and thirty-five points between 2002 and 2018, out of a possible 150.

For minority students who take the NCEE in the Chinese language, namely the MKH group, preferential policies in Xinjiang have also involved complex arrangements since the 1980s. The MKH is an important category of minority students: because the proportionality principle requires that half of all students admitted by Chinese colleges outside Xinjiang be minorities, the MKH group benefits disproportionally from their proficiency in Chinese. Table 8.3 shows the maze of admission policies for the various MKH subgroups. There are similar policies for admission to high schools and continuing education programs at college levels. For comparative reference, in regular provinces where minority members go to regular public schools, the bonus points range between a high of twenty to twenty-five points for those reside in minority-concentrated areas and a low of five to ten points for those who live in Han areas. For China's college admissions, where every point counts, the bonus points for minority members who live in Han areas are so controversial that a few provinces have begun to reduce or even eliminate them in early 2017.

It is worth noting that while the bonus points for minority students are ethnically based, those for Han students are regionally based (at least until 2019). A ten-point bonus to Han students who go to ethnic schools is due to their residence in remote and rural areas where no regular school is available. A ten-point bonus to Han students in southern Xinjiang is due to the region's lower level of development and poorer quality of schools. By contrast, all MKH students with two or just one minority parent(s), regardless of their regional and economic backgrounds, have received bonus points. This suggests that preferential policies in college admissions aim more at protecting ethnic prerogatives than compensating for minority disadvantages.

In the 2019 admission cycle, however, there is a notable change in the bonus points policy in favor of integration. For the first time, a minority student (from one of the eleven groups) with one Han parent receives five bonus points more than a student with two minority parents. Moreover, anyone who is *not* from one of the eleven minority groups, meaning Han and other groups, can receive twenty extra points (the highest bonus) if they major in a local ethnic language. These changes are in line with Chen Quanguo's overall policy in Xinjiang. It remains to be seen whether and how these two changes may promote intermarriages and the study of local ethnic languages by Han and other students who are not from one of the eleven local minority groups.

TABLE 8.3 *Bonus points by ethnic group in college admissions in Xinjiang (maximum NCEE score = 750)*

Year	Bonus points	Type of ethnic students receiving bonus points[11]
1985	10	Hui; Han students who go to ethnic schools
	30	MKH with one parent from one of the 11 minority groups[12]
	100	MKH with two parents from one of the 11 minority groups
1987	10	Hui; Han students who go to ethnic schools
	80	MKH with one parent from one of the 11 minority groups
	100	MKH with two parents from one of the 11 minority groups, applying to colleges outside Xinjiang
	150	MKH with two parents from one of the 11 minority groups, applying to colleges in Xinjiang
2002–3	10	Hui students; MKH with one minority parent
	70	MKH with two parents from one of the 11 minority groups or with one such parent *and* from southern Xinjiang[13]
2018	10	Hui and MKH with one parent from one of the 11 minority groups; anyone from southern Xinjiang not eligible for other bonus points
	20	MKH, bilingual, and HKM students with one parent from one the 11 minority groups and from southern Xinjiang
	50	MKH with two parents from one of the 11 groups
2019	5	Hui students
	10	Anyone from southern Xinjiang not eligible for other bonus points
	15	MKH with two parents from one of the 11 minority groups
	20	MKH with one Han parent and one parent from one of the 11 groups; Anyone not from one of the 11 minority groups but with prospective college major in an ethnic language

Note: HKM refers to Han students taking college admission tests in a minority language.
Source: For 1985–2003, *Xinjiang Education Yearbook*, cited in Li (2009a), 163; for 2018, *Xindong fang* (2018); for 2019, *Gaosan* (2019).

[11] In various years, ten to twenty bonus points have been given to ethnic categories. From 2002 to 2015, ten to twenty points were awarded to athletes who placed within the top six in major national competitions. In recent years, ten points are awarded to returned expatriates and their offspring, martyrs' offspring, decorated ex-servicemen and ex-servicemen who did not receive state-assigned jobs.

[12] These include Uighur, Kazakh, Mongol, Kyrgyz, Tajik, Sibe, Uzbek, Tatar, Daur, Tibetan, and Russian.

[13] Southern Xinjiang refers to Aksu, Hotan, Kashgar, and Kizilsu Kyrgyz Autonomous Prefecture.

Adverse Impact on Education

Large-scale preferential policies in college admissions have had adverse consequences for the state's own purposes. With millions of eligible students from lower to higher education, Xinjiang is the region with the largest minority population to benefit from those policies. But the negative effects have been duly noted by local scholars (Cheng 2016; Zulhayat 2009 and 2011; Ma 2006, 2007, 2009a, 2009b, 2009c, and 2009d; Li 2005a, 2009a, and 2009b; Ren 2003). From the perspective of this study, the preferential policies help to undermine the state's own goal of expanding higher education for minority members, by weakening the quality of educational outcomes and preparation for the job market.

Preferential admissions, above all, affect motivation and drive for the protected student groups at all levels of schooling. A common complaint among local teachers and school principals is that those policies cultivate a mentality of dependency, increase rather than bridge academic gaps, and stigmatize minority students as underachievers. In middle and high schools, many minority students already feel that they do not need to work hard, since they will be admitted to college anyway. They are used to the idea that as minorities they are entitled to protection and have low expectations about the grades they should get. At all levels of the educational system, minority students in ethnic schools are insulated from the competitive pressure that normally motivates students to perform and improve. On minority dominant campuses, according to a faculty member of a college in Gulja/Ili, a lack of preparation and motivation can be so prevalent that serious students are looked upon as "odd" (Cheng 2016: 159). In my conversations with Uighur and Tibetan students, the academic achievers among them are usually critical of preferential admissions, because they stigmatize them as underachievers and harm their less motivated peers.[14]

Preferential policies have had similar effects on protected Han student groups in Xinjiang. Of three heavily Uighur prefectures in southern Xinjiang, two – Hotan and Kashghar – have preferential policies for Han students for high school and college admissions, while Asku does not. The result is that Han schools in Aksu have had much better academic records (Li 2009a: 173). Interestingly, siblings within the same family can perform differently depending on the ethnicity under which they have been grouped. In one extended family with mixed Uighur-Han parentage, for example, siblings and their children who are officially registered as Han or have Han last names work harder and perform better than those who are not registered as Han. They cite social expectations and admission incentives as the main reasons.[15]

14 Conversations with eight Uighur students on an Aksu college campus, summer 2011, one of whom went on to be the top score achiever in her county's teachers' certifying exam in 2015. Also conversations with two Tibetan students from the TAR studying in New York City, fall 2015.

15 Conversations with two sisters with Uighur and Han parents who were married in the 1950s. Their children went to college in the 2000s and the early 2010s. Conversations with a family whose grandparent is Uighur. Fall 2013 and summer 2015 respectively, southern Xinjiang.

TABLE 8.4 *Results of high-school admission tests in Urumqi: 2003–5*

		Math (maximum = 150)		Physics (maximum = 100)		Chemistry (maximum = 100)	
Year	School system	Average score	% passing	Average score	% passing	Average score	% passing
2003	Regular	98.7	68.5	58.4	64.4	44.7	n/a
	Uighur	74.7	35.8	49.3	42.5	39.5	65.7
	Kazakh	53.1	13.3	36.0	12.8	32.9	44.3
2004	Regular	89.7	56.1	61.7	71.9	44.0	77.9
	Ethnic	40.3	4.6	39.1	20.1	33.3	45.6
	Bilingual	66.7	26.9	53.2	52.1	39.6	67.9
2005	Regular	85.1	n/a	60.3	n/a	41.4	n/a
	Ethnic	46.2	n/a	43.3	n/a	30.8	n/a

Source: "Xinjiang weiwu'er zizhiqu jiaoyuju diaocha baogao" [Investigative report of the department of education of XUAR], cited in Ma (2009b: 42).

Table 8.4 shows results from high-school admission tests for Urumqi's public schools in 2003–5. These were the last three years before bilingual programs were implemented in the city's ethnic schools in 2006. The middle school students from the regular school system and those from the ethnic school system took different tests, with the tests for ethnic schools easier in content. Nevertheless, as the columns show, more than half of the students from ethnic schools consistently failed the three subject tests – with the exception of the chemistry test in 2003 for Uighurs and in 2004 for students of bilingual programs (where math and science courses are taught in Chinese). The real gap was yet larger than the test scores would suggest, since the test contents for ethnic schools were easier. Language alone could not explain the difference in performance, since the tests for ethnic schools were in the languages in which the subjects were taught. Two decades later, a considerable gap still exists in the academic performance in those two types of schools. In the 2018 high-school admissions tests in Urumqi, the qualifying scores for top-tier high schools in the regular system averaged about 150 points more than those for their ethnic counterparts, out of 750 possible points (*Wuyoukao wang* 2018).

Another impact of preferential policies has been the college majors for minority students and their segregated experiences in college. Because of underpreparation in math and science, a large proportion of them choose to major in their native language, history, or philosophy. This physically separates them from the disciplines where Han students are concentrated. Different learning and residential experiences can reinforce this separation. Minority freshmen would usually take remedial Chinese classes in the first year, academic classes in ethnic languages in the next two years, and classes in

Chinese are encouraged in the in the final two years. The textbooks for academic classes in ethnic languages are locally compiled and less rigorous than the nationally uniform textbooks in the regular programs.

Moreover, dormitories on Chinese campuses are usually assigned by their students' academic department and entering class, so that being separate from the academic disciplines where Han students are concentrated also entail separate dorms for ethnic students. Along with different exams and evaluation standards, minority and Han students may go through college in separate worlds. After a partial reform in 2002, minority students who passed their remedial Chinese class can take their math and science classes in regular programs in college. Still, many struggle in such classes and rarely use Chinese outside the classrooms. Han students, who often consider minority students to be poorly prepared, are reluctant to mingle with them (Zulhayat 2009: 101–10; Cheng 2016: 158, 159). The problem of separate college experiences therefore persists.

Yet another effect of preferential admissions may be responsible for a vicious circle in the educational system, especially before the universal teachers' certification exams were instituted in 2015. Because many minority graduates of higher education became teachers in lower grades at ethnic schools, they affect the quality of education in these grades. This is especially true of the teaching staff in the math and science subjects. The percentage of college-educated minority teachers tends to be higher than that of their Han counterparts in Xinjiang's middle and high schools, and they also compare well in China as a whole. Yet the admission scores of their students tell a different story. School authorities in Xinjiang concede that teachers with "superficial" degrees is a major problem in ethnic schools (Li 2009a: 173). Even in regular elementary schools of southern Xinjiang, ethnic teachers may write answers on the blackboard for their students during tests, so as to save themselves the embarrassment and penalty for a low-performing class. As a common practice in Xinjiang's public schools, teachers whose class scores the lowest average points among classes in the same grade may see a one-third deduction in their basic salary (e.g., ¥750 out of ¥3,000/ month), hence the pressure to cheat.[16]

Preferential policies in college admissions have also led to various efforts to game the system, suggesting that those policies do adversely affect student incentives. In Xinjiang, some Han or Hui students have changed their ethnic status to Uighur or Kazakh for the purpose of college admissions. Some students from interior provinces relocate to Xinjiang to benefit from the lower admission standards. These practices were serious enough to prompt Xinjiang's government to issue a special document in March 2003 in order to tighten the verification of college applicants' ethnic status and to punish students and

[16] Conversations with two public school teachers in a rural county of southern Xinjiang, fall 2013 and summer 2015.

bureaucrats involved in fraud. Still, "fake" minority members are not uncommon on Xinjiang's college campuses (Cheng 2016: 158).

The practice also occurs in multiethnic provinces where blurred boundaries make it relatively easy to register as minority members. Fierce pressure for all college applicants renders the scheme a "worthwhile" shortcut. In Chongqing, the head of the college admissions bureau in one county arranged to change his son's ethnic status from Han to Tujia in 2009 before the college application process. His son eventually scored high enough to qualify for the top college in China without the ethnic bonus points, but was disqualified after the fraud was exposed. In that year alone, a total of thirty-one officials in the city were disciplined for the same fraud. In fact, the size of the Tujia people has increased exponentially nationwide and especially in Chongqing in the reform era. From a previously unrecognized and indistinct group before the CCP's classification campaign, the Tujia is now the sixth largest minority group in China. This growth has elevated Chongqing's standing to sixth place nationwide in the share of minority population. Abuse in this regard lends further evidence for the distorting effects of preferential admission policies.

For the real minority members of Xinjiang, the educational benefits of preferential policies have been paradoxical. While there is greater access to education, this does not mean good preparation for the state's own goal: integration into the new job market.

Adverse Effects on Employment

State protection of minority students at the pre-college and college levels does not translate into their protection in the new market economy. On the contrary, minority college graduates in Xinjiang have faced a grave job market, due to expansion of higher education on the one hand and preferential admission policies on the other. Both developments, in turn, help to create new pools of job candidates with expectations and skills ill suited to the new economy.

This mismatch can be seen from myriad official data sources. Between 1998 and 2002, or the first five years after the enrollment expansion of 1997, unemployed graduates of all colleges in Xinjiang – from regular colleges to alternative programs – increased to nearly 100,000; while another 750,000 college students who had graduated since 2002 remained unemployed a decade later (Zhang 2013a). In the very year when the system of job assignments ended in Xinjiang, namely 2003, these problems were manifest. According to employment data from Xinjiang's Bureau of Education in 2003, 80.07 percent of the college graduates and 58.83 percent of the two-year college graduates in the Mandarin-speaking group were able to find an employer, but the percentages were 38.16 percent and 26.34 percent respectively for ethnic language speakers (Wang 2006: 35). Surveys by local scholars confirm the hiring gap: just 33.72 percent of surveyed minority college graduates in

TABLE 8.5 *Minority enrollment in colleges and specialized schools: 2000 and 2013*

Type of school/year	Four-year college	Two-year college	Specialized secondary school	Vocational high school	Technical school
2000	31,989	834,390	62,572	34,992	12,260
2013	116,256	956,057	86,810	53,971	26,261
% increase	263	14.6	38.7	54.2	114.2

Source: Adapted from Umuk (2016: 68).

Xinjiang found employment in 2005 (Wang 2006: 35; Qi and He 2007: 165). The big jump in four-year college enrollment, as seen in Table 8.5, prolonged the problem. After the Urumqi riot of 2009, local state drives to improve employment and integration – from expanding the civil service to increasing preschool and bilingual programs – have boosted job rates for minority college graduates. In 2010, 74.04 percent of minority college graduates in Xinjiang found jobs, and the rate exceeded 80 percent for the first time in 2012 and reached 81.14 percent in 2014. Still, the jobless rate of 18.86 percent for minority graduates doubled the rate of 9.24 percent for Han graduates in Xinjiang in 2014 (Umuk 2016: 68).

Although all minority students complain about discrimination in the labor market in various surveys, aggregate data and field conversations suggest a complex picture of skill match or mismatch in the marketplace. The overall pattern that emerges in Xinjiang is that it is easier for students who go to regular high schools and take the college entrance exams in Mandarin to find jobs than the MKH group, and easier for the MKH group to find jobs than the MKM group. The MKM graduates mostly major in the humanities in their ethnic languages, where the job market is already saturated and new opportunities are few. Perceived gaps in the academic rigor and technical skills of each group thus make a key difference. Data from Aksu Prefecture's Employment Center is illustrative. In 2003, the year when Xinjiang ended state assignment for college graduates, about 5,650 graduates registered here for job placement. Among them, 88 percent were minorities, 65 percent were female, 61 percent graduated from vocational schools, 38.6 percent graduated from two-year colleges, and 7 percent graduated from college (Li 2009a: 175). By contrast, among graduates from Xinjiang's colleges with a high concentration of Han students, such as technical and medical colleges, employment rates upon graduation were around 80 percent (Qi and He 2007: 165).

For employers in the new market economy, business interests are leading considerations in hiring, minorities included. Among their concerns are the academic preparation of students who benefited from preferential admissions, fear of ethnic tensions in the firm, past experiences with minority hires, worries about the inconvenience of Muslim customs, and not least, Mandarin proficiency. Uighur and Kazakh students agree that employer apprehension about their abilities and attitudes hurt their job prospects, while Han students' options for finding jobs in interior provinces put them at further disadvantages in job searches (Zulhayat 2009: 105). Even Uighur students who attended boarding schools and colleges in interior provinces experience difficulties in finding jobs in and out of Xinjiang in the nonstate sector (Reyilai 2013; Tohti 2014). This suggests that Mandarin proficiency per se is not the biggest hurdle, since these graduates have high proficiency here.

Indeed, a host of educational and political factors account for unemployment among Uighur college graduates. Structural factors in the education of minority students include inadequate college majors, poor training in college, poor preparation in secondary schools, reliance on the government for jobs, aversion to the private sector and temporary jobs, and poor communication skills and social networks. In a survey of minority college graduates on a Xinjiang campus in 2006, a combined 79.64 percent picked government agencies and public institutions as their top choice of place to work, while just 14.62 percent picked the private sector or other forms of employment (Qi and He 2007: 168). A decade later, in 2016, a survey of minority college graduates in the STEM field shows that while employment prospects are very good in their professional fields, the most enthusiastic preference among the students was still a civil service job (Li et al. 2017: 241). Among political factors for higher minority unemployment, "expansion and oversupply" of minority college graduates may be most important. That is, Uighur students' high expectations for government jobs are due in important part to the expansion of higher education in Xinjiang. Specialized, trade, and technical schools, which have experienced less expansion (see Table 8.5), would serve minority students better. As the oversupply of minority college graduates is not met with a corresponding expansion of the job market they desire, state policies to push more and more minority students into college have become a self-defeating effort (Renaguli et al. 2011).

Rather than emphasizing academic standards or skills, local educational agencies have responded with bilingual education programs in recent years. From the point of view of those who criticize "expansion and oversupply," this new strategy remains ill designed, since the emphasis is still on higher education rather than vocational schools. The latter would be better suited to producing a Uighur industrial class for Xinjiang's expanding partner assistance projects, where Mandarin proficiency may not be crucial.

BILINGUAL EDUCATION AS A RESPONSE

The ups and downs of Mandarin instruction in Xinjiang's ethnic schools have exemplified the centralizing dynamics of the autonomous system. During the radical years of the 1960s, ethnic and Han schools were merged to promote class universalism. In the early post-Mao era, or the late 1970s and the early

1980s, the integrated schools were separated in an effort to restore ethnic prerogatives. Integrated schools at the secondary level declined from 156 in 1981 to 44 in 1984, while ethnic schools expanded and totaled 780 in 1984. In production corps, where Han members compromised the majority, ethnic schools grew from thirty-eight in 1981 to forty-seven in 1985 at the secondary level, and 169 at the elementary level by 1985 (Li X. 2001: 23). As part of this initiative, ethnic schools ceased to teach Mandarin in the 1980s, but resumed it as a second language in the early 1990s (SEC 1995: 337, 808). The decade left an impact: the departure of Mandarin teachers and a generation of ethnic students growing up without learning any Chinese. This gap in part contributed to a Great Leap Forward strategy in bilingual education two decades later.

The restoration of ethnic schools has helped to increase the teaching of ethnic languages to minority children, but it has also had side effects. One has been the quality of education, due to a lack of well-qualified teachers and textbooks in ethnic languages. Another was the coincidence of resumed ethnic schools with the onset of economic liberalization, when Mandarin proficiency became important in the job market. Rural areas have been disproportionally affected by the problems of ethnic schools, because children of Uighur officials and professionals have been attending better schools in urban centers or in regular public schools. One county elementary school I have visited in southern Xinjiang, for example, is the only regular elementary school in the county seat. Half of the school children are Uighur, mostly offspring of the county's cadre and professional class. Finally, the shrinkage of mixed schools has reduced venues for intermingling among ethnic groups, further increasing cultural and language gulfs.

Draconian Bilingual Education

Programs to strengthen Chinese language instruction began as experiments in 2000 and were implemented in major cities in Xinjiang from 2004. That year, two models of so-called bilingual education were decreed by Xinjiang's provincial government: the *complementary* model, which treats Mandarin and an ethnic languages as parallels, and the *immersion* model, which treats Mandarin as the principal language and the ethnic language as supplementary.

The *complementary* model strikes a balance between state goals and ethnic prerogatives. It is aimed at southern and western Xinjiang where Uighurs and Kazakhs are respectively concentrated. All humanities classes (language and literature, moral education, history, geography) are taught in a minority language, while math and science classes (plus English where available) are in Mandarin. This model was implemented from 2004 in 20 percent of Xinjiang's ethnic schools. By the end of 2005, about 2.9 percent of all minority students were enrolled in this model. The program is popular with students and parents, drawn by improved chances of transferring to regular schools and for preschool children, meal subsidies, and daycare benefits (Zulhayat 2011: 9). More importantly, the model does not threaten to overwhelm the minority language. Under similar pressures of unemployment and restiveness among minority graduates, the TAR and Inner Mongolia have also sped up this model of bilingual education in their ethnic school systems.

The *immersion* model is far more one-sided. It is aimed at urban areas where Mandarin is in greater use. All subjects would be taught in Mandarin, while one ethnic language course is offered. In its 2004 plans, the stated goal of Xinjiang's provincial government was to implement this model in major cities by 2010, in cities and counties of northern and eastern Xinjiang (where the Han people are concentrated) by 2013, and in all other regions by 2016. Since 2006 the immersion model has been implemented in ethnic schools in Urumqi, Xinjiang's capital city, and subsequently in other major cities. By 2006, 114,869 or 6.6 percent of minority students in Xinjiang were enrolled in the immersion model and by 2009 the ratio increased to 13.66 percent (Zulhayat 2011: 10). This model is highly controversial as it aggressively promotes the state goal of integration and threatens to replace the ethnic language.

Staff shortage and logistical difficulties might have tempered further progress of the immersion model, but the Urumqi riots of 2009 inopportunely led authorities to assert more state intervention. A CCP Central Committee symposium on Xinjiang, held on May 17–19, 2010, led to an aggressive proposal to push the immersion model. Hu Jingtao and Wen Jiabao, the country's top party and state leaders respectively at the time, instructed that the immersion model be implemented in Xinjiang's preschools by 2012 and across ethnic schools by 2015. The emphasis on all *preschools* entailed that children would begin learning Mandarin two years before elementary school, thus adding a whole new group to Xinjiang's bilingual agenda. Hu and Wen's instructions were probably made without understanding the cultural and political implications of such an aggressive agenda, or its practical difficulties. But compliant local officials scuttled into action. The provincial government set as its new political target that all preschool children between the ages of five and six years old must enter "bilingual classes" by the end of 2010.

Thereupon responsibilities were put on the layers of local bureaucracy to implement state goals, regardless of local concerns and technical feasibility. Indicators for appraising results were established and pressure was placed on educational authorities at lower levels to achieve them. The provincial government demanded that implementation be complete by September 2010 and appraisals be given in the following month. These new demands, on top of Xinjiang's 2004 plans to implement the immersion model across all grades in ethnic schools, created tremendous pressure for staffing and logistics (Ma 2011c: 167–8). A lack of qualified Mandarin teachers and teachers competent to teach subject courses in Mandarin already plagued the complementary model in many parts of Xinjiang, especially the heavily ethnic south, which lacks a Mandarin-speaking environment. The Great Leap Forward to the immersion model would now literarily entail a complete retraining of existing teachers or simply their replacement.

In the political climate after the Urumqi riot, political goals trumped logistical practicality. Earlier, to prepare for Xinjiang's original 2004 plan for phased transition to the immersion model, full-time training for minority teachers had already been going on at a difficult pace. These teachers had been sent to prefectural capitals for training, but the programs were ineffective as they were designed to help trainees meet certification standards. Outside the classrooms, trainees still communicated with one another in ethnic tongues and lacked an environment to speak Mandarin or retain what they had learned during training. After one or two years of training, they still had difficulty teaching a class in Chinese or getting their students to understand a class taught in Chinese. Students ended up learning less in terms of the subject content and becoming frustrated with bilingual education (Li and Cai 2012: 86; Zhang M. 2009: 98). The result was to worsen rather than improve the overall quality of education.

The preschool targets of Hu Jingtao and Wen Jiabao, since mid-2010, entailed yet more challenging problems. Because most preschool programs for minority children did not have bilingual teachers at the time, teaching staff had to be pulled from elsewhere to fulfill the local governments' political goals. For example, in the southern prefectures of Aksu and Kashgar, educational authorities pulled out teachers from higher grades who were teaching subject courses in Chinese (in the complementary model) as well as Chinese-language teachers in ethnic schools (in the traditional model), placing them in kindergartens. To make up for the loss of bilingual teachers in the higher grades, the workload of the remaining teachers was increased (Ma 2011c: 167–8). In language training programs for teachers, draconian methods were used as well. Some local bureaus of education would charge an "assurance deposit." Trainees who failed their monthly evaluations would have their deposit taken away and be required to put down another one. Trainees who failed the final evaluations were required to pay part of the training costs (Ma 2009b: 57–9). Such measures were intended to motivate trainees to do well, but they caused much anxiety and resentment among the teachers.

From 2010 to 2015, more resources and hiring were invested to expand preschool bilingual programs and the immersion model, especially in the rural south. Several billions in US dollars were spent on constructing bilingual kindergartens, including 2,523 new ones in rural areas (Mao 2018). A variety of measures and incentives were used to lure bilingual teachers to the rural south, including the expansion of hiring quotas for bilingual teachers, the dispatch of teachers from outside local areas on a rotating basis, the recruitment of college students to intern as teachers, and an increase of stipends for rural teachers. By 2015, the number of bilingual teachers in Xinjiang's preschools, elementary schools, and middle schools exceeded

119,900, an increase of over 83,300 or 43 percent. Over 100,690 of these bilingual teachers are minority members, accounting for 61.09 percent of all minority teachers (over 175,000) at those three levels of schools in Xinjiang. However, as Uighur scholars and teachers concede, two major problems continue to plague bilingual education in ethnic schools (Memet and Halewjan 2018: 35–8; Memet 2018: 41–2). First, the problem of poor Mandarin for many minority teachers persists, which is more serious than before because in the immersion model they have to teach subject courses in Mandarin. Second, students in ethnically concentrated areas, where bilingual education is most urgently needed, do not have an environment in which to speak Mandarin outside the classroom.

Despite these problems, the immersion model has been brought to full fruition under Chen Quanguo's rein since August 2016. That is, its implementation across all ethnic schools and at all grade levels. According to data from the SEAC, in 2017 the "national language" became the language of instruction for 82.8 percent of all minority students – or 1.889 million – enrolled in Xinjiang's public schools. This was a 79.1 percent increase over the preceding year, when the number was 1.0547 million. By August of 2018, the ratio rose to 100 percent, that is all minority students, totaling 2.9419 million, in Xinjiang's public schools are now taught in Mandarin in all subjects (SEAC 2018). An ethnic language is offered and mandated for minority students, as the immersion model originally entails. To ensure that this course would not be sidelined, students enrolled in the immersion model are required to take the ethnic language test as part of their high-school admission and graduation tests, as well as their college entrance exams (Mao 2018). Despite these measures in defense of ethnic languages, the pressure of integration is clear in Xinjiang's accelerated transition to the immersion model. By comparison, although over 96 percent of public school students receive bilingual education in Tibet, the complimentary model remains in use (SEAC 2018).

With the spread of the immersion model in Xinjiang, the reality of bilingual education creates more intimate threats than cultural marginalization. Among Uighur teachers, silent bitterness is driven as much by resistance to cultural assimilation as by intense resentment at the draconian methods of implementation.

Bilingual Education and Its Discontents

Among Uighur cultural and intellectual elites, a key source of anxiety about the immersion model is the replacement of the ethnic language by a "transition" to the Chinese language. The complimentary model does not cause such anxiety because it aims to preserve the ethnic language. Although the immersion model may have the lofty goal of better integrating Uighurs and enhancing their job prospects, the tensions between the demands of integration and ethnic prerogatives are not easily reconciled.

For those who worry about the waning of the Uighur tongue, the immersion model is misguided because a lack of Mandarin proficiency is not the reason for Uighur students' underachievement. Thus the benefits of bilingual education may not outweigh the costs. Citing the consistent poor performance of the MKH group (minorities whose native tongue is Chinese and who go to regular schools), Zulhayat argues candidly, it is preferential policies that deprive minority students of the incentive to work hard and compete with their Han peers. For this Uighur scholar, who is among the most pro-modernization among Uighur intellectuals, Uighurs have a legitimate and genuine concern about the potential adverse effects on ethnic children's cultural values and identity (2009: 93, 111–16). Thus she only cautiously supports the state's new bilingual program. Tohti (2014) is more skeptical, arguing that the state promotion of bilingual education is viewed in Uighur communities as monolingual education, amounting to accelerated and forced assimilation by political methods and potentially the elimination of the Uighur people culturally. Worries about cultural assimilation and language extinction were also frequent topics on the website that Tohti founded, Urghurbiz.com. These worries are reinforced by frequent Chinese obliviousness to those concerns. During one of my visits to a local college in southern Xinjiang, Chinese-language teachers expressed genuine bewilderment that Uighur faculty members would subtly discourage Uighur students from learning Chinese. To them, any opportunity to improve skills and increase learning is a positive thing: good for individuals and society. This lack of empathy to see the other side's point of view only adds to Uighur resentment. If "subtle discouragement" was the sentiment in the early 2010s, one can only imagine Uighur faculty's bitterness in the late 2010s when the immersion model was implemented much more aggressively.

Another contentious point is the local governments' campaign-style approach to bilingual education, a reflection of the centralizing dynamics of the autonomous system. In their zeal to get fast results, local officials give out extreme commands that distort the meaning of bilingual education and make teaching impossible. One Uighur teacher in a village school complained about such a Uighur official from the local educational bureau, who sternly told teachers at a meeting: "pre-school bilingual education means teaching Chinese; not one lesson of the ethnic tongue can be taught and not one word of it can be uttered!" This made any teaching impossible for her, since her preschool pupils did not understand a word of Chinese while she was not supposed to say a word of Uighur. The result was that the children could learn neither Chinese nor Uighur. Another Uighur teacher complained about similar distortions at an Ili middle school. While she agreed with the benefit of bilingual education, she found that the program became monolingual since she was not supposed to use Uighur in the classroom (Zhang M. 2009: 98). Such problems appear to vary with local bureaucracies and schools, but they especially affect preschools' bilingual programs, since their main purpose is to introduce ethnic children to Mandarin.

The one-sidedness in bilingual education embodies the centralizing dynamics of the autonomous system at its worst. Despite its two-way implication, the intensified push for bilingual education is intended for minority students to learn Chinese, not for Mandarin speakers to learn a local ethnic language. Though this one-way direction is driven by practical considerations, it fails even the utilitarian test. In southern Xinjiang, where Uighurs comprise over 80 percent of the local population, it makes more sense for the numerically smaller Chinese group to learn Uighur and even use Uighur as the official language. But researchers' suggestions for optional classes in ethnic languages for Han students are frequently brushed aside by local educational authorities, who are only concerned with answering the latest calls from Beijing. The Uighur or Kazakh tongues also have wider utility in Central and West Asia, which would help tremendously in China's "Belt and Road" venture. The new Silk Road project, indeed, is among the dynamics that have driven two prefectures, Ili and Kashgar, strategically situated as gateways to Central Asia, to experiment with ethnic language offerings in regular schools. Here Han students may take it as an elective, while it is a requirement for minority students (Mao 2018).

Covert or blatant pragmatism is undoubtedly another problem that condones centralized diffusion and undermines ethnic autonomy. In my field experiences in southern Xinjiang, the perception that languages in small circulation are useless has led many Han Chinese to underappreciate the seriousness of Uighur anxieties. The generations of locally born Han Chinese in the post-Mao period mostly do not bother to learn Uighur, dismissing it as useless. Schoolteachers sometimes betrayed their dismissive attitude by referring to "backward languages." Among Han bilingual teachers, some have majored in Uighur in college, but their spoken Uighur is usually worse than the Mandarin of their Uighur colleagues, since they do not bother to practice. Among (non-Uighur) minority intellectuals whose native tongue is Chinese, there tends to be support for the utility of languages in wide national and international circulation, in other words Mandarin and English. When asked if they would want to learn three languages – that is, an ethnic tongue, Mandarin, and English – they seem to have not thought about the question, yet they expect those with "useless" mother tongues to do so.

The inland boarding school program has also fallen victim to draconian bilingual education. Established in 2000 for Xinjiang, the program sends selective MKH students to top-tier high schools in inland Chinese cities. These cities and Xinjiang's government share the bulk of the student's expenses, while the families shoulder the rest. After one year of remedial courses in Chinese, English, math, and science in their inland schools, a Xinjiang class follows the regular curricula and takes all classes in Chinese. Graduates take the national college entrance exam in Chinese. Qualifying scores and admission quotas are separately established for this group, namely, separate from the Chinese students in their inland schools and from ethnic students back in Xinjiang. That is, the cut-off points for college admissions for this group are lower than their Han counterparts in interior provinces but higher than their ethnic peers at home. With 1,000 students in the first year of the program in 2000 (out of 20,000 applicants), enrollment grew annually to 36,000 by 2010. However, in another example of a draconian approach, Xinjiang's Bureau of Education assigns admission targets to local middle schools and uses success rates to evaluate their performance. Schools with a low number of students who qualify for inland school admissions would be levied a financial penalty.[17]

Such interventionist approaches only aggravate Uighur anxiety about the impact of the program. The perceived taking of Uighurs' best and brightest young minds to interior provinces for training has created qualms among Uighur intellectuals and parents about cultural erosion. Some view those students as "a stolen generation," worrying that their immersion in interior cities will make them gradually forget their ethnic culture or even identity. One graduate of such a class confessed to having been vigilant about the program, despite personal improvement in professional competence (Reyilai 2013).

Alternative Models

Needless to say, the draconian approach to bilingual education in Xinjiang represents the worst of the institutional tensions of the autonomous system. That is, centralization but ethnicization: the state's approach is highly centralizing, while the purported goal is to increase job access and economic integration for Uighur students. In ethnic regions where radicalism and violence are not paramount threats, those institutional tensions can be mitigated by more leeway for local decision making.

In ethnic regions where local receptivity to bilingual education is high and coercion is low, bilingual education has proceeded much more successfully. After all, resource allocation alone would be a strong incentive to embrace the program. In the Yanbian Korean Prefecture, absence of central intervention has allowed local educators to come up with their methods and textbooks. Ethnic public schools for Korean Chinese, especially those based in Korean-concentrated areas, use the ethnic immersion model. That is, subject courses are taught in Korean, with Chinese and English as language courses usually taught by Mandarin-speaking teachers. In urban Yanbian, these schools can be so well run that some Han parents regularly choose to send their children there. The leading primary school in Yanbian is one of the top ten schools in the entire country. Its curricula and campus layout proudly teach and celebrate different aspects of Korean culture in a way that is inconceivable in Xinjiang. The school maintains a waiting list for Han applicants and Han students comprise about

[17] Conversations with four local teachers of a rural county, southern Xinjiang, summer 2015.

4–5 percent of the student body.[18] In Tibetan regions of Qinghai and Gansu provinces, local educational authorities and schools are allowed to pick the models of instruction most appropriate for local conditions, which range from student choices and faculty resources to local vernacular conventions (Ge 2011: 72). Local authorities in Qinghai have also responded accommodatingly to Tibetan students' protests against the Mandarin immersion model.

Practical utility is another incentive often ignored by authorities in their push for bilingual education in Xinjiang. In ethnic regions where bilingual skills are in need, minority groups are motivated to choose bilingual education or even monolingual education on their own. In Yanbian's case, a high presence of Chinese residents within the prefecture – 59.29 percent Hans versus 37.7 percent Koreans (2010 census) – entails a linguistic milieu that uses Chinese as a convenient and necessary means of communication. In the same way, some Han parents choose Korean ethnic schools for their children because they feel that proficiency in the Korean language will give their children more academic and career options in the future. Even within Xinjiang, Uighur parents who are professionals and urbanites routinely send their children to regular schools and boarding schools in interior provinces. In Chengdu, the closest metropolis for the Tibetan regions of western Sichuan and the TAR, many resourceful Tibetans come to buy residential properties so that their children can attend local schools for a better education.[19]

By the same token, for outer peripheral regions where Uighurs and Tibetans are concentrated, the impracticality of learning Chinese raises serious issues about the state's push for Mandarin proficiency, especially through the immersion model. In a study by Padma Thundrup, director of Qinghai's Center for Religious Affairs, bilingual education is found to be feasible in urban areas of Qinghai but remains a daunting challenge in rural and pastoral areas, due to logistic difficulties that are worse than those in southern Xinjiang. Foremost is a shortage of teachers who are conversant in both Chinese and Tibetan and capable of teaching math and science or competent to teach Mandarin. Unlike Xinjiang, where the central government spends generously on bilingual programs, many localities in Qinghai have no resources to retrain their teaching staff. With students scattered around vast mountain regions, it is difficult to establish schools of scale or to attract teachers willing to stay (Thundrup 2012). In this context, it makes little sense to implement universal bilingual programs, when 98 percent of the local population is Tibetan in many counties.

The points raised above challenge the state's expansion of education in outer peripheral regions. The central state promotes education – bilingual education included – as a means to professional development and national integration, but

[18] Field visits to several Korean schools in Yanbian, including this school, in fall 2013.

[19] Field observations in Wuhouci area of Chengdu, where Tibetan settlers congregate. July 2017 and 2018.

the end results may not always serve the local communities in a way that genuine autonomy may require. One problem is the weakening of the native language for ethnic students who focus on a Chinese-medium education. Another is the lack of jobs for graduates who pursue majors in ethnic mediums. As Adrian Zenz (2013) has shown, Tibetans view the market economy as the greatest threat to their ethno-cultural survival, as the young generation are lured into Chinese-medium education by better career prospects while Tibetan-medium graduates face dire employment prospects. This problem, Thundrup (2012) suggests, implies that the state's goal of education should be shifted. Instead of means to career advancement, education may also be treated as a means to personal and intellectual enrichment. Over the past three decades the state has been trying to draw out waves of ethnic youths from pastoral and rural regions to modern education. It would make more sense to draw them back to renovate and diversify the pastoral or rural economy. In other words, the central drive in expanding education may not always be feasible for the outer peripheral regions.

In this context, it is little wonder that in southern Xinjiang, many rural parents find public school to be "useless" for their children, since it is hard for them to find desired jobs despite their education. To these parents, learning the Koran is at least better for the children's upbringing. In many rural areas in the south, the job of the school principal and teachers in the morning is simply to go to the children's homes and bring them to school. In one case encountered by a Hong Kong-based reporter, a school principal was beaten up by a parent, with scratches all over his face and a big cut on his ear. The parent felt that a certificate of graduation from the public school is "un-Muslim" and useless (Zhang C. 2014). Outside the gates of some public elementary schools, public notices used to be posted warning parents not to withdraw their children on false pretexts, referring to the sending of children to underground madrassas. For the secularly and achievement-oriented Han people, such parental behavior is beyond comprehension. When a local Han resident told me similar stories of obstructive Uighur parents, he angrily uttered, "[W]e treat them too well! Our policies are too lenient!" He cared little about what the local parents thought or wanted, and would in any event have dismissed their thinking as "backward." In recent years, the increase of "work-in-residence" teams in the rural south has added to state power to ensure public education, by making it a routine practice to go to villagers' homes in the morning to make sure their school-age children go to school that day.

The Cost of Low Autonomy

Additional consequences ensue from the state's heavy hand in promoting bilingual education in Xinjiang. As in the economic arena, it forces the state to take on more responsibilities in order to solve the problems created by itself. That is, bilingual education will increase young Uighurs' expectation about employment. However, if this expectation is not met in the real world, they are likely to feel doubly frustrated about the state's draconian drive.

In both Xinjiang and the TAR, local governments have taken up the task of finding jobs for minority members. In Xinjiang, local governments have tried to create "public welfare jobs," such as providing loans for entrepreneurship, offering incentives for companies to hire minorities, contracting firms in coastal provinces to hire minorities, or sending graduates for professional training and internship (Li 2012a: 26). In the two years from 2012 to 2013, Xinjiang's government agencies hired more Uighurs than in the ten years combined prior to the Urumqi riots of 2009. Downsized workers who had waited over a decade for retirement benefits have now received them. Efforts have also been made to provide employment to at least one adult child for each household. According to a local Uighur, once his unemployed relatives were provided with jobs, they became hopeful about their future, making plans to get married and buy housing, and most of all, they stay away from illicit activities (Yao 2014b). Since Chen Quanguo's arrival in Xinjiang in August 2016, Xinjiang has moved into full gear to create jobs not only for minority college graduates but even Uighur villagers, through government hiring and partner assistance programs.

In the TAR, the local government has also undertaken elaborate efforts to provide employment after the Lhasa riots of 2008. The region has adopted a policy of guaranteeing employment for at least one adult child in each Tibetan household, so as to provide stabilizing and exemplary effects in the family. The local government encourages college graduates to work for medium and small companies by offering financial incentives: it pays back college tuition and loans for those who work for such companies for five years or more; it pays a stipend to those who accepts employment in nonstate firms; it expends travel expenses (¥1,000) and a monthly stipend (¥300) for those who take up employment outside the TAR; and it requires partner assistance projects to hire a certain number of TAR college graduates. With these measures, the TAR managed to have an 84 percent employment rate for its college graduates between 2006 and 2010 (*Xizang ribao* 2012).

After Chen Quanguo assumed power in the TAR in 2011, he reintroduced the policy of guaranteed job assignment for college students of TAR residency and Tibetan descent. This resulted in full employment for these students during his tenure in the TAR, from 2012 to mid-2016. Huge state subsidies and a small population made the various job incentives possible in the TAR. There were 16,600 college students in 2011 in the TAR, compared with Xinjiang's 70,000 that year (*Xinhua* 2012; *Xinjiang ribao* 2011). In other words, stability in the two sensitive regions is going to be bought whatever the costs, but state intervention itself will not yield. Nevertheless, job guarantees for Tibetan college students ended after Chen's departure, signifying that the policy is not sustainable. This puts into question how long Chen's bilingual education and full employment drive will be sustainable in Xinjiang.

Ultimately, the grave tensions between centralization and ethnicization, as manifested in Xinjiang's bilingual programs, demonstrate a dearth of autonomy, particularly in ethnic regions, that pose threats to political integration. This dearth is devastating because its impact is perceived to threaten the ethno-national survival of a distinct cultural community. The scenario is similar to, yet even more serious than, a case that has become emblematic of the problem of missing autonomy: the reconstruction of Kashgar's old town. Here authorities demolished the historical Uighur town to reconstruct a modern replica, causing much controversy over the destruction of a traditional Islamic city. In bilingual education, as in the Kashgar case, local governments failed to consult with local Uighur communities. Plans were devised and imposed from the top down. Uighur resentment over damages to their traditional culture is thus unsurprising. In the Kashgar case, at least there were justifications for reconstruction, such as a lack of safety, sanitation, and water supply in the old architectural structures. The local state did also take steps to negotiate with former residents about compensation, and their evacuation proceeded with more civility than in Han regions. In China's context, the negotiations already seemed "democratic" enough.

However, there was no genuine autonomy for native Uighurs in decision making over bilingual education or Kashgar's urban reconstruction. In the latter case, negotiations with local residents took place after decisions about reconstruction had already been made (Yao 2009). Local communities did not really have a choice over *whether* the reconstruction should proceed, but only what arrangements they would have after their relocation.

SUMMARY

In this chapter I look at why policies for education and language have increased ethnic tensions in the reform era, drawing largely on Xinjiang's case. Rather than emphasizing tensions caused by state assimilation and ethnic nationalism, I treat these tensions as integral to the institutional dynamics of the autonomous system: the central imperatives of integration and development determine educational priorities and strategies, while the ethnic prerogatives of preferential policies undermine those state goals.

This chapter shows that the tensions between those central imperatives and ethnic prerogatives are heightened by the new market economy. The state can no longer align central imperatives with ethnic prerogatives in terms of job guarantees, when the market favors competitive skills and disadvantages minority students. A combination of state policies – expanded higher education, market reforms, preferential admissions, and bilingual programs – have created educational patterns that heighten ethnic grievances at the expense of integration. Driven by the paradigms of development and integration, the state has been oblivious to these problems. Instead of adjusting its paradigms, the state simply intensifies its policy mechanisms to further enhance them. My analysis in the chapter shows the dubious role of the state and of its policy designs. It is the state's self-avowed good intentions to promote its developmental and egalitarian drive that have justified its heavy intervention in minority education. Preferential admission policies, while aimed at lifting minorities, fail to consider the variety of educational needs and the fitness of educational programs for different student types, experiences, and cultural backgrounds. The modernizing, secularizing, and integrative role of public education is assumed, even while this is not always backed by realities in culturally and linguistically distinct outer peripheral regions.

As shown in Xinjiang's case, the adverse effects of the state's educational and language policies have a socially volatile side. Minority students nurtured by preferential admissions are enraged by a lack of desired employment. Parents impoverished by college tuition are angered by a lack of expected returns. Teachers accustomed to set ways of instruction are pressured to improve in subjects or language where they are weak. A draconian bilingual program has been imposed overnight on ethnic children. That the Chinese language seems to be the cause of all this trouble provides a strong emotional rallying point.

CONCLUSION

From Empire to Nation State: Lessons and Reforms

In concluding, this chapter will draw together the findings and implications from this study. First, it will weigh the feats and faults of the autonomous system in achieving the transition to the nation state for China. Second, it will assess proposals and prospects for improving China's nation state building. Finally, the chapter will consider the implications of ethnic issues for a rising China.

SOCIALIST AUTONOMY AND TRANSITION TO NATION STATE

Has socialist autonomy allowed the Middle Kingdom to make a successful transition from empire to nation state? The official Chinese view is a definitive but not entirely confident yes: China has found the solution in the autonomous system. The findings from this study present a more complicated picture.

The socialist system of autonomy did help China to largely inherit the territorial boundaries of the last imperial dynasty and avoided secessionist wars during the transition to a modern nation state. This was a significant achievement. Although China's imperial system differed from the global expansion of empire in the nineteenth century, its disintegration was spurred by the same forces that impelled the spread of the nation state during the twentieth century. That is, modern nationalism, or the idea that states should be governed by a nationally defined people. As Wimmer and Min argue, insofar as the nationalist doctrine triggers competing projects of state building, the transition from empire to nation state has often been associated with secessionist civil war or internal strife against political exclusion by subordinated ethnic groups (2006: 874–7). In other words, the global spread of and transformation to the nation state is itself a major cause of war.

The macrohistorical dynamics of nation state formation have applied to the Chinese case as well. There were secessionist moves in China's outer peripheries in the first half of the twentieth century, namely Mongolia, Tibet, and Xinjiang. To the extent that China avoided secessionist wars and saw just one region break away (Outer Mongolia), the socialist system of ethnic autonomy can be seen as successful. In fact, if we count India as a civilization whose princely states were united as a multination state only in colonial times, China would be the only ancient empire that has made the transition to a (multi)nation state, notwithstanding periodic strains in the two outer peripheral regions.

At the same time, having "inherited" imperial domains does not mean that China will automatically hold them forever. What happened in the USSR after 1991 is an acute reminder of this. Moreover, because of the large demographic/territorial core that China has also inherited, holding the two outer peripheral regions for now – at extremely high costs – cannot be considered a complete success or perhaps even a success at all.[1] Furthermore, China's transition to a modern state was contingent upon a few contextual factors, which by definition are not constant. Those contextual factors are reviewed in Chapters 1–3. The first was the presence of external invasions, which threatened the territorial integrity of the heartland as well as the hinterland, forcing ethnic elites to choose loyalties and alliances. The co-optation of native elites by the Republican regimes temporarily secured key alliances, at the expense of alienating the oppressed ethnic masses. The second contextual factor was the CCP's universalizing ideology and strategy of class struggle, which helped to rally ethnic masses against their co-ethnic oppressors as well as Han rulers and foreign invaders. The third contextual factor was the socialist redistributive state, which delivered for the ethnic proletariat and created new ethnic elites allegiant to the state. In addition, the socialist economy mediated the longstanding ecological rivalry between agrarian and nomadic societies, bringing modern professionals and projects to the pre-modern hinterland while sending natural resources to the industrial heartland, finally rendering the core and peripheral regions complimentary.

However, as a strategy necessitated by revolutionary and wartime experiences, socialist autonomy did not necessarily provide a long-term stable or optimal response to the macroinstitutional transition to the (multi)nation state. As the socialist state retreated and resource battles heat up in the post-Mao era, the nation state has been put under serious strains by challenges from the outer peripheral regions.

Incomplete Transition

Why have ethnic mobilization and violence occurred only in the outer peripheral regions? This study suggests that the system of autonomous regions, with its one-size-fits-all institutional order, has done a tenuous job of incorporating the two outer peripheral regions. The institutional dynamics or built-in tensions of the system, I have shown, have combined with

[1] I thank Professor Dingxin Zhao for suggesting these points.

changing contextual factors to foster discontents and destabilizing factors. In other words, China's transition to the nation state, on a deep level, is incomplete.

First, in terms of institutional dynamics, the autonomous system has attempted to achieve national integration and ethnic incorporation, *not through mechanisms of political autonomy*, but through a mix of centralization and ethnicization. The former entails a uniform system of ethnic governance under the centralized party leadership, while the latter entails institutionalized ethnic and geographical markers supplemented by policy benefits. This institutional order makes ethnicity politically relevant by grounding political identity, state administration, and policy benefits on the ethnic criterion. The inherent tensions therein – between reduced political autonomy but enhanced centralization and politicized identities – were mitigated during the Mao era by class politics, but they have since been intensified by the state's sponsorship as well as suppression of identity politics in the post-Mao era.

The institutional dynamics of centralization and ethnicization, triggered by as well as resulting from state policies, are particularly conducive to ethnic tensions and conflict in the outer peripheral regions. The dynamics of centralization particularly conducive to ethnic tensions include those that threaten ascriptive features of ethnic groups and impose their transformation, such as religion and language; those that impose transformation of pre-modern and agrarian or egalitarian societies into secular, urban, and competitive ones, such as economic modernization and economic liberalization; and those that marginalize minority representation and participation, such as the centralized political system. Conversely, the institutional dynamics of ethnicization particularly conducive to ethnic tensions in the outer peripheral regions include those that facilitate or constrain identity expression, such as state sponsorship or suppression of cultural expression and ethnic conventions; those that foster ethnic prerogatives, such as ethnically based policy benefits; and those that result in socioeconomic marginalization, such as developmental drives.

The dynamics of centralization and ethnicization have affected the outer peripheral regions in particular, thanks to a mix of historical and contemporary factors. Above all, these regions had very different historical relations with the heartland, yet the autonomous system treats all culturally distinct groups as "ethno-nations," regardless of those historical differences, alternatively exaggerating or understating ethnic differences. In either case, potential for ethnic mobilization is elevated by the state's overaccommodation or underaccommodation of disparate ethnic communities. That is, overaccommodation of those in the inner peripheries (through cultural tools and policy benefits) but underaccommodation of the outer peripheral regions (insufficiency of self-governing rights).

At the same time, because of their greater centrifugal tendencies, resource allocation and state intervention are far more intensive in the outer peripheral regions. This ironically involves the state directly and principally as the culprit for their contemporary woes. When underaccommodation of political rights combines with greater barriers to participation in the modern economy, ethnic mobilization materializes. In other words, although politicized identity and the lack of political autonomy are constant in all autonomous regions, variance in the type of ethnic regions and the substance of government policies make a difference to how the institutional dynamics of socialist autonomy play out at the local level. Only in the two outer peripheral regions, again, do ascriptive features amount to key barriers to market participation and has inland migration induced serious ethnic conflict.

Second, the demise of the universalizing class ideology has deprived the central state of the institutional principles of legitimate government to project universal legitimacy among its multiple ethno-nations. This affects the outer peripheral regions in particular, because their fragile historical and cultural affinity with the heartland had entailed that social class solidarity played a crucial role in their integration with the new nation state. A breakdown of the redistributive state, which was based on social class solidarity, further undermines the social foundation of ethnic support for the central state. That is, when economic reforms transformed the rules and norms by which economic resources were allocated, the old "social contract" between the state and ethnic members also broke down. Under market transition and the western development drive, the forces of national and global integration threaten as well as marginalize the ascriptive endowments (ethnic language and culture) formally protected by the autonomous system, which are acute issues in the two outer peripheral regions. Whereas previously minorities were equal members of the proletarian class, now they are the primary victims of a new developmental ideology. In other words, the working classes in minority regions have had the most to lose during the reform era, costing the state its most important allies that were critical to its legitimate rule in sensitive minority regions.

The situation is worsened by a critical generational shift. Minority youths born after the late 1970s, when the reform era began, have experienced drastically different formative years than their precursors. Instead of the political and economic liberation experienced by their parents and grandparents, and the collective communes and state jobs that provided for them, minority youths with distinct ascriptive features now face frustration in finding employment. For these ethnic youths left behind by market reforms, they may find recourse in the monasteries and madrassas or on the streets. Either way they can be easily susceptible to the rhetoric of ethnic finger pointing, rendering social discontent seemingly driven by ethnic divisions. This problem is especially true of Tibetan and Uighur youths because of greater linguistic, cultural, and educational barriers to competing in the market economy. In other words, ethnic members who have grown up in the reform era do not have the reference frames of their older co-ethnics to feel "grateful" to the state or allegiant to it.

Third, socialist autonomy has created ethnically distinct political elites, especially in the titular groups. Those elites, Philip Roeder (1998) argues based on the Soviet case, were accountable to central authorities but also controlled access to scarce public goods, such as education, economic resources, and entrance to coveted professions. These benefits facilitate what Roeder calls the creation of "ethnic machines," along with entrenched interests and state dependency. Although ethnic elites may be accountable to the state, the ethnic machines, privileges, and dependency make it difficult for the state to alter local practices and incentives. "It was in this way that ethnicity became politically relevant; titular ethnic groups came to believe that they had unique political rights and unique access to resources distributed in the political arena" (Crawford and Lipschutz 1998: 523).

In the Chinese case, "ethnic machines" have enhanced identity politics among ethnic elites in general, but intensity varies with politically sensitive and nonsensitive groups, or outer versus inner peripheral ones. Overall the shaping of one's life chances and opportunities along ethnic lines does lead to the sustenance of ethic elites for whom "autonomy" means the political and economic distribution of public goods for their own group. For politically nonsensitive groups, this orientation helps to weaken or neutralize political demands, because those public goods render political demands secondary or superfluous. For the politically sensitive groups, however, "carrots" alone may not be insufficient to neutralize autonomy demands, because the political price to pay is an acceptance of the state prerogatives of political centralization and integration, which undermine ethnic expression at best and ethnic survival at worst. This is particularly the case for the Uighurs. Indeed, at academic forums in China it is routine to hear a bifurcation of ethnic elites (*jingying*) and ethnic commoners. The former is keen on emphasizing ethnic distinctions and identities, while the latter is mainly interested in everyday livelihood. To the extent that ethnic elites play a far greater role in representing ethnic interests and opinions, they reinforce the "ethnic machines" created by the state itself, along with entrenched interests and identity politics.

Finally, China's massive modernization and developmental drive has turned the longstanding ecological rivalry between the heartland and the hinterland upside down. Reversing the historical trend, the hinterland has now become the reservoir of resources and developmental frontiers sought and predated upon by the needy heartland. The onslaught of encroachment into resource-rich peripheries by state firms, enterprising businesses, and migrants from the heartland, feeds a dynamic of ethnic exclusion that undermines ethnic autonomy in those regions, thus inciting ethnic mobilization.

In short, while a trade-off between autonomy and preferential policies may be acceptable in the inner peripheral regions, it may not be so easy in outer peripheral regions where historically central–peripheral relations were weak and cultural distances significant. These dynamics are even at play in Beijing's relations with Hong Kong and Taiwan, two culturally Chinese territories that have yet to politically integrate with mainland China. Despite ample economic inducements offered by the mainland, a majority of people in those two territories seem unwilling to make concessions on autonomy and identity. Through Hong Kong's anti-extradition protests in 2019 and Taiwan's Sunflower Movement in 2014, the young people of these two regions protested vehemently against greater integration with the mainland. The road to China's self-image of a complete nation state remains arduous.

Whether Stability

Chinese concerns for national integration, even state dissolution, have been heightened by the collapse of the Soviet-type ethno-federations in the post-socialist world. Chinese academic books and articles abound that draw lessons from the Soviet and Yugoslav cases.

The most concerned analysis is offered by Ma Rong (2011a), the Hui scholar at Beijing University. In answering a question posed by himself – "Is China vulnerable to separatism in the 21st century?" – Ma argues that the autonomous system has nurtured all the institutional conditions for separatism: construction of national identities, ethnically based territorial units, and ethnic elites as representatives of particularistic group interests. These factors have become ideological and political foundations for politicizing socioeconomic and cultural issues in ethnic regions, he argues, leading to ethnically mobilized discourse and violence. Politicized ethnic discontent, in turn, causes overvigilance and distorted reaction on the part of the state, delaying proper solutions to everyday problems and feeding a vicious cycle that breeds separatism. In other words, the emphasis here is on the institutionalization of minority prerogatives that has politicized identities and threatened national integration.

The alternative view blames the weakening of the state apparatus for the disintegration of the Soviet system. Barry Sautman dismisses Ma's argument as a misconception of ethno-federalism's role. "The notion that it necessarily leads to state dissolution is based on the *post hoc propter hoc* fallacy that separatist movements arose, several ethno-federalist states dissolved, and therefore separatist movements caused the dissolutions." The Soviet Union fell apart, Sautman argues, "mainly because its government was already severely weakened by central political decisions not directly connected with ethnic mobilization" (2010: 91–2).

Other factors that contributed to the dissolution of ethno-federal systems may be conceived of as "sufficient conditions." These include core ethnic regions (i.e., regions with ethnic majorities) (Hale 2004), the weakening of institutions that upheld previous social contracts (Crawford and Lipschutz 1998), and democratization (Mansfield and Synder 1995; Synder 2000). Of these three conditions, the first two have been present in China while the third is not yet. The first condition, "core ethnic regions," favors China at first glance. It has just one such region, the TAR, with over 92 percent of Tibetans. But China has a dozen of ethnic majority regions at the prefectural level. Among these, Uighur-majority prefectures include Hotan (97 percent), Kashgar (90 percent), Aksu (72 percent), Turpan (70 percent), and Kizilsu Kirghiz (64 percent). Of these, not surprisingly, Hotan and Kashgar have been most restive. Outside the TAR, Tibetan-majority prefectures include Yushu (97 percent), Golog (91 percent), Garzê (78 percent), Huangnan (66 percent), Hainan (62 percent), Ngawa (54 percent), and Gannan (51 percent). However, these Tibetan prefectures are located in areas that had broken off from Lhasa's rule from the ninth century, so separatism per se is relatively weak. Beijing has another important advantage in the Tibetan case: its Tibetan cadre tends to find the exile government a challenge to their authority and hence has vested interests in maintaining the status quo. Nevertheless, strengthened by the state's own creation of a homogenized identity and frustrated by its political and religious restrictions, ethnic agitation is conceivable without the Tibetan cadre, especially in the age of social media. The second sufficient condition for the dissolution of ethno-federalism, namely the demise of the social contract of the socialist era, has been present in the post-Mao era and played a major role in brewing ethnic unrest.

Only the third condition, democratization, is missing in China's case. This means that China's authoritarian system plays a critical role in holding the multinational state together. The ubiquitous patrol vehicles and squads on the streets of Xinjiang's urban centers, especially in the south, easily remind one how stability is being achieved. It does not conversely mean, of course, that democratization will necessarily lead to state dissolution of the Soviet kind. Realistically, the nationalistic bent and demographic weight of China's majority population will make such a scenario difficult. As Wang Lixiong (2006) notes, the bottom line of the Han majority is that there will be no independence, and improved forms of autonomy are preferable to bloodshed.

Indeed, the small demographic weight of the sensitive regions almost precludes state dissolution in China's case. Together the population of Tibet and Xinjiang comprises just 2 percent of the Chinese population nationwide, or a mere 1 percent if only the titular groups are counted. This demographic context made China the only pre-modern empire that was able to retain most parts of its territory in the transition from empire to modern nation state and allowed the central government (both Republican and Communist China) to never take serious measures to construct a pan-Chinese identity until recently. China's demographic context has also made the currently expensive money transfers to the two minority regions still affordable, and leaves them with very slim chances for independence.[2] Nevertheless, the fact that the two

[2] I thank Professor Zhao for raising the points in the last sentence of this paragraph.

regions continue to induce much anxiety and attention on the part of the state suggests an as yet incomplete transition to nation state in China's case. Any meaningful integration will require more than money transfers.

REFORMING THE SYSTEM

In debating reforms, China's three contending schools – liberal autonomists, integrationists, and socialist autonomists – have shown a basic agreement about the current system of ethnic autonomy. That is, autonomy remains defined in terms of what the state wants: substantive rights in development and distribution, rather than procedural rights in political choices and decision-making powers. The nominally procedural rights granted at local levels – by way of local legislative power – are still designed to protect the type of substantive rights defined by the state. These rights – largely developmental and distributional – are intended to serve rather than challenge the central imperatives of interethnic parity and national integration.

The simultaneously constraining but indulgent nature of the current system gives rise to the institutional tensions of the autonomous system. Given these contradictions, it is unsurprising that reform proposals have been at odds as to what should be done. The three contending schools disagree on the conception and delivery of autonomy as well as its consequences. The liberal autonomists castigate it for lacking political rights, yet without repudiating the ethnic prerogatives in the official version of autonomy. The integrationists criticize it for politicizing ethnic identity, yet without rejecting the institutional limits on political autonomy. The prevailing minority opinion tolerates the trade-off between political autonomy and ethnic prerogatives, though it is less than fully content with the current implementation of socialist autonomy. Reform proposals, thus, offer diverse or even contrary remedies. The liberal autonomists seek more ethnic rights in policy making and cultural spheres. The integrationists want to reduce ethnic prerogatives and replace the autonomous system with the regular provincial system. The socialist autonomists prefer to preserve and improve the current system.

These competing reform proposals have had some meaningful impact on public policy and discourse. In the first few years after the Lhasa riots of 2008 and the Urumqi riots of 2009, a heightened political climate allowed the integrationist discourse to dominate in popular, media, and policy forums. Ma Rong was a frequent presence at major pundit forums and his calls for enhancing bilingual education in Xinjiang helped contribute to an acceleration of bilingual programs in local schools during 2010 and 2011. Between 2010 and early 2014, Hu Angang and Zhu Weiqun, two leading integrationists of the statist variant, published widely noted articles promoting a new generation of ethnic policy. Together, they call for weakening or ending the three pillars of the autonomous system: political fixity of ethnic identities, territorialized ethnic governance, and ethnically based allocation of policy benefits (Ma 2011a, 2013a; Hu and Hu 2010, 2011; Zhu 2012 and 2015). In their stead, they advocate regional criteria and citizenship rights that are ethnically neutral. Writing in 2013, James Leibold senses an emerging consensus for reform in the direction of strengthening national integration and promoting ethnic assimilation, although he does not see radical policy change as likely.

However, the momentum of the integrationists caused a major backlash among the socialist autonomists. Strongly opposed to the integrationists, the socialist autonomists launched robust counteroffensives during 2012–14, organizing symposiums and publishing high-profile articles to rebut them (Hao 2012; Pei 2012). In response to the nationalistic high ground of the integrationists, socialist autonomists appeal to the party's ideological platform: "socialism with Chinese characteristics." Socialist norms should continue to define redistributive policy on ethnic grounds, they argue, and more importantly, to justify state protection of minority members from the onslaught of the market economy. They also attack the "melting" consequences of integrationist policies and criticize convergence as Darwinist. At the same time, even while they continue to emphasize the developmental needs of ethnic groups, socialist autonomists say nothing about greater autonomy in terms of self-governance. For layers of the state apparatus in charge of ethnic affairs or studying the subject, it is bureaucratically rational to remain socialist autonomists and politically expedient to toe the ideologically correct line. Granted, some are genuinely devoted to the idea of ethnic equality and national integration through socialist autonomy, but others are privately sympathetic to the liberal autonomists. Ethnic elites worry less about proposals for turning autonomous regions into regular provinces, since the CCP is unlikely to take that risk at present. Animosity between the integrationists and defenders of the autonomous system can be so tense that they pound on the table at conferences, and refuse to talk to each other in private.

The ideological platform of the Xi Jinping administration since late 2012, a commitment to the "core value system of socialism" has helped the socialist autonomists to triumph politically. The CCP's 6th Conference on Minority Work, held in September 2014, responded to the debate on ethnic policy by incorporating the "socialist ethnic theory" advanced by the socialist autonomists. Xi Jinping's speech at the conference affirmed the autonomous system as the source of China's ethnic policy and pledged more developmental policies for minority regions. It pointedly refuted the (integrationists') assertion that China's autonomous system was based on the Soviet model and that ethnic policy must be depoliticized. The conference did answer the integrationists with calls to strengthen a common national identity, but left little opening for reform in the direction of reducing ethnic particularism. With Ilham Tohti put away for life two months before the 2014 conference and the integrationists rebuked at the conference, the socialist autonomists prevailed ideologically and politically.

Public discussion of ending the autonomous system is now off the table, if not outright banned.

A new trade-off appears to have emerged. That is, more developmental and distributional benefits but also more national integration. For the first part of the new bargain, the state has added a new grand project to its earlier western development initiative for minority regions: the thirteenth Five-Year Plan for Frontier Development and Enrichment (*xingbian fumin*). A host of existing state developmental and assistance programs continues to intensify in minority regions. For the second part of the new bargain, the state promotes identification with the "community of the Chinese nation" (*zhonghua minzu gongtongti*). This new identity, unlike the ideas of civic nationalism and equal citizenship advocated by liberal integrationists, is based on the common "Chinese dream" or the "rejuvenation of the Chinese nation," through "shared development and prosperity" (Tao 2018). These ideas, along with another new slogan, "interethnic unity like a family" (*minzu tuanjie yijiaqin*), harken back to the Mao era when collective interests and socialist brotherhood were emphasized.

It remains to be seen if the "community the Chinese nation" can serve as a new universalism that transcends ethnicity. Confucian universalism was tolerant of alternative faiths. Class universalism was exclusive, but of a small group of former ethnic elites, which did not get in the way of interethnic coalition. Developmentalism, on which the "community of the Chinese nation" is based, has been divisive interethnically or otherwise and requires large state outlays. More importantly, Confucianism spread through "cultural osmosis," not state imposition. Class universalism spread through a social revolution participated in and of benefit to the ethnic masses. Developmentalism, by contrast, has been promoted top down, and from inland to ethnic regions. Finally, the idea of the Chinese nation (*Zhonghua minzu*) remains contentious among ethnic intellectuals within China, not least because the state itself continues to use the term "nationality" to refer to its domestic ethnic groups. Because of the demographic dominance of the Han people and the central stipulation of the "Chinese dream," the "Chinese nation" may be easily taken as represented by the Han nation.

Specific policy measures remain in flux. Locally, some incremental changes are taking place in the direction of the integrationists' platform. Beginning in 2017, several regular provinces began to reduce or eliminate preferential policies in college admissions for minority students who live in Han areas, including Beijing, Jiangsu, Heilongjiang, Tianjin, and Shandong (*Gaosan* 2017; *Qi wanbao* 2017). On July 28, 2017, Xinjiang's local legislature voted to end preferential policies in family planning for local minority members. Under old policies, Han couples could only have one child in urban areas and two children in rural areas, whereas the permitted numbers were two and three for minority couples respectively. New policies allow Han couples to have the same number of children as minority couples, that is two children for urban couples and three for rural couples (XUAR 2017). The policy change is seemingly symbolic, since the relaxation of the one-child policy nationally in 2016 already allows Han couples to have two children, while the number of rural Han residents in Xinjiang is very small. Nevertheless, different localities may still have different preferential policies for minority members, such as allowing four children for rural Uighur families. At the national level, major changes in preferential policies remain unlikely. In the foreseeable future, socialist autonomy will probably remain dominant, due both to the regime's concern with stability and to the ideological high ground and politically entrenched base of the socialist autonomists.

All this means that there is no place for the liberal autonomists' visions of reform, at least for now. These visions concern in particular the two outer peripheral regions. They assume added relevance in recent years, given the deteriorating situation for Uighurs in Xinjiang. An "eight phrases" reform platform, outlined by Ilham Tohti, is reflective of the aspirations of an otherwise subdued Uighur intelligentsia. Mindful of improbable independence, Tohti concedes that not every "nationality" needs to have a "nation state." His reform proposal thus aims at restoring genuine autonomy within the current territorial arrangement, including (1) Uighur involvement in the policy-making and developmental processes that affect them; (2) Uighur rights over resources, religion, and language; (3) political trust in Uighurs that can be reflected in their appointment to the top leadership position in Xinjiang; (4) equality or no discrimination of Uighurs; (5) respect for Uighurs as cultural equals rather than as inferiors; (6) recognition for Uighurs' view of their history and of Xinjiang's history; (7) improved standards of living; and (8) democracy.[3] Tohti's autonomy thus diverges from socialist autonomy in its priorities: whereas socialist autonomy emphasizes material progress, Tohti places it at the near bottom of his list, or number 7. Instead, he prioritizes Uighurs' right to decide the kind of progress they want and how they want it. Rebiya Kadeer, the Uighur leader in exile, states the Uighur people's goal as seeking the right to "self-rule" and "self-determination," which she does not regard as "separatist" (RFE 2011). Both Uighur leaders concur on the primacy of autonomy rights, an elusive goal under China's current system and political climate.

For the TAR, no coherent vision parallel to Tohti's has emerged from Tibetan areas of China. Rather, high autonomy has been proposed by Tibetan exiles. The idea includes a self-governing territory comprising areas inhabited by all ethnic Tibetans across four neighboring Chinese provinces, restrictions on non-Tibetans entering the Tibetan areas, and decision-making power in all issues except defense and foreign relations. This autonomous government would make policy on education, religious practice, and the use of natural resources. The Dalai Lama assures that it would not force out Han Chinese who have already settled on the Tibetan plateau, but would place limits on

[3] Conversations with Tohti, Minzu University of China, Beijing, December 2012.

future migration (Wong 2009). His envoys have presented this idea of Tibetan autonomy to Beijing, but China rejects the "Greater Tibet" concept on historical grounds and chastises its potential for ethnic cleansing. Wang Lixiong (2012a) argues that the exiles have exhausted their political strategy of relying on international pressure to induce concessions from China, so that any future vision and strategy for change will need to come from within Tibetan regions of China. Wang's own proposals vary from indirect representation to village autonomy (2006; 2012b).

The conceptual barrier to improving autonomy, ironically, is the very idea of sovereignty that China learned from the West. Questions about indigenous rights and self-governance are often moot in the Chinese discourse because of the staunch Chinese insistence on sovereignty. The average officials and scholars in China, as well as the general public, easily get defensive over Western criticisms about Chinese policies in Tibet and Xinjiang, routinely turning around to attack Western records or intentions. They hold sacred that all of China's territories belong to the whole country so there is little room for liberal guilt. On the contrary, many believe that the rest of the country has done much to help the TAR and Xinjiang and that China's developmental programs are genuinely good for ethnic regions. Teng Xing, a prominent scholar of ethnic studies, testily told me in a conversation that he had lived in a native American tribe for two years and studied its conditions first hand, so "don't lecture to me about autonomy." Guided by this attitude and aided by developmentalism, ultra-modern infrastructure, resource capacity, and a maximalist state, the integrationists will likely prevail by default over the long run. But it remains to be seen what the costs will be.

Viable Alternatives

In the short and intermediate run, neither de-ethnicization nor high autonomy is likely under the current regime. For the layers of the state apparatus in charge of ethnic affairs, it is bureaucratically rational to remain socialist ethno-federalists and politically expedient to toe the ideologically correct line than to challenge it. But some are genuinely devoted to the idea of ethnic equality and national integration through socialist autonomy, while others are privately sympathetic to dissident autonomists. For individual ethnic members, incentives diverge: those who do well without affirmative action programs, or otherwise have strong identification with the state, are more critical of socialist autonomy and supportive of integration. Those whose cultural and linguistic attributes do not serve them well in the market economy understandably resist any perceived move toward de-ethnicization.

In the other direction, China's current climate of hyper-antiseparatism forecloses prospects for liberal autonomy. Any devolution of power will be looked down upon with mistrust from the center. Moreover, as Philip Roeder's (1991) study of Soviet disintegration shows, local ethnic officialdom was willing to challenge and break away from the central Soviet state *only* when the latter no longer had the ability to deliver economic benefits. As long as Beijing can deliver such benefits, it is unlikely to be seriously challenged. But this does not mean that Beijing is without serious challengers. Instead of the local officialdom in the Soviet case, in China's case it is the cultural and intellectual elites, particularly from the more culturally distinct communities and the post-Mao generations. Threatened by the homogenizing effects of modernization, these elites are concerned with the preservation and reconstruction of their ethnic culture and history. This is particularly true of outer peripheral regions with core ethnic groups, namely the TAR and Xinjiang. In moments of political liberalization, they are most likely to be political entrepreneurs mobilizing along ethnic lines.

Given the infeasibility of drastic reforms in either direction, it is more realistic to discuss mid-range reforms under current political conditions. The optimal scenario will be a mix of reforms that simultaneously enhances national integration and real autonomy.

Differentiating National and Ethnic Minorities

One of the central flaws of the ethnic classification campaign was to lump together groups of divergent sizes, histories, cultural attributes, and geographic distances as "nationalities." As some Uighurs rightly complain, "small and isolated primitive tribes" in remote hills are hardly comparable to large communities associated with major civilizations (Chen 2012: 34).

A differentiation of China's minority groups will do much to help devise better governance forms and public policies. Most importantly, the definition of Tibetans and Uighurs as "national minorities" would entail that their rights to territorial autonomy and its prerogatives be better respected. The Mongols may be added as a national minority. The so-called "isolated primitive tribes" are analogous to "indigenous peoples," whose land and cultural rights should be respected, although the varying degrees and lengths of historical incorporation and interaction will not make a definitive classification easy. Culturally at least, the minority communities that fall in China's inner peripheral zone can simply be called "ethnic groups," rather than "nationalities." In place of preferential policies, policies promoting inclusion, representation, and sensitivity may be more appropriate for these groups.

Indeed, China's regular school curriculum and public media are notorious in being Han-centric and state-centric. Most students go through public school curricula without learning about the minority origins of many Chinese dynasties and cultural heritages. Public representation of minority groups and cultures, meanwhile, often amounts to a "stereotyping" and "simplifying" project (Davis 2005), which helps to reinforce the biased perception that minority regions need outside help to develop. To the extent that preferential policies help reinforce those biases, their replacement by universal anti-poverty programs on the one hand, and policies of ethnic sensitivity on the other, may more effectively reduce entry barriers for ethnic groups.

Special Autonomous Zone (SAZ)

A SAZ may be a feasible option modeling after China's coastal Special Economic Zones, which are territorial enclaves with policy flexibilities within a larger administrative unit. For the new SAZ, Hu Yaobang's idea of high autonomy may be experimented with: the central state will have authority in just three areas: defense, diplomacy, and veto power over internal policy. This will help tune down the "maximalist" state that contemporary China has become in Xinjiang and Tibet.

Such a SAZ can be experimented with in southern Xinjiang. Granted, the central state will resist any new arrangement filled with uncertainties. Perhaps the only possible way to induce a compromise from the central state would be to render Xinjiang a regular province, while preserving the existing autonomous units within it. Such a mixed system could avoid making the central state overly insecure about separatism and religious radicalism, as it allows state intervention and Han exit if ethnic cleaning were to occur. Uighur political and cultural elites would surely oppose any retreat from the idea that a Uighur autonomous region does not mean the whole of Xinjiang. But given political realities, if a localized SAZ can be shown to work well first, a SAZ that includes the whole of southern Xinjiang or even entire Xinjiang will be more feasible later on.

A Xinjiang province with a SAZ within it will be more like Qinghai or Yunnan. In fact, Qinghai, while a regular province, contains autonomous units covering 98 percent of its territories. In this arrangement, the absence of one titular ethnic group has mitigated, at least at the provincial level, titular identity politics and the alignment of small minority groups against it. Within the proposed SAZ, the local minority government will have power over such issues as resources, employment, education, language, and employment that now concern Uighurs. The central and local governments may negotiate policies to prevent non-Uighurs from the fate of Russian minorities in former Soviet republics after independence. Local ethnic elites, especially secular elites, will likely need to make coalitions with the Han and the small minority groups as well as with the central government to keep the modern sectors thriving and religious radicalism in check. Their priorities may not be all that different from Beijing's, even if their strategies are. The parallel existence of a SAZ and autonomous areas within Xinjiang would allow healthy competition between two models of autonomy. In those autonomous areas outside the experimented SAZ, improved autonomy may focus on indigenous groups' rights where relevant, political and cultural inclusion, voluntary bilingual education programs, bilingual usage in public services and signage, and if possible, forms of autonomy according to local popular preferences.

For the TAR, a legal framework for high autonomy already exists, namely the 17-Point Agreement reached between Beijing and Lhasa in 1951. While the Tibetan government-in-exile has repudiated it, a return to that framework would entail a much higher degree of political autonomy than at present. This includes preservation of Tibet's pre-1952 system of government (Point 4), the status, functions, and powers of the Dalai and Panchen Lamas (Point 6), and freedom of religion (Point 7). The central government, meanwhile, would take charge of Tibet's defense and external affairs (Points 2, 8, and 14). The Greater Tibet concept has less legal foundation, but deserves no less autonomy. To promote more autonomy in eastern Tibetan regions, Wang Lixiong's ideas of "indirect representation" (2006) and "village autonomy" (2012b) hold more political realism at present.

Bilingual Education as Two-Way Electives

In all bilingual programs that currently exist, it is both practical and technically feasible to offer different models of bilingual education as elective classes for all students, rather than only mandatory programs for minority students. Offering options is a necessary attendant of autonomy and the best way to diffuse opposition. Logistically it is easier than a blanket transition to Chinese-medium instruction. Conversely, offering ethnic languages in regular schools, as elective substitutes to foreign languages, will give incentives for Mandarin speakers to take such courses. For Mandarin speakers in ethnic regions, it makes more sense to learn a local ethnic language than a foreign language, which is now mandated. If bonus points are given for taking an ethnic language test for college admissions or for civil service jobs, there will surely be more interest in learning ethnic languages.

Indeed, in this age of fast transformation and globalization for China, protection of cultural heritages – including ethnic languages – should be among its national priorities. Thanks to a long history of ethnic fusion and acculturation, most Chinese have a relaxed attitude about cultural assimilation. This insensitivity is worsened by a seemingly Darwinist approach to what may be assimilated. "Advanced" cultures are warmly embraced, while "backward cultures" are shunned. Symbols of Western culture, from Christmas to Valentines' Day and from birthday cakes to white wedding gowns, have become commonplace in China. Urban Chinese parents eagerly push their children to learn English and for those who can, to attend high schools and colleges in Western countries. Concerned intellectuals lament that many Chinese youths now spend more time learning English than Chinese, but few Han parents seem to hold deeper cultural misgivings. Several US holidays are celebrated by the Chinese public with fanfare, but few Han Chinese care or know about the holidays and other cultural traditions of their own "backward" minorities. In their frenzy to develop and modernize, local officials have no qualms about demolishing traditional architectures, ancient walls, or even historical landmarks. But resistance to such destructive efforts from minority groups should give pause to China that its own modernization bias may be at fault.

Overcoming Social Darwinian Bias

Battling this bias will be a daunting task, but a necessary part of any serious Chinese rethinking on ethnic policy and governance. Although minority intellectuals and commoners generally embrace material progress, many are disconcerted about being categorized as backward. Beijing's efforts to transplant inland models to ethnic regions certainly assumes the superiority of its models. Promotion of economic development by the Han-dominated government and inland regions, moreover, lends itself to perceptions of Sinification, even if integrationists insist that modernization is not Sinification. With a growing recognition of the folly of this one-way dissemination, there should be more room for bottom-up initiatives from ethnic communities. As a well-placed SEAC researcher boldly criticizes, the state's policies of development in minority regions eschews a diverse view of human evolution and have a Darwinian logic, for they use the "advanced" majority group as a measure by which minority groups are gauged. Viewing minority societies as inferior, the advanced group is convinced of its "responsibility" to help the weak groups (Ming 2012: 9–10; 2015). Such views move beyond earlier criticisms that fault technical infeasibilities of transplanting inland models. Criticizing Han cultural biases brings the argument to a higher, normative plane and can lead to a new level of public understanding. As a first step, elimination of references to "backward" and "advanced" regions will help moderate a superiority complex among Han individuals and instill respect for ethnic differences.

Protection Based on Rights

The integrationists offer a potentially revolutionary platform of reform by proposing equal citizenship. Although the original intention is to get rid of the state's positive discrimination, any discourse on political equality will have to confront the realities of societal discrimination suffered by distinct minority groups. Societal discrimination arises from sources that state policies have sought to remedy: language, religion, culture, or levels of development. How would a reform platform for equal citizenship protect minority rights (Uighurs and Tibetans specifically) in job searches, hotel stays, taxi rides, airport searches, passport applications, religious worship, etc.? Some integrationists duly recognize these problems, but are short on specific solutions. They pay attention to legal battles in America that seek to roll back affirmative action policies, but they neglect legal battles that seek to fight back against various forms of racial discrimination. Ma Rong ends many of his articles praising the American model of ethnic integration and views the segmental effects of the autonomous system as virtual segregation (2010a). However, China's integrationists seldom if ever touch on anti-discrimination laws in America.

With improved rule of law in China, anti-discrimination law will be the natural alternative to state policies of positive discrimination.

The SEAC and its local branches will be best poised to enforce such a law. This transition of SEAC functions will assuage fears about job loss from the demise of preferential policies, thus securing support for reforming socialist autonomy. To enforce equal citizenship, any statutes will also need to cover other common prejudices in China, such as those involving age, appearance, gender, and disabilities in hiring. Such a broadly based law may indeed prove to be better protection for all Chinese citizens in the long run.

IMPLICATIONS FOR THE INTERNATIONAL ARENA

The international implications of China's ethnic woes revolve around constraints on China's security and foreign policy behavior as well as on its international reactions. As sporadic unrest in China's ethnic regions has involved violence, in some cases massive violence, ethnic strife could erupt into greater distractions in times of China's external crisis. Moreover, when some of China's ethnic policies receive international attention as human rights abuses, as in the international uproar over the treatment of Uighurs, China's international image and soft power suffer significantly.

One constraint on China's security behavior has been the foreign policy implication of placating restive groups at home. This has entailed expensive financial subsidies and other policy payouts that place burdens on China's global rise. Stabilizing restive regions has required more security apparatus than might otherwise be necessary. It has become notorious that China's expenditure for domestic "stability maintenance" now exceeds that for national defense. In the international arena, Beijing has had to use economic incentives, such as free-trade zones, investment, and export opportunities, to induce other countries to cancel political activities organized by exiled groups (Dreyer 2005: 78). Even a simple meeting with exiled leaders by western politicians can make Beijing highly nervous, as this may send encouraging messages to restive minority groups at home. More recently, Chinese investments have helped to silence complaints regarding Xinjiang's reeducation camps from Muslim countries in African, Asia, and the Middle East (Perlez 2019). Finally, sporadic unrest and suppression generate international criticism and pressure to improve human rights conditions (Sautman 2005). Extreme measures such as the surveillance state and reeducation camps multiply such criticism and pressure.

Insofar as the financial and security costs can be absorbed internally, the moral costs would matter more for the international environment of China's rise. Reports of excruciating ethnic policies unleash criticisms of human rights abuse, internal colonialism, and political oppression as well as a deep mistrust of the nature and intentions of the Chinese regime. The reeducation camps in Xinjiang have therefore caused growing concern in Western capitals about what China's domestic crackdown means for international security and the liberal international order. As one European analyst puts it, US Vice President Mike Pence set the tone for the West's China discourse when he argued at the Hudson Institute in 2018 that "a country that oppresses its own people rarely stops there." In this view, China's turn toward a more repressive stance domestically – with internment camps in Xinjiang and proliferation of high-tech surveillance – and an increasingly aggressive foreign policy, are not coincidental developments, but different manifestations of the same trend (Nyrén 2019). Even preferential policies may invite mistrustful judgments that they are ploys to buy off restive minorities. Ethnic exiles are sentimentally charged by ethnic unrest in China, and public opinions and politicians in the West will remain influenced by these exile sources.

International support for ethnic insurgence should constitute a grave concern for a rising China. Such support not only internationalizes ethnic conflict but can also influence its intensity and outcome (Saideman 2001, 2002). A range of factors, including China's regime type, its relative power and ideology, the charisma of ethnic leaders, as well as the domestic constituents of supporting countries, will likely increase the level of international support for China's restive minority groups, that is Tibetans and Uighurs. As Saideman's studies show, when separatism of a minority group strengthens and popular support for such strife visibly rises within the group in question, the perceived intensity and popular base can influence international support even in violent conflicts. Such a minority group in an undemocratic regime and a strong state, moreover, is likely to receive broader external support. These factors weigh significantly in Western support for Tibet, although the importance of economic relations has also offset sentimental concerns.

Implications for Western Policies

For Western policies, the implications from this study entail improving China's understanding of the roots of its ethnic problems as well as of the nature of Western support for minority human rights in China. Misunderstanding of this support is the biggest source of misperception on the Chinese part of a Western – especially American – conspiracy to destabilize China. Lacking an understanding of Western (especially American) pluralistic domestic politics, many in China – including some serious analysts – equate the support that exiled ethnic leaders enjoy in the West to Western governments' political support for separatism and even "terrorism" in China. It is important that those misunderstandings be dispelled, as they have become a major source of misconceived conspiracy theories and hypernationalism in China.

It is not uncommon in popular or semi-official discourse in China to blame "Western forces" for being "behind-the-scene actors" in China's restive minority regions. In the most notorious case, Dai Xu, a professor at China's National Defense University and a popular commentator in China's nationalistic media forums, has become a populist propagandist of American conspiracies to derail

China through subversive activities in China's neighboring countries as well as Tibet and Xinjiang (*HQSB* 2009). His most extreme comments have been deleted from the Chinese internet, but the idea of a Western conspiracy lingers in the sensationalist media and the popular imagination, especially the populist paper *Global Times* (e.g., *HQSB* 2014), where Dai Xu's opinions have also appeared. Influenced by the state's nationalistic education, it is easy for less informed Chinese citizens to fall for conspiracy theories, stimulating hypernationalism and further misunderstandings.

Despite the absurdity of conspiracy theories, they linger in some form in the official Chinese understanding of Western support for China's ethnic exiles. The American government's reluctance to label violent incidents in Xinjiang as "terrorism" has further fueled the perception that the Tibet and Xinjiang issues are being used by the US government as foreign policy tools to tie down China's hands. This (mis)perception has in important part led to the "sovereignty anxiety" that contributes to China's extensive efforts at integration in those sensitive minority regions. These efforts in turn backfire, causing more tensions in those regions and creating a vicious cycle. It is also among the reasons for China's hypersensitivity to the Dalai Lama's meetings with Western governments. Driven by this misconception and hypersensitivity, China has been willing to spend generously on commercial deals to dissuade foreign governments from supporting or harboring so-called "separatist forces." In the process it has also become a hostage of its own mistaken perceptions and policies.

Western governments would do well to convey the authenticity and sincerity of their human rights concerns. It is routine for serious Chinese analysts – and likely policymakers as well – to dismiss those Western concerns as moral posturing. In a report on America's Xinjiang policy written by researchers at the Chinese Academy of Sciences, the authors refer to the Xinjiang issue as a "card" available for America to play against China. As the USA increasingly relies on Chinese cooperation in the areas of global financial crises, anti-terrorism, and anti-nuclear proliferation, the report argues, the cards in America's hands have dwindled, making the Tibet and Xinjiang issues more important (Gu et al. 2012). The rationale for this line of argument is utter realism: the report dismisses the moral concerns of the human rights discourse as spurious, since these concerns largely come from circles not directly relevant to foreign policy making in America. More recently, discomfort with excessive security measures has made many Han intellectuals in Xinjiang see the point of Western criticisms about human rights issues in China. But ordinary Han residents in Xinjiang remain supportive of those measures and indifferent to Western criticisms, despite onerous burdens on themselves. They and those who visit Xinjiang from inland provinces, simply marvel at how safe the province has become under Chen Quanguo's rein, with little regard for the cost to Uighurs.

It is useful to help Chinese policy analysts and policymakers understand the pluralistic domestic political processes in America. Unlike in China where the ruling party and its leadership dominate, multiple actors play important roles in the US policy processes – not only the Congress but also nongovernmental organizations, academia, and the general public. It is especially important to remind China that using China's paradigm of "sovereignty" to understand Western concerns for human rights is misguided. Because of China's mental trap in the "hundred years" of humiliation at the hands of imperial powers, it holds sovereignty issues as overriding, unconvinced that the West can possibly take human rights issues seriously. Using this lens to understand American concerns and policies, however, can be specious, because the liberal, individualistic, and postmodern values of the American civil society genuinely lead to a valuation of individual liberties and rights over sovereign rights. In America's open political process, this civil society has a bearing on foreign policy making, unlike the closed political system of China.

It is also important to educate China about why the so-called "anti-China forces" among American politicians are "anti-China." What are their motives? Are they really ill-intended? For American politicians on the left and the right, criticizing China's human rights records, or pressuring the country to democratize or abandon its authoritarian system, is not equivalent to being "anti-China." After all, the Chinese Communist Party is not equivalent to China the country, even though the CCP often blurs the distinction. Likewise, even those sympathetic to separatism among Western politicians are not necessarily "anti-China" per se: for they do not support separatism for its own sake but out of human rights concerns. In other words, if some minority groups do not feel well protected in terms of their rights and liberties, what then is the meaning of sovereignty for them? In interesting ways, the lack of concern for China's human rights issues shown by the Trump administration disappoints conspiracy theorists in China, as it contradicts their belief system about America. Of course, the Trump administration's "anti-China" stance on trade has aroused new conspiracy theories, this time about America's efforts to contain China's rise by halting China's "Made in China 2025" Plan or Huawei's 5G dominance. Much as Chinese (mis)perceptions of American intentions on human rights issues, the Chinese leadership and the general public have difficulty viewing China's heavy state subsidies for its state enterprises as abuse of international trade rules. In such cases, education about non-Chinese perspectives will be useful.

Finally, with Western countries' rich experiences in dealing with minority incorporation and autonomy, it would be productive to share with China those effective policies that can balance the goals of national integration, group autonomy, individual rights, and social equality. Needless to say, the rise of homegrown terrorism in western Europe and the polarization of identity politics in America have cast doubts on the credibility of Western experiences. In this context, it is more useful to make concrete and feasible proposals for reform than simply championing the abstract concepts of freedom and rights. It is more prudent to show Chinese leaders specifically why a stifling of local input and dissent leads to bad policies that feed greater and broader social disaffection. China needs to be convinced that domestic separatism and terrorism are largely products of its own policy dynamics, and that it needs to adjust domestic policies to fundamentally stem the destabilizing forces.

Ultimately, China needs to be convinced that state largesse on the one hand, but state control on the other, will not resolve fundamental problems of national integration. Such contradictory efforts serve to drain the dividends from its remarkable economic development, as long as the sources of integration's discontents persist. Most of all, the moral costs associated with draconian policies, such as the reeducation camps in Xinjiang, irreparably damage the national image of a rising China.

Bibliography

SOURCES IN ENGLISH

Akçam, Taner. 2004. *From Empire to Republic: Turkish Nationalism and the Armenian Genocide*. London: Zed Books.

2013. *The Young Turks' Crime against Humanity: The Armenian Genocide and Ethnic Cleansing in the Ottoman Empire*. Princeton, NJ: Princeton University Press.

Anand, Dibyesh. 2003. "A Contemporary Story of 'Diaspora': The Tibetan Version." *Diaspora* 12.2: 211–29.

Anderson, Benedict. 1983. *Imagined Communities*. London: Verso.

Bakke, Kristin M. and Erik Wibbels. 2006. "Diversity, Disparity and Civil Conflict in Federal States." *World Politics* 59 (October). 1–50.

Barfield, Thomas J. 1989. *The Perilous Frontier: Nomadic Empires and China*. Oxford: Blackwell.

2001. "The Shadow Empires: Imperial State Formation Along the Chinese-Nomad Frontier." *Empires*. Eds. Susan E. Alcock et al. Cambridge: Cambridge University Press. 11–41.

Barkey, Karen and George Gavrilis. 2016. "The Ottoman Millet System: Non-territorial Autonomy and Its Contemporary Legacy." *Ethnopolitics* 15.1: 24–42.

Barnett, Robert. 1994. *Resistance and Reform in Tibet*. London: Hurst.

2009. "The Tibetan Protests of Spring, 2008." *China Perspective* 3: 6–23.

Beckett, Gulbahar H. and Gerard A. Postiglione. 2012. *China's Assimilationist Language Policy: The Impact on Indigenous/Minority Literacy and Social Harmony*. London and New York: Routledge.

Becquelin, Nicholas. 2000. "Xinjiang in the Nineties." *The China Journal* 44: 65–90.

2004. "Staged Development in Xinjiang." *The China Quarterly* 178 (June): 358–78.

Bellér-Hann, Ildikó et al. 2007. *Situating the Uighurs between China and Central Asia*. Farnham: Ashgate Publishing.

Benson, Linda. 2004. "Education and Social Mobility among Minority Populations in Xinjiang." Ed. Starr. 190–215.

Benson, Linda and Ingavar Svanberg. 1998. *China's Last Nomads: The History and Culture of China's Kazaks*. Amonk, NY: M.E. Sharpe.

Benton, Lauren. 2001. *Law and Colonial Cultures: Legal Regimes in World History, 1400–1900*. New York: Cambridge University Press.

Bhala, A. S. and Qui Shufang. 2006. *Poverty and Inequality among China's Minorities*. London: Routledge.

Bovingdon, Gardner. 1998. "From *Qumulluq* to *Uyghur*: The Role of Education in the Development of a Pan-Uyghur Identity." *Journal of Central Asian Studies* 3.1: 19–29.

2002. *Strangers in Their Own Land: The Politics of Uyghur Identity in Chinese Central Asia*. PhD dissertation, Cornell University.

2004. *Autonomy in Xinjiang: Han Nationalist Imperatives and Uyghur Discontent*. East-West Center. *Policy Studies* 11.

2010. *The Uyghurs: Strangers in Their Own Land*. New York: Columbia University Press.

Bulard, Martine. 2009. "China's Wild West." *Le Monde diplomatique*, August 2. http://mondediplo.com/2009/08/02china.

Bunce, Valerie. 1999. *Subversive Institutions: The Design and Destruction of Socialism and the State*. New York: Cambridge University Press.

Cavalli-Sforza, L. Luca. 1998. "The Chinese Human Genome Diversity Project." *PNAS* 95.20: 11501–3.

CECC (Congressional-executive Committee on China). 2005. *China's Regional Ethnic Autonomy Law: Does It Protect Rights*. Washington, DC: US Government Printing Office.

Cederman, Lars-Erik, Luc Girardin, and Kristian Skede Gleditsch. 2009. "Ethnonational Triads: Assessing the Influence of Kin Groups on Civil Wars." *World Politics* 61.3: 403–37.

China Daily. 2016. "Xinjiang Issues China's First Local Counterterrorism Law." *China Daily*, August 5.

Clarke, Michael. 2007. "China's Internal Security Dilemma and the 'Great Western Development': The Dynamics of Integration, Ethnic Nationalism and Terrorism in Xinjiang." *Asian Studies Review* 31.3: 323–42.

Cliff, Thomas. 2016. "Interethnic Conflict as a Function of the Economic 'Normalization' of Southern Xinjiang." Eds. Hillman and Tuttle. 122–50.

Connor, Walker. 1984. *The National Question in Marxist-Leninist Theory and Strategy*. Princeton, NJ: Princeton University Press.

Crone, Patricia. 1989. *Pre-industrial Societies: New Perspectives on the Past*. Oxford: Wiley-Blackwell.

Crawford, Beverly. 1998. "Explaining Cultural Conflict in the Ex-Yugoslavia: Institutional Weakness, Economic Crisis, and Identity Politics." Eds. Crawford and Lipschutz. 197–260.

Crawford, Beverly and Ronnie D. E. Lipschutz. 1998. *The Myth of "Ethnic Conflict": Politics, Economics and "Cultural Violence."* Berkeley, CA: University of California Press.

Davis. Sara L. M. 2005. *Songs and Silence*. New York: Columbia University Press.

Deutsch, Karl W. 1953. *Nationalism and Social Communication*. Cambridge, MA: M.I.T. Press.

Di Cosmo, Nicola. 1994. "Ancient Inner Asian Nomads: Their Economic Basis and Its Significance in Chinese History." *The Journal of Asian Studies* 53.4: 1092–126.

2002. *Ancient China and Its Enemies: The Rise of Nomadic Power in East Asian History*. London and New York: Cambridge University Press.

Dillon, Michael. 1999. *China's Muslim Hui Community: Migration, Settlement and Sect*. New York: RoutledgeCurzon.

2002. "We Have Terrorists Too." *The World Today* 58.1: 25–7.

2004. *Xinjiang: China's Muslim Far Northwest*. London: RoutledgeCurzon.

Dreyer, June Teufel. 1976. *China's Forty Millions: Minority Nationalities and National Integration in the People's Republic of China*. Cambridge, MA: Harvard University Press.

2005. "China's Vulnerability to Minority Separatism." *Asian Affairs: An American Review* 32.2: 69–86.

2006. "Economic development in Tibet under the People's Republic of China." Eds. Sautman and Dreyer. 411–30.

Duara, Prasnejit. 1997. *Rescuing History from the Nation: Questioning Narratives of Modern China*. Chicago: Chicago University Press.

Dwyer, Arienne. 2005. "The Minorities of China." *The Encyclopedia of the World's Minorities*. Ed. Carl Skutsch. New York: Routledge. 286–94.

Fairbank, John King. 1983. *The United States and China*. Cambridge, MA: Harvard University Press.

Fearon, James. 2006. "Ethnic Mobilization and Ethnic Violence." *Oxford Handbook of Political Economy*. Eds. Barry R. Weingast and Donald Wittman. Oxford: Oxford University Press. 852–68.

Fei, Xiaotong. 1988. "Plurality and Unity in the Configuration of the Chinese Nation." *Tanner Lectures*, November 15 and 17. Web.

Fischer, Martin Andrew. 2002. *Poverty by Design*. Montréal: The Canada Tibet Committee.

2005. *State Growth and Social Exclusion in Tibet: Challenges of Recent Economic Growth*. Copenhagen: NIAS Press.

2012. "The Geopolitics of Politico-Religious Protest in Eastern Tibet." *Hot Spot Forum, Cultural Anthropology Online*, April 2. Web.

2013. *The Disempowered Development of Tibet in China: A Study in the Economics of Marginalization*. Lanham, MD: Lexington Books.

Fuller, Grahm E. and N. Jonathan Lipman. 2004. "Islam in Xinjiang." Ed. Starr. 320–52.

Gellner, Ernest. 1983. *Nations and Nationalism*. Ithaca, NY: Cornell University Press.

Gladney, Dru. 1990. "The Ethnogenesis of the Uighur." *Central Asian Survey* 9.1: 1–28.

1991. *Muslim Chinese: Ethnic Nationalism in the People's Republic*. Cambridge, MA: Harvard University Press.

1995. "Economy and Ethnicity: The Revitalization of a Muslim Minority in Southeastern China." *The Waning of the Communist State: Economic Origins of Political Decline in China and Hungary*. Ed. Andrew Walder. Berkeley, CA: University of California Press. 242–66.

1998. "Clashed Civilizations: Muslim and Chinese Identities in the PRC." *Making Majorities: Constituting the Nation in Japan, Korea, China, Malaysia, Fiji, Turkey and the United State*. Ed. Dru Gladney. Palo Alto: Stanford University Press. 105–31.

2009. "Freedom Fighters or Terrorists? Exploring the Case of the Uighur People." Testimony to US Congress Committee on Foreign Affairs, Subcommittee on International Organizations, Human Rights and Oversight. June 16.

Goldstein, Melvyn et al. 2006. "Development and Change in Rural Tibet: Problems and Adaptations." Eds. Sautman and Dreyer. 193–213.

Goodman, David. 2002. "The Politics of the West: Equality, Nation-Building and Colonization." *Provincial China* 7.2: 317–34.

2004. "The Campaign to 'Open Up the West': National, Provincial-Level and Local Perspectives." *The China Quarterly* 178 (June): 317–34.

Gustafsson, Björn and Li Shi. 2003. "The Ethnic Minority–Majority Income Gap in Rural China during Transition." *Economic Development and Cultural Change* 51.4: 805–22.

Hale, Henry E. 2004. "Divided We Stand: Institutional Sources of Ethnofederal State Survival and Collapse." *World Politics* 56 (January): 165–93.

Han, Enze. 2016. *Contestation and Adaptation: The Politics of National Identity in China*. New York: Oxford University Press.

Han, Enze and Christopher Paik. 2014. "Dynamics of Political Resistance in Tibet: Religious Repression and Controversies of Demographic Change." *The China Quarterly* 217 (March): 69–98.

Harrell, Stevan. 1995. "Civilizing Projects and the Reactions to Them." *Cultural Encounters on China's Ethnic Frontiers*. Ed. Stevan Harrell. Seattle, WA: University of Washington Press. 3–36.

2001. *Ways of Being Ethnic in Southwest China*. Seattle, WA: University of Washington Press.

Harrell, Stevan and Li Yongxiang. 2003. "The History of the History of the Yi." *Modern China* 29.3: 362–96.

Harris, Rachel A. 2008. *The Making of a Musical Canon in Chinese Central Asia: The Uyghur Twelve Muqam*. Farnham: Ashgate Publishing.

Heberer, Thomas. 1989. *China and the National Minorities: Autonomy or Assimilation?* Amonk, NY: M.E. Sharpe.

2005. "Ethnic Entrepreneurship and Ethnic Identity: A Case Study among the Liangshan Yi (Nuosu) in China." *The China Quarterly* 182 (June): 407–27.

Henry, Clemence. 2016. "The Chinese Education System as a Source of Conflict in Tibetan Areas." Eds. Hillman and Tuttle. 92–121.

Hillman, Ben. 2016. "Unrest in Tibet and the Limits of Regional Autonomy." Eds. Hillman and Tuttle. 16–39.

Hillman, Ben and Gary Tuttle, eds. 2016. *Ethnic Conflict and Protests in Tibet and Xinjiang*. New York: Columbia University.

Hizb ut-Tahri, Taqiuddin an-Nabhani. 1998. *The Islamic State*. London: Al-Khilafah Publications.

Ho, Ping-ti. 1998. "In Defense of Sinicization." *Journal of Asian Studies* 57.1: 123–55.

Howell, Anthony and C. Cindy Fan. 2011. "Migration and Inequality in Xinjiang: A Survey of Han and Uyghur Migrants in Urumqi." *Eurasian Geography and Economics* 52.91: 119–39.

Içduygu, Ahmet, Şule Toktas, and Ali B. Soner. 2008. "The Politics of Population in a Nation-building Process: Emigration of Non-muslims from Turkey." *Ethnic and Racial Studies* 31.2: 358–89.

ICT (International Campaign for Tibet). 2018. "Self-immolation by Tibetans." www.savetibet.org/resources/fact-sheets/self-immolations-by-tibetans/. Last updated December 10, 2018.

The Independent. 2006. "A Meeting of Civilisations: The Mystery of China's Celtic Mummies." *The Independent*, August 28. Web.

Ilhati. 2015. "Voices from the Dark Cell." *Boxun*, July 15. www.boxun.com/news/gb/china/2013/07/ 201307151423.shtml.

Jagchid, Sechin and Van Jay Symons. 1989. *Peace, War and Trade along the Great Wall.* Bloomington, IN: Indiana University Press.

Jin, Li, Li Hui, and Wen Bo. 2005. "Genetic Composition of the Han: The Demi-Based Diffusion of Han Culture." *Journal of Dr. Sun-Yat-sen Memorial Hall*, May 16: 110–17.

Kaup, Katherince Palmer. 2000. *Creating the Zhuang*. Boulder, CO: Lynne Rienner.

Khazanov, Anatoly M. 1984. Nomads and the Outside World. "Cambridge and New York: Cambridge University Press." Asia Research Center, Murdoch University.

2001. "Nomads in the History of the Sedentary World" Nomads in the Sedentary World. Eds. Anatoly M. Khazanov and André Wink. London: Routledge 1–23.

Kim, Si Joong. 2003. "The Economic Status and Role of Ethnic Koreans in China." *Korean Diaspora in the World Economy*. Eds. C. Fred Bergsten and Inbom Choe. London: Eurospan.

Koch, Jessica. 2006. "Economic Development and Ethnic Separatism in Western China: A New Model of Peripheral Nationalism." Working Paper No. 134. Asia Research Center, Murdoch University.

Kradin, Nicolai N. 2002. *The Hunnu Empire* (in Russian). Moscow: Logo.

2005. "From Tribal Confederation to Empire: The Evolution of the Rouran Society." *Acta Orientalia Academiae Scientiarum Hungaricae*. 58: 149–61.

Kissinger, Henry. 2011. *On China*. New York: Penguin Books.

Lapidus, Gail W. and Victor Zaslavsky, with Philip Godman, eds. 1992. *From Union to Commonwealth: Nationalism and Separatism in the Soviet Republics*. New York: Cambridge University Press.

Lattimore, Owen. 1940. *The Inner Asian Frontiers of China*. New York: American Geographical Society.

Leff, Skalnik Carol. 1999. "Democratization and Disintegration in Multinational States." *World Politics* 51.2 (January): 205–35.

Leibold, James. 2013. "Ethnic Politics in China: Is Reform Inevitable?" *Policy Studies* No. 68. Honolulu: East-West Center.

2016. "Interethnic Conflict in the PRC: Tibet and Xinjiang as Exceptions?" Eds. Hillman and Tuttle. 223–50.

Leibold, James and Yangbin Chen. 2014. *Minority Education in China: Balancing Unity and Diversity in an Era of Critical Pluralism*. Hong Kong: Hong Kong University Press.

Levenson, Joseph R. 1971. *Revolution and Cosmopolitanism: The Western Stage and the Chinese Stages*. Berkeley, CA: University of California Press.

Li, Hui and Kenneth Kidd et al. 2009. "Genetic Landscape of Eurasia and 'Admixture' in Uyghurs." *American Journal of Human Genetics*. 85.6 (December): 934–7.

Lipman, Jonathan N. 1998. *Familiar Strangers*. Seattle, WA: University of Washington Press.

Litzinger, Ralph A. 2000. *Other China: The Yao and the Politics of Belonging*. Durham, NC: Duke University Press.

Losel, Rigzin. 2011a. "Come to Tibet with an Open Mind." *New York Times*: "Room for Debate" (online). September 1, 2011. Web.

Ma, Rong. 2003. "Population Distribution and Relations between Ethnic Groups in the Kashgar Prefecture. Xinjiang Uyghur Autonomous Region, China." *China's*

Minorities on the Move. Eds. Robyn Iredale, Naran Bilik, and Fei Guo. New York: M. E. Sharpe. 106–22.

2006. "Education of Ethnic Minorities in Contemporary China." Paper presented at the International Symposium on China's Positive Policies in Minority Education: Plural Perspectives. Dickinson College, April 14–15. 1–20.

2007. "Bilingual Education for China's Ethnic Minorities." *Chinese Education and Society*. 40.2: 9–25.

2010a. *Population and Society in Contemporary Tibet: Population and Society in Tibet*. Seattle, WA: University of Washington Press.

Mackerras, Colin. 1994. *China's Minorities: Integration and Modernization in the Twentieth Century*. New York: Oxford University Press.

2018 "Religion and the Uyghurs: A Contemporary Overview." *The Uyghur Community: Diaspora, Identity and Geopolitics*. Eds. Güljanat Kurmangaliyeva Ercilasun and Konuralp Ercilasun. Palgrave Macmillan. 59–84.

MacPherson S. and G. H. Beckett. 2008. "The Hidden Curriculum of Assimilation in Modern Chinese Education: Fuelling Indigenous Tibetan and Uygur Cessation Movements." *Cultural Education/Cultural Sustainability: Identity, Tolerance, and Multicultural Issues in Minority, Diaspora, and Indigenous Education*. Eds. Z. Bekerman and E. Kopelowitz. Mahwah, NJ and London: Lawrence Erlbaum Associates.

Mann, Michael. 1986. *Sources of Social Power: Volume I, a History of Power from Beginning to A.D. 1760*. New York: Cambridge University Press.

Mansfield, Edward and Jack Synder. 1995. "Democratization and War." *Foreign Affairs* 74.3 (May/June): 79–95.

Martin, Terry. 2001a. *The Affirmative Action Empire: Nations and Nationalism in the Soviet Union, 1923–1939*. Ithaca, NY: Cornell University Press.

2001b. "An Affirmative Action Empire: The Soviet Union as the Highest Form of Imperialism." Ed. Suny and Martin. 67–89.

McCarthy, Susan K. 2009. *Communist Multiculturalism: Ethnic Revivalism in Southwest China*. Seattle, WA: University of Washington Press.

MCP. 2020. "Multiculturalism Policy Index." www.queensu.ca/mcp/.

Millward, James. 2000. "Historical Perspectives on Contemporary Xinjiang." *Inner Asia* 2.2: 121–35.

2007. *Eurasian Crossroads: A History of Xinjiang*. New York: Columbia University Press.

Millward, James and Peter C. Perdue. 2004. "Political and Cultural History of the Xinjiang Region Through the Late 19th Century." Ed. Starr. 27–62.

Minogue, Kenneth and Beverly Williams. 1992. "Ethnic Conflict in the Soviet Union: The Revenge of Ethnic Particularism." Ed. Motyle. 225–42.

Moneyhon, Matthew D. 2002. "Controlling Xinjiang: Autonomy on China's 'New Frontier'." *Asia Pacific Law and Policy Journal*, 3.1: 120–52.

2004. "China's Great Western Development Project in Xinjiang: Economic Palliative or Political Trojan Horse?" *Denver Journal of International Law and Policy* 31.3: 491–525.

Motyle, Alexander J., ed. 1992. *Thinking Theoretically about Soviet Nationalities*. New York: Columbia University Press.

Moyo, Dambisa. 2010. *Dead Aid: Why Aid Is Not Working and How There Is a Better Way for Africa*. Vancouver, BC: Douglas & Mcintyre Ltd.

Mullaney, Thomas. 2010a. *Coming to Terms with the Nation: Ethnic Classification in Modern China*. Berkeley, CA: University of California Press.

2010b. "Seeing for the State: the Role of Chinese Social Scientists in China's Ethnic Identification Projects." *Asian Ethnicity* 11.3 (October): 325–42.

Norbu, Dawa. 2001. *China's Tibet Policy*. Surrey: Curzon Press.

Norbu, Jamyang. 2008. "Running Dog Propagandists." Phayul, July 14. www.phayul.com/news/article.aspx?id=21945.

Nyrén, Pär. 2019. "China's Liberal Hawk: Yan Xuetong's Vision for Chinese Benevolent Dominance." *The Diplomat*, June 28. Web.

Olson, James Stuart. 1998. *An Ethnohistorical Dictionary of China*. Westport, CT: Greenwood Publishing Group.

Perdue, Peter. 2005. *China Marches West: The Qing Conquest of Central Asia*. Cambridge, MA: Harvard University Press.

Perlez, Jane. 2019. "China Wants the World to Stay Silent on Muslim Camps. It Is Succeeding." *The New York Times*. September 25.

Petech, L. 1990. *Central Tibet and the Mongols* (Serie Orientale Roma 65). Rome: Instituto Italiano per il Medio ed Estremo Oriente.

Pirie, F. 2005. "Segmentation Within the State: The Reconfiguration of Tibetan Tribes in China's Reform Period." *Nomadic Peoples* 9.1–2 (June–December): 83–102.

Pye, Lucian W. 1976. "China: Ethnic Minorities and National Security." *Current Scene* 14.12 (December): 1–17.

Qarluq, Abduresit Jelil and Donald Hugh McMillen. 2011. "Towards a 'Harmonious Society'? A Brief Case Study of the Post-liberation Settlement in Beijing of Uyghur Intellectuals and Their Relations with the Majority Society." *Asian Ethnicity* 12.1 (February): 1–31.

Quataert, Donald. 1983. *Social Disintegration and Popular Resistance in the Ottoman Empire 1881–1908*. New York: New York University Press.

Rawski, Evelyn. 1996. "Re-envisioning the Qing: The Significance of the Qing Period in Chinese History." *Journal of Asian Studies* 55.4: 829–50.

Reuters. 2016. "Three Suicide Bombers Killed by Police in China." December 28. Web.

RFA. 2014. "Xinjiang's Half a Year of Intensified Crackdown." RFA, November 25. Web.

RFE (Radio Free Europe). 2011. "Interview: 'I Can't Say the Struggle Will Always Be Peaceful,' Says Uyghur Advocate Kadeer." February 27. Web.

Riga, Liliana. 2012. *The Bolsheviks and the Russian Empire*. New York: Cambridge University Press.

Roeder, Philip. 1991. "Soviet Federalism and Ethnic Mobilization." *World Politics* 43.2 (January): 233–56.

1998. "Liberalization and Ethnic Entrepreneurs in the Soviet Successor States." Eds. Crawford and Lipschutz. 78–107.

2004. "The Triumph of Nation-States: Lessons from the Collapse of the Soviet Union, Yugoslavia and Czechoslovakia." *After the Collapse of Communism: Comparative Lessons of Transition*. Eds. Michael MacFaul and Kathryn Stoner-Weiss. New York: Cambridge University Press.

Rozman, Gilbert. 1987. *The Chinese Debate about Soviet Socialism: 1978–1985*. Princeton, NJ: Princeton University.

Rudelson, Justin Jon. 1997. *Oasis Identities: Uyghur Nationalism along China's Silk Road*. New York: Columbia University Press.

Sautman, Barry. 1998. "Preferential Policies for Ethnic Minorities in China: The Case of Xinjiang." *Nationalism and Ethnic Politics* 4.1–2: 86–118.
1999. Ethnic Law and Minority Rights in China: Progress and Constraints. *Law & Policy* 21.3 (July): 283–314.
2005. "China's Strategic Vulnerability to Minority Separatism in Tibet." *Asian Affairs: An American Review* 32.2 (July): 87–118.
Sautman, Barry and June Teufel Dreyer. 2006. *Contemporary Tibet: Politics, Development and Society*. Armonk, NY: M.E. Sharpe.
2010. "Scaling Back Minority Rights? The Debate about China's Ethnic Policies." *Stanford Journal of International Law* 46.1: 51–120.
Saideman, Stephen M. 2001. *The Ties that Divide: Ethnic Politics, Foreign Policy, and International Conflict*. New York, NY: Columbia University Press.
2002. "Discrimination in International Relations: Analyzing External Support for Ethnic Groups." *Journal of Peace Research* 39.1: 27–50.
Sakwa, Richard. 1998. *Soviet Politics in Perspective*. London: Routledge.
Schein, Louisa. 2000. *Minority Rules: The Miao and the Feminine in China's Cultural Politics*. Durham, NC: Duke University Press.
Schwartz, Ronald D. 1994. *Circles of Protest: Political Ritual in the Tibetan Uprising*. London: Hurst.
SCMP. 2017. "Armed Police Out in Full Force After Deadly Xinjiang Terror Attack." *South China Morning Post*. February 15. Web.
Seymour, James D. 2000. "Xinjiang's Production and Construction Corps and the Sinification of Eastern Turkestan." *Inner Asia* 2: 171–93.
Shakya, Tsering. 2008a. "The Gulf between Tibet and Its Exiles." *Far Eastern Economic Review*. May 8.
2008b. "Tibetan Questions." *New Left Review*, 51 (May–June): 5–27.
2012. "Self-Immolation: The Changing Language of Protest in Tibet." *Revue d'Etudes Tibètaines* 25 (December): 19–39.
Slezkine, Yuri. 1994. "The USSR as a Communist Apartment or How a Socialist State Promoted Ethnic Particularism." *Slavic Review* 53.2 (Summer): 414–52.
Smith, Anthony D. 1992. "Ethnic Identity and Territorial Nationalism in Comparative Perspective." Ed. Motyl. 45–65.
Stalin, Joseph. 1913. "Marxism and the National Question." J. V. Stalin Archive. www.marxists.org/reference/archive/stalin/works/1913/03.htm.
Starr, S. Frederick, ed. 2004. *Xinjiang: China's Muslim Borderland*. Armonk, NY: M.E. Sharpe.
Stein, Justin J. 2003. "Taking the Deliberative Turn in China: International Law, Minority Rights and the Case of Xinjiang." *Journal of Public and International Affairs* 14 (Spring): 13–14.
Sun, Yanfei. 2017. "The Rise of Protestantism in Post-Mao China: State and Religion in Historical Perspective." *American Journal of Sociology* 122.6: 1664–725.
Suny, Ronald Grigor. 1992. "State, Civil Society and Ethnic Consolidation in the USSR: Roots of the National Question." Eds. Lapidus and Zaslavsky. 22–42.
1993. *The Revenge of the Past: Nationalism. Revolution and the Collapse of the Soviet Union*. Stanford, CA: Stanford University Press.
Suny, Ronald Grigor and Terry Martin, eds. 2001. *A State of Nations: Empire and Nation-making in the Age of Lenin and Stalin*. New York: Oxford University Press.

Synder, Jack. 2000. *From Voting and Violence: Democratization and Nationalist Conflict*. New York: W.W. Norton and Company.
Took, Jennifer. 2005. *Native Chieftaincy in Southwest China*. Leiden: Brill Academic Publishing.
Topgyal, Tsering. 2011. "Insecurity Dilemma and the Tibetan Uprising in 2008." *Journal of Contemporary China* 20.69: 183–203.
Treisman, Daniel. 1997. "Russia's 'Ethnic Revival': The Separatist Activism of Regional Leaders in a Post-Communist Order." *World Politics* 49 (January): 212–49.
Ungor, Ugur Umit. 2012. *The Making of Modern Turkey: Nation and State in Eastern Anatolia, 1913–1950*. New York: Oxford University Press.
Van Wie Davis, Elizabeth. 2008. *Uyghur Muslim Ethnic Separatism in Xinjiang, China*. Asia-Pacific Center for Security Studies. January 2008. www.apcss.org/uyghur-muslim-ethnic-separatism-in-xinjiang-china/.
Wang, Juan. 2017. *The Sinews of State Power: The Rise and Demise of the Cohesive Local State in Rural China*. New York: Oxford University Press.
Wang, Lixiong. 2002. "Reflections on Tibet." *The New Left Review* 14 (March–April): 79–111.
2006. "Indirect Representation Versus a Democratic System: Relative Advantages for Resolving the Tibet Question." Eds. Sautman and Dreyer. 107–28.
2012a. "What Else If Not Self-Immolation?" *Tibet Telegraph*. December 29. www.tibettelegraph.com/2012/12/what-else-if-not-self-immolation.html.
Wellens, Koen. 2009. "Negotiable Rights? China's Ethnic Minorities and the Right to Freedom of Religion." *International Journal of Minority and Groups Rights* 16.3: 433–54.
Wen, Bo, et al. 2004. "Genetic Evidence Supports Demi Diffusion of Chinese Culture." *Nature* 431.16 (September): 302–5.
White, Sydney D. 1998. "State Discourse, Minority Policies, and the Politics of Identity in the *Lijiang Naxi* People's Autonomous County." *Nationalism and Ethnoregional Identities in China*. Ed. William Safran. Portland, OR: Frank Cass. 9–27.
Williams, Erin Elizabeth. 2008. "Ethnic Minorities and the State in China: Conflict, Assimilation, or a 'Third Way'?" CPSA 2008. www.cpsa-acsp.ca/papers-2008/Williams.%20Erin.pdf.
Wimmer, Andreas and Min, Brian. 2006. "From Empire to Nation State: Explaining War in the Modern World: 1816–2001." *American Sociological Review* 71.6: 867–97.
Wong. Edward. 2009. "Autonomy Is the Solution for Tibet, Dalai Lama Says." *New York Times*. May 28.
Wu, Xiaogang and Song Xi. 2014. "Ethnic Stratification amid China's Economic Transition: Evidence from the Xinjiang Uyghur Autonomous Region." *Social Science Research* 44: 158–72.
Wu, Xiaogang and Donald J. Treiman. 2004. "The Household Registration System and Social Stratification in China, 1955–1996." *Demography* 41.2: 363–84.
Wylie, Turnell V. 1977. "The First Mongol Conquest of Tibet Reinterpreted." *Harvard Journal of Asiatic Studies* 37.1: 103–33.
Yang, Fenggang. 2006. "The Red, Black and Grey Markets of Religion in China." *Sociological Quarterly* 47.1: 93–122.
2012. *Religion in China: Survival and Revival under Communist Rule*. New York: Oxford University Press.

Yash, Ghai. 2000. *Autonomy and Ethnicity: Negotiating Competing Claims in Multi-ethnic States*. New York: Cambridge University Press.

Yeh, E. T. 2003. "Tibetan Range Wars: Spatial Politics and Authority on the Grasslands of Amdo." *Development and Change* 34.3: 499–523.

Zang, Xiaowei. 2010. "Affirmative Action, Economic Reforms, and Uyghur-Han Variation in Job Attainment in Urumqi." *The China Quarterly* 202 (June): 307–26.

2012. "Age and the Cost of Being Uyghurs in Ürümchi." *The China Quarterly* 210 (June): 419–34.

Zaslavsky, Victor. 1992. "The Evolution of Soviet Separatism Under Gorbachev." Eds. Lapidus and Zavslasky. 71–97.

Zenz, Adrian. 2013. *"Tibetanness" Under Threat? Neo-integrationism, Minority Education and Career Strategies in Qinghai, P.R. China*. Leiden: Global Oriental.

2018a. "'Thoroughly Reforming Them Towards a Healthy Heart Attitude': China's Political Re-education Campaign in Xinjiang." *Central Asian Survey* 28.4: 347–60.

2018b. "New Evidence for China's Political Re-Education Campaign in Xinjiang." *China Brief* 18.10 (May 15). Web.

Zhang, Zhuoni and Wu Xiaogang. 2017. "Occupational Segregation and Earnings Inequality: Rural Migrants and Local Workers in Urban China." *Social Science Research* 61: 57–74.

Zhao, Dingxin. 2001. *The Power of Tiananmen: State-Society Relations and the 1989 Beijing Student Movement*. Chicago: University of Chicago Press.

2015. *The Confucian-Legalist State: A New Theory of Chinese History*. New York: Oxford University Press.

Zhao, Y. B. et al. 2011. "Ancient DNA Evidence Supports the Contribution of Di-qiang People to the Han Chinese Gene Pool." *American Journal of Physical Anthropology* 144.2: 258–68.

Zhou, Minglang. 2003 *Multilingualism in China: The Politics of Writing Reforms for Minority Languages, 1949–2002*. Berlin: Walter de Gruyter.

2012. "Historical Review of the PRC's Minority/Indigenous Language Policy and Practice: Nation-State Building and Identity Construction." Eds. Becket and Postiglione. 18–30.

Zhou, Minglang and Sun Hongkai, eds. 2004. *Language Policy in the People's Republic of China*. Boston, MA: Kluwer Academic Publishing.

Zhou, Zunyou. 2017. "China's Strategy for De-radicalization." *Terrorism and Political Violence*, DOI:10.1080/09546553.2017.1330199.

SOURCES IN CHINESE

Abdugheni. 2011. *Zaijing weiwu'erzu liudong renkou diaocha yanjiu* [A study of Uighur migrants in Beijing]. PhD dissertation, Minzu University of China.

Ao, Junde. 2001. "Minzu quyu zizhifa shi zenme xiugai de?" [How was the law on ethnic autonomous regions amended]. *Zhongguo minzu* 4: 4–7.

Azad, M. 2010. "Zui furao de tudishang de yili weiwu'e ren de xiagang daijia" [The price of being laid off for Uighurs in the endowed land of Ili]. *Uighurbiz.net*, April 13. www.uighurbiz.net/html/2010/0413/13435.html.

Bingtuan. 2013. "Xinjiang nanbeijiang renkou chayi jiqi yu quyu xietiao fazhan de yingxiang" [Demographic differences in northern and southern Xinjiang and their impact on regional development]. *Bingtuan sheke guihua ban*, July 1. Web.

Cai, Caidan. 2008. "Menyuan hanzu de laiyuan" [Sources of Han People in Menyuan]. *Qinghai Xinhua net*, May 21. Web.

Cao, Ying and Suhua Liu. 2004. "Lun zaoqi weixinpai de zhuquan guan" [On the early reformers' conception of sovereignty]. *Changsha ligong xuebao* 19.4 (December): 86–94.

CCP (Central Committee). 1980a. "Guanyu zhuanfa 'Xizang gongzuo huiyi jiyao' de tongzhi" [Notification on Forwarding the Minutes of Work Symposium on Tibet], April 7. In CCP (Document Research Center).

CCP (Central Committee Secretariat). 1980b. Zhongyang shujichu taolun Xinjiang gongzuo wenti de jiyao" [Minutes from the CCP Central Committee Secretariat's Discussion of its Work on Xinjiang]. July 16. www.people.com.cn/item/20years/newfiles/c1030.html.

CCP (Central Committee and the State Council). 1991. "Zhonggong zhongyang, guowuyuan guanyu jinyibu zuohao zongjiao gongzuo ruogan wenti de tongzhi" [The CCP Central Committee and the State Council notification on several issues regarding improvement of religious work]. 1991[6], February 5. http://cqlx.pkulaw.cn/fulltext_form.aspx.

2001b. *Mao Zedong Xizang gongzuo xuanbian* [Selected collection of Mao Zedong on Tibet (related) work]. Beijing: Zhongyang wenxian chubanshe.

2005. *Xizang gongzuo wenxian xuanbian* [Selected collection of documents on Tibet (related) work]. Beijing: Zhongyang wenxian chubanshe.

2018. "Zhonggong zhongyang guowuyuan guanyu shishi xiangcun zhenxin zhanlue de yijian" [CCP Central Committee and the State Council opinion on implementing the strategy to revive rural villages]. February 5. Web.

CCP (Document Research Center). 1982. *Sanzhongquanhui yilai zhongyao wenxian xuanbian* [Selected important documents since the 3rd plenum]. Vols. 1 and 2. Beijing: Zhonggong zhongyang wenxian chubanshe.

CCP (Organization Department). 2001a. *2000–2001 zhongguo diaocha baogao: xin xingshi xia de renmin neibu maodun* [2000–2001 investigative report on China: contradictions among the people in new times]. Beijing: Zhongyang bianyi chubanshe.

CCTB (Central Compilation and Translation Bureau). 1989. *Gongchan guoji dashiji* [Major events of the Comintern]. Ha'erbin: Heilongjiang renmin chubanshe.

CCTV1. 2018. "Xinjiang: Jujiao nanjiang sidi.sanzhou jingzhun tuopin" [Xinjiang: precision anti-poverty in the four prefectures of southern Xinjiang]. *Wanjian xinwen*, August 9.

CE *(Zhongguo jingji wang)*. 2013. "Xizang ge dishi shuji, shizhang (xingshu zhuanyuan) mingdan + jianli" [Names and resumes of party secretaries and chief executives at prefectural and municipal levels in the TAR]. Last updated July 2013. http://district.ce.cn/zt/rwk/sf/xz/ds/201206/15/t20120615_23410337.shtml.

2019. "Xinjiang gedi shuji, shi/zhou (xingshu zhuanyuan) mingdan + jianli" [Names and resumes of party secretaries and chief executives at prefectural and municipal levels in Xinjiang]. Last updated January 11, 2019. http://district.ce.cn/zt/rwk/sf/xj/ds/201206/14/t20120614_1269253.shtml.

Chang, An. 2010. "Qingmo minchu xianzheng shijie zhong de 'wuzu gonghe'" ['The Five-nation republic' in the constitutional worldview of the late Qing and early republican period]. *Beida falu pinglun* 2: 343–71.

Chang, Bao. 2011. "Xunzhao guojia: Qingmo minguo shiqi menggu difang jingying guojia rentong de yanbian yu xingcheng" [Looking for the state: The evolution and formation of national identity among local elites in Mongol areas during the late Qing and the Republican eras]. *Minzu shehuixue yanjiu tongxun* 78 (January): 1–17.

Chen, Fang. 2015. "Xinjiang qu jiduanhua diaocha" [Investigation of Xinjiang's deradicalization campaign]. *Ifeng*, October 12. http://news.ifeng.com/mainland/special/xjqjdh/.

Chen, Pengfei. 2014. "1978–1989 nian dangde minzu zhengce yanbian fenxi" [An analysis of the evolution of the party's ethnic policy during 1978–1989]. MA thesis, Xinjiang Teachers' College.

Chen, Tianhua. 2002. *Meng houtou, jingshi zhong* [Forcefully turn head to warn the world]. Beijing: Huaxia chubanshe.

Chen, Weiren. 1980. "Xizang kaocha ji" [A report on (Hu Yaobang's) investigative tour to Tibet]. *Lilun dongtai* 217 (July 15): 1–24.

Chen, Xinlin. 2010. "Cong zuqun dao minzu difang rentong yu guojia fenlei de boyi yu huhui – Tanqi shequ de shizheng yanjiu" [From ethnic groups to nationalities – competition and interaction between local identity and state classification – a case study of the Tanqi community]. *Zhongnan minzu daxue xuebao* 6: 38–42.

Chen, Xinyuan. 2012. "Wode liangwei weizu shangji" [My two Uyghur superiors]. *Minzu shehuixue yanjiu tongxun* 125 (December): 24–36.

Chen, Yuning. 1994. *Zhongguo minzu ningjuli de lishi tansuo* [A historical exploration of ethnic cohesion in China]. Kunming: Yunnan renmin chubanshe.

Chen, Zhibin and Sun Xiao. 2011. "Yita shijian: 1962 nian 60 wan Xinjiangren pantao sulian neimu" [The Yili-Tacheng incident: the inside story of the escape of sixty thousand Xinjiang residents to the Soviet Union in 1962]. *Gongshi wang*, November 7. www.21ccom.net/articles/lsjd/lccz/article_2011110748308.html.

Cheng, Min. 2013. "Wu Jinghua shengqian pibo 'Deng Liqun zishu: shi'er ge chunqiu" [Wu Jinghua's refutation of Deng Liqun's memoir]. *Hybsl*, July 11. www.hybsl.cn/ybsxyj/shengpingyusixiang/2013-07-11/38587.html.

2014a. "'Liangshao yikuan' zhengce de xingcheng guocheng" [The formation of the policy of "two less and one lax"]. *Hybsl*, March 17. www.hybsl.cn/zt/smnhy/ssssss1/2014-03-17/45297.html.

2014b. "Cheng Min: 80 niandai shi Xinjiang diqu zui wending de shiqi" [The 1980s was the most stable period in Xinjiang]. *Hu Yaobang shiliao xinxi wang*, March 28. www.cssn.cn/mzx/llzc/201404/t20140404_1058615.shtml.

2014c. "Yaobang tongzhi yu Kunming baokong an youhe guanxi?" [What does Comrade Yaobang have to the Kunming terror case?]. *Hybsl*, May 9. www.hybsl.cn/zt/smnhy/ssssss1/20140509/46192.html.

Cheng, Xuejiao. 2016. "Xinjiang shaoshu minzu gaokao jiafen zhengce cunzai de wenti ji duiche" [Problems of Xinjiang's preferential policies in college admissions and solutions]. *Lilun yanjiu* 6: 158–9.

China. 2017. "Zhijing Xinjiang fanbaokong xisheng de yinglie" [Salute to Xinjiang's heroes who died fighting terror]. April 4. https://military.china.com/11103358/20170404/30386580.html.

Chinacourt. 2014. "1979 nian Chen Yonggui weihe ma Hu Yaobang shi 'Hu Luanbang'?" [Why did Chen Yonggui call Hu YaoHuabang "Hu the wrecker" in 1979]. September 6. http://mqxfy.chinacourt.gov.cn/article/detail/2014/09/id/1433540.shtml.

Chinanews. 2014. "Xinjiang jiang choudiao 20 wan ming jiguan ganbu xiajiceng sannian fugai wancun" [Xinjiang will send 200,000 officials from state agencies to grass-roots for three years covering 10,000 villages]. February 15. www.chinanews.com/gn/2014/02-15/5841799.shtml.

Chopel, Khedrup. 2005. "Dang de zongjiao zhengce zai Xizang de guanche zhixing" [Implementation of the party's ethnic policy in Tibet]. *Zhongguo zangxue* 3: 158–68.

Dai, Xiaoming. 1999. "Xin zhongguo minzu fazhi jianshe: Shiji zhijiao de huigu yu qianzhan" [Construction of law on minorities in China: Looking back and forward at the turn of the millennium]. *Minzu yanjiu* 5: 21–32.

Dajia bao. 2016. "2016 nian Xinjiang xinnongcun hezuo yiliao xin zhengce" [New policies for Xinjiang's new cooperative healthcare in 2016]. March 8. www.dajiabao.com/zixun/20299.html.

Dang, Yulin and Zhang Yuxi. 2003. *Dangdai Xinjiang jianshi* [A brief history of Xinjiang]. Beijing: Dangdai zhongguo chubanshe.

Deng, Liqun. 2006. *Deng Liqun zishu: shi'erge chunqiu (1975–1987)* [Deng Liqun's memoir: *Twelve* years (1975–1987)]. Hong Kong: Dafeng chubanshe.

2008. "Deng Liqun zishu li dui 1980 nian Xizang wenti de huiyi" [Deng Liqun's recollection of the Tibet issue in 1980 in his memoir]. *Makeszhuyi pinglun*, April 28. www.reviewing.cn/2008/0428/8318.html.

Dong, Bumin. 2019. "Shequ jiaozheng de fazhan lishi ji xianzhuang" [Evolution and current state of community correction]. July 10. http://china.findlaw.cn/lawyers/article/d722752.html.

Du, Yongbin. 2005. "Han yiben 2005 nian ban qianyan – ge'ersitan: meiguo de 'xizang tong" [Forward to the 2005 edition – Goldstein: America's Tibet expert]. *Lama wangguo de fumie* [*The Demise of the Lamaist State*]. *Mei Ge'ersitan* (Melvin Goldstein). Beijing: Zhongguo zangxue chubanshe.

Duan, Qiming. 2012. "Guanche 19 hao wenjian de deyushi" [Gains and losses in implementing Document 19]. *Kexue yu wushen lun* 4: 14–22, 64.

Dute wang. 2017. "2017 nian Xinjiang fanfu zuixin xiaoxi, Xinjiang tanguan mindan daquan" [Latest anti-corruption news of 2017 from Xinjiang: A complete list of corrupt officials]. January 9. www.9d4d.com/lianghui/211894.html.

EdB. 1979. Editorial Board of Modern Chinese History, ed., *Zhongguo jindai shi* [Contemporary Chinese history]. Beijing: Zhonghua chubanshe.

1986. Editorial Board of Encyclopedia Sinica, ed., *Zhonghua da baike quanshu (minzu ji)* [Encyclopedia Sinica: collection on ethnic groups]. Beijing: Zhongguo baike chubanshe.

1987. Editorial Board of Guangxi Zhuangzu Autonomous Regions, ed., *Guangxi zhuangzu shehui lishi diaocha* [A historical investigation of the Zhuang community of Guangxi]. Nanning: Guangxi Minzu Press.

1989. Editorial Board of Chronicles of Work on Ethnic Affairs, ed., *Dangdai zhongguo minzu gongzuo dashiji* [Major events in ethnic work in contemporary China]. Beijing: Minzu chubanshe.

1993. Editorial Board of Contemporary China, ed., *Dangdai zhongguo minzu* [Ethnic groups in contemporary China]. Beijing: Dangdai zhongguo chubanshe.

2009. Editorial Board of Tibet in Contemporary China, ed., *Dangdai zhongguo de Xizang* [Tibet in contemporary China]. Beijing: Dangdai zhongguo chubanshe.

Edu.sina. 2004. "2004 nian gedi gaokao luqu fenshuxian" [The 2004 cut-off scores for college admissions in all provinces]. Undated. http://edu.sina.com.cn/focus/04gkcf/.

2006. "Xinjiang zhaoweihui gongbu 2006 nian zuidi toudang kongzhi fenshuxian" [Xinjiang College Admissions Committee announces the lowest qualifying scores for 2006]. June 28. http://edu.sina.com.cn/exam/2006-06-28/135444006.html.

EOL (Zhongguo jiaoyu zaixian). 2018. "Xinjiang linian gaokao fenshuxian" [The cut-off scores for college admissions in Xinjiang in past years]. April 8. http://gaokao.eol.cn/xin_jiang/dongtai/ 201804/ t20180408 _1594248.shtml.

Fan, Ke. 2011. "'Bianjiang fazhan' xian yi" [Disputing "frontier development"]. *Zhongnan minzu daxue xuebao* 1: 1–7.

Fei, Xiaotong. 1980. "Guanyu woguo minzu de shibie wenti" [On the problem of ethnic classification in our country]. *Zhongguo shehui kexue* 1: 147–63.

Fu, Maoji. 1954. "Yunnan shaoshu minzu yuwen de yiban qingkuan" [The general state of Yunnan's minority languages]. *Xin Jianshe*, March 1954.

Gao, Tianding. 2015. *Hu Yaobang yu xinshiqi fan yuanjia cuoan yanjiu* [Hu Yaobang and rectification of wrongful cases in the new era]. PhD dissertation, the Central Party School.

Gao, Zhonglun and Mu Jianglong. 2011. "Quanguo duikou zhiyuan xia Xinjiang jingji shehui fazhan de sikao" [On Xinjiang's economic and social development under partner assistance programs]. *Dangdai jingji* 1: 88–9.

Gaosan. 2017. "2017 gaokao shaoshu minzu jiafen zhengce jiedu" [Explaining bonus points policy for college admissions in 2017]. June 20. www.gaosan.com/gaokao/153823.html.

2019. "2019 Xinjiang gaokao jiafen ji youxian luqu zhengce" [Preferential policies in college admissions for Xinjiang, 2019]. May 21. www.gaosan.com/gaokao/245559.html.

Ge, Fengjiao. 2011. "Quanguo shaoshu minzu diqu shuangyu jiaoxue qingkuang gaishu" [An overview of bilingual education in minority regions]. *Xinjiang jiaoyu xuebao* 27.1: 69–76.

Gong, Xuezeng. 2003. "Xinzhongguo chuli minzu wenti de lilun yu shijian" [The theory and practice of new China in dealing with minority issues]. *Zongjiao yu minzu* 2: 2–26.

Gong, Zhixiang. 2009. *Minzu zhengce guocheng ji shizheng fenxi* [Minority policy decision making and an empirical analuysis]. Beijing: Zhongyang minzu daxue chubanshe.

Gongwuyuan. 2016. "2016 nian Xinjiang gongwuyuan kaoshi jianzhang" [Guidelines to Xinjiang's 2016 civil service exam]. March 21. https://gongwuyuan.eol.cn/difang/skzx/201603/t20160321_1378459.shtml.

Gu, Guoliang, et al. 2012. *Meiguo duihua zhengce zhong de Xinjiang wenti* [The Xinjiang issue in American policy towards China]. Beijing: Shehui kexue wenxian chubanshe.

Guan, Kai. 2007. *Zuqun zhengzhi* [Ethnic politics]. Beijing: Zhongyang minzu daxue chubanshe.

2011. "Manzu minzuxing: Diguo shidai de zhengzhihua jiegou yu houdiguo shidai de qu zhengzhiuhua jiegou" [The Manchus' ethnicity: politicization during imperial times and depoliticization in post-imperial times]. *Minzu shehuixue yanjiu tongxun* 78: 18–27.

2013. "Zhongguo de minzu zhengce: Bubian de huayu yu bianhua de shijian" [China's ethnic policy: unchanging discourse and changing realities]. *Wenhua zongheng* 6: 26–33.

Guan, Wei. 2004. "Lun zhongguo jindai guojifa guannian de zhaoxing" [On the rise of the concept of international law in modern China]. *Zhengfa luncong* 3: 84–9.

Guan, Yanbo. 2007. "Lun tangdai neidi yu bianjiang de 'hushi' he 'chaogong' maoyi" [On the trading and tribute system between the interior and frontier regions during the Tang dynasty]. *Heilongjiang minzu congkan* 4: 84–8.

Guancha. 2014a. "Xinjiang yanda baokong bannian: dadiao kongbu tuanhuo 115 ge, jiupu 334 ming zaitao xianyiren" [Half a year of intensified crackdown in Xinjiang: crushed 115 terror groups, arrested 334 suspects]. November 25. www.guancha.cn/local/2014_11_25_301560.shtml.

2014b. "Kelamayi jiang juban zizhiqu yundonghui, jinzhi wuzhong yizhuang renyuan chengzuo gongjiao" [Kelamayi will hold XUAR's sports meet and ban five types of dressing styles from public busses]. August 5. www.guancha.cn/local/2014_08_05_253709.shtml.

2015. "Xinjiang hetian shiwei fu shuji, shizhang Adeli Nu'ermaimaiti bei shuangkai" [Deputy Party Secretary and Mayor of Hotan Adeli Nurmehmet faced double expulsions]. February 19. www.guancha.cn/FaZhi/2015_02_19_ 309936.shtml.

2016. "Xinjiang: Jinzhi jiazhang youdao, qiangpo haizi canjia zongjiao" [Xinjiang: Prohibit parents from goading or forcing their children to participate in religious activities]. October 13. https://news.qq.com/a/20161013/001198.htm.

2019. "Yangshi bochu zhenhan shipin! Tashuo: ruguo meiyou jiaopei, wo dengdai de keneng shi diyu" [CCTV broadcasts rattling video clips from Xinjiang: He says, without the education and training center, I may be in hell]. March 19. www.guancha.cn/politics/2019_03_19_ 494248.shtml.

Guliyan. 2010. "Xuexiao jinzhi zongjiao huodong de falü yiju" [The legal basis for banning religious activities in schools]. *Xinjiang shehui zhexue kexue wang*, September 13. https://wenku.baidu.com/view/e4529e6048d7c1c708a14539.html.

Ha, Zhengli. 2009. "Dangdai zhongguo shaoshu minzu zongjiao zhengce jianping" [A brief analysis of policies towards minority religions in contemporary China]. *Zhonggong jinan shiwei dangxiao xuebao* 2: 102–6.

Han, Ting. 2015. *Dangde Xinjiang minzu zhengce de lishi diaocha* [An investigation of the party's ethnic policy in Xinjiang]. MA thesis, Xinjiang sifan daxue.

Hao, Shiyuan. 2012. "Hao Shiyuan Pingxi 'di'erdai minzu zhengce' shuo jiexuan" [Excerpts of Hao Shiyuan's comments on the second generation of minority policies]. *Zhongguo minzu bao*, February 3, 10, and 17; March 2, 9, and 16; April 13 and 30; May 11.

Hao, Shiyuan, Zhang Haiyang, and Ma Rong. 2013. "Goujian xinxing minzu guanxi" [Building a new type of ethnic relations]. *Lingdaozhe* 53 (August): 79–100.

He, Fang. 2009. "Hu Yaobang yu minzu quyu zizhi" [Hu Yaobang and autonomy in minority regions]. *Ai sixiang*, August 24. www.aisixiang.com/data/29752.html.

He, Junfang. 1998. *Zhongguo minzu shuangyu wenti yanjiu: Lishi yu xianshi* [A study of bilingual education in China: history and reality]. Beijing: Zhongyang minzu daxue chubanshe.

He, Longqun. 2010. "Zhou Enlai yu Guangxi minzu diqu de fazhan" [Zhou Enlai and development of minority areas in Guangxi]. *Zhongguo qingnian wang* April 28. Web.

HQSB (*Huangqiu shibao*). 2009. "Dai Xu: Xizang Xinjiang chuyu meijun banxiaoshi huoli daji quannei" [Dai Xu: Tibet and Xinjiang located within half an hour of American military attack]. August 20, 2009.

2014. "Sheping: Baigong gai cheng Xinjiang 'kongbuxiji' zhide guli" [Op-ed: The White House deserves to be commended for reversing itself and referring to Xinjiang's "terrorist attack"]. May 24.

Hu, Anang and Hu Lianhe. 2010. "Yushijujin tuidong minzu jiaorongyiti shi guojia changzhijiu'an de zhiben zhi ce" [Changing with the times and promoting ethnic integration is the fundamental policy to ensure China's long-term stability]. *Tansuo* 5: 151–5.

2011. "Di'erdai minzu zhengce: cujin minzu jiaorong yiti he fanrong yiti" [The second generation of ethnic policy: Promoting ethnic integration and common prosperity]. *Xinjiang shifan daxue xuebao* 5: 1–13.

Hu, Hongbao and Zhang Limei. 2009. "Minzu shibie yuanze de bianhua yu minzu renkou" [Changes in criteria for classifying ethnic groups and ethnic populations]. *Xinan minzu daxue xuebao* 30.4: 9–13.

Hu, Lingming. 2011. "Guanyu xiugai wanshan 'minzu quyu zizhifa de jidian sikao'" [Some reflections on amending "Law on Autonomy of Ethnic Regions."]. *Minzu luntan* 11: 17–20.

Hu, Youze and Cheng Rong. 2016. "Xinshiqi 'liangshao yikuan' minzu zhengce yanjiu" [An analysis of the "two less and one lax" policy in the new era]. *Qinghai minzu yanjiu* 27.2: 81–5.

Hualv. 2012. "Shequ jiaozheng de yiyi younaxie?" [What is the significance of community correction]. February 8. www.66law.cn/topic2010/sqjzdyy/2063.shtml.

2019. "Xinjiang pinkunhu biaozhun" [Allowances for poor households in Xinjiang]. January 16. www.66law.cn/laws/735363.aspx.

Huang, Guangxue and Si Lianhu. 2005. Zhongguo de minzu shibie [China's ethnic classification]. Beijing: Minzu chubanshe.

Huang, Mu and Wu, Keya. 2001. "Zhongguo gudai shaoshu minzu chaogongzhi chutan" [A preliminary analysis of the tribute system for ethnic minorities in ancient China]. *Qinghai minzu yanjiu* 12.4: 33–5.

Huang, Rongqing. 2009. "Xibu shaoshu minzu renkou yu fazhan" [Ethnic populations and development in western China]. *Zhongguo renkou* January 12: 1–29.

Huang, Wei. 2008. "Minzu zizhi difang zhengfu yu qita difang zhengfu xingzheng quanli de bijiao yanjiu" [A comparison of the administrative powers of local governments in autonomous and other regions]. *Minzu yanjiu* 3: 1–10.

Huang, Xingtao. 2002. "Minzu zijue yu fuhao rentong" [Ethnic self-consciousness and identity markers]. *Zhongguo shehui kexue pinglun* (Hong Kong) February Web.

Huang, Zhangjin. 2011. "Kemu de xuanze" [Kemu's choice]. *Fenghuang zhoukan* September 5. Web.

2012. "Xinjiang weizu shehui zheng xianru shenzhong weiji" [Xinjiang's Uighur society in deep crisis]. *Yangguang shiwu zhoukan* (Hong Kong), 35 (December): 42–22.

2013. "Shizi lukou de Xinjiang" [Xinjiang at crossroads]. *Fenghuang zhoukan* 478 (July 25). Web.

2014. "Xinjiang minzu zongjiao wenti de youlai he xianzhuang" [The origin and state of Xinjiang's ethnic and religious problems]. March 28. https://cinacn.blogspot.com/2014/03/blog-post_28.html.

Huatu. 2011. "Xinjiang gongwuyuan kaoshi zuire zhi 1100 baokao, 280 ge 'lingbaokao'" [The most popular civil service job attracts 1,100 applicants, while 280 openings receive zero applicants]. May 3. www.huatu.com/a/gwy/news/xinjiang/2011/0503/84449.html.

Jia, Youjun, Qi Qungao, and Wang Yingzi. 2006. "Xinjiang shaoshu minzu daxuesheng jiuye wenti yu chengyin fenxi" [Analyzing obstacles to employment for minority students in Xinjiang]. *Jiaoyu yu zhiye* 14: 55–6.

Jian, Zhixiang. 2006. *Zuqun guishu de ziwo yu shehui dingyi* [Self-identification and social definition of ethnic belonging]. Beijing: Minzhu chubanshe.

2009. "Zuqun youhui zhengce yu zuqun rentong" [Ethnic preferential policies and ethnic Identity]. Ed. Ma (2009a). 141–58.

2011. "Ma Qi de shenfen zhuanhuan yu zhengzhi jueze – jianyi minguo shiqi difang geju shili de guojia yishi" [Ma Qi's identity transformation and political choice: national identity of local warlords during the Republican era]. *Minzu shehuixue yanjiu tongxun* 78: 28–39.

Jiang, Ping and Huang Zhu, eds. 1994. *Zhongguo minzu lilun yu shijian* [Theory and practice of China's minorities]. Beijing: Zhongyang dangxiao chubanshe.

Jin, Wei. 2008. "Duikou yuanzu yu Xizang de jingji fazhan" [Partner assistance and Tibet's economic development]. *Xibei minzu yanjiu* 59.4: 10–19.

2010a. *Xizang: Yuanzu yu fazhan* [Tibet: Aid and *development*]. Lhasa: Xizang renmin chubanshe.

2010b. "Ganbu yuanzang de chengjiu yu juxian" [The achievements and limitations of cadre assistance to Tibet]. *Kexue shehui zhuyi* 6: 66–8.

2011. "Guangxi minzu wenti diaocha baogao" [Investigative report on ethnic problems in Guangxi]. *Kexue shehui zhuyi* 5: 131–4.

2016. "Xizang's de shouyuan yu kechixu fazhan" [Aid to Tibet and its sustainable development]. *Xibei minzu yanjiu* 2: 5–14.

Kuximake, Parr hatti, and Gulnar WufuLi, 2008. "Yanjiu pipan Yizabute: Daxue laoshi de zeren" [College faculty's responsibility to study and criticize *Hizb ut-Tahrir*]. *Kashgar shifan xueyuan xuebao* 29:2: 80–4.

LAER. 2001. *Zhonghua renmin gongheguo minzu quyu zizhi fa* [PRC Law on Ethnic Autonomous Regions]. *Zhongguo zhengfu menhu wangzhan*. Web.

Li, Fanwen. 2005. *Xixia tongshi* [A general history of west Xia]. Yinchuan: Ningxia remin chubanshe.

Li, Hongliang. 2017. "Xinjiang weiwu'er daxuesheng jiuye jiazhi quxiang de yindao cuoshi" [Measures to guide employment preferences of Xinjiang's Uighur students]. *Caizi* 5: 165.

Li, Jianglin. 2010. "Qinghai 'Xunhua shijian' shimo" [The origin of the Xunhua incident]. http://biweeklyarchive.hrichina.org/article/307.html.

Li, Jiansheng. 2004. "Dangqian Xinjiang diqu de feifa zongjiao huodong jiqi e'zhi he yufang" [Illegal religious activities in Xinjiang at present and their curtailment and prevention]. *Xinjiang sifan daxue xuebao* 2: 32–6.

Li, Junqing. 2009. *Chonggou yu chaoyue: Minzu diqu gonggong guanli xianzhuang diaocha yu fenxi* [Restructuring: An investigation of public administration in ethnic regions]. Beijing: Renmin chubanshe.

Li, Shiyu. 2001. "Cong kangqian minzu zhengce kan xibu kaifa" [Ethnic policies during Emperors Kangxi and Qianlong and the development of western regions]. *Guizhou daxue xuebao* 19.4: 73–80.

Li, Shuguang and Cai Wanling. 2012. "Xinjiang shaoshu minzu xiaoxue shuangyu jiaoyu cunzai de wenti ji duice" [Problems in bilingual education at Xinjiang's ethnic elementary schools and remedies]. *Hetian shifan zhuanke xuexiao xuebao* 31.3: 85–7.

Li, Xiaoqiang, Long Kui, and Lü Weixuan. 2017. "Xinjiang gongke yuanxiao shaoshu minzu tongxue jiuye quxiang tezheng yanjiu" [A study of job destinations for minority graduates from Xinjiang's STEM colleges]. *Keji feng*, September (I): 241.

Li, Xiaoxia. 2001. "Xinjiang minhan hexiao de yanbian yu fazhan qianjing" [The evolution and future of mixed Han and ethnic schools in Xinjiang]. *Xinjiang daxue xuebao* 29.2: 22–8.

2005a. "Xinjiang gaokao zhaosheng zhong de shaoshu minzu kaosheng youhui zhengce fenxi" [An analysis of preferential policies for minority students in Xinjiang's college admissions]. *Xinjiang daxue xuebao* 33.1: 77–88.

2009a. "Xinjiang gaokao zhaosheng zhong de shaoshu minzu kaosheng youhui zhengce fenxi" [An analysis of preferential policies for minority students in Xinjiang's college admissions]. Eds. Ma and Guo. 154–91.

2009b. "Xinjiang daxue shaoshu minzu dazhongzhuan biyesheng de jiuye wenti" [The employment issue for minority graduates of four-year and two-year colleges in Xinjiang]. Ed. Ma (2009a). 387–93.

2011a. "Nanjiang weihan nongmin de shengchan jiaowang diaocha" [An investigative report of interaction among Uighur and Han farmers in southern Xinjiang]. *Minzu shehuixue yanjiu tongxun* 84: 1–15.

2011b. "Xinjiang minzu guanxi zouxiang jiqi yingxiang yinsu fenxi" [An analysis of the factors affecting trends in ethnic relations in Xinjiang]. *Minzu shehuixue yanjiu tongxun* 94: 1–9.

2012a. "Xinjiang shehui jingji fazhan diaocha baogao" [An investigative report on social and economic development in Xinjiang]. *Minzu shehuixue yanjiu tongxun* 108: 21–9.

2012b. "Xinjiang zongjiao shiwu guanli zhengce fenxi" [An analysis of state regulation of religious affairs in Xinjiang]. *Minzu shehuixue yanjiu tongxun* 117: 1–8.

2012c. "Xinjiang: kuayueshi jingji fazhan xia ruhe shixian changzhi jiu'an" [Xinjiang: How to ensure long-term stability under leap-forward economic development]. *Minzu shehuixue yanjiu tongxun* 125: 14–22.

2013a. "Xinjiang e'zhi feifa zongjiao huodong zhengce fenxi" [An analysis of state policies to contain illegal religious activities in Xinjiang]. *Minzu shehuixue yanjiu tongxun* 140: 23–31.

2013b. "Xinjiang zongjiao shiwu guanli zhengce fenxi – yi jinzhi siban jingwen ban weili" [An analysis of state regulation of religious affairs in Xinjiang – the case of banning private madrasas]. *Minzu shehuixue yanjiu tongxun* 140: 32–40.

2013c. "Xinjiang zongjiao shiwu guanli zhengce fenxi – yi zongjiao jiaozhi renyuan shenghuo butie weili" [An analysis of state regulation of religious affairs in Xinjiang – the case of subsidies for the clergy], *Minzu shehuixue yanjiu tongxun* 136: 11–19.

2015. "Xinjiang shaoshu minzu chanye gongren fazhan ji xianzhuang fenxi" [An analysis of the evolution and status of minority industrial workers in Xinjiang]. *Minzu shehuixue yanjiu tongxun* 187: 29–40.

2016. "Xinjiang zongjiao jiduan sixiang chuanbo tedian ji diyu zhengce fenxi" [An analysis of the spread of religious extremism in Xinjiang and counter strategies]. *Minzu shehuixue yanjiu tongxun* 213: 1–7.

2017. "Xinjiang jiceng zuzhi jianshe yu shehui wending guanxi huisu" [The relationship between building rural governance and social stability]. *Minzu shehuixue yanjiu tongxun* 240: 29–36.

Li, Weiwei. 2012. "Jiangsu Yixing de shequ jiaozheng zhongxin hen renxinghua" [The community correction centers in Yixing, Jiangsu, are very humane]. Sina blog. May 5. http://blog.sina.com.cn/s/blog_7ccbc9ef01013thx.html.

Li, Yongfeng. 2013. "Minjian jingwen xuexiao: zuoyou Xinjiang weilai de an'liu" [The undercurrent that will determine Xinjiang's future: private madrassas]. *Fengsheng*, November 6. http://fengshenghk.blogspot.com/2013/11/blog-post_6.html.

Li, Yueming. 2010. "Gedi duikou zhiyuan Xinjiang qingkuang yilan" [Provincial distribution of partner assistance to Xinjiang]. *Shishi qiushi* 3: 115.

Li, Yunquan. 2006. "Chaogong zhidu de lilun yuanyuan yu shidai tezhen" [The theoretical sources of the tribute system and its characteristics in different historical periods]. *Zhongguo bianqiang shidi yanjiu* 16.3: 37–48.

Li, Yuwei. 2004a. "Minguo shiqi guomindang zhengfu de minzu zhengce ji neimenggu de minzu wenti" [Ethnic policies of the KMT government and the ethnic problem in Inner Mongolia during the Republican era]. *Zhongyang minzu daxue xuebao* 1: 81–7.

2004b. "Beiyang zhengfu de minzu zhengce yu neimenggu de minzu wenti" [Ethnic policies of the Beiyang government and the ethnic problem in Inner Mongolia]. *Nengmenggu shehui kexue* 2: 14–17.

Li, Zonghua and Li Yankai. 1992. *Anduo zangshi lue* [A brief history of Amdo]. Xining: Qinghai remin chubanshe.

Liang, Jinglun. 2014. *Beijing duikou zhiyuan Xinjiang Hetian diqu shijian yanjiu* [A study of Beijing's partner assistance to Hotan]. MA thesis, Minzu University of China.

Liang, Qichao. 1901/1963. "Guojia sixiang bianqian yitong lun" [A comparative study of changes in the conception of the state]. *Xinhai geming qianshinian shi lunwenji* [Collection of essays on the decade before the revolution of 1911]. Beijing: Sanlian shudian.

Lin, Da. 2009. "Sifa bugong shi Xinjiang wenti de yinbao dian" [Judicial unfairness is the tipping point for Xinjiang's problems]. *Yazhou zhoukan* 30: 35.

Lin, Huixiang. 1936. *Zhongguo minzu shi* [Ethnic history of China]. Beijing: Shangwu yinshuguan.

Liu, Dan. 2010. "Xinjiang yimin wenti fenxi" [An analysis of the migration problem in Xinjiang]. *Xibei renkou* 31.6: 115–19, 125.

Liu, Tong. 1998. *Tangchao jimi fuzhou yanjiu* [A study of loose rein prefectures in the Tang dynasty]. Xi'an: Xibei daxue chubanshe.

Liu, Weijun. 2010. *Xiyu wenhua jingcui* [Cultural essentials of western regions]. Vols. 1–2. Hong Kong: Zhonghua wenhua chubanshe. (Vols. 3–4, 2011).

2011. "Shui shi tianshan de yuanzhumin" [Who are the original inhabitants across the Tianshan areas?]. Paper presented at the conference on the development of Chinese ethnology at Xinjiang University, July 11–12.

Liu, Yuelan. 2007. "Xinjiang jianshe bingtuan renkou qianyi yanjiu" [A study of migration patterns in Xinjiang's PCCs]. *Xibei renkou* 28.2: 111–15.

2009a. "Gaige kaifang yilai dangde minzu zongjiao zhengce zai Hetian de chenggong shijian" [Successful implementation of the party's ethnic and religious policy in Hetian in the reform era]. *Zhonggong yili zhouwei dangxiao xuebao* 2: 53–5.

Liu, Yuelan and Wang Xuehua. 2008. "1954–2005 nian Xinjiang bingtuan renkou fazhan tedian ji zhiyue yinsu fenxi" [Characteristics and constraining factors in the demographic growth of Xinjiang's PCCs, 1954–2005]. *Xibei renkou* 29.1: 98–102.

Liu, Yujin. 2014. "Xizang jiaqiang he chuangxin simiao guanli gongzuo cujin zongjiao hemu" [Tibet strengthens and innovates regulation of monasteries, promoting religious harmony]. *Xizang ribao*, December 24.

Liu, Yuewu. 2009b. "Zhongguo chuantong zongfan tizhi shulun" [On the Suzerain-vassal system in traditional China]. *Nanjing Shifan daxue xuebao* 6: 42–8.

Losel, Rigzin. 2011b. "Ruhe gei xifang ren jiang Xizang wenti" [How to explain the Tibet issue to westerners]. *Lingdaozhe* (April): 22–8.

Losel, Rigzin and Huang Weizhong. 2012. "Cong zai neidi de zangzu liudong renkou zhuangkuan kan hanzang minzu guanxi: yi chengdu liudong renkou weili" [A look at the Han–Tibetan relations through the migratory population in interior China: The case of Chengdu]. *Zhongguo zangxue* 101.2: 6–8.

Lü, Simian. 1935. *Zhongguo minzu yanjin shi* [A history of the evolution of China's ethnic groups]. Shanghai: Yazhou shukan.

Luo, Changpei and Fu Maoji. 1954. "Guonei shaoshu minzu yuyan wenzi gaikuang" [An overview of minority language and scripts in our country]. *Zhongguo yuyan* 3.

Luo, Zhijia. 2016. *Dang zai Xinjiang de wenhua zhili de lishi jincheng ji jiben jiaoxun yanjiu* [A study of the history and lessons of the party's cultural management of Xinjiang]. PhD dissertation, Shaanxi Normal University.

Ma, Dazheng. 2002. *Guojia liyi gaoyu yiqie: Xinjiang wending wenti de guancha yu sikao* [The supremacy of national interests: Observations and reflections on the issue of stability in Xinjiang]. Urumqi: Xinjiang renmin chubanshe.

Ma, Dazheng and Xu Jianying. 2006. *"Dong tujue sitan guo" mimeng de huangmie* [The passing of the illusion of East Turkestan]. Urumqi: Xinjiang remmin chubanshe.

Ma, Pinyan. 2003. "Xinjiang fandui feifa zongjiao huodong yanjiu" [A study of Xinjiang's fight against illegal religious activities]. *Xinjiang shehui kexue* 4: 72–8.

Ma, Rong. 1996. *Xizang renkou yu shehui* [Tibet's population and society]. Beijing: Tongxin chubanshe.

2001. "Zhongguo ge minzu zhijian de zuji tonghun" [Interethnic marriages in China]. *Minzu yu shehui fazhan* [Ethnic groups and social development]. Beijing: Minzu chubanshe. 161–224.

2004. "Lijie minzu guanxi de xin silu" [New thinking in understanding ethnic relations]. *Beijing daxue xuebao* 6: 122–3.

et al. 2005. "Xinjiang Wulumuqi liudong renkou jiegou tezhen yu jiuye zhuangkuan" [The structure and employment of migrant population in Urumqi, Xinjiang]. *Xibei minzu yanjiu* 3: 5–42.

2008a. "Sidalin shifou zai minzu wenti shang fanle lishixing cuowu?" [Did Stalin make a historical mistake on the ethnic issue?]. *Minzu shehu xue yanjiu tongxun* 46: 1–8.
2008b. "Xizang zizhiqu renkou de jiegou yu bianhua" [The structure and transformation of Tibet's population]. *Zhongguo Xizang* 3: 167–83.
2009a. Ed. *Shaoshu mionzu shehui fazhan yu jiuye* [Development and employment in minority society]. Beijing: shehui kexue wenxian chubanshe.
2009b. "Xinjiang minzu jiaoyu de fazhan yu shuangyu jiaoyu de shijian" [Development of minority education and implementation of bilingual education in Xinjiang]. Eds. Ma and Guo. 30–64.
2009c. "Xinjiang minzu jiaoyu yu daxuesheng jiuye wenti zuotanhui jilu zhengli" [Minutes from symposium on minority education and employment for Xinjiang's college students]. Ed. Ma (2009a). 394–406.
2009d. "Neimenggu chaoyuan muqu de menghan guanxi yanbian ji yingxiang yinsu – yi ximengdongwu qi yige muye shequ wei ge'an" [The dynamics of the Han–Mongolian relations in pastoral areas of Inner Mongolia: A case study of Ximengdongwu Banner]. *Xibei minzu yanjiu* 4: 8–31.
2010a. "Zhongguo shehui de linyilei 'er'yuan jiegou'" [Another "dual structure" in Chinese society]. *Beijing daxue xuebao* 47.3: 93–103.
2010b. "Zhongguo chuantong 'zuqun guan' yu xianqin wenxian 'zu' zi shiyong qianxi" [A brief analysis of traditional Chinese conceptions of ethnicity and the use of "zu" in pre-Qin classic texts]. Ed. Xie. 205–38.
2011a. "Er'shiyi shiji zhongguo shifou cunzai guojia fenlie de fengxian" [Is China vulnerable to separatism in the twenty-first century?]. *Lingdaozhe* (February and April): 88–108 and 72–85.
2011c. "Xinjiang chengzhen fazhan yu shuangyu jiaoyu jincheng" [Urban development and progress in bilingual education in Xinjiang]. *Xibei minzu yanjiu* 69.2: 159–72.
2011d. "Xizang shehui fazhan yu shuangyu jiaoyu" [Tibet's social development and bilingual education]. *Zhongguo zangxue* 2 (February): 114–45.
2011e. "Minguo shiqi shaoshu minzu jingying: Lijie zhongguo cong 'tianxia diguo' zhuanxiang 'minzu guojia' de yaoshi" [Minority elites during the Republican era: Understanding the key to China's evolution from a "celestial empire" to a "nation-state"]. *Minzu shehuixue yanjiu tongxun* 78 (January): 1–5.
2012. "Zhongguo de minzu wenti yu 20 shiji 50 niandai de 'minzu shibie'" [China's current minority problems and the "ethnic classification" of the 1950s]. *Xibei minzu yanjiu* 74.3: 13–28.
2013a. "Guanyu dangqian woguo minzu wenti de jinyibu taolun – yetan 'di'erdai minzu zhengce'" [Further thinking on ethnic issues in China – on the "second-generation ethnic policy"]. *Zhongyang minzu daxue xuebao* 4:5–10.
2013b. "Xinjiang duikou zhiuyuan xiangmu shishi qingkuan diaocha" [An investigation of the implementation of partner assistance projects in Xinjiang]. *Minzu shehui xue yanjiu tongxun* 147 (November): 1–12.
Ma, Rong and Drolop Tenzin. 2008. "Lasa liudong renkou de diaocha baogao" [An investigative report on Lhasa's migratory population]. *Xibei minzu yanjiu* 4: 124–71.
Ma, Rong and Guo Zhigang, eds. 2009. *Zhongguo xibu diqu shaoshu minzu jiaoyu de fazhan* [Development of minority education in China's western regions]. Beijing: Minzu chubanshe.

Ma, Yao. 2001. *Minzuxue yu minzu gongzuo lunwen ji* [Collection of papers from ethnic studies and ethnic work]. Kunming: Yunnan minzu chubanshe.

Ma, Yin. 1984. *Zhongguo shaoshu minzu changshi* [General knowledge about China's ethnic groups]. Beijing: Zhongguo qingnian chubanshe.

Mao, Weihua. 2018. "Xinjiang 'shuangyu' jiaoyu de duominuogu xiaoyin" [The domino effect of Xinjiang's bilingual education]. *China Daily*, May 16. Web.

Meiwen wang. 2017. "2007 nian Xinjiang gongkai kaoshi luqu gongwuyuan, gongzuo renyuan gonggao" [Public announcement for Xinjiang's 2007 civil service exam]. May 11. www.wenjiwu.com/doc/klpgni.html.

Memet, Adil and Guljawer Halewjan. 2018. "Shilun Xinjiang shuangyu jiaoyu cunzai de wenti yu duice" [Problems in Xinjiang's bilingual education and solutions]. *Xibu xuekan* 71.2: 35–8.

Memet, Dilshati. 2018. "Jiaqiang Xinjiang shuangyu jiaoyu, cujin shaoshu minzu rencai peiyang" [Strengthen bilingual education in Xinjiang, promote training of minority talent]. *Dangdai jiaoyu lilun yu jiaoxue shijian* 4: 41–2.

Mi, Shoujiang and You Jia. 2004. *Zhongguo yisilan jiao* [Islam in China]. Beijing: Zhongguo zhouji chubanshe.

Min, Yuan. 2014. "Yu Zhu Weiqun tan Xinjiang qingzhensi shuliang wenti" [Debating Mr. Zhu Weiqun on the number of mosques in Xinjiang]. *Zhongguo shuzi shidai*, May 1. Web.

Ming, Hao. 2012. "Minzu 'shijue' huhuan yushijujin – tan dangqian minzu yanjiu zhong de redian huati" [Enhancing the "ethnic perspective" in contemporary ethnic studies]. *Yunnan minzu daxue xuebao* 29.5: 5–21.

2015. "Qiangdiao duoyang xing youhe 'guofen'" [What is excessive about emphasizing diversity?]. *Zhongguo minzu bao*, July 17.

Mo, Yueyan. 1996. "Li Weihan dui jiejue zhongguo minzu wenti daolu de tansuo" [Li Weihan's search for solutions to China's ethnic problems]. *Minzu yanjiu* 3: 1–9.

MOE (Ministry of Education). 1983. "Jiaoyubu guanyu zhengque chuli shaoshuminzu diqu zongjiao ganrao xuexiao jiaoyu wenti de yijian" [Ministry of Education on properly handling the problem of religious interference in public school education in minority regions]. February 17. www.china.com.cn/guoqing/zwxx/2011–10/02/content_23540452.htm.

1998. "Mianxiang 21 shiji jiaoyu zhenxing xingdong jihua" [A plan of action for strengthening education for the twenty-first century]. December 24. http://old.moe.gov.cn//publicfiles/business/htmlfiles/moe/moe_177/200407/2487.html.

MOF (Ministry of Finance). 1993–2017. *Zhongguo caizheng nianjian* [Finance yearbook of the PRC]. Beijing: Zhongguo caizheng zazhishe.

MUF (Ministry of United Front). 1991. *Minzu wenti wenjian huibian* [Collection of documents on ethnic issues]. Beijing: Zhongyang dangxiao chubanshe.

Na La. 2010. *Qingmo minguo shiqi Xinjiang youmu shehui yanjiu* [A study of Xinjiang's pastoral society in the late Qing and Republican eras]. Beijing: Sheke xueshu chubanshe.

NFRB (Nanfang ribao). 2009. "6.26 Shaoguan shijian wei faxian waibu shili he heishehui chashou" [No external forces or organized crime involved in the 6.26 Shaoguan incident]. July 7. Print.

NFZM (Nanfang zhoumo). 2007. "1990–2007: Zhongguo fanji dongtu 17 nian" [1990–2007: 17 Years of fighting East Turkistan]. January 11. Print.

Nijatkar. 2012. "2012 Xinjiang weiwu'er zizhiqu gongwuyuan kaoshi: Jueda duoshi gangwei xianding hanzu" [Xinjiang's 2012 civil service exams: most positions require Han applicants]. August 27. www.uighurbiz.net/archives/5151.

Niyaz, Abiz. 2004. "Dangqian Xinjiang fan fenlie douzheng yu Yisilanjiao guanxi de jige wenti" [Several issues in the linkages between Xinjiang's battles against separatism and Islam). *Xinjiang shifan daxue xuebao* 2 (June): 15–20.

Pan, Jiuyan. 2009. *Quanguo yuanzang jingji fenxi* [The whole country assists Tibet: An economic analysis]. Chengdu: Sichuan daxue chubanshe.

Pan, Jiuyan and Zhou Hongfang. 2010. "'Quanguo yuanzang': Gaige lujing yu zhengce huiyin" [On "the whole country assists Tibet": Reform paths and policy responses]. *Zhonggong Sichuan shengwei shengji jiguan dangxiao xuebao* 2: 61–4.

Pei, Shengyu. 2012. "Jianchi zhongguo tese minzu lilun zhengce, pibo 'di'erdai minzu zhengce' shuo" [Uphold Chinese ethnic theory and policy, criticize proposals for the "second generation of ethnic policy"]. *Yunnan minzu daxue xuebao* 3.2: 163.

Peng, Jianying. 2004. *Zhongguo gudai jimi zhengce de yanbian* [The evolution of loose rein policies in ancient China]. Beijing: Zhongguo shekeyuan chubanshe.

People's Daily. 2017. "Xinjiang jiaoyuting yuan tingzhang Sattar Sawut deng qiren jieshou diaocha" [Head of Xinjiang's department of education Sattar Sawut and six others under investigation]. February 9. http://politics.people.com.cn/n1/2017/0209/c1001-29070296.html.

Qi, Qungao and He Jianzhong. 2007. "Xinjiang shaoshu minzu daxuesheng jiuye xingshi yu duice fenxi" [An analysis of employment trends for minority students in Xinjiang and coping policies]. *Jiaoyu yu zhiye* 3: 165–7.

Qi, Ruoxiong. 2000. "Wushi niandai zhongguo gongchandang chuli Xinjiang shaoshu minzu zongjiao wenti de fangzhen yu shijian" [The principles and practices of the party in dealing with minority religious issues in Xinjiang in the 1950s]. *Zhonggong dangshi yanjiu* 6: 39–45.

Qi wanbao. 2017. "Shandong jinxia gaokao buzai fen yierben, quxiao shaoshu minzu jiafen" [Shandong eliminates two-tier college admissions and bonus points for minorities this summer]. March 25.

Qin, Heping. 2013. "56 ge minzu de laili bingfei yuanyu minzu shibie" [Origin of the 56 nationalities did not originate from the classification project]. *Minzu xuekan* 19.5: 34–48.

Ren, Xinli. 2003. "Guanyu dizhi zongjiao dui jiaoyu shentou de duice yanjiu" [On policies to constrain the infiltration of religion in the educational field]. *Xinjiang shifan daxue xuebao* 24:3: 29–31.

Renaguli, Xiakere, et al. 2011. "Shaoshu minzu xuesheng jiuye wenti fenxi" [An analysis of employment issues for minority students]. *Meili zhongguo* 5: 525–6.

Renmin ribao. 2019. "Diqici quanguo duikou zhiyuan Xinjiang gongzuo huiyi zhaokai, Wang Yang chuxi bing jianghua" [The seventh national conference on partner assistance to Xinjiang convenes, Wang Yang attends and speaks]. July 7. Print.

Reyilai. 2013. "Shinian hou, huigu Xinjiang 'neigao ban'" [Looking back at the Xinjiang class a decade later]. *Minzu shehuixue yanjiu tongxun* 147: 33–5.

Sakhon, Samut Erken. 2010. "Lun xinshiqi 'liangshao yikuan' xingshi zhengce de guanche ji wanshan – yi Xinjiang diqu de sifa shijian weili" [On implementing and improving the "two less and one lax" policy in the new era – The case of Xinjiang's judicial practice]. *Fazhi yu shehui* 11 (November): 108–10.

SBG (Statistics Bureau of Guangxi). 2001. 2003. 2010. *Guangxi tongji nianjian* (Statistical yearbook of Guangxi). Beijing: Zhongguo tongji chubanshe.

SBIM (Statistics Bureau of Inner Mongolia). 2001. 2003. 2010. *Neimenggu tongji nianjian* [Statistical yearbook of Inner Mongolia]. Beijing: Zhongguo tongji nianjian.

SBN (Statistics Bureau of Ningxia). 2001. 2003. 2010. *Ningxia tongji nianjian* [Statistical yearbook of Ningxia]. Beijing: Zhongguo tongji nianjian.

SBS (Statistics Bureau of the State). 2006. *Zhongguo tongji nianjian* [Statistical yearbook of China]. Beijing: Zhongguo tongji nianjian.

SBT (Statistics Bureau of Tibet). 1989–2010. *Xizang tongji nianjian* [Statistical yearbook of Tibet]. Beijing: Zhongguo tongji chubanshe.

2011. "Xizang zizhiqu 2010nian diliuci quanguo renkou pucha zhuyao shuju gongbao" [Major data on the TAR from the 6th national census in 2010]. *Xizang ribao*, May 4.

SBS and SEAC, eds. 2003. *2000 nian renkou pucha zhongguo minzu renkou ziliao* [Data for China's ethnic populations from the 2000 national census]. Beijing: Zhongguo tongji chubanshe.

SBX (Statistics Bureau of Xinjiang). 1995. 1997. 1999. 2003. 2006. 2010. *Xinjiang tongji nianjian*. Beijing: Zhongguo tongji chubanshe.

SCCO and SBS (State Council Census Office and Statistics Bureau of the State). 1985. *Zhongguo 1982 nian renkou pucha ziliao* [The 1982 national census of China]. Beijing: Zhongguo tongji nianjian.

1993. *Zhongguo 1990 nian renkou pucha ziliao* [The 1990 national census of China]. Beijing: Zhongguo tongji nianjian.

2002. *Zhongguo 1982 nian renkou pucha ziliao* [The 1982 national census of China]. Beijing: Zhongguo tongji nianjian.

SEAC. 1991. SEAC Educational Bureau, *Xin shiqi minzu jiaoyu shouce* [Manual on minority education in the new era]. Beijing: Minzu daxue chubanshe.

2002. "Guojia minwei, guojia jingmaowei, gong'anbu, guojia lǚyouju, guojia gongshang guanliju guanyu jiuzheng xiaji shaoshu bingguan fandian lǚdian jujue shaoshu minzu renyuan ruzhu tongzhi" [Notification on rectifying a small group of hotels' practice of denying service to minority members by the SEAC, the State Commission on Economy and Trade, the Ministry of Public Security, the State Tourism Bureau and the State Bureau for Regulation of Commerce and Industry]. 2002[123], November 27. www.chinalawedu.com/falvfagui/fg22598/15565.shtml.

2007a. "Xin zhongguo minzu gongzuo shijiang zhisi, jinxing minzu shibie, queren 56 ge minzu chengfen" [The fourth of ten lectures on ethnic work in new China: Ethnic classification and establishment of 56 categories]. March 14. www.seac.gov.cn/art/2007/3/14/art_2011_69495.html.

2007b. "Xin zhongguo minzu gongzuo shijiang zhiwu, jianding buyi di shixing minzu quyu zizhi" [The fifth of ten lectures on ethnic work in new China: Firmly carry out autonomous governance in ethnic regions]. March 14. http://ww.seac.gov.cn/art/2007/3/14/art_2011_69494.html.

2018. "Shuangyu jiaoyu, rang meihao weilai chushou keji" [Bilingual education: the bright future is within reach]. *Zhongguo minzu bao*, October 30.

SEAC and SBS. 2007. SEAC Economic Development Bureau and SBS National Economy Statistics Department, eds., *Zhongguo minzu nianjian 2006* [2006 yearbook of China's nationalities]. Beijing: Zhongguo tongji nianjian.

SEC (State Education Commission). 1995. Office of Minority Education, ed., *Shengshi zizhiqu shaoshu minzu jiaoyu gongzuo wenjian huibian 1977–1990*. [Collected documents on minority education work from provinces, metropolises and autonomous regions 1977–1990]. Chengdu: Sichuan Minzu chubanshe.

Shan, Xun. 2013. "Wangzhen jiangjun sixing Xinjiang yu wuci Xinjiang gongzuo huiyi" [General Wang Zhen's four trips to Xinjiang and the fifth work conference on Xinjiang]. *Liaowang dongfang zhoukan*, July 27. Web.

Shen, Haimei. 2013. "Minzu guojia yu guishu de xingbie zhengzhi: jiyu Yunnan minzu shibie de taolun" [The nation state and the gender politics of belonging: A discussion based on ethnic classification in Yunnan]. *Minzu shehuixue yanjiu tongxun* 142: 33–44.

Shen, Zhihua. 1999. "Zhongsu jiemeng yu sulian Xinjiang zhengce de bianhua" [Sino-Soviet alliance and changes in Soviet policy towards Xinjiang]. *Jindai shi yanjiu* 3: 213–27.

Shi, Chunyan. 2012. *Gongchandang Xinjiang minzu gongzuo* [The CCP's ethnic work in Xinjiang]. PhD dissertation, Suzhou University.

Shu, Yun. 2017. "Neimenggu shengchan jianshe bingtuan zujian shimo" [The origins of the founding of PCCs in Inner Mongolia]. *Chongqing ribao*, December 21.

Si, Jianxing. 2003. "Guojifa de shuru yu zhongguo jindai zhuquan guannian de faren" [The influx of international law and the rise of the concept of state sovereignty in modern China]. *Nanping shizhuan xuebao* 3: 46–50.

Sohu. 2004. "Xinjiang nongcun gaishui shidian hui zhaokai, wunian quanmian quxiao nongye shui" [Conference on experimental tax in rural Xinjiang convenes, agrarian taxes to be eliminated in five years]. July 9. http://news.sohu.com/20040907/n221911729.shtml.

2016. "Zuixin Xinjiang renkou shuju" [Xinjiang's latest demographic data]. December 20. www.sohu.com/a/122066430_534679.

2017. "Zhejiang lianshou Xinjiang Akesu gongjian yinran chanye yuan" [Zhejiang partners with Aksu to establish dyeing industries]. November 28. www.sohu.com/a/207316662_807353.

2018. "Beijing jiang duikou zhiyuan 220 ge yuanjiang fupin xiangmu" [Beijing's partner assistance to Xinjiang will provide 220 anti-poverty projects]. May 8. www.sohu.com/a/230835131_381534.

Song, Guoqing. 2015. "Ningxia yuanjia cuo'an pingfan tedian" [Characteristics of reversing wrongful cases in Ningxia]. *The Maoist Legacy*, June 24. www.maoistlegacy.uni-freiburg.de/zh/2015/06/24/.

State Council of the PRC. 1992. *Xizang de zhuquan guishu yu renquan zhuangkuang* [Tibet's sovereignty and human rights conditions]. White Paper. September 1. Web.

1994a. "Zhongrenmin gongheguo jingnei waiguoren zongjiao huodong guanli guiding" [The PRC regulations for religious activities of foreign individuals in China]. 1994[144]. January 31. http://waishi.gznc.edu.cn/info/2004/2762.htm.

1994b. (Bureau for Religious Affairs). "Zongjiao changsuo guanli tiaoli" [Regulations for places of worship]. Document 1994 [145]. April 13. www.ebaifo.com/fojiao-27083.html.

1999. *Zhongguo de shaoshu minzu zhengce jiqi shijian* [China's minority policy and practice]. White Paper. September 27. Web.

2009a. *Xinjiang de fazhan yu jinbu* [Development and progress in Xinjiang]. White Paper. September 21. Web.

2009b. *Zhongguo de minzu zhengce yu geminzu gongtong fanrong fazhan* [China's ethnic policy and common prosperity and development among ethnic groups]. White Paper. September 27. Web.

2014. *Xinjiang shengchan jianshe bingtuan de lishi yu fazhan.* [History and development of Xinjiang production and construction corps]. White Paper. October 5. Web.

2017a. "Guowuyuan bangongting guanyu yinfa xingbian fumin xingdong 'shisanwu' guihua de tongzhi" [State Council notification on the 13th five-year plan for frontier development and enrichment]. May 28. Web.

2017b. *Xinjiang renquan shiye de fazhan jinbu* [Development and progress in human rights in Xinjiang]. White Paper. June 1. Web.

State Council of the PRC (Census Office). 2000. "Diwuci renkou pucha shuju" [Data from the fifth national census]. www.stats.gov.cn/tjsj/ndsj/renkoupucha/2000pucha/pucha .htm.

Su, Keqin. 1960. "Guanyu shaoshu minzu shehui lishi diaocha yanjiu de shinian" [A decade of investigating and studying minority society and history]. *Shinian minzu gongzuo chengjiu*. Beijing: Minzu chubanshe.

Sun, Longji. 2004. *Lishi xuejia de jingwei xia*n [The latitude and longitude of historians]. Nanning: Guangxi shifan xueyuan chubanshe.

Sun, Yong. 2015. *Weihu Xizang diqu shehui wending duice yanjiu* [A study of policies to safeguard Tibet's social stability]. Lhasa: Xizang renmin chubanshe.

Sun, Yueliang. 2006. *Xizang nongcun pinkun wenti fupin kaifa yanjiu* [A study of *poverty* issues in Tibet and anti-poverty development]. MA thesis, Suzhou University.

Tang, Lijiu. 2014. "Xinjiang wenti shengcheng de yuanyou he qiujie zhilu" [Origins of the Xinjiang problem and paths to solutions]. *Gongshi wang*, March 6. www .21ccom.net/articles/zgyj/dfzl/article_2014030610179 8.html.

Tao, Wenzhao. 2018. "Zai gongtong fazhan zhong zhulao zhonghua minzu gongtongti yishi" [Solidifying a sense of the community of the Chinese nation through common development]. *Guangming ribao*, January 5, 2018.

TAR. 1987. *Xizang zizhiqu fojiao simiao minzu guanli zhangcheng* [TAR regulations for democratic management of Buddhist monasteries]. Lhasa: Xizang minzu zongjiao weiyuan hui.

1991. "Xizang zizhiqu zongjiao shiwu guanli zanxing fa" [Temporary Regulations for Religious Affairs in the TAR]. September 20. http://code.fabao365.com /law_460447_1.html.

Teng, Xing and Wang Jun. 2002. *Ershi shiji zhongguo shaoshu minzu yu jiaoyu lilun yu shijian* [Theory and practice of China's minority education in the 20th century]. Beijing: Minzu chubanshe.

Tenzin and Zhang Xiangming, eds. 1991. *Dangdai zhongguo Xizang* [Tibet in contemporary China]. Beijing: Dangdai zhongguo chubanshe.

Thundrup, Padma. 2012. *Qinghai muqu shuangyu jiaoyu fazhan wenti yanjiu baogao* [A report on problems in developing bilingual education in Qinghai's pastoral regions]. *Xibei minxu yanjiu* 1: 14–28.

Tian, Fanping. 2010. "Lun minzu zizhi difang zizhi jiguan xieshang minzhu juece jizhi de wanshan" [On perfecting the decision-making mechanisms of consultative democracy in ethnic autonomous regions]. *Minzu yanjiu* 4: 12–21.

TS (Tianshan wang). 2006. "Kongke cun geng xuyao zaoxue jizhi" [Hollowed-out villages have greater need for blood-generating capability]. March 6. Web.

2017a. "Xinjiang weiwu'er zizhiqu qu jiduanhua tiaoli" [XUAR regulations on deradicalization]. March 29. www.xjxnw.gov.cn/c/2017–03–30/1154866.shtml.

2017b. "Jinian duikou yuanjiang gongzuo zouguo guanghui 20 nian" [Two glorious decades of partner assistance to Xinjiang]. July 11. www.chinaxinjiang.cn/zixun/xjxw/201707/t20170711_555121.htm.

Tianya luntan. 2015. "Dui zuogunmen gongji Hu Yaobang liangshaoyikuan zhengce de huifu" [Response to the leftist hitters' attacks on Hu Yaobang on the policy of double legal standards]. November 20. http://bbs.tianya.cn/post-no110–15453549–1.shtml.

Tohti, Ilham. 2009. "Zhongguo de minzu zhengce buxuyao fansi ma?" [Should we not reassess China's ethnic policy?]. October 29. www.chinesepen.org/blog/archives/101462.

2013. "Weiwu'er ren heyi you yizhong cuobai gan?" [Why do Uighurs feel a sense of defeat?]. June 7. http://cn.rfi.fr/.

2014. "Dangqian Xinjiang minzu wenti de xianzhuang ji jianyi" [The state of Xinjiang's ethnic problems at present and suggestions]. Archived at https://groups.google.com/forum/#!msg/2ncn/EbFlM7TnixA/rVIxbBLZuawJ.

Tseten, Dorjie. 1995. *Xizang jingji jianshi* [A brief history of Tibetan economy]. Lhasa: Xizang renmin chubanshe.

Tulak, Hankis. 2013. "Weiwu'erzu nongmingong neidi chengshi shengcun yu shiyin yanjiu – yi Wuhanshi weiwu'erzu nongmingong weili" [Uighur rural migrants' survival and adaptation in interior China: The case of Uighur rural migrants in Wuhan city]. *Minzu shehuixue yanjiu tongzxun* 137: 1–25.

2014. "Weiwu'erzu liudong renkou de neidi chengshi rongru de yanjiu – jiyu Wuhanshi de diaocha" [A study of Uighur migrants' integration in an interior city: Investigation based on Wuhan city]. *Zhongnan minzu daxue xuebao* 4: 63–9.

2012b. "Minzu zhengce bu cunzai fanxiang qishi" [There is no reverse discrimination in current ethnic policy]. *Huanqiu shibao*, March 16. http://opinion.huanqiu.com/1152/2012-03/2529409.html.

2013. "Xinjiang hanwei guanxi de bianqian ji zhengjie" [The evolution and root problem of Uighur–Han relations in Xinjiang]. *Yangguang shiwu* 54 (May 9): 37–9.

2014. "Nanjiang yuanjiaozhi zhuyi diaocha biji" [A field research report on the rise of fundamentalism in southern Xinjiang]. *Zhongguo xinwen zhoukan* 611 (May 29): 58–63.

Tursun, Turgunjun. 2012a. "Shaoshu minzu weihe nanyi danren diyibashou?" [Why is it difficult for minorities to become the top office holder?]. *Blog.sina*, January 18. http://blog.sina.com.cn/s/blog_60f25ed70102dw9y.html.

Umuk, Sawuresh. 2016. "Xinjiang shaoshu minzu daxuesheng jiuye xianzhuang wenti yu duice" [Problems of employment for Xinjiang's minority college graduates and solutions]. *Xiandai qiye* 4: 68–9.

Wang, Chen and Dong Yungu. 2011. *Xizang zhishi jieda* [Questions and answers about Tibet]. Beijing: Renmin chubanshe.

Wang, Daiyuan. 2012. *Quanguo zhiyuan Xizang gongzuo de jingji xiaoyi yanjiu* [A study of the economic effects of the whole country's assistance to Xinjiang]. Lhasa: Xizang guji chubanshe.

Wang, Dongli. 2014. "Li Weihan dui zhongguo minzu quyu zizhi zhidu de gongxian" [Li Weihan's contribution to China's system of autonomy in ethnic regions]. *Zhongguo tongyi zhanxian* 271 (July): 33–4.

Wang, En'mao. 1997. *Wang En'mao wenji* [Collected works of Wang En'mao]. Vol. 2. Beijing: Zhongyang wenxian chubanshe.

Wang, Jinbao. 2013. "Zhu Weiqun: yige shiqi de cuoshi shidang shi Xinjiang zongjiao wenti de bufen yuanyin" [Zhu Weiqun: Policy mistakes during a certain period is partially the reason for Xinjiang's religious problems]. *Zhongguo xinwen zhoukani*, August 21. Web.

Wang, Ke. 2003. "'Minzu': yige laizi riben de wuhui" ["Minzu": A misunderstanding from Japan]. *Ershiyi shiji* 77.6: 73–83.

Wang, Lixiong. 2001. "Ruhe kandai 17 tiao xieyi" [How to look at the 17 Point Agreement]. May 26. www.chinesepen.org/blog/archives/107048.

2007. *Wode xiyu, nide dongtu* [My western region, your eastern land]. Taipei: Locus Publishing.

2009. *Tianzang* [Celestial Burial]. Taipei: Locus Publishing.

2012b. "Ranshao de yiyan – Zangren yinhe zifen?" [Burning last words: Why do Tibetans self-immolate?]. December. http://woeser.middleway.net/2012/12/blog-post_18.html.

Wang, Luolin and Zhu Ling. 2005. *Shichanghua yu jiceng gonggong fuwu – Xizang an'li yanjiu* [Marketization and public service at grass-roots: The case of Tibet]. Beijing: Minzu chubanshe.

Wang, Shusheng. 2001. "Ulanfu he shaoshu minzu diyige dangzhibu" [Ulanfu and the first minority party branch]. *Dadi*, Vols. 12–13. Web.

Wang, Tongling. 1934. *Zhongguo minzu shi* [Ethnic history of China]. Beiping: Wenhua xueshe.

2010. *Zhongguo minzu shi* [Ethnic history of China]. Changchun: Jili chubanjituan youxian gongsi.

Wang, Xiaobin. 2012. "Zhenshi yu xuwang – ping Mei Ge'ersitan's baofeng qian de ningjing' ji jianlun zangxue yanjiu de xinsilu" [Truth and Myth – commenting on Melvin Goldstein's "Calm before the Storm" and on new thinking in Tibetan studies]. *Xizang minzu xueyuan xuebao: Zhexue shehui kexue ban* 33.5: 25–32.

Wang, Xi'en. 2008. "Dangdai zuji renkou liuqian yu minzu guocheng" [Interethnic migration in today's China and the ethno-national process]. *Xinan minzu daxue xuebao* 5: 1–11.

2009. "Yetan zai woguo minzu wenti shang de 'fansi' yu 'shishiqiushi'" [Also on "reassessment" and "seeking truth from facts" on the ethnic issue in our country]. *Xinan minzu daxue xuebao* 1: 1–17.

Wang, Xindeng. 2003. "Kangzhan shiqi sulian dui Xinjiang de kuozhang shentou yu 'sanqu gemin'" [Soviet expansion in Xinjiang during the Anti-Japanese War period and the "tri-region revolution"]. *Ili jiaoyu xueyuan xuebao* 16.2 (June). www.shehui.pku.edu.cn/upload/editor/file/20180627/20180627101342_1595.pdf.

Wang, Yingzi. 2006. "Shaoshu minzu xuesheng jiuye wenti de diaocha fenxi" [An investigation and analysis of minority students' employment problems in Xinjiang]. *Zhongguo daxuesheng jiuye* 16: 35–8.

Wang, Yu. 1998. "Dangde zhengzhi luxian de zhanlue zhuanbian zai Qinghai de weida shijian" [Implementation of the party's strategic political transformation in Qinghai]. *Gaige qiushi chuangxin – Qinghai jinian dangde shiyijie sanzhong quanhui ershi zhounian youxiu lunwen ji* [Collected essays in commemoration of the 20th anniversary of the 3rd plenum of the 11th party conference]. Ed. Yuan Tian. Xining: Zhonggong Qinghai shengwei. 261–71.

Wang, Zuo'an. 2003. *Zhongguo de zongjiao wenti he zongjiao zhengce* [China's ethnic problems and ethnic policy]. Beijing: Zongjiao wenhua chubanshe.

Wen, Jun. 2006. *Xizang nongye ke chixu fazhan zhanlue yanjiu* [A study of a sustainable strategy for Tibet's agriculture]. Lhasa: Xizang renmin chubanshe.

Wu, Chi-ne. 2009. "Minzu zizhi yu zhongyang jiquan" [Ethnic autonomy and centralized authoritarianism]. *Zhongyang yanjiuyuan jindai yanjiushi jikan* (Taiwan) 65 (September): 81–137.

2013. "Renqun de fenlei yu guozu zhenghe" [Classification of ethnic groups and integration of a nation]. *Minzu shehuixue yanjiu tongxun* 138: 1–32.

2014. "Zhonghua minzu zongzu lun yu zhonghua minguo de bianjiang zizhi shijian" [The clan theory of the Chinese nation and the implementation of frontier autonomy in the Republic Era]. *Minzu shehuixue tongxun* 158: 38–59.

Wu, Chuke. 2005. *Bianjiang zhengzhi xue* [The political science of frontiers]. Beijing: Zhongyang minzu daxue chubanshe.

2011. "Goujian zhongguo xin diyuan anquan zhanlue de lilun zhunbei yu sikao" [Theoretical reflections on China's new geopolitical security strategy]. *Wujing xueyuan xuebao* 27.3: 5–12.

Wu, Dahua. 2005. "Lun 'liangshao yikuan' de shaoshu minzu fanzhui xingshi zhengce" [On the policy of "two less and one lax" for minority offenders]. *Fanzuixue luncong* 3: 105–14.

Wu, Fuhuan. 2001. "'Sange zhuyi' dui Xinjiang jiaoyu lingyu de shentou ji duice" [Infiltration of the "three-ism" into Xinjiang's educational arena]. *2001 niandu guojia sheke jijin tebie weituo xiangmu* [Special project of the national social science foundation in 2001]. http://bianjiang.blogspot.com/2013/08/blog-post_4961.html.

Wuyoukao wang. 2018. "2018 nian Xinjiang Wulumuqi zhongkao luquxian yi gongbu" [The qualifying scores for high school admissions in Urumqi, Xinjiang, are announced]. August 3. www.51test.net/show/9024642.html.

WYZX. 2009. "Weishenme wo buman Hu Luanbang" [Why do I complain about Hu Luanbang?]. *Wu You Zhi Xiang*, November 13. http://zlk.wyzxsx.com/Article/lishi/2010/09/138846.html.

2013. "Jianzheng Xinjiang you zhi dao luan" [Witnessing Xinjiang turning from governance to chaos]. *Wu You Zhi Xiang*, November 6. www.wyzxwk.com/Article/lishi/2011/08/243037.html.

Xia, Liyang. 2001. "Lun shaoshu minzu gongmin xingshi fanzhui anjian zhong xingfa ji 'liangshao yikuan' zhengce de shiyong" [The application of criminal law and the policy of "two less and one lax" in criminal cases involving minority citizens]. *Zhongnan minzu xueyuan xuebao* 21.2: 25–8.

Xiao, Yang. 1996. *Zhongguo xingshi he celue wenti* [Criminal offense and policy matters in China]. Beijing: Falu chubanshe.

Xiaohe, 2007. "1952 nian Wang Zhen zao pipan hou chezhi likai Xinjiang neimu jiemi" [The inside story of Wang Zhen's departure from Xinjiang after censure and demotion]. *Wenshi jinghua*, December.

Xie, Lizhong, ed. 2010. *Lijie minzu guanxi xin silu: Shaoshu minzu wenti de qu zhengzhi hua* [New thinking in understanding ethnic relations: De-politicization of minority issues]. Beijing: Shekewenxian chubanshe.

Xinhua. 2011. "Shenglaobingsi you butie: Xizang nongmin xisuan 'youhui zhengce' zhang" [There are subsidies for all aspects of life: Tibetan farmers calculate benefits from preferential policies]. May 8. http://news.ifeng.com/c/7fZfwn9Xl2n.

2012. "Xizang 2011 nian yinjie gaoxiao biyesheng jiben shixian quanbu jiuye" [Full employment for TAR's college graduates of 2011]. January 11. http://news.cntv.cn/20120111/108740.shtml.

2019. "Jianli meili Xinjiang" [Building beautiful Xinjiang]. August 1. http://shenlan.haiwainet.cn/n/2019/0801/c3544063-31602900.html.

Xinjiang ribao. 2011. "Xinjiang zizhiqu 2011nian gaoxiao biyesheng chuci jiuyelü da 71.25%" [71.25% employment rate for XUAR's college graduates of 2011]. November 14. www.gov.cn/gzdt/2011-11/14/content_1992316.htm.

2019. "2019 nian Xinjiang gaokao fenshuxian gongbu" [The cut-off scores in Xinjiang's college admissions for 2019 announced]. June 27. www.xjbs.com.cn/news/2019-06/27/cms2171331article.shtml.

Xinnonghe. 2013. "Xinjiang zaici tiaogao xinnonghe renjun chouzi biaozhun" [Xinjiang raises insurance premiums for new cooperative healthcare]. March 4. www.xinnonghe.org/show_title.php?id=172.

Xindong fang. 2018. "2018 nian Xinjiang gaokao jiafen zhengce" [Bonus points for college admissions in Xinjiang, 2018]. May 7. http://gaokao.xdf.cn/201805/10778807.html.

Xiong, Kuixin and Yan Qing. 2006. "Hongjun changzheng de shengli yeshi dangde minzu zhengce de shengli" [The victory of the Long March is also a victory of the party's ethnic policy]. *Zhongguo minzu* 11: 35–8.

Xizang ribao. 2012. "Xizang daxuesheng 'quan jiuye' toushi: Gongzhi gangwei zhan bacheng" [Full employment for college graduates of TAR residency, 80% of it in public sectors]. December 26.

Xjass (Xinjiang Academy of Social Sciences). 2010. "Xinjiang weiwen xin siwei: Fan baoli, jiang fazhi, jiang zhixu" [New thinking for maintaining social stability in Xinjiang: Oppose violence, respect law and order]. December 27. www.xjass.com/zy/content/ 2010–12/27/content_182660.htm.

Xu, Lili. 2005. *Lun minzu guanxi yu minzu guanxi wenti* [On ethnic relations and problems in ethnic relations]. Beijing: Minzu chubanshe.

Xu, Lili and Yu Xiaofeng. 2009. "Lun bianjiang minzu diqu fei chuantong anquan wenti ji yindui" [Non-traditional security problems in frontier ethnic regions and coping strategies]. *Minzu yanjiu* 5: 34–43.

Xu, Xiaoping and Jin Xin. 2008. *Zhongguo minzu wenti baogao* [Report on China's ethnic issues]. Beijing: Zhongguo sheke chubanshe.

XUAR. 1988. "Xinjiang weiwu'er zizhiqu zongjiao huodong changsuo zanxing guize" [XUAR temporary regulations for regulating places of religious activities]. XUAR Chair, 1988[2]. November 9. www.pkulaw.cn/fulltext_form.aspx.

1994. "Xinjiang weiwu'er zizhiqu zongjiao guanli tiaoli" [XUAR regulations for regulating religion]. XUAR People's Congress, July 16. Expired January 1, 2015. www.law-lib.com/law/law_view.asp.

1997. "Guanyu jieding feifa zongjiao huodong de yijian" [Opinions on defining illegal religious activities]. XUAR Party Committee, 1997[1]. https://wenku.baidu.com/view/f32a694a767f5acfa1c7cd44.html.

2011. "Guanyu jieding feifa zongjiao huodong de yijian" [Opinions on defining illegal religious activities]. XUAR Party Committee, 2011[1]. www.doc88.com/p-7456857262981.html.

2013. "Guanyu jinyibu yifa zhili feifa zongjiao huodong e'zhi zongjiao jiduan sixiang shentou gongzuo de ruogan zhidao yijian" [Guiding opinions for regulating illegal religious activities according to law and curtailing infiltration of religious extremism]. XUAR Party Committee, 2013[11]. http://qmx.xjkunlun.cn/tzgz/zcfg/2014/515095.htm.

2014a. "Xinjiang weiwu'er zizhiqu zongjiao shiwu tiaoli" [XUAR Regulations on Religious Affairs]. XUAR Party Committee, November 28. www.xinjiang.gov.cn/2017/05/15/130318.html.

2014b. "Shibie zongjiao jiduan huodong (75 zhong juti biaoxian) jiben zhishi" [Basic knowledge for distinguishing (75 specific manifestations of) extremist religious activities]. November www.taodocs.com/p-169649155.html.

2014c. "Guanyu jinyibu jiaqiang he wanshan yisilanjiao gongzuo de ruogan yijian" [Several opinions on further strengthening and improving our work regarding Islam]. XUAR Party Committee, 2014 [28]. www.zaidian.com/jiaoshiwenzhang/453918.html.

2017. "Xinjiang weiwu'er zizhiqu renkou yu jihua shengyu tiaoli" [XUAR regulations for population and family planning]. XUAR *weisheng jiandu*, August. www.xjwsjd.gov.cn/flfg/jgsyfg/xjwwezcgbb/14509.htm.

Xue, Xiantian. 2008. "Shi tuidong gemin haishi weihu zishen anquan? Guanyu sulian tiaoting sanqu gemin de minzu yinsu" [Promoting revolution in Xinjiang or protecting its own security? Ethnic factors in the Soviet mediation of the tri-region revolution]. *Zhonghua minguo shi yanjiu sanshinian 1972–2002* [Three decades of research into the Republican era 1972–2002]. Ed. CASS. Beijing: Sheke wenxian chubanshe. 345–59.

Xuezi. 2015. "Zangzu daxuesheng jiuye yixiang wenjuan diaocha baogao" [A survey report on job preferences among Tibetan college students]. *Xuezi* 10 (October). www.shehui.pku.edu.cn/upload/editor/file/20180829/20180829111208_895 3.pdf.

Yan, Canghong, Li Anhui, and Wu Shoubin. 2012. "Lun minguo shiqi de minzu zhengce" [On ethnic policies during the Republican era]. *Lanzhou daxue xuebao*, 40.1: 2–7.

Yan, Fu. 1986. "Lun shibian zhi ji" [On the urgency of reform]. *Yan Fu ji* [Collection of Yan Fu], Vol. 1. Beijing: Zhonghua shuju.

Yang, Fuqiang. 2011. "'Duikou yuanjiang' zhengce huigu yu fansi" [Reflections on the policy of partner assistance for Xinjiang]. *Xibei minzu daxue xuebao* 5: 109–15.

Yang, Minghong. 2014. "Duikou yuanzang youxiaoxing de lilun renshi yu shixian lujing yanjiu" [Analyzing theoretical understanding and practical paths to effective partner assistance to Tibet]. *Zhongguo Zangxue* 3: 126–32.

Yang, Shu, Li Jie, and Cao Wei. 2019. "Dui 'sanqugeming' de chongxin renshi yu pingjia" [Reassessing the "tri-revolution"]. *Xinjiang yanjiu tongxun* 6: 1–7.

Yang, Xuechen, 1993. "Qingchao de minzu zhengce" [Ethnic policy of the Qing dynasty]. *Zhongguo lidai minzu zhengce* [Ethnic policies of Chinese imperial dynasties]. Eds. Tian Jizhou et al. Xining: Qinghai renmin chubanshe. 309–55.

Yang, Yongjun. 1999. "Gudai zhongguo zhongguo jimi zhengce de bianqian jiqi yuanyin tanjiu" [On the transformation of loose rein policies in ancient China and its causes]. *Xibei shidi* 2: 43–50.

Yao, Xinyong. 2009. "Minzu zhengce de cuoluan yu zuqun chongtu de jihua" [Distorted ethnic policy and intensified ethnic conflict]. *Er shi yi shiji* 12: 58–66.

2012. "Shishi'erfei de minzu ganbu yibashou queshi lun" [The dubious issue of a shortage of minorities holding the top office]. *Blog.sina*, January 18. http://blog.sina.com.cn/s/blog_60f25ed70102dw9y.html.

2013a. "Hanzu zhishifenzi yanzhong de Xinjiangren: Lansan de Xinjiangren" [The idle people of Xinjiang – Xinjiang's people in the eyes of Han intellectuals]. *Yangguang shi wu zhoukan* 54 (May 9). Web.

2013b. "Di'erdai minzu zhengce: guojia zhongzu zhuyi de gaobai" [The second generation of ethnic policy: Confession of state racism]. *Blog.sina*, June 6. http://blog.sina.com.cn/u/2614085431.

2014a. "Zhuanzhi yaobude, minzu zizhi yexu shenxing" [No to authoritarianism but also caution on ethnic autonomy]. *Gongshi wang*, March 17. www.21ccom.net/articles/gsbh/2014/0317/102562.html.

2014b. "Yu yiwei weiwu'erzu pengyou tan qiwu zhihou Xinjiang jiuye deng de jiji bianhua" [Talking to a Uighur friend about positive changes in employment after the 7.5 incident]. *Blog.sina*, May 12. http://blog.sina.com.cn/s/blog_60f25ed70102eimy.html.

Yi, Fuxian. 2009. "Xinjiang 7.5 shijian de renkou jingjixue yinsu" [Demographic economics in the 7.5 incident of Xinjiang]. *Blog.sina*, July 10, 2009. http://blog.sina.com.cn/s/blog_5d98d17f0100e7j7.html.

Yu, Zidong. 2003. "Lun Qingchao de shaoshuminzu jiaoyu zhengce" [On the Qing dynasty's educational policy for ethnic minorities]. *Minzu jiaoyu yanjiu* 14.3: 39–43.

Zeng, Wenwu. 1936. *Zhongguo jingyin xiyu shi* [A history of China's management of western regions]. Beijing: Shangwu yinshuguan.

Zhang, Chi. 2013a. "Xinjiang jiduan shili neikong baogao" [A report on curbing extremist forces in Xinjiang]. *Fenghuang zhoukan* 472 (June 14). Web.

2013b. "Xinjiang: Baoshou sichao de weixian xinhao" [Xinjiang: Dangerous signs of conservatism]. *Fenghuang zhoukan* 492 (December 16). Web.

2014. "Kongbao luxiang shentou Xinjiang" [Videos about violence and terror spread widely in Xinjiang]. *Fenghuang zhoukan* 508 (March 2). Web.

Zhang, Haiyang. 2014a. "Buyao gei 'liangge fanshi' maidan" [Stop paying price for the "two whatevers" policy]. *Gongshi wang*, March 26. www.21ccom.net/articles/sxwh/shsc/article_2014032610311 5.html.

2014b. "Minzu wenti de genzi zai nali?" [What is the root of ethnic problems] *Fenghuang daxuewen*, August 13. https://i.ifeng.com/news/news?aid=87711835.

Zhang, Ligang. 2010. "Lun 'liangshao yikuan' zhengce" [On the "two less and one lax" policy]. *Shandongsheng qingnian ganbu guanli xueyuan xuebao* 143.1: 97–101.

Zhang, Mei. 2009. "Xinjiang shaoshu minzu shuangyu jiaoyu moshi jiqi yuyan shiyong wenti" [Models of bilingual education for minority students in Xinjiang and the problem of language use]. *Minzu jiaoyu yanjiu* 20.4: 96–101.

Zhang, Shanyu. 1997. *Zhongguo renkou dili* [Demographic geography of China]. Shanghai: Shangwu yinshuguan.

Zhang, Shanyu, Peng Jizuo, and Mao Aihua. 2006. "Xibu diqu renkou qianyi xingshi jiqi yingxiang fenxi" [An analysis of migration trends in western regions and their impact]. *Neimenggu shehui kexue* 27.1: 95–9.

Zhang, Shiming. 2004. "Qingdai zongfan guanxi de lishi faxue duowei toushi fenxi" [A historical and legal analysis of the suzerain–vassal state relationships in the Qing dynasty]. *Qingshi yanjiu* 1 (February): 21–8.

Zhang, Shuangzhi. 2003. "Nanjing minguo zhengfu de minzu sixiang he zhengce" [Ethnic doctrine and policy of the Republican government of Nanjing]. *Zhongguo zangxue* 64.4: 46–53.

Zhang, Shuangzhi. 2010. "Qingchao waifan zhizhinei de chaojin nianban yu jingong zhidu" [The annual pilgrimages and the tribute system for vassal states in the Qing Dynasty]. *Qingshi yanjiu* 3 (August): 106–15.

Zhang, Taiyan. 1977. "Du ribenguo zhi" [On reading Annuals of Japan]. *Zhang Taiyan zhenglunwen ji* [Collection of Zhang Taiyan's political essays]. Vol. 1. Beijing: Zhonghua shuju.

Zhang, Wenguang. 2010. "Minzu diqu caizheng tizhi gaige fangxiang tanxi" [Exploring directions of reforming the fiscal system in ethnic regions]. *Minzu yanjiu* 3: 25–34.

Zhang, Xiuming. 2009. *Xinjiang fan fenlie touzheng he wending gongzuo de shijian yu sikao* [Reflections on battles against separatism and maintenance of social stability in Xinjiang]. Urumqi: Xinjiang renmin chubanshe.

Zhang, Yunde. 2009. "Qiantan 'yizabute' zai Xinjiang shentou pohuai de benzhi" [Analysis of the nature of infiltration and sabotage activities in Xinjiang by Hizb-ut-Tahrir]. *Xinjiang shehui kexue* 2: 58–64.

Zhang, Zhengming. 1990. "Lun heqin zhengce" [On policy of kinship alliances]. *Zhongguo gudai bianjiang zhengce yanjiu* [A study of frontier policy in ancient China]. Ed. Ma Dazheng. Beijing: Zhongguo shehui kexue chubanshe.

Zhao, Rukun. 2012. "Er'shi shiji wuliushi niandai de zhongguo bianjiang yimin" [China's frontier immigration in the 1950s and 1960s]. *Zhonggong dangshi yanjiu* 2: 52–64.

Zhao, Yancai and Wei Kaifang. 2003. "Zhongguo chuantong zongfan zhidu jiben tezhen shulun" [On the basic features of China's traditional suzerain-vassal system]. *Yunnan shehui kexue* 1: 81–95.

Zheng, Changde. 2013. "2000 nian yilai zhongguo shaoshu minzu renkou zengzhang yu fenbu" [The growth and distribution of China's minority population since 2000]. *Xibei renkou* 2.34: 1–5.

Zheng, Yongnian. 2012. "Weishenme ziyuan sheng biancheng le wenti sheng?" [Why have resource rich provinces become problem provinces]. *Lianhe zaobao*, January 10.

Zhonggong jiaoyu. 2017. "Kepu: Gongwuyuan, shiye danwei he cangong shi shenme?" [What is a civil servant, a public service entity and a quasi-civil servant?]. October 17. www.zgsydw.com/shanghai/20171017/332210_1.html.

2018. "Linian Xinjiang gongwuyuan kaoshi fenshuxian" [The cutoff scores for the civil service exams in Xinjiang in the past years]. February 24. http://xj.offcn.com/html/2018/02/41580.html.

Zhongguo ribao wang. 2014. "Kunming kongbu xiji nübaotu yi qingxing bing zhaogong, nübaotu zhengmianzhao baoguang jin 16 sui" [Female assailant in the Kunming terror attack woke up to give confession, only 16 years old]. March 6. Reposted at http://news.e23.cn/content/2014-03-06/2014030600007.html.

Zhou, Enlai. 1957a. "1957 nian 3 yue 25 ri zhongguo renmin zhengzhi xieshang huiyi guanyu Guangxi zhuangzu zizhiqu wenti zuotanhui shang de jianghua" [Speech at the CPPCC symposium on the Zhuang autonomous region on March 25, 1957]. *Guangxi minzu gongzuo dang'an xuanbian* 1950–65 [Selected records of Guangxi's ethnic work]. Ed. Guangxi Autonomous Region Bureau of Archives. Beijing: Zhongguo dang'an chubanshe. 457–70.

1957b. "Guanyu woguo minzu zhengce de jige wenti" [Several issues in our country's ethnic policy], *Hebei sheng minzu shiwu weiyuanhui*, August 4. www.hebmzt.gov.cn/html/jdls/20181206/783.html.

Zhou, Jinghong. 2005. "Nanjing guomindang zhengfu chuqi shinian bianjiang minzu shiwu guanli jizhi he zhengce" [Governance mechanisms and policies for minorities in the first decade of the KMT government in Nanjing]. *Zhongguo bianjiang shi yanjiu* 15.3: 46–56.

Zhou, Ping. 2008a. "Woguo de bianjiang yu bianjiang zhili" [China's borderlands and their governance]. *Zhengzhixue yanjiu* 2: 67–72.

2008b. "Zhongguo bianjiang zhili yanjiu" [Studying China's frontier governance]. *Xueshu tansuo* 2 (April): 28–34.

2008c. "Zhongguo de bianjiang zhili: Zuji zhuyi haishi quyu zhuyi" [China's frontier governance: An ethnic or regional approach]. *Sixiang zhanxian* 3:34: 25–9.

Zhou, Weizhou. 1985. *Tuyuhun shi* [A history of Tuyuhun]. Yinchuan: Ningxia renmin chubanshe.

Zhu, Peimin. 2004. *Zhongguo gongchandang yu Xinjiang minzu wenti* [The Chinese communist party and Xinjiang's ethnic problem]. Urumqi: Xinjiang renmin chubanshe.

Zhu, Weiqun. 2012. "Dui dangqian minzu lingyu wenti de jidian sikao" [Some reflections on the problems in the ethnic front at present]. *Xuexi shibao*, February 13.

2015. "Zhu Weiqun: Minzu gongzuo zhong yao gengduo qiangdiao zhonghua minzu de gongtongxing he yizhixing" [More emphasis should be placed on the commonalities of the Chinese nation]. *People's Daily*, March 11. http://theory.people.com.cn/n/2015/0311/c40531–26674807.html.

Zou, Rong. 1958. *Geming jun* [Revolutionary army]. Beijing: Zhonghua shuju.

Zulhayat, Simayi. 2009. "Shaoshu minzu jiaoyu yu chenggong: Yi Xinjiang shuangyu jiaoyu weili" [Minority education and its success: The case of Xinjiang's bilingual programs]. Ed. Ma (2009c). 84–133.

2011. "Jiaoyu youhui zhengce: Xinjiang de shuanggui jiaoyu zhidu fenxi" [Preferential policies in education: An analysis of Xinjiang's dual educational system]. *Minzu shehuixue yanjiu tongxun* 97: 1–12.

Index